2.90

W9-BRZ-273

W.E. McCullen
195 So Coy

★

AMERICAN WRITERS SERIES
★
HARRY HAYDEN CLARK
General Editor

★

★ AMERICAN WRITERS SERIES ★

Volumes of representative selections, prepared by American scholars under the general editorship of Harry Hayden Clark, University of Wisconsin

WILLIAM CULLEN BRYANT, *Tremaine McDowell, University of Minnesota*

JAMES FENIMORE COOPER, *Robert E. Spiller, University of Pennsylvania*

JONATHAN EDWARDS, *Clarence H. Faust, University of Chicago, and Thomas H. Johnson, Lawrenceville School*

RALPH WALDO EMERSON, *Frederic I. Carpenter, formerly of Harvard University*

BENJAMIN FRANKLIN, *Frank Luther Mott, University of Missouri, and Chester E. Jorgenson, Wayne University*

ALEXANDER HAMILTON AND THOMAS JEFFERSON, *Frederick C. Prescott, Cornell University*

BRET HARTE, *Joseph B. Harrison, University of Washington*

NATHANIEL HAWTHORNE, *Austin Warren, University of Iowa*

OLIVER WENDELL HOLMES, *S. I. Hayakawa, Illinois Institute of Technology, and Howard Mumford Jones, Harvard University*

WASHINGTON IRVING, *Henry A. Pochmann, University of Wisconsin*

HENRY JAMES, *Lyon Richardson, Western Reserve University*

HENRY WADSWORTH LONGFELLOW, *Odell Shepard, Trinity College*

JAMES RUSSELL LOWELL, *Norman Foerster, formerly of University of Iowa, and Harry H. Clark, University of Wisconsin*

HERMAN MELVILLE, *Willard Thorp, Princeton University*

JOHN LOTHROP MOTLEY, *Chester P. Higby and B. T. Schantz, University of Wisconsin*

THOMAS PAINE, *Harry H. Clark, University of Wisconsin*

FRANCIS PARKMAN, *Wilbur L. Schramm, University of Iowa*

EDGAR ALLAN POE, *Margaret Alterton, late of University of Iowa, and Hardin Craig, Stanford University*

WILLIAM HICKLING PRESCOTT, *William Charvat, Ohio State University, and Michael Kraus, College of the City of New York*

SOUTHERN POETS, *Edd Winfield Parks, University of Georgia*

SOUTHERN PROSE WRITERS, *Gregory Paine, University of North Carolina*

HENRY DAVID THOREAU, *Bartholow Crawford, University of Iowa*

MARK TWAIN, *Fred Lewis Pattee, Rollins College*

WALT WHITMAN, *Floyd Stovall, North Texas State Teachers College*

Southern Prose Writers

REPRESENTATIVE SELECTIONS, WITH
INTRODUCTION, BIBLIOGRAPHY, AND NOTES

BY

GREGORY PAINE

Professor of English
University of North Carolina

AWS

AMERICAN BOOK COMPANY

New York · Cincinnati · Chicago
Boston · Atlanta · Dallas · San Francisco

E. P. 1

Paine's SOUTHERN PROSE WRITERS

MADE IN U.S.A.

PREFACE

The purpose that has guided the choice of selections for this volume has been to make available to students of American literature southern literary materials not readily available in convenient form elsewhere and to present these materials in units sufficiently large to be genuinely representative of the authors chosen. This has meant a rigid limitation in the number of authors considered and has made the problem of selection very difficult, for it is easier to select small units from many authors than to choose a few authors to be represented by relatively large units. The latter seems worth doing, however, for although a collection which devotes only a page or two to each author may be entertaining for an ocean voyage, it is poorly adapted for college study.

The main limitation set has been the obvious one of chronology. Recent writers, whose works are readily available and generally well known, have been omitted. While no rigid terminal date has been set, the selection of authors has been confined, in the main, to those whose important work was done in the nineteenth century.

Within the time limits established, the selection has been guided by the desire to choose the most representative writers of each genre, and, on the whole, to lean toward an emphasis on belles-lettres rather than on the more utilitarian—though often powerful—prose which has occupied so much of the attention of gifted Southerners.

Since Poe, as both story writer and critic, could not be covered in the few pages that might be spared for him, and since there is an excellent Poe volume in the American Writers Series, I have felt obliged, though with misgivings, to omit selections from his works.

In the editorial aids accompanying the selections, I have been mainly concerned with the difficult task of ascertaining facts, for in the discussions of southern literature heretofore there has been an abundance of interpretation by writers of varying degrees of enlightenment, but amazingly little in the way of ascertained facts of biographical and literary history. The statesmen and politicians have fared very well at the hands of their biographers, but nearly every author of essays and fiction needs a new biography, a bibliography of his writings, and some competent critical evaluation based upon full information. Here is a rich, untilled field for many students.

I am indebted, however, to a few careful literary historians of the older generation—men like Baskervill, Henneman, Trent, and C. Alphonso Smith—who tried to give accurate information, and to a number of living men and women, usually professors in southern universities, who are sound, careful scholars and critics.

Some excellent studies of southern authors are to be found in theses and dissertations written by graduate students in recent years. Such studies have been a great help in compiling the present volume—a help which I have gratefully tried to acknowledge.

At every turn I have been made aware of work to be done, of new lines of investigation, of gaps in our knowledge which must be filled in before any important synthesis can be made in the field of southern literature. It is my hope that this volume may suggest some new topics of interest to students of southern literature and that its very deficiencies may be a stimulus to further study in an important phase of American cultural life.

GREGORY PAINE

ACKNOWLEDGMENTS

For permission to reprint material from the works of authors listed below, the editor expresses grateful acknowledgment to the publishers and individuals indicated.

JAMES LANE ALLEN: The selection from *The Reign of Law* is printed by permission of The Macmillan Company, publishers.

WILLIAM BYRD: The selections from Byrd's *Histories of the Dividing Line Betwixt Virginia and North Carolina* are printed through the courtesy of the North Carolina State Department of Archives and History, publishers.

O. HENRY: "Thimble, Thimble" is printed by permission of Doubleday, Doran & Company from *Options*, by O. Henry, copyright 1908, 1909, 1925 by Doubleday, Page & Company.

SYDNEY LANIER: The selections from *Retrospects and Prospects* and from *Music and Poetry* are printed by consent of Charles Scribner's Sons, publishers.

THOMAS NELSON PAGE: "How Jinny Eased Her Mind" is reprinted from *Pastime Stories*, by permission of Charles Scribner's Sons, publishers.

WALTER HINES PAGE: The selections from *The Southerner*, by Nicholas Worth (Walter Hines Page) are printed through the courtesy of Arthur W. Page, Esq., for the Page family.

WOODROW WILSON: The passages from "Mere Literature" are reprinted from *Mere Literature and Other Essays*, published by Houghton Mifflin Company, 1896, copyright by Woodrow Wilson, by permission of Houghton Mifflin Company.

The passages from the Address on Robert E. Lee are reprinted from *The Public Papers of Woodrow Wilson. College and State*, Edited by Ray Stannard Baker and William E. Dodd, through the courtesy of Mrs. Woodrow Wilson.

CONTENTS

Biography of Patrick Henry

INTRODUCTION

I. RACES AND CLASSES

The first white settlements in the South were necessarily along the seaboard, where ships could enter deep water harbors or creep up the wide rivers of the coastal plain. The Spaniards entered the St. Johns River of Florida to establish settlements on its banks, and the French sailed up the tortuous outlets of the Mississippi. After the ill-fated Raleigh settlement on Roanoke Island, still the subject of historical conjecture and fanciful legend, the London Company established the settlement of Jamestown on a malarial peninsula of the James River. Of the three hundred adventurers who came to Jamestown in 1607–1609, ninety-five were designated as "gentlemen." According to John Smith, they were more fitted "to spoyle a commonwealth than to begin or maintain one," and there were "many unruly gallants packed thither by their friends to escape ill destinies." But these "gallants" had slight influence on the later fortunes of the colony, for "of the persons alive in Virginia in October, 1609, all but sixty had died by May of the following year."[1] By 1624 the Company had sent over fourteen thousand persons, of whom nearly thirteen thousand died from exposure or disease, or at the hands of the Indians. By 1715 there were seventy-two thousand whites, besides twenty-three thousand Negroes, in the colony, and during this century of expansion thousands of men had left Virginia to settle in adjacent colonies, especially North Carolina.[2]

Some of the starving settlers were saved by eating corn—the maize obtained by barter from the Indians or easily raised

[1] T. J. Wertenbaker, *Patrician and Plebeian in Virginia* (Charlottesville, Va.: 1910), pp. 7–8.

[2] John Fiske, *Old Virginia and Her Neighbors* (Boston: 1897), II, 169.

—and to this day corn is the most widely produced grain of the South, from the dunes of the coast to the steep slopes of the Smokies. But it was tobacco that made Virginia prosperous. The plant was cultivated easily, and ships carried the dried yellow leaves to the ports of England, where factors paid good prices. A staple crop was developed which would bring in double repayment for the hundred thousand pounds expenditure by the London Company. The raising of tobacco spread up the fertile tongues of land along the James, York, Chickahominy, and Potomac rivers. Its culture required the labor of many hands, working most of the year in planting, cultivating, curing, and marketing. On his fertile acres the successful plantation owner, with natural gifts of initiative and industry, directed his servants or his slaves in raising the staple crop. The annual yield was loaded from his private river wharf upon ships which carried the golden weed to England. In the autumn the planter might take passage on the vessel to sell his product at the highest prices, or to spend the winter in London or on the Continent. His son might accompany him to study law at the Inns of Court or to enter a university. The returning vessel was not empty, but brought back new tools and stock, furniture and tapestries, clothing and jewelry, wines and liquors, paintings and books. Back on his estate, among his friendly neighbors, the Virginia planter might receive political recognition through appointment to offices by the crown, or by election to the House of Burgesses or the Council.

In the seventeenth century the laborers on the tobacco plantations were chiefly white servants, but in the eighteenth century the Negroes did the field work. Many of the white servants were "free-willers," who sold their services voluntarily for a term of years to pay for the passage to the New World. Life was so hard and mere existence so precarious for the agricultural laborers and the miners of England that they would gladly sell a few years of life to reach the land of opportunity so glowingly described by plantation owners and masters of vessels. Some were debtors forced by severe English laws to flee from the clutches of their creditors. Others were political prisoners, the patriots of lost causes, guilty only of having been defeated by the Cromwellian Commonwealth or by the Stuarts in power. Others, who did not labor in the tobacco fields, signed articles of indenture to work on the plantations as tailors, weavers, blacksmiths, or as other artisans, or even to tutor the young masters and mistresses. These servants were of a fairly good class, generally, but there were some criminals, the number of which is still a sore point. We recall the remark of Dr. Johnson, who scorned all Americans: "Why, they are a race of convicts, and ought to be thankful of anything we allow them short of hanging!" Since there were three hundred offenses in the English code punishable by death, even hardened judges sought transportation as a compromise. Some criminals were sent to the colonies, including Virginia, but the colonial authorities met the attempts to send jail-birds to them with vigorous, and generally successful, opposition.

The number of white servants was surprisingly large, for there was an annual immigration of from fifteen hundred to two thousand, in the period from 1635 to 1705, "making a total for these decades of from 100,000 to 140,000."[3] This was in Virginia alone, and to Maryland and other colonies came many more.

Contrary to popular belief, seventeenth-century Virginia was not divided into large plantations, but was possessed by hundreds of small farmers, with holdings of from fifty to one hundred acres each. At the end of the century two-thirds of the free-holders cultivated their own plantations without slaves.

[3] T. J. Wertenbaker, *The First Americans, 1607–1690* (New York: 1927), p. 25.

The growth of large plantations in the next century was based upon slave labor, which, although it was less efficient than that of indentured servants, cost only one-third as much as white labor, and the supply of slaves was ample. In 1690 there were not more than four thousand slaves in Virginia. Even such wealthy Virginians as Robert Wormsley, Robert Beverley, Mrs. Elizabeth Digges, John Carter, William Fitzhugh, and the first William Byrd had few slaves, usually fewer than a hundred each. Although William Fitzhugh had plantations of twenty-three thousand acres in 1686, he owned only twenty-nine slaves and a few white servants.[4]

The eighteenth century brought great changes to Virginia. The Tidewater planters formed an aristocratic class, which dominated the colony. With an insatiable hunger for land, and more land, some planters increased their holdings until they commanded thousands of acres.

Beyond the seventeenth-century plantations along the Virginia rivers, there stretched a vast and mysterious wilderness. Indian traders and land scouts brought back reports of the rough Piedmont area beyond the fall line, and of high mountain ridges in the West. Various explorers, especially John Lederer, led expeditions to the summits of the Blue Ridge, and told fabulous tales of "silver tomahawks, Amazonian Indian women, peacocks, lakes 'ten leagues broad,' and barren sandy deserts." In 1716 Governor Spotswood led a band of gentlemen, rangers, and servants over the Blue Ridge into the Great Valley and took possession of the region in the name of King George I.

[4] J. T. Adams, *Provincial Society, 1690–1763* (New York: 1927), p. 30. See also F. A. Bruce, *Economic History of Virginia in the Seventeenth Century* (New York: 1896), 2 vols.; L. G. Tyler, *England in America, 1580–1652* (New York: 1904); H. S. Osgood, *The American Colonies in the Seventeenth Century* (New York: 1904, 1907), 3 vols.; Mary N. Stanard, *Colonial Virginia; Its People and Customs* (Philadelphia: 1917).

Emancipated servants were granted their "head-rights" of fifty acres each along the branches of rivers in the "upcountry." Some of these upcountry families reared sons who became leaders in colonial affairs. In 1732 Peter Jefferson patented a thousand acres at the foot of the Blue Ridge, and in 1743 his son Thomas was born. Patrick Henry was born and grew to manhood in the foothills. Into the Shenandoah Valley came groups of dissenters who later aided in destroying the Anglican establishment. Down from Pennsylvania came a stream of Scotch-Irish, Germans, English Quakers, and Welsh Baptists to scatter over the Piedmont of Virginia and the Carolinas and to press westward into the Appalachians.

A most important racial group were the Scotch-Irish, democratic, liberty-loving, religious, virile, and Indian-hating. The Scotch-Irish were the descendants of Scotch Presbyterians whom James I had settled in Ulster, in northern Ireland, to turn the country from Catholicism. By the end of the seventeenth century their position as dissenters in opposition to James II and William III had become intolerable, and many emigrated to America. Their chief port of entry was Philadelphia. After they had taken up the best lands of western Pennsylvania, they crept along the wilderness roads by wagons and pack-horses into the Shenandoah Valley, down into the fertile valleys of Piedmont North Carolina, and over into the hill country of South Carolina and Georgia. Other groups landed at Charleston, and moved up the banks of the rivers to join their kin in the uplands of the Carolinas. Thousands came annually during the middle decades of the eighteenth century. Their sufferings had intensified their piety and stern religious faith, which was founded on the theology of Calvin and Knox. Their love of learning led to the establishment of schools and colleges. Exalting the importance of individual man, they were democratic and liberty-loving. Too warlike to fear the Indians and too greedy for land to live at peace with them, they were Indian-haters and bold frontiersmen, forming a bulwark of security to the Tidewater settlers. On the tombstone of one of them is this character-revealing epitaph: "Here lies the remains of John Lewis, who slew the Irish lord, settled Augusta County, located the town of Staunton, and furnished five sons to fight the battles of the American Revolution."[5] Loving the pioneer life with its perils and rewards, the sons of the Scotch-Irish settled in the coves and valleys of the Appalachian Highlands and passed beyond the mountains to lay the foundations of Kentucky and Tennessee. From this stock came such presidents as Jefferson, Monroe, Jackson, the Harrisons, Polk, Buchanan, Johnson, and Wilson, also scores of southern leaders.

Another racial group, the Germans, also migrated into the Piedmont of Virginia and North Carolina, where they established compact communities on the rich lands of the river bottoms. They built plain, comfortable cabins on well-kept farms, which were worked by both men and women. Their industrial life was based on free white labor, for seldom did they buy slaves. Although law-abiding and patriotic, they took little interest in politics. In their homes, schools, and churches they spoke German, for the English language came slowly. Firm in simple piety they zealously supported their local churches of Lutherans, German Reformed, and Moravians. Of these the Moravian Brethren, followers of John Huss, made the largest settlements. In 1752 Bishop Spangenburg led an exploring party from Edenton, North Carolina, to the summit of the Blue Ridge and selected a tract of ten thousand acres in the Piedmont. Another land-looking party of twelve "single brethren" made a journey from Bethlehem, Pennsylvania, in a large covered wagon drawn by six horses. The Moravians brought a large tract "of wild rugged country into a high state of population and improvement," and established centers

[5] Quoted by Adams, *ibid.*, pp. 172–173.

of marketing, industries, and education, of which the chief was Salem.[6]

Maryland, Virginia's neighboring colony on the Chesapeake, dates from 1643, when the *Ark* and the *Dove* anchored near the mouth of the Potomac with twenty gentlemen and two hundred laborers to found the town of St. Mary's. The economy of the colony was like that of Virginia, therefore, in establishing one class, an aristocracy of planters and traders, and another of servants. Although Maryland had been planted under Catholic auspices, it was tolerant of other Christian sects, even welcoming a thousand Puritans from southern Virginia. Baltimore, founded in 1729 on the Susquehanna, became a port for the shipment of furs, flour, and farm produce.

South Carolina, which was settled later than Virginia, but earlier than North Carolina, was peopled by groups of Englishmen, not only from England, but from the Bahamas, Barbados, Virginia, and New England, and by French Huguenots, a few Scotch, and the Scotch-Irish. One William Sayle planted a colony on "the first highland" (1670–1671) on the peninsula at the junction of the Ashley and Cooper rivers, the site of the Charleston of today. The unhealthy swamp lands along the rivers, where extensive indigo and rice plantations extended, drove the planters to the coast during many months of the year, leaving their plantations to the care of overseers. Some planters were also traders and merchants. Such prominent Charlestonians as Gabriel Manigault, Isaac Mazyck, Henry Laurens, and John Rutledge exported provisions to the West Indies, the staples rice and indigo to England or to the continent

[6] See Elkanah Watson, *Men and Times of the Revolution* (New York: 1856), p. 255. See also C. R. Hanna, *The Scotch-Irish* (New York: 1902), 2 vols.; P. J. Hamilton, *The Colonization of the South* (Philadelphia: 1904); J. W. Wayland, *The German Element of the Shenandoah Valley of Virginia* (Charlottesville, Va.: 1907); M. L. Hansen, *The Atlantic Migration, 1607–1860* (Cambridge, Mass.: 1940); Adelaide L. Fries, *The Road to Salem* (Chapel Hill, N.C.: 1944).

south of Finisterre, and brought back articles of English manufacture and other commodities.[7]   Manigault was a Huguenot,
an able representative of the French exiles who came to America
after the revocation of the Edict of Nantes in 1685.   Many of
these refugees came to the northern colonies, especially New
York, and groups of several hundred each came to Virginia,
establishing themselves along the James River and later dis-
persing over the colony.[8]   But to South Carolina came the
largest number of Huguenot exiles, who made six separate
settlements, largely on the Santee and Cooper rivers.   After
an early inter-racial friction, they were rapidly accepted in
commercial and political life.   Some became merchant princes,
for example, Isaac Mazyck, Stephen Godin, René Ravenel,
Solomon Legaré, and Gabriel Manigault.   Although they probably did not constitute more than a tenth of the population,
they "have exercised an influence beyond their proportional
numbers," as D. D. Wallace states, and "their influence has
been due to their moral and intellectual fibre being so rigidly
tested as to eliminate those unable to endure suffering for their
convictions, and to the discipline of their misfortunes."[9]   Of
the leading soldiers, politicians, and literary men of South
Carolina, Francis Marion, Henry Laurens, Washington Allston,
and Hugh Swinton Legaré came of this stock.

The early settlers of North Carolina were land-seeking Virginians, largely freed servants, who crossed the boundary to
settle on the rich bottom lands along Albemarle Sound.   Probably many of these "lubbers" were worthless, and were marked
by laziness and animality, as William Byrd II asserted in his
History of the Dividing Line.   In the eighteenth century English-

[7] C. L. Becker, *Beginnings of the American People* (Boston, Mass.:
c. 1915), p. 166.
[8] H. M. Jones, *America and French Culture* (Chapel Hill, N.C.:
1927), p. 95.
[9] *The History of South Carolina* (4 vols.; New York: 1934–1935),
I, 150.

men of a better class established plantations along the tidal rivers for the raising of tobacco, rice, and cotton by the work of slaves. Dr. John Brickell, a physician of colonial North Carolina, wrote approvingly of these planters in *The Natural History of North Carolina*, first published in 1737. These later English settlers may have been prosaic and unromantic, but they had "hard common sense, courage, foresight, and determination."[10]

Besides the English there were four other racial streams that entered North Carolina—French Huguenots, Scottish Highlanders, Scotch-Irish, and Germans. In 1691 some Huguenots settled on the Pamlico River and later on the Neuse, Trent, and Cape Fear rivers. They were unimportant in numbers and influence in comparison with the picturesque Scottish Highlanders, who came by way of the ports of Wilmington and Charleston in the middle decades of the eighteenth century. Along the Cape Fear River the Scotch prospered, suffering the severest hardships, rivaling the Indians as hunters, and retaining their native customs and language. One of the paradoxes of their colorful life is that, after their persecutions by monarchial government in Scotland, they were loyalists in the Revolution, and suffered defeat at Moore's Creek Bridge in 1776. The legends of the romantic Flora MacDonald still survive, notably in Paul Green's play *The Highland Call*, presented annually in Fayetteville, North Carolina.[11]

Georgia, the last of the thirteen colonies to be founded, had "as cosmopolitan a population as could be found in America." It became a sort of cross-roads of the world, for within a half dozen years after the beginning there could be found in the colony Piedmontese, Swiss, Salzburgers, Moravians, Germans,

[10] R. D. W. Connor, *Race Elements in the White Population of North Carolina* (Raleigh, N.C.: 1920), p. 12.

[11] Published by the University of North Carolina Press, Chapel Hill, N.C.: 1941.

Jews, Scotch Highlanders, and English."[12] The Board of Trustees sent over about twenty-five hundred debtors from English prisons, who settled Savannah; from Austria came twelve
hundred Lutheran Salzburgers, who settled at Red Bluff on
the Savannah; Lieutenant Hugh Mackay brought two hundred
Highland Scots, who settled at New Inverness, later Darien,
on the Altamaha; in 1733 forty Jews came to Savannah, where
they took "some noticeable part in the affairs"; several groups
of Moravians came from Saxony, but these pacifists would not
take up arms against the Spaniards, and soon left for Pennsylvania. The few indentured servants from England, Wales,
and Germany were discontented, lazy, and criminal, playing
an insignificant part in the settlement. Several hundred Puritans came by way of South Carolina and Massachusetts, and
prospered with their slaves on rice and indigo plantations at
Sunbury; refugee Acadians stopped on their way from Nova
Scotia to Louisiana and France.

Outside of the original thirteen colonies, in the frontier
regions of Florida and Louisiana the Spaniards and French
struggled to found and maintain settlements and to acquire
large territories for their crowns. Each region was explored
and settled by colorful men whose exploits are the glory of
historians and romancers. To the peninsula of Florida came
Ponce de Leon, Narvaez, and Menéndez to make discoveries
and plant settlements. The French Huguenots who attempted
to colonize on the St. Johns River were massacred. From 1762
to the close of the Revolution Florida was in the possession of
England and was staunch and true during the conflict. At the
end of the war Florida was returned to Spain in exchange for
the Bahama Islands, and in 1819 it was ceded to the United
States. Its colonial period was marked by Indian warfare, and

[12] E. M. Coulter, *A Short History of Georgia* (Chapel Hill, N.C.:
1833), p. 29. See also Reba C. Strickland, *Religion and the State in
Georgia in the Eighteenth Century* (New York: 1939).

by border conflict with South Carolina and Georgia and with the French to the west.

In Louisiana's romantic history, the reader is stirred by De Soto's expedition from Florida across the wilderness to the Mississippi, by La Salle's expedition down the Great River, and by Bienville's long career in the building of forts which later became cities. There was Spanish rule in Louisiana from 1763 to 1802, only a year before the Louisiana Purchase by Jefferson. Thus there were rival peoples in New Orleans, and a confusion of tongues and traditions which contrasted with the prevailing English pattern of the eastern seaboard, and later supplied varied materials for a southern literature.

The movement of the English, Scotch-Irish, and others across the Appalachians into the transmontane South began very early. First went the fur traders, following with their long pack trains the trading paths from Charleston and the English forts on the James River into the Cherokee country and beyond, meeting always the bitter rivalry of the French, who traded northward from the Gulf Coast and held the allegiance of the Creek nation. Then came the "long hunters," like James Knox, Dr. Thomas Walker, and Daniel Boone, who spent more than one consecutive hunting season in the wilderness without returning home, and who, through their explorations, learned much of the country and its resources. Later these men were able to locate valuable lands for the eastern land speculators who took up vast tracts and opened them for settlement. After the Treaty of Fort Stanwix in 1768, the pioneers went over the mountains in large numbers to settle in Kentucky and Tennessee. Famous names belong to this epic story—Daniel Boone and John Sevier, frontier heroes; George Washington and Thomas Jefferson, who early saw the significance of English settlement in the Great Valley; Andrew Jackson, great exponent of the region; and many others. To mention them and to recall the movements in which they participated is to realize a basic factor in the cultural life of the South—the juxtaposition of the older plantation economy and the newer, ever-moving, increasingly aggressive frontier.

II. PLANTATION AND FRONTIER

During the eighteenth century the plantation and frontier systems produced opposed economic and cultural groups in the southern colonies. In seventeenth-century Virginia the word *plantation* had the meaning of the modern word *colony*, but later it meant an agricultural unit where the work was divided among groups of slaves who worked in routine under overseers and foremen to produce the staple commodity of tobacco for sale. In southern North Carolina, and in South Carolina a valuable staple crop was rice. The plantation system produced, besides its staple crop, a wealthy class of landed, slave-owning, office-holding gentry, who rebelled against England in the Revolutionary War, established a sectional, antinorthern "Cotton Kingdom" in the Old South, and suffered defeat in the War Between the States.

The frontier system developed on the borders of the plantations, receded to the Piedmont and Appalachian regions, and still survives in the back country of the hills and mountains. The settlers farmed small holdings and seldom owned slaves. As U. B. Phillips states: "Frontier industrial units were on an average still smaller, comprising in many cases only a single person; agriculture was pursued only to supply necessaries, attention was often given mainly to hunting or Indian trading, and the individual or group was in many emergencies concerned with the protection of life more than the accumulation of property."[13] These frontiersmen were not "poor whites," but, as we have indicated, sturdy Scotch-Irish, resourceful Germans, and other groups of vigorous men.

[13] *Plantation and Frontier* (Cleveland, Ohio: 1910), I, 73. See also V. W. Crane, *The Southern Frontier, 1670–1732* (Philadelphia: 1929).

Some of the planters in Tidewater Virginia, Maryland, and North Carolina were Cavaliers, connected with the best families of England, but most of them were middle-class men who came to the New World because it had limitless land. The planters in Tidewater Virginia obtained holdings by royal grants, and by treaty or theft from the Indians. They increased their holdings by purchases from their neighbors through bankrupt sales, and by marrying heiresses. By the English laws of entail and primogeniture successive elder sons built up mammoth home plantations. A successful planter might own a dozen plantations in half a dozen counties.

The methods of tobacco culture were ruinous to many plantations, for the system was fundamentally wasteful, with the despoiling of fertility, ignorance of scientific methods of agriculture, use of unreliable labor, and thriftlessness. Believing incorrectly that tobacco must be grown on new ground, the planter "girdled" and burned big trees of valuable timber and set out the plants among the stumps. No fertilizer was used, the rains washed away and leached the topsoil, and new forest ground must be painfully grubbed. The work was done almost entirely by hand tools, for the few plows were drawn by oxen. The planters continually grumbled about the worthlessness of overseers and the laziness of the slaves. Most planters borrowed money on each crop and were in frequent danger of bankruptcy. A few planters prospered, however, because of greater skill and intelligence, aided by diversified farming and the sale of horses and stock—and even slaves. They developed princely estates along the tidal rivers, with mansions and spacious grounds. Some of these exist today in much of their former grandeur.

This small number of planters established "a class so wealthy, so powerful, its members so bound to one another by marriage and other ties, and so intrenched in influence with the various authorities as to set them apart in quite a different way from

that in which the moderate distinctions of wealth had operated earlier."[14]

Even Professor Wertenbaker, who often questions the
"Cavalier tradition" and the glorification of the First Families
of Virginia, speaks well of planters, stating that "if they were
men of means and purchased or developed considerable estates,
they had to take upon themselves the responsibility of controlling, directing, and caring for their servants and slaves.
This developed in them a sense of self-reliance, self-respect and
the power of command." [15]

Like the greatest squire in an English parish the planter assumed leadership in the local religious and political groups.
A citizen like Nicholas Spencer, Richard Lee, Robert Beverley,
Adam Thoroughgood, or William Byrd owned the principal
pew in the parish church and was senior warden of the vestry,
sat at the head of the justices on the county bench, and paraded
as colonel of the militia on muster days. He might represent
his county in the House of Burgesses at Williamsburg, serve
on the Council, or even receive an important office through
appointment by the royal governor.

The planter-gentleman class was entirely aristocratic in its
assumption of superiority in social graces, learning, business
acumen, and political sagacity. The planters educated their
own children, but were not willing to tax themselves for universal education. They controlled local and state politics by
limiting voting to freeholders, and by distributing patronage.
The frontiersmen in the Piedmont and the great valleys beyond
the Blue Ridge resented the proud arrogance of the planters,
and on the eve of the Revolution there was lack of sympathy
and coöperation between the West and the East, between the
low country and the back country.

Physiographically separated from the coast country, the far-

[14] Adams, *Provincial Society*, p. 215.
[15] *Patrician and Plebeian in Virginia*, p. 397.

mer-pioneers were untouched by its social traditions and were often hostile to its political activities. When the planters and the "Buckskin Men" met in Williamsburg, Edenton, or Charleston, they were far apart in appearance, speech, and ideas. The gentlemen were dressed in breeches and hose, colored waistcoats, lace and ruffles; the plain people in skins and canvas. The cultured speech of men trained at Oxford, Cambridge, and the Inns of Court was answered in the dialects of the Scotch-Irish and German-Americans. Suave, artificial imperiousness was too often met by frank, rude resentment. Above all, the Piedmont West hated the political domination by the Tidewater East, secured by unequal representation in the colonial assemblies. The unbalanced political representation in Virginia led to threats of state dismemberment, which were not allayed until 1816, when a compromise was reached. In North Carolina the Piedmont West, infuriated by Royal and planter officers and by unequal taxes, revolted in a Regulator uprising which led to skirmishes and battles. Later the quarrels between East and West were partially quieted by the arbitrary division of the state into two sections by counties, and the election of the governor from the sections for alternate terms with no re-election. At the time of the Revolution the wealthy planters and merchants of South Carolina, who numbered 26,644 whites, elected twenty senators and seventy representatives, whereas the upcountry, with 111,534 whites, elected only seventeen senators and fifty-four representatives.[16] Resentful as the upcountry men might be, they were usually powerless, for the plantation aristocracy produced the ablest leaders to dominate both the state capitals and the principal market towns. It remained for the American Revolution to unite the opposing interests and to give the back country a voice through its "forest-born Demosthenes," Patrick Henry.

[16] David Y. Thomas, *Studies in Southern History and Politics* (New York: 1914), p. 253.

III. EARLY WRITING AND PUBLISHING

The Englishmen who established or visited the first settlements along the Chesapeake and Albermarle Tidewater wrote
much about the wonders and resources of the New World.
Their "true reports" and "Good News" were written to attract emigrants from the British Isles or to defend themselves
against false accusations.   The letters and journals contain
marvelous accounts of the natural resources and amazing wonders of the New World, and lively narrative of escapes from
hurricanes and "salvages."

The dozen letters and histories by Captain John Smith make
good reading.   His latest editor, A. G. Bradley, staunchly
asserts: "It is not too much to say that Smith's writings afford
a liberal education in the methods, manners, sentiments, and
hopes of the men who were in the forefront of English coloni-
sation in the stirring age."[17]   Of his dozen writings three are
of especial importance: *A True Relation* (1608), which is a
forty-page letter giving an account of the Jamestown settlement; *A Map of Virginia* (1612), for its incidents of settlement
and Indian life; and the *Generall Historie* (1624), in which he
wrote all about the Virginia that he knew.   Smith's chief contribution to the legends of Virginia is the story of his escape
from death by Powhatan's axe-man through the intervention
of that "Numpareill of Virginia," the Indian girl Pocahontas.
The historians of the colonial period repeated in all seriousness
Smith's story, but later the legend became a persistent romantic
theme in stories, novels, poems, and plays.   John Davis, an
English-American sailor, poet, traveler, and tutor introduced
the story in a short story, a novelette, and a novel, *The First
Settlers of America* (1805).   Since then, it has been treated in at
least six novels, twenty-nine plays, and thirty-five narrative
poems by Americans; English writers have added more.

[17] *Captain John Smith* (London: 1905), pp. 222–223.

The horrors of the hurricane which overwhelmed Sir Thomas
Gates and his companions in the shipwreck of the "Sea-Ven-
ture" on the Bermuda Islands were related by several sur-
vivors, especially William Strachey, Richard Rich, and Silvester
Jourdan, whose accounts reached the ears or eyes of Shakespeare to be immortalized in *The Tempest*.

All of the colonial pamphlets and books were printed in
England, under the successive licensing acts, as were Robert
Beverley's *A History of the Present State of Virginia* (1705),
John Lawson's *New Voyage to Carolina* (1709), later published
as the *History of North Carolina*, Hugh Jones's *The Present
State of Virginia* (1724), and William Stith's *History of the
First Discovery and Settlement of Virginia* (1747). Several of
the best writings by colonial Virginians remained in manuscript
for a century or more. The excellent prose and verse of the
"Burwell Papers," probably written by John Cotton of "Queen's
Creek," were not printed until 1814. Colonel Henry Norwood
told about the thrilling incidents of a remarkable voyage in
1649 in a manuscript which was published two centuries later
in Force's *Historical Tracts*.

The numerous manuscripts of William Byrd II, recorded in
shorthand by his secretary, were not deciphered for a hundred
years, and they were not printed until the middle of the nineteenth century. In 1841 was published *The Westover Manuscripts*, containing *The History of the Dividing Line*, based upon
the 1728 survey, which remains his best work on account of
its descriptions of frontier life and its racy style. In the same
volume was *A Journey to the Land of Eden, A. D. 1733*, a descriptive account of Byrd's rich, fruitful lands, open to settlers,
in northwestern North Carolina, also *A Progress to the Mines*,
a journey to iron mines in central Virginia. In 1901 J. S. Bassett edited these *Writings*, retaining the manuscript peculiarities of the orthography of Byrd's secretary, prefixing an able
introduction, and adding an appendix which lists the books in

Byrd's library, the largest colonial library in the South. In 1929 William H. Boyd edited Byrd's *Histories of the Dividing Line*, which prints on opposite pages the previously-published *History of the Dividing Line*, and the *Secret History*, a shorter narrative which contains unfavorable comments on Byrd's Virginia colleagues. The recent publication of the first and second parts of *The Secret Diary of William Byrd* has renewed interest in Byrd's varied life.

The British government and its despotic agents, the royal governors, did not want printing presses set up in the colonies, for they feared that treasonous, seditious writings would lead to political uprisings against authority. Governor William Berkeley's remark in 1671 was the secret thought of a dozen royal governors: "I thank God we have not free schools nor printing and I hope we shall not have these hundred years. For learning has brought disobedience and heresy and sects into the world; and printing has divulged them and libels against the government. God keep us from both." When John Buckner, a merchant and landowner, brought to Jamestown a printer named William Nuthead to print the laws of 1680, without license, there arose a flurry of excitement in the governor's palace. Lord Culpeper reproved Buckner and Nuthead, and they "entered into bond in £100 not to print any thing thereafter." With his commission as governor, Lord Effingham received a royal order that "no person be permitted to use any press for printing upon any occasion whatsoever."

Printers and presses, however, slowly and delayed, entered the southern colonies. Even the royal governors invited them, advertised for them, and paid printers well to print decrees and laws for distribution. After his trouble at Jamestown, William Nuthead was invited to St. Mary's City, the capital of Maryland, where he was paid in 1685, "five Thousand five Hundred and fifty pounds of Tobaccoe." For a time William

Parks was official printer for both Maryland and Virginia, and was paid £200 by each "in country produce." The government of South Carolina advertised £175 sterling as aid to the first printer. Almost immediately three appeared—George Webb of unknown residence, Eleazir Phillips, Jr. from Boston, and Thomas Whitemarch from Philadelphia. Each served briefly as colonial printer, and each died of yellow fever within a year or two. Acknowledging that he was "printer to his majesty," Whitemarch printed a long notice in the first number of his *South Carolina Gazette*, warning contributors of "Essays, whether in Prose or Verse . . . that the Purport of them be not too manifestly opposite to the Principles laid down in the following lines. . . .

I'm not High Church, nor Low Church, nor Tory nor Whig,
No flatt'ring young Coxcomb, nor formal old Prig:
Not eternally talking, nor silently quaint,
No profligate Sinner, nor pragmatical Saint.
. . . .
To no party a Slave, in no squabbles I join
Nor damn the opinion that differs from mine.
Evil tongues I contemn, no mob Treasons I sing,
I dote on my Country, and am Liege to my King."

A later editor of the *South Carolina Gazette*, Lewis Timothy, was a man of great force in his advocacy of freedom and liberty in the ante-Revolution period. The Stamp Act, which he bitterly opposed, caused him to suspend the publication of his paper. James Johnston, a Scotchman, received £100 sterling as the first printer of Georgia, and issued *The Georgia Gazette* from 1763 to 1776.

Perhaps the following listing of the first printers in the South will help in understanding the establishing of printing.

Maryland, St. Mary's City, 1685, William Nuthead.
Virginia, Williamsburg, 1730, William Parks.

South Carolina, Charleston, 1731, George Webb.
North Carolina, New Bern, 1749, James Davis.
Georgia, Savannah, 1762, James Johnston.
Louisiana, New Orleans, 1764, Denis Braud.
Florida, St. Augustine, 1783, John Wells and Charles Wright.
Kentucky, Lexington, 1787, John and Fielding Bradford.
Tennessee, Rogersville, 1791, George Roulstone and Robert
    Ferguson.
Mississippi, Fort Hill, 1798, Andrew Marschalk.
Alabama, Fort Stoddert, 1811, Samuel Miller and John B. Hood.
Texas, Galveston, 1817, Samuel Bangs.
Arkansas, Arkansas Post, 1819, William E. Woodruff.[18]

The early printings were proclamations, records of legislative bodies, laws, and other official documents. Parks printed a new tobacco law, the Bradfords printed *The Kentucke Almanack*, and in Mississippi the first printing is supposed to have been a ballad, "The Galley Slave," of which no copy exists. If one should scan carefully the twelve volumes of Evans's *American Bibliography*, which is a listing of printings in the United States from 1639 to 1800, the study would reveal few pamphlets or books of belletristic nature printed in the South.

The colonial printers usually established weekly newspapers to keep the press working and to bring in money. William Parks established the *Maryland Gazette* (1727) in Annapolis and the *Virginia Gazette* (1736) in Williamsburg. Phillips started the *South Carolina Weekly Journal* (1732) in Charleston, and had an immediate rival in Whitemarsh's the *South Carolina Gazette*. Davis started the *North Carolina Gazette* (1751) in New Bern, Johnston the *Georgia Gazette* (1763) in Savannah,

[18] Lawrence C. Wroth, *The Colonial Printer* (2d ed.; Portland, Maine: 1938). See also the pamphlets by Douglas C. McMurtrie on early printing in each of the southern colonies and states, and his *A History of Printing in the United States: Middle Atlantic States* (New York: 1936).

Wells and Wright the *East-Florida Gazette* (1783) in St. Augustine, John Bradford the *Kentucke* (later *Kentucky*) *Gazette* (1783) in Lexington, and Roulstone and Ferguson the *Knoxville Gazette* (1791). When Louisiana was under French rule, Louis Duclot founded *Moniteur de la Louisiane* (1794) in New Orleans. There is little known about the *Mississippi Gazette* (1800) started at Natchez by Benjamin M. Stockes, or the *Mobile Centinel* (1811) at Fort Stoddert by Miller and Hood, or the *Arkansas Gazette* (1819) by Woodruff at Arkansas Post. An important citizen of Texas by the name of Samuel Bangs founded the *Texas Republican* (1819) at Nacogdoches.

These first papers were not newspapers in the modern sense. Although announcing "Containing the freshest Advices both Foreign and Domestick," there was little news printed, and the early colonial papers carried no advertisements. They were called *gazettes*, and, in imitation of the English gazettes, were official in printing the proclamations of governors and the proceedings of councils. The editor, who was usually a better printer than journalist, welcomed contributions of letters and articles, even jokes and poems. These helped him fill up his space—and they furnished a publishing medium for literary aspirants.

The colonial newspapers were hard hit by the Stamp Act of 1765, for it taxed each issue and every advertisement. Jonas Greene, a later editor of the *Maryland Gazette*, printed his last edition in mourning rules, with "The Times are Dismal, Doleful, Dolorus, and Dollarless" around a death's head. Other papers were suspended until the next year when the hated tax was removed.

When the war began in 1775 ten newspapers were being published in the South: two in Maryland, two in Virginia, two in North Carolina, three in South Carolina, and one in Georgia.

The Revolution, the foundation of the Republic, and the

clashes of the Federalist and Democratic (Anti-Federalist) parties made newspapers so important that in 1810, when Isaiah Thomas made his compilation, there were one hundred and eleven newspapers in the South.[19]

Journalism went over the Alleghenies when John Bradford of Virginia brought a printing-press to Lexington, Kentucky, started the *Kentucky Gazette* and became state printer. It took him a year to transport press and supplies from Philadelphia to Lexington, by wagon over the mountains to Pittsburgh, by flat boat down the Ohio to Maysville, by pack horse, from which it "fell into pi," to Lexington. His *Kentucky Gazette* was the only paper in all the West. Each copy, too precious for personal use, was sent by a post rider to distant places, even into Ohio and Tennessee. When a copy reached a settlement the best reader mounted a stump and read to the "assembled multitude" every word in the *Gazette*, including advertisements. John Bradford became a leader in his section. Although a Jeffersonian Democrat and a member of the Democratic Society of Lexington, he was not too violent a partisan to admit to his paper the writings of opponents.

Jeffersonian democracy had a more mettlesome champion in Thomas Ritchie (1778–1854) who edited the *Richmond Enquirer* from 1804 to 1845. The advocates of states' rights looked upon him as their oracle, and the Whigs hated him.[20]

In the succeeding decades the southern newspapers became increasingly partisan and sectional. Richie's opponent in Richmond was John Hampden Pleasants, who founded the *Richmond Whig* in 1827 and edited it until his death in 1846. The conservative planters and merchants of the Tidewater, who advocated greater control by the national government,

[19] Isaiah Thomas, *The History of Printing in America* (2d ed.; Albany, N.Y.: 1874), II, 296–305.

[20] G. F. Mellen, "Southern Editors," *The South in the Building of the Nation*, VII, 472.

supported Pleasants. His career ended in tragedy, for he was killed in a duel by Thomas Ritchie, Jr., who was editing his father's *Enquirer*.

In the decades before 1861 hundreds of newspapers arose and fell in the South. With each leader and faction starting a newspaper as a mouthpiece, with many leaders in politics and religion, the press spread from town to town. Within a large city, where only one or two papers are printed today, there were many competing daily; thus New Orleans had a dozen and Raleigh had ten. Gradually weak papers succumbed or were absorbed by stronger rivals, and there are now fewer than twenty leading newspapers that have passed the century mark. Many of the most powerful newspapers today have been started within fifty years.

The newspapers gladly welcomed contributions of verse and prose; yet their contents have not been thoroughly examined to show the volume and excellence of this literary matter. In her study of colonial newspapers Miss Cook has included the discussion of the *Maryland Gazette*, the *Virginia Gazette*, and the *South Carolina Gazette*.[21] The editors of these gazettes reprinted poems, essays, stories, and even plays from British books and periodicals. In the *Maryland Gazette*, as shown in ten extant issues, were the "Plain Dealer" essays, which include fables in verse and prose, fairy stories, legends, and old tales, such as Chaucer's "Man of Law's Tale" under a new guise. In its fragmentary pages there is evidenced "the periodical essay in an advanced form, much tolerable verse in direct imitation of current English forms, [and] a great regard for Pope and Addison,—Milton as well."

The *Virginia Gazette* is even more important for its contents. In twenty-two numbers appeared an essay-serial "The Monitor." In imitation of Addison and Steele's *Spectator* an omni-

---

[21] Elizabeth C. Cook, *Literary Influences in Colonial Newspapers, 1704–1750* (New York: 1912).

present commentator is created in the Monitor, who accepts six young ladies as news-gatherers. Their reports on "Remarks, Letters, Poems, Billet-Doux" each week are in the vein of light social satire.

In the *South Carolina Gazette* there was a large amount of literary material, including quotations or reprints from the *Spectator*, the "Meddler's Club" essays, criticisms of plays, an original epilogue of Otway's *Orphan*, and lists of books for sale. In the words of Miss Cook, "the original essays and poems of the *Gazette* . . . prove that this little paper . . . was attempting literature."

William Wirt's numerous essays first appeared in Richmond newspapers. The *Letters of the British Spy* were published in the *Virginia Argus* in 1803. To Thomas Ritchie's *Richmond Enquirer* Wirt and his friends contributed the ten essays of *The Rainbow* in 1804, the nine essays of *The Rainbow: Second Series* in 1804–1805, and one number of *The Rainbow: Third Series* on April 19, 1805. To the *Richmond Enquirer* Wirt and his collaborators contributed twenty-eight essays of *The Old Bachelor*. Although the essayists imitated many of the devices employed in the *Spectator*, they showed an awareness of current Virginia life.

Most of the humorous sketches by Augustus Baldwin Longstreet and his successors were first published in newspapers. Longstreet contributed the sketches, later collected as *Georgia Scenes*, to the Milledgeville *Southern Recorder*, and later to the Augusta *State Rights Sentinel*, which he established and edited, 1834–1836. William Tappan Thompson, who published the sketches about Major Jones, was associated with Longstreet on the Augusta *Sentinel*.

The student of the drama of Williamsburg, Charleston, Richmond, New Orleans, and Baltimore turns to the weekly and daily newspapers of the cities for advertisements, play bills, and critical reviews. The literary treasures in southern newspapers have been only partially uncovered and await the careful investigation by many students.[22]

IV. LIBRARIES

In the colonial and ante-bellum periods the collecting, reading, and writing of books was done by the planters and the professional classes, and to a greater extent than is generally realized. The planters of Virginia, North Carolina, and South Carolina made notable collections of valuable imported books. From wills and county inventories, for books were valuable property, the contents of over a hundred Virginia plantation libraries have been listed. Besides the royal governors and the rich planters, who often pasted handsome armorial bookplates in their quartos and folios, there were other men who valued and collected books. The parsons of the Anglican Church brought literary tastes from their English homes and universities; physicians, lawyers, and tutors, even music teachers and dancing masters, had books.

We can mention only a few of the owners of large libraries. Perhaps the use of "large" in reference to a library of a hundred or a few hundred volumes may bring a smile to the student who wanders among a million books, housed in a million-dollar building. But leather-bound octavos and folios in the seventeenth century were much prized. Ralph Wormeley II left in 1701 "the largest and best-selected library brought together in Virginia in the seventeenth century," consisting of three hundred seventy-five separate titles. Richard Lee left in 1714 a "scholar's library" of three hundred titles, including many books in Greek, Latin, French, and Italian. Robert Beverley, the historian, bequeathed about two hundred fifty books,

[22] See M. S. Shockley, "American Plays in the Richmond Theatre, 1819–1838," *Studies in Philology*, XXXVII, 100–119 (1940); W. S. Hoole, "Two Famous Theatres of the Old South," *South Atlantic Quarterly*, XXXVI, 273–277 (1937), "Charleston Theatres," *Southwest Review*, XXV, 193–204 (1940).

although the inventory has been lost. "King" Carter collected a library of three hundred titles. The largest libraries of the late eighteenth century, those of John Waller (1755), Ralph Wormeley (1763), Ralph Carter (1772), with over six hundred titles, and William Fleming (1789) "contain a much greater percentage of classic and literary works than do the smaller collections."[23] The most avid book collector was William Byrd II, whose library at "Westover" on the James River numbered over thirty-six hundred titles. His secretary-librarian, William Proctor, arranged the books in cases and shelves by subject matter. The cases contained history, biography, travels, law books, religious works, scientific and mathematical treatises, and miscellaneous works "on almost every phase of man's life and intellectual pursuits." In a large and important section classified as "Entertainment, Poetry, Translations, etc." were to be found books by most of the great writers in English literature, especially the works of the Elizabethan and Restoration dramatists. His classical library included nearly three hundred works, not only by the better-known writers but by most of the minor authors. The rceently-published *Secret Diary* shows that Byrd not only collected books but read them. He disciplined his mind by daily readings in Hebrew and Greek. Rarely does he mention a title, but he read from Anacreon, Cassius Longinus, Herodian, Homer (*Odyssey*), Josephus, Pindar, Plutarch, and Thucydides. During the day he read in Latin from Horace, Petronius, Sallust, Terence, and Milton (Latin poems). In the evening he frequently read Italian. Contemporary London literature reached him promptly, and he read the *Tatler*, poetry, travel books, and sermons, usually those of Archbishop Tillotson.

[23] G. K. Smart, "Private Libraries in Colonial Virginia," *American Literature*, X, 32 (1938). See also Louis B. Wright, *The First Gentlemen of Virginia* (San Marino, Calif.: 1940); Mary Newton Stanard, *Colonial Virginia: Its People and Customs* (Philadelphia: 1917).

A large percentage of the books collected by Virginia gentlemen were utilitarian—law books for reference in buying and transferring property; books in husbandry, medicine, and practical arts for guides in homes isolated from neighbors and towns; books in religion and divinity for the meditative hours. About one-fourth of the books were in the classics. The humanistic tradition of the Renaissance, with its insistence that every educated person should be able to read Greek and Latin, persisted through three centuries of the South. Certainly the colonial planters who collected books believed that wisdom came from the classics; therefore they hired tutors who could teach the young masters the lore of Cicero, Plutarch, Seneca, Virgil, Pliny, Homer, Aristotle, and Plato.

The planters possessed fewer books in belles-lettres. Although Chaucer, Spenser, Shakespeare, Bacon, and Milton were not uncommon, there were more books by the lesser poets. Perhaps Butler's *Hudibras* was more popular than any other poem. The plays of Jacobean and Caroline playwrights were numerous, especially in the library of William Byrd II.

A study of the literary interests and libraries of later Virginians of the early national period would include such men as George Mason of "Gunston Hall," Richard Henry Lee, Madison, Marshall, Monroe, and John Randolph of Roanoke.

Thomas Jefferson was the greatest bookman of the South, for he collected three successive libraries, each of considerable size. To his father's library at Shadwell he added books gathered as a law student in William and Mary College under George Wythe, and as a member of the House of Burgesses. In the burning of the Shadwell home he lost nearly all his books, which he estimated had cost £200. At Monticello he built up a library of nearly ten thousand volumes, classified on the basis of Bacon's division of the mental faculties, of which the three grand divisions were Memory, Reason, and Imagination. After the British had destroyed the Library of Congress in 1814,

Jefferson, much in need of money, offered Congress his collection. After some bickering about the atheistical nature of some of the books, Congress bought six thousand five hundred books at less than half their cost, for $23,950. A fire in 1851 burned two-thirds of these books. By his will Chancellor Wythe bequeathed to Jefferson his large library, which almost filled the vacant shelves. Although past seventy, he set about buying in Europe the newer books, engaging for this purpose young George Ticknor of Massachusetts, whom he called "the best bibliograph I have met."

If we pass over the dividing line into North Carolina we learn that no private libraries were itemized until after the beginning of royal rule in 1725, which turned the emigration of a planter class to the Albemarle region.[24] From this date to 1790, seven private libraries in North Carolina were outstanding —those by Edward Moseley, Henry Snoad, Jeremiah Vail, John Eustace, David Milner, James Reid, and that of the Johnston family. Edward Moseley was the foremost man in Tidewater North Carolina for nearly half a century. Although he built up a large law practice, he managed a plantation of twenty-five thousand acres and a hundred slaves. He collected a library of four hundred volumes, mostly in law. The Johnston library was built up from the libraries of Governor Eden, Governor Gabriel Johnston, and Governor Samuel Johnston (1733–1816), and comprised four thousand five hundred volumes.

Mr. Weeks finds traces of nearly forty large private libraries collected in North Carolina before the Revolution, and he speaks well of the literary culture of the colonials. "I think it accurate to say that the political leaders of the colony of North Carolina at the time of the Revolution were better ac-

[24] See Stephen B. Weeks, "Libraries and Literature in North Carolina in the Eighteenth Century," *Report American Historical Association 1895*, pp. 171–261.

quainted with the literature of their time than the leaders of political North Carolina are today [1895] with either contemporary English or American literature.[25]

The merchant princes and rice planters of South Carolina had large book collections. Many had been educated abroad and spoke several languages. Their literary tastes led them to collect books and to establish public libraries. Henry Laurens covered the walls of his library with books of literature, history, art, and travel, and his friends claimed that he had read every one of them. Charles Pinckney had a library of twenty thousand volumes written in six languages, reading each language with ease. John Rutledge built up a large library which was burned during the Revolution. Such historians as William Henry Drayton, David Ramsay, Alexander Hewat, Arthur Middleton, John Laurens, William Moultrie, and Alexander Garden, had extensive private libraries. In a later day, Simms collected a large library at "Woodlands," which narrowly escaped fire in 1862 and was totally lost in 1865 by fire from Sherman's stragglers.

The earliest public libraries in the southern colonies were established by the Reverend Thomas Bray (1656–1730) of the Church of England, who saw that "Standing libraries will signifie little in the Country, where Persons may ride some miles to look into a Book; . . . but *Lending Libraries*, which come home to 'em without charge, may tolerably well supply the Vacancies in their own studies."[26] Through his efforts in connection with "The Society for Promoting Christian Knowl-

[25] *Ibid.*, p. 200.
[26] Quoted by Bernard C. Steiner, "Rev. Thomas Bray and the American Libraries," *American Historical Review*, III, 59–75 (1896). See also J. T. Wheeler, "Thomas Bray and the Maryland Parochial Libraries," *Maryland Historical Magazine*, XXXIV, 246–265 (1939); Edgar Pennington, "The Beginnings of the Library in Charles Town, South Carolina," *Proceedings American Antiquarian Society*, XLIV, 159–189 (1935).

edge," he founded thirty-nine libraries to aid the good and suitable, but poor, men that he sent out as missionaries. Of these libraries, thirty were established in Maryland, the "premier library" of over a thousand volumes being sent to Annapolis, *De Bibliotheca Annapolitana*. The other Bray libraries were sent to Virginia, North Carolina, South Carolina, and Georgia. Most of these books were religious, but some were in history, language, natural science, classics, and even poetry. Since the readers did not add many volumes by gift, the books were soon worn out or lost, and others moulded in the corners of vestry rooms. Few of the Bray volumes are now in existence.

The first public library founded in the southern colonies and still in active existence is that of the Charleston Library Society. According to its 1826 catalogue, compiled by Stephen Elliott, "the Charleston Library Society owes its origin to seventeen young men, who, in the year 1748, associated for the purpose of raising a small fund to 'collect such new pamphlets' and magazines as should occasionally be published in Great Britain."[27] Chartered in 1754, with the provision that each person should pay £50 to become a member, with weekly dues of five shillings, it prospered until the Revolution. In 1765 the generosity of Gabriel Manigault, who had been president for several years, prompted him to lease a building and furnish it for library use. In 1771, another active worker, John McKenzie, left a thousand books in the care of the Society. Disaster came in 1778 with the burning of all the books, except fewer than two hundred, and part of the McKenzie collection. The catalogue of 1811 indicated seven thousand volumes, and in 1850 there were twenty thousand volumes, of which many were injured or lost during the War of Secession.

By 1859, when Rhees made his listing, over seven hundred libraries had been established in the southern states since 1800,

---

[27] Quoted by William J. Rhees, *Manual of Public Libraries* (Philadelphia: 1859), p. 451.

besides those of the eighteenth century. The college libraries begin with that of William and Mary College, founded in 1693 through the efforts of Commissary James Blair. He bequeathed to it his own private library, and other donors of books were distinguished men. The library suffered during the Revolution, by fire in 1850, and almost total destruction of its eight thousand volumes in the Civil War. One is tempted to go through the list of the many state universities and colleges to cite interesting facts about the history of their libraries. In many institutions were literary or debating societies, each with its collection of books, often considerable, presented by "generous and enlightened" donors. It would be pertinent to analyze the contents of the library of the University of Virginia, originally selected and arranged by Jefferson. We note that Baltimore was the chief city of libraries, having twenty-one in 1859. The city had received in 1857 the gift of $350,000 from George Peabody to establish the Institute in his name, and one of the objects of his desire was "an extensive library."

Of the tens of thousands of books in these hundreds of public libraries, many were lost by misuse and ill care. The mildew and insects of the South love books. We read in a catalogue of the Apprentices' Library of Charleston that "the old books, and those not often consulted, unless bound with Russia leather, are apt to be injured by insects. They may be saved by taking them out every week or two, and striking the backs together." During the War Between the States, libraries were closed for the insects to enjoy the books, or they were ravaged by straggling soldiers. Only a fraction of ante-bellum public library books are now in existence.

V. REVOLT AND LIBERALISM

The southern aristocrats of colonial days generally adhered to the conservative opinions of eighteenth-century Tory Englishmen in their views about politics, religion, and education.

Their language united them closely to the empire; their political units, codes of laws, and religious organizations were modeled on English forms. They were "Provincials," in its stricter, better meaning, as Canadians are today, proud of their allegiance to the mother country. But the issues and conflicts of the late eighteenth century developed able men, especially in Virginia and South Carolina, who united or compromised with similar men of the North in radical, revolutionary action against England and in the establishing of a democratic form of government. The men of the Revolution and the founding fathers were great thinkers and powerful leaders.

Even in the seventeenth century bold men had revolted against certain despotic loyal governors, and had resented the English trade laws. As early as 1660 navigation acts had been enacted which restricted colonial exports to British or colonial ships, manned by British masters and seamen, and sailing to British ports. The British crown and ministry looked upon the colonies as *dependencies*, "not as integral and fully privileged members of the growing parent state," and as *possessions* "subject to exploitation for the benefit of the poeple who remained at home."[28]

By 1763, which marks the treaty at the close of the French and Indian War, the southern planters had not only gained confidence in themselves but they were protesting against the increasing commercial restrictions of the British ministry. They had fought successfully against the French and Indians on the Allegheny border, and these wilderness expeditions had inspired mutual confidence among soldiers from different sections and had developed military ability in the colonial leaders, especially Washington.

The proposed Stamp Act in 1763 aroused the colonies to heated remonstrance. When it became known in Virginia in

[28] G. E. Howard, *Preliminaries of the Revolution, 1763–1775* (New York: 1905), p. 47.

1764 the House of Burgesses promptly forwarded a remonstrance, but in its session in 1765 there prevailed a feeling that the act should not be resisted and that a compromise should be arranged. The House was dominated by John Robinson, who in the words of William Wirt, was "one of the most opulent men in the colony, and the acknowledged head of its landed aristocracy,"[29] and by Peyton Randolph, Richard Bland, George Wythe, and Richard Henry Lee. Before this able group arose Patrick Henry from the Virginia Piedmont, "an obscure and unpolished rustic . . . who bearded them in their den."[30] Henry introduced resolutions against the Stamp Act, denying the right of Great Britain "to impose any taxation whatsoever" upon the colony. After a "most bloody" debate, in the statement of Jefferson, the resolutions were carried by one vote. The Virginia Resolves were published and widely circulated in northern newspapers, and led to the calling of a Stamp Act Congress in New York in October. First to accept an invitation was South Carolina under the influence of the fiery Christopher Gadsden, successful planter and merchant, who said, "We do not hold our rights from them [the British lawmakers]; we should stand upon the broad, common ground of those natural rights that we all feel and know as men and as descendants of Englishmen."[31] In the seaboard cities of the South opposition to the Stamp Act led to riots. In Charleston the people would not permit the stamps to be brought into the city from British ships, and they burned effigies, each bearing a label of "The Stamp Seller." In Savannah mobs marched through the streets denouncing the Act and threatening to burn the stamps.

Rebellion was rife, as indicated by the acts and resolutions

---

[29] *Sketches of the Life and Character of Patrick Henry* (9th ed.; Philadelphia: 1836), p. 63.

[30] *Ibid.*, p. 72.

[31] *The South in the Building of the Nation*, II, 27.

in the legislatures of the southern colonies, especially in the House of Burgesses of Virginia. The southern colonies sent delegates to the continental congresses in Philadelphia, and the congress of 1776 adopted the Declaration of Independence, which was drafted by Jefferson, with some revisions by the other members of the Committee of Five.[32] This historic document contains the "natural rights" philosophy of government, with the doctrinal assertions that "all men are created equal," that they are "endowed by their Creator" with the rights to "life, liberty, and the pursuit of happiness," that governments, instituted to preserve these rights, "derive their just powers from the consent of the governed," and that the people have the right of revolution in altering or abolishing any government "which becomes destructive of these ends." These doctrines of natural rights, social contract, popular sovereignty, and the rights of resistance were not original with Jefferson or the other members of the Committee of Five, but had been worked over by the popular leaders of revolution in the seventeenth century, and had been advanced by various English and French political theorists for two centuries. Tom Paine in his pamphlet *Common Sense*, which had been issued a few months before July, 1776, to tens of thousands of readers, had prepared the American people for the Declaration of Independence. Jefferson expressed "the common sense of the subject" in the "sentiments of the day," to use his own phrases, and as Professor Becker says: "Where Jefferson got his ideas is hardly so much a question as where he could have got away from them."[33]

Since 1776, however, the political assumptions have been attacked by both friends and foes of the American Revolution and by conservatives and liberals in political thinking. Probably

[32] See Carl Becker, *The Declaration of Independence* (New York: c. 1922), Chapter IV.
[33] *Ibid.*, p. 27.

only one article of the Jeffersonian philosophy is accepted in American democracy—that governments "derive their just powers from the consent of the governed," with the right of the majority to rule. The theory that "all men are created free and equal," glorious in idealistic abstraction, caused trouble to the aristocratic rulers when common men without property asked for the vote. The constitutions of Alabama, Arkansas, Kentucky, Mississippi, and Texas have changed the phrase "all men, when they form a social compact, are equal," to "all *freemen*, when they form a social compact, are equal."[34] Thus, with the usual provision that freemen who wish to vote must own land, the rights of property were protected. Jefferson, although an aristocrat by birth and a planter, accepted equalitarianism, for he was a sincere believer in the natural intelligence and good will of all men high and low. In a later generation Andrew Jackson was to bring the doctrine of equalitarianism and political democracy to the men of the frontier. On the other hand, John C. Calhoun was to speak out with downright plainness against the equality of men.

These glowing abstractions about man's rights and privileges in an imaginary pre-historical era were troublesome in their practical applications. Liberal men of the South, led by Jefferson, tried to carry them out in the Articles of Confederation of 1777 and in the constitutional conventions. It might naturally be assumed that the frontiersmen from the Piedmont and eastern slopes of the Appalachians would be the leaders in the feeling for democracy and in revolution against Great Britain, but U. B. Phillips asserts that the aristocratic planters were the leaders.[35]

In the struggle over the drafting and adoption of the Constitution, the leaders were Tidewater planters. Virginia had such able men as Washington, who presided at the 1787 convention,

34 *Ibid.*, p. 240.
35 *The Course of the South to Secession* (New York: c. 1929), p. 15.

Madison, who bore a leading part, Marshall, with his forceful arguments, George Mason and Edmund Randolph, who refused to sign it. In South Carolina such down-country men as John Rutledge, Charles Cotesworth Pinckney, Charles Pinckney (his cousin), and Pierce Butler were representative. In the words of the South Carolina historian, D. D. Wallace, "her delegates were typical wealthy, aristocratic southern Federalists," who were "in favor of a strong government, a strong one-man executive, and the guardianship of the interests of the lower South."[36] Liberal for their time they certainly were, and yet, with Washington as president and conservative men from Virginia and South Carolina supporting him, liberalism was soon checked in high places. These same conservatives, however, were leaders in the abolishing of entails and primogeniture, a revolutionary change which destroyed landed privilege, and they were strong proponents of "liberty of conscience."

In religion the planters generally adhered to the Church of England, which was established by law in Maryland, Virginia, North Carolina, and South Carolina. The spirit of liberty brought about by the Revolution swept away every establishment. The parsons and other Tories left the country, and the church, discredited and disintegrating, was slowly built anew under a Protestant Episcopal organization.

Deism, or natural religion, as opposed to the revealed religion of Catholics and Protestants, had many believers in eighteenth-century America.[37] In outward forms Jefferson was an Episcopalian, for he was baptized, married, and buried by parsons with prayer-books in hand, but his expressed religious views were deistic or Unitarian. The deists and skeptics read Tom Paine, Voltaire, and Volney. "Parson" Weems sold Paine's *The Age of Reason* in Virginia. The colleges and uni-

[36] *The South in the Building of the Nation*, II, 40.
[37] See H. M. Morais, *Deism in Eighteenth Century America* (New York: 1934).

versities were accused as being centers of infidelity. Bishop Madison, president of William and Mary College from 1777 to 1812, was such a tolerant churchman that he was suspected of being a freethinker, and George Wythe, professor of law, was a liberal. In the newly-founded universities of North Carolina and Georgia were professors who were accused of skepticism and infidelity.[38]

The Presbyterians of the hill country rose to power in their fight against the Established Church in Virginia before the Revolution, with Patrick Henry as their champion in the "Parson's Cause."

The irreligion of the frontier was checked by the waves of evangelism which established the growing Methodist and Baptist churches.

In the education of the masses, during the colonial period, the South lagged behind even the inadequate systems of other sections, but its upper classes enjoyed unusual educational advantages, many of them attending European universities or northern colleges. Lack of interest in public education in the South was due to a number of factors—the scattered nature of the population, the marked class distinctions, and an aristocratic conception of education on the part of the Established Church. With the rise of the Presbyterians to influence, on the eve of the Revolution, numerous small colleges were established, mainly in the Piedmont.

Thomas Jefferson, with his plan for universal free education in Virginia ("A Bill for the More General Diffusion of Knowledge"), introduced in the state legislature in 1779, "was in advance of anything known in the country at the time." Simultaneously, as Virginius Dabney states,

he turned his attention to his alma mater, William and Mary. As a trustee of the institution, he virtually made over the cur-

[38] See Clement Eaton, *Freedom of Thought in the Old South* (Durham, N.C.: 1940) for a thorough study of the growth of liberalism.

riculum, emphasizing scientific and social studies, then almost universally neglected, and arranged to allow the students a larger degree of freedom in choosing their subjects. The reform he instituted at William and Mary, while Continentals and Red-coats were still struggling for supremacy, were in many ways similar to those he was to make effective on a larger scale some forty years later with the establishment of the University of Virginia.[39]

Shortly after the Revolution, a number of state universities were chartered in the South, the University of Georgia being the first chartered and the University of North Carolina the first to open its doors to students. But although higher education received early attention, free public education was long in coming. It is important to note, however, Jefferson's early stand on public education as essential in a democracy. "Enlighten the people generally," he said in a letter to Dupont de Nemours, "and tyranny and oppressions of body and mind will vanish like evil spirits at the dawn of day."

"One may state without fear of contradiction," says Gilbert Chinard of Jefferson's plan of education, "that no system so complete, so logically constructed, so well articulated had ever been proposed in any country in the world. . . . it preceded by more than fifteen years the plans of the French Convention. As the first charter of American public education it is an astonishing document and deserves more attention than it has hitherto received."[40]

In the last decades of the eighteenth century some planters had misgivings about slavery. There was a growing opinion that the traffic in slaves from Africa should be stopped. The Revolution suspended the traffic, and after the war many states laid heavy import duties or even prohibitions on slaves. North Carolina laid a duty in 1787, and Virginia and Maryland

[39] *Liberalism in the South* (Chapel Hill, N.C.: 1932), p. 45.

[40] *Thomas Jefferson; The Apostle of Americanism* (Boston: 1929), p. 99.

enacted prohibition laws. Humane sentiment, which sometimes prompted these pieces of legislation, was reinforced by economic interest. In South Carolina, "the men of established wealth and conservative attitude"—Ralph Izard, John Rutledge, David Ramsay, Edmund Pendleton, the Pinckneys, and Rawlins Lowndes—"argued that permission of imports would reduce the price of slaves already possessed, or at least prevent their values from rising; that it would . . . heighten the proportion of blacks in the population, and intensify the danger of slave insurrection."[41] The legislature passed a prohibition law, which, however, was repealed in 1803, and forty thousand slaves came in within four years.

Many of the great Virginians of the Revolutionary generation were in favor of emancipation. The most effective utterance was by Jefferson in 1781: "The whole commerce between master and slave is a perpetual exercise of the most boisterous passions. . . . The parent storms; the child looks on, catches the lineaments of wrath, puts on the same airs in a circle of smaller slaves. . . . Indeed, I tremble for my country when I reflect that God is just; that His justice cannot sleep forever." In later years Jefferson was far more temperate in his utterances. Professor St. George Tucker of William and Mary College gave each year to his law students a "melancholy review" of the persistence in Virginia of "that partial system of morality which confines rights and injuries to particular complexions," and he proposed a plan of emancipation by transportation. Madison spoke of slavery as a "dreadful calamity," and Monroe took steps toward the repatriation of the blacks transported to Africa. Some slaveholders even emancipated their slaves, of whom notable examples were George Washington, "Councillor" Carter, Robert Pleasants, General Horatio Gates, and John Randolph of Roanoke. In Maryland two

[41] U. B. Phillips, *The Course of the South to Secession* (New York: c. 1939), p. 91.

great aristocrats, Charles Carroll of Carrollton and William Pinkney, gave some support to Quaker projects for manumission.

Although many planters were having misgivings about slavery, the great majority of them believed that slavery was right and at times wrote in defense of it.

In his *Arator* essays, first published in 1803, John Taylor of Caroline discussed slavery and answered Jefferson. "Negro slavery is a misfortune to agriculture," because the use of slaves by overseers has impoverished the land. The free Negro class, "cut off from most of the rights of citizens, and from all the allowances of slaves" harm and embarrass the agriculturist. Congress should purchase "lands sufficient for their subsistence in states where slavery is not allowed." Mr. Jefferson's assertions "were written in the heat of a war for liberty; the human mind was made still hotter by the French revolution. . . . To me it seems, that slaves are too far below, and too much in the power of the master, to inspire furious passions. . . . The chapter on the manners of slave-holders [by Jefferson] before quoted concludes with an intimation, that the consent of the masters to a general emancipation, or their own extirpation, were the alternatives between which they had to choose. Such a hint from a profound mind is awful. It admits an ability in the blacks, though shackled by slavery, to extirpate the whites."[42] Thus Taylor visions the ugly possibility, shudderingly apparent to Southerners, of the uprising of Negroes, reverting to animal savagery. In this and later writings Taylor states that chattel slavery has been accepted by the Constitution and cannot be abolished legally.

In the Revolutionary period, then, the South, with her able political leaders fighting for liberty, played a decisive part in formulating and adopting the great documents of the period, the Declaration of Independence and the Constitution of the

[42] *Arator* (third ed.; Baltimore: 1817), pp. 40–47 *passim*.

United States, and the Bill of Rights. In this period, too, we see the beginnings of the great lines of cleavage in national and sectional thought, which have governed the course of southern history.

VI. AGRARIANISM

Basic in southern thought has been the belief that agriculture is the foundation of economic and political well-being. This view is best expressed in the writings of Thomas Jefferson and John Taylor of Caroline. In his *Notes on Virginia* (1782) Jefferson wrote a few powerful sentences in favor of rural life.

Those who labour in the earth are the chosen people of God, if ever He had a chosen people, whose breasts he has made his peculiar deposit for substantial and genuine virtue. It is the focus in which he keeps alive that sacred fire, which otherwise might escape from the face of the earth. Corruption of morals in the mass of cultivators is a phaenomenon of which no age nor nation has furnished an example.[43]

On December 20, 1787, he wrote to Madison that "our governments will remain virtuous for many centuries; as long as they are chiefly agricultural; and this will be as long as there shall be vacant lands in any part of America. When they [the people] get piled upon one another in large cities, as in Europe, they will become corrupt as in Europe."[44]

On December 9, 1795, he wrote to Volney: "For my part I have no fear of a people, well informed, easy in their circumstances, dispersed over their farms, and occupied on them. I say *over their farms*, because these constitute the body of our citizens, the inhabitants of towns are but zero in the scales."[45]

To Jefferson the commercial cities were centers of evil and

[43] *Writings.* Edited by Paul Leicester Ford. (10 vols.; New York: 1892–1899), III, 268–269.

[44] *Writings*, IV, 479–480.

[45] *Volney et L' Amérique . . . Correspondance avec Jefferson.* Trans. Gilbert Chinard. (Baltimore: 1923), p. 35.

he spoke of "the mobs of great cities," which are like "sores
. . . to the strength of the human body." This extreme opinion
in 1782 was modified in 1805; yet he wondered if "their labor
in their trade [handicraftsmen of the old cities of Europe] is
worth more than their labor on the soil." His democracy en-
visaged a nation of farmers with small land-holdings, and with
cheap and plentiful land to secure a wide distribution of property.[46]

Like Jefferson, Taylor believed that life on the plantation or
farm, far removed from cities, was the best life for Southerners.
He was almost rhapsodic in his praise of rural life.[47]

Taylor believed that in the life of the nation agriculture is
"our greatest interest" and toward its improvement the entire
political and economic life of the country should be exclusively
directed. The brother interest to agriculture is that of the
"mechanicks," the carpenters, blacksmiths, and other artisans in
little towns. Opposed to these interests are the "alien stock-
jobbers," the nonproductive capitalists, who have maintained
political strength by "intricate frauds and ideal credit." Agriculture should be rich and powerful "to discharge faithfully
the obligation she owes to society by constituting the majority."

[46] This view is held by Charles Beard, *Economic Origins of Jeffersonian Democracy* (New York: 1915) and A. J. Nock, *Jefferson* (New
York: 1926), but it is opposed by Frederick C. Prescott in *Alexander
Hamilton and Thomas Jefferson*, American Writers Series (New York:
1934). Another moot issue is the influence of the Physiocratic
group on Jefferson. Parrington stresses this influence, stating that
"the major principles of the school sank deep into his mind and
creatively determined his thinking." (*Main Currents of American
Thought*, I, 346–347; also II, 10–11). But Richard Hofstader states
that "a high valuation upon agricultural life . . . generally antedated Physiocratic influence" and that Jefferson's *Notes on Virginia*
were published "five years before his contact with the Physiocrats."
See "Parrington and the Jeffersonian Tradition," *Journal of the History of Ideas*, II, 391 ff. (October, 1941).

[47] *Arator*, pp. 179–181.

We farmers and mechanicks have been political slaves in all countries, because we are political fools. We know how to convert a
wilderness into a paradise, and a forest into palaces and elegant
furniture; but we have been taught by those whose object is to
monopolize the sweets of life, which we sweat for, that politicks
are without our province, and in us a ridiculous affection
[affectation].[48]

The worst drain upon agriculture is the protective tariff,
building up under the pretext of encouraging manufactures a
"capitalist interest . . . which instantly seizes upon the bounty
taken by law from agriculture."

E. T. Mudge states that in Taylor's later works "the argument is based on a theory of natural sovereignty or natural
self-government and the implications derived therefrom for
the doctrine of states' rights, for a limitation of the power of
the Supreme Court, for a reorganization of the banking system,
for a nullification of the protective tariff, and in general for the
removal of the repressions which impede the growth of agriculture."[49]

Other eminent Virginians and the majority of Southerners
held this view—and some still hold it. The tobacco, cotton,
sugar, and rice planters, the small farmers from Tidewater to
the Appalachians, believed in a rural economy. They disliked
and feared the capitalists and the masses in cities. All that was
pure and wholesome came from the soil; much that was dirty
and evil came from the reeking streets of towns. From the soil
came the great staples upon which southern well-being depended—staples for which the northern states and European
lands clamored. Presently one of these staples was to rear an
economic kingdom which would condition life and literature
for many generations.

[48] *Arator*, p. 27.
[49] *The Social Philosophy of John Taylor of Caroline* (New York:
1939), pp. 34–35.

VII. THE COTTON KINGDOM

In 1789, when Washington became president, the South was a political entity which made its representatives very influential in the national capital. Economically there was less unity. Tobacco was of decreasing importance in the Tidewater because of uncertain prices and unskillful culture. Farming was becoming diversified, especially in the Piedmont. Over in Kentucky and Tennessee the settlers were opening up a new country of fertile lands raising varied crops. The slave economy was becoming less profitable, and many planters were freeing or selling their slaves.

It is reasonable to assume that at this time slavery might have been abolished to the satisfaction of the planter, who had a big stake in the "peculiar institution," with the declining value of tobacco, the rapid development of small farms, and the influence of liberal leaders. Thus the terrible war between the plantation and industrial sections of the country might have been averted. The increasing and immense profits of a new plantation economy of cotton culture, however, made slave labor indispensable, developed the Lower South from Georgia to Texas, and created an aristocracy to rule a "Cotton Kingdom."[50] From decade to decade, and especially from 1830 to 1860, this section of the South became more assertive of its economic importance and of its political domination.

Green seed, short staple cotton was known in the early days of Jamestown, and had been grown in the Tidewater for two centuries with only moderate success. The lint had to be separated from the seed by plucking fingers, the huge bales were hauled to the ships in the seaports with difficulty, and the foreign markets were uncertain. Cotton was easily grown,

[50] For a discussion of the attitude toward slavery see W. S. Jenkins, *Pro-Slavery Thought in the Old South* (Chapel Hill, N.C.: 1935), Chap. II.

however, and the area of production was reaching back into the Piedmont. Black seed, long staple cotton came from the Bahama Islands to Georgia in 1786. Trials proved that it could be grown satisfactorily only within a few miles of the ocean. On the "sea islands" of John's Island, Edisto, St. Helena, and others, the long staple cotton throve. The production continued to expand in this region and down into Florida for thirty years, reaching an annual yield of ten million pounds, to be sold at prices up to one or two dollars a pound.

The invention of the cotton gin in 1793 made cotton growing increasingly profitable. The newly-invented and constructed spinning and weaving machines in the factories of England and New England manufactured huge quantities of ginned cotton. Cotton as a staple crop rapidly surpassed in value tobacco and rice.

The area of culture rapidly extended. In Virginia cotton was grown with only moderate success, for late frosts often ruined a promising crop. In North Carolina there was fairly successful growing and costly marketing. But the chief region was in the Lower South.

This section was in a "black belt" of fertile, level valleys and plains, of good available shipping ports on the Atlantic and the Gulf, and under liberal favorable laws for the buying of plantations and the holding of Negroes in slavery. The Indians of Georgia, Alabama, and Mississippi were living a semi-agricultural life upon good lands available for cotton. The covetous planters took these lands by doles of money or by promises of reservations beyond the Red River. Even before the complaining, and usually fighting, Indians had crossed the Mississippi, the cotton planters looked longingly upon the prairies to the southwest and began a vigorous campaign for the annexation of Texas. Jefferson had made available to them in 1803 the wide valley of the lower Mississippi, but that was not enough. Later they approved the Mexican War so that new territories might be acquired to which they could bring their slaves. The broad alluvial tracts on either bank of the Mississippi were known to be lastingly fertile, but their liability to flood had caused them to be shunned. After long levees had been built at public expense, the planters took over the region. Jackson, Natchez, and Memphis grew rapidly as cotton ports.

The story of the migration of planters, settlers, and squatters from the older states to the Cotton Kingdom is both glowingly romantic in its incidents of successful fortune and also depressingly realistic with the sad tales of ruined men. The raising of cotton was always a gamble. As U. B. Phillips writes: "A cotton crop in western prospect became a golden fleece. From Maryland to Mississippi, from Virginia to Alabama, from Missouri to Texas, every whence every whither, people took ship or flatboat, or set forth in carryalls or covered wagons, with tinkling cattle and trudging slaves if they had them."[51] The price of cotton was always fluctuating from ruinous lows to golden highs, but in the fifteen years before the War Between the States it tended to rise steadily. In the early decades of the century an annual export of a million bales was high, but in the years from 1850 to 1860 the crop increased from 2,500,000 to 5,000,000 bales.

Since cotton was best cultivated by Negroes, even by less intelligent and skillful slaves than in the tobacco and rice fields, slavery flourished. In Virginia, Maryland, and the Carolinas there were too many slaves, with a million in the early nineteenth century and the number doubling every twenty years. Thousands of planters emigrated to the cotton belt with their slaves. From Virginia in numbers, from the Carolinas, down from Kentucky and Tennessee they hurried to Eldorado. The planters remaining in Virginia kept from bankruptcy by selling their slaves in the markets to traders who would transport them down South, and the slaveholders of Kentucky and Tennessee

[51] *Life and Labor in the Old South* (Boston: 1930), p. 100.

sold surplus Negroes "down the river."[52] The richest planters had several plantations of a thousand or more acres each, worked by upwards of a hundred slaves. But most plantations were more profitably worked in smaller units with from twenty to sixty slaves each. By 1860 Georgia was second only to Virginia of the fifteen slave-owning commonwealths and had over forty thousand slaveowners holding 435,000 slaves. If the average was less than a dozen to a master, most of the units must have been farms and not plantations. But there is more information available about such wealthy men as Colonel Joseph Bond, John Basil Lamar, and the Howell Cobbs, father and son. Some of the wealthiest were of aristocratic families, but many rose from lowly rank. Such a man was Colonel Farish Carter, who started as a small-town merchant and became "probably the wealthiest man in the state."[53] His early fortune was acquired as a war-profiteer on government contracts during the War of 1812 and the subsequent troubles with the Spaniards and Indians. Soon he purchased a plantation at Scottsborough, in Baldwin County, and afterwards the "Mills Plantation"; he went up to Virginia and bought sixty slaves; he acquired a rich plantation in the Cherokee Indian lands and another over in Alabama; and in 1845 he owned 426 slaves and 33,293 acres.[54]

On the eve of the war there were not over twenty-five hundred slaveholders who owned over a hundred slaves each. Each state had a few wealthy men like Samuel Hairston of Virginia, who owned nearly seventeen hundred slaves. There were perhaps eleven thousand others who possessed fifty or more slaves each and a hundred thousand who owned from ten to fifty each.

[52] See J. Winston Coleman, *Slavery Times in Kentucky* (Chapel Hill, N.C.: 1940). Chaps. V–VIII.

[53] Ralph Betts Flanders, *Plantation Slavery in Georgia* (Chapel Hill, N.C.: 1933), p. 126.

[54] *Ibid.*, p. 122.

In a vast region extending from Baltimore deep into Texas, from the Allegheny Mountains to the Gulf and Atlantic coasts, even to St. Louis and Kansas City, and pressing farther west, the planter was in supreme power, with his hold upon land and slaves. As master of his manor, he was the social model and arbiter of his section. As holder of any political office he desired, he controlled the taxes which fed education and public improvements. The power of the planter aristocracy was stated by Richard Taylor, a lieutenant-general in the Confederate army:

We set up a Monarch, too, King Cotton, and hedged him with divinity surpassing that of earthly potentates. To doubt his royalty and power was a confession of ignorance or cowardice. This potent spirit, at the nod of our Prosperos, the cotton-planters, would arrest every loom and spindle in New England, destroy her wealth and reduce her population to beggary. The power of old England, the growth of eight hundred years, was to wither as the prophet's gourd unless she obeyed its behests.[55]

In the pyramid of Southern society one-third of the people formed the slave-holding, aristocratic class. The other two-thirds had no direct connection with slavery. On the small farms around the big plantations or in larger numbers in the Piedmont were hundreds of thousands of poor farmers. In the labor competition against slaves they were usually crushed to dire poverty; only a few succeeded in acquiring lands and slaves. They were envious of their rich neighbors, and the ambitious hoped to meet them some day as equals. Many were kinsmen, just poor relations. From their small fields and flocks they sold surplus poultry, dairy and garden products at the "big houses." They were usually illiterate, therefore they collected no books and they wrote nothing. They appear in

[55] *Destruction and Reconstruction* (New York: 1879), p. 234.

literature usually in the writings of travelers and of visitors in the plantation homes.

Another class of whites lived in the villages and were supported by the planter class. They were the factors and merchants with whom the moneyed people traded; the lawyers who drew up their deeds, mortgages, and wills; the physicians who cured their diseases; the parsons and preachers who exhorted them to righteous living and incidentally quoted Scripture as authority for slavery; and the "mechanicks," as Taylor had called them, the carpenters, blacksmiths, and other skilled artisans.

The ante-bellum planters were native Americans, generations removed from the English, Scotch, Huguenots, Spaniards, and French of the coastal plain and from the Scotch-Irish, Germans, and Moravians of the Piedmont, commingled and combined into an agrarian commonwealth based upon tobacco, rice, sugar, and cotton plantations worked by slaves. The troublesome menaces of the Abolitionists and the assumptions of the northern industrialists gradually forced the planters to closer association which extended over state lines and led them to confederation and self-protection.

It was undoubtedly the growing threat of industrial domination and the increasing political tension which turned many of the best minds of the period away from belles lettres to the more practical arts of oratory and debate.

VIII. THE MOVEMENT TOWARD SECESSION

In the decades before the Civil War the South developed able orators who in legislative halls expressed opposition to tariffs, and belief in states' rights, nullification, slavery, and secession. South Carolina produced such brilliant leaders as Robert Y. Hayne, who debated against Webster in 1830 in the United States Senate; George McDuffie, who was a vehement advocate of nullification; and John Henry Hammond, who championed slavery from his offices as Governor and United States Senator.[56]

Another South Carolinian, John C. Calhoun, the greatest figure in the long controversy, "became by virtue of intellect and character, driven by an apostolic zeal, the master political mind of the South."[57] Calhoun had had a long political career even before he was elected vice-president under John Quincy Adams in 1824. In 1827 he defeated a higher-tariff bill by his casting vote. At the request of W. C. Preston and other South Carolinians, he wrote the "South Carolina Exposition," in which he asserted the unconstitutionality of a federal tariff law and maintained the power of a state "to estop the enforcement of an unconstitutional act." After South Carolina passed the ordinance of nullification in 1832, he resigned the vice-presidency in order to be appointed to the Senate where he might do effective work for his state. He became convinced that slavery was a permanent institution in the South, and that each new state in the West should be open to slavery. Calhoun's last address in the Senate, in 1850, was a vigorous reply to Clay's Omnibus Bill. After hearing Webster's great speech of compromise, he still thought it "difficult to see how two peoples so different and hostile can exist together in one common Union."

Calhoun's political ideas are best expressed in his posthumous *A Disquisition on Government*, and *A Discourse on the Constitution and Government of the United States*. Opposed to Jefferson in the natural-rights theory of government, he condemned the hypothesis of a pre-historical "state of nature" and the origin of government by means of a contract. Rejecting the attitudes of Jefferson and Paine that the less government the

[56] See G. A. Wauchope, *The Writers of South Carolina* (Columbia, S.C.: 1910), pp. 192–196; 216–222; 279–281.

[57] V. L. Parrington, *Main Currents in American Thought* (New York: 1927), II, 69. In a dozen pages (69–92) Parrington, with his Jeffersonian adherence, analyzes some strong positions and more weaknesses in Calhoun's political philosophy.

better, Calhoun maintained that government is necessary to society and that society is necessary to man. As individuals are selfish they must be restrained by government, and as governments are selfish they must be restrained by constitutions. The greatest of political problems is the establishing of the responsibility of rulers. Suffrage fixes this responsibility, but there is imminent danger that the majority will become despotic, tending toward oppressive and absolute government. The "tyranny of the majority" can be curbed by the recognition of varied and diverse interests, which he calls the "concurrent majority." This "concurrent majority" can force compromise—even veto or nullify a law. It is evident that Calhoun's argument leads to a veto power to be granted to the southern states against the enforcement of protective tariff laws and of unfavorable slavery laws.

Calhoun departed further from Jefferson in defending slavery. He attacked the theorem that "all men are created equal" by stating vigorously: "Taking the proposition literally, there is not a word of truth in it." He asserted that "there has never yet existed a wealthy and civilized society in which one portion of the community did not, in point of fact, live on the labor of the other," and that this relation may be regarded "as the most solid and durable foundation on which to rear free and stable institutions."

Calhoun's basis for secession rested upon his theory of the sovereignty of the states. After the adoption of the Constitution it was generally held that there existed a divided sovereignty in that the national government was sovereign in certain matters and the states were sovereign in others. He maintained that the constitution-making power, which rested in the states, was superior to the law-making power of the federal government. The states, therefore, are supreme, and may at any time rightfully assert their sovereignty and withdraw from the Union.

In summarizing the changes in Calhoun's political philosophy, Parrington states that "in the end the political philosopher turns partisan to a cause. . . . Espousing the ideal of democracy, he yielded to the seductions of a Greek republic. Beginning as a Jeffersonian, he ended as the philosopher of a slave aristocracy. . . . [He believed] that property will rule by reason of its inherent power, and that political justice is attainable only by a nicely calculated system of checks and balances, which provides each important group with a defensive veto."[58]

The influence of Calhoun in leading the southern states to secession is a matter of divided opinion. He was not a pioneer in the defense of slavery, for before his Congressional activity there were such powerful leaders as Senator William Smith, Governor George McDuffie, Dr. Thomas Cooper, and Thomas R. Dew. Agreeing with his principles were such ardent Secessionists as Robert Barnwell Rhett, W. L. Yancey, Albert Gallatin Brown, Senator Louis Wigfall, Jefferson Davis, Roger Pryor, and Robert Toombs. It is a false, and somewhat bitter, exaggeration of his leadership to place upon him alone the responsibility for the continuation of slavery and for the events following the firing on Fort Sumter. He was the ablest spokesman of the ideas held by most of the plantation aristocracy.

IX. FICTION IN THE OLD SOUTH

These ideas of the plantation aristocracy were not wholly philosophic, political, or economic in origin. The contents of old libraries, the records of book purchases, and the reviews in periodicals indicate that literary Southerners a century ago purchased and read extensively the romantic fiction produced in Great Britain and the North. Of all the foreign authors Scott was the most popular. In the first decade of the century *Marmion*, *The Lady of the Lake*, and Scott's other metrical

[58] *Op. cit.*, II, 81–82.

tales were read and quoted. They were also arranged for the
stage, to be presented in the theatres of Richmond, Charleston,
New Orleans, and other cities. Scott's novels, imported from
Great Britain or in pirated editions, were sold in large quantities. Miss Grace W. Landrum states that "The novels were
obtainable in 1828 at seventy-five cents a volume, but by May
3, 1845, one could secure the whole number for two dollars
and a half!"[59] Not only men of letters, like Kennedy and
Simms, read Scott; but such leaders as Henry Clay, Commodore
Matthew Fontaine Maury, Raphael Semmes, Jefferson Davis,
and Robert E. Lee have left records of the spell of his poetry
and fiction. When Scott died in 1832 the *Richmond Enquirer*
for November 20 "edged its columns heavily with black as in
honor of a departed figure of national importance."[60]

Undue emphasis upon Scott's vogue in the South may lead
students to disregard the rival popularity of other British
novelists, especially G. P. R. James and Bulwer-Lytton. Encouraged by the success of Scott, James wrote a hundred novels
and tales between 1825 and 1850, of which a dozen deal with
the period of chivalry. As Mr. G. Harrison Orians states:
"Above all, his *History of Chivalry* (1831), published in the
'Harper's Family Library,' makes James's record a potentially
imposing one for affecting the temper of the South."[61]

By citations from the criticisms in southern magazines Miss
Landrum has emphasized the craze in the South for Bulwer-
Lytton's novels.[62] *Pelham* (1828), a society novel, "took the
South by storm," especially the lady readers. The demand for
historical romances was so lively, with the reading of *Dever-
eaux*, *The Last Days of Pompeii*, *Rienzi*, *The Last of the Barons*,

[59] "Sir Walter Scott and His Literary Rivals in the Old South,"
American Literature, II, 258 (November, 1930).

[60] *Ibid.*, pp. 260–261.

[61] "Walter Scott, Mark Twain, and the Civil War," *South Atlantic
Quarterly*, XL, 346 (October, 1941).

[62] *Op. cit.*, pp. 270–272.

and *Harold*, that it caused one critic to assert that "these works of Bulwer are in every hole and corner of the land." Even in the heat of the Civil War there was a demand for a serialization of his *Strange Story*, and "The influence of this 'most gifted and most remorseless, the most imaginative and seductive of novelists' was far-reaching for at least thirty-five years."[63]

Besides James and Bulwer-Lytton, there were Byron and Carlyle, who affected the thinking of Southerners, but the influence of Scott has been stressed since Mark Twain blasted at Scott in Chapter XLVI of his *Life on the Mississippi* (1883).

Mr. Orians refutes all of the charges against Scott by Mark Twain and other critics rather convincingly, and maintains that "His works led them [the Southern aristocrats] to desire a more chivalric order; and inasmuch as courtliness ran counter to no deep-seated prejudice, disrupted no economic state, disturbed no social development, there was little to hinder or retard the development of a culture of social charm and manners."[64]   But the truth remains that, in the words of Miss Landrum, "Whatever be the cause, or causes, literary or economic, Jeffersonian simplicity in the South clearly evolved into aristocratic predilections."[65]

Such writers of southern fiction as Dr. William Alexander Caruthers, John Pendleton Kennedy, William Gilmore Simms, Beverley Tucker, and John Esten Cooke wrote to some extent in the Scott tradition. Turning to the past for colorful heroes, as Scott had done, the novelists penned the exploits of leaders in victorious skirmishes and battles against the background of colonial and revolutionary days. The chief characters were gentlemen and ladies with codes of honor and manners, acting and talking artificially; and the common people, who dressed roughly and spoke rustic dialect, were used as foils to the aristocrats or in humorous incidents. It was hoped that the novelists might even surpass Cooper, who had fictionized

[63] *Ibid.*, p. 272.   [64] *Op. cit.*, p. 350.   [65] *Op. cit.*, p. 262.

gentlemen and pioneers, heroes and villains, patriots and Tories, in such romances of the Revolution as *The Spy*, *The Pilot*, and *Lionel Lincoln*. These and other tales by Cooper were read with approval by Southerners and were reviewed favorably by Poe and Simms.

John Pendleton Kennedy was a versatile man of many accomplishments, wide literary friendships, and varied literary production. His *Swallow Barn* (1832) is in the literary tradition of both Scott and Irving. Kennedy and Irving were lifelong friends, and the reader familiar with *The Sketch Book* and *Bracebridge Hall* will find a familiar pattern in *Swallow Barn*. It is perhaps the first book in the plantation tradition,[66] with its pictures of the estates of "Swallow Barn" and "The Brakes," the characterization of the gracious gentleman, Frank Meriwether, incidents of the county court, fox and 'possum hunts, and concluding chapters of "the quarter" and the story of a Negro mother. Virginia plantation life seems happy and successful with kind, able masters and loyal slaves. As Mr. J. B. Hubbell states: "*Swallow Barn* is social history of the truest kind. Had Kennedy chosen to write a novel instead of a Virginia sketch-book, he would have found it more difficult to paint an accurate picture."[67]

Kennedy's *Horse-Shoe Robinson* and *Rob of the Bowl* are in the Scott-Cooper tradition. Published in the same year (1835) as Simms's *The Partisan*, and dealing with the same material, *Horse-Shoe Robinson* may be less valuable for its historical incidents but is superior in the creation of individual characters. The gentry are favorably represented in such characters as General Francis Marion, Major Arthur Butler, Philip Lindsay, and his daughter Mildred; the lower classes are vividly pre-

[66] See Francis Pendleton Gaines, *The Southern Plantation* (New York: 1925), for an excellent analysis of the conception of the plantation in literature.

[67] Introduction, *Swallow Barn*. American Authors Series (New York: 1929), pp. xxix–xxx.

sented in John Ramsay, Mary Musgrove, and the real hero, Galbraith Robinson, a blacksmith.[68]

Other ante-bellum Virginia novelists, of whom Caruthers was the preëminent example, looked back sentimentally to the colonial times under the sway of the "Cocked Hat Gentry." He exalted the Cavaliers, and remarked that his stories dealt "with the generous, fox-hunting, wine-drinking, duelling, and reckless race of men, which gives so distinct a character to Virginians wherever they may be found." In *Cavaliers of Virginia* (1834–1835) he told an energetic story of Bacon's rebellion against Berkeley in 1676, in which rough, vigorous men, the ancesters of later revolutionaries, opposed the tyranny of a royal governor. But Caruthers defied the historians in representing Bacon and his men, not as small farmers and frontiersmen, but as Cavaliers. The *Knights of the Horse-Shoe* (1845), deals with Governor Spotswood's famous expedition from Williamsburg west into the Valley of Virginia, and is a series of pictures of happy colonial life. There is a mystery-enshrouded hero, a beautiful wooden heroine, a well-portrayed Spotswood, a humorous mountaineer who uses the dialect of the poor whites, and Negroes speaking their dialect. In viewing the troubles in the South during the thirties Caruthers had tendencies toward liberalism and reconciliation, which are shown in his *Kentuckian in New York; or, the Adventures of three Southrons* (1834), which Parrington calls "an excellent contribution to the cause of intersectional good-will."[69]

Nathaniel Beverley Tucker, son of St. George Tucker and half-brother of John Randolph of Roanoke, was "the epitome of Virginia Cavalier, the Secession Movement incarnate."[70]

[68] For excellent criticism, see Ernest E. Leisy's Introduction to *Horse-Shoe Robinson* (New York: 1937).

[69] *Main Currents in American Thought*, II, 41. Parrington views this "Virginia liberal" sympathetically.

[70] See the Introduction by Carl Bridenbaugh to *The Partisan Leader* (Americana Deserta edition; New York: 1933).

He revolted against President Andrew Jackson for his proclamation in the South Carolina Nullification controversy, for his leveling of classes, and for his shibboleth of the common man. In his Tory thinking he approved the views of his colleague Professor Thomas R. Dew at William and Mary College, who accepted slavery and the inequality of men. For his vehement adherence to state sovereignty he was called "Virginianissimus" and the "Virginia Fire-Eater." In 1836 Tucker printed anonymously and secretly in Washington a few copies of *The Partisan Leader; A Tale of the Future.* In 1861 a new edition of thousands of widely-circulated copies was published in New York. As revealing the ideas and temper of Virginians in 1836, *The Partisan Leader* is an amazing book. This partisan leader is not of the Revolution, but of the cause of Virginia and the South against the Union. Young Douglas Trevor, son of Hugh Trevor, a high-minded Virginian, and a West Point officer, leads his men in rebellion against federal forces. The Scott influence is seen in the slow-moving introductory chapter of a lonely horseman coming to a camp of armed mountaineers near the Blue Ridge, the aristocratic society of gentlemen and their Negro slaves, the charming, timid "females," and the lurking spies and villains. Through the speeches of a Mr. B—— and other landed gentlemen the states' rights doctrine is ardently advocated. The story ends abruptly, with Douglas Trevor a prisoner, and his rescue about to be attempted. In this propaganda novel the author expresses suspicion, hate, and defiance of the federal government under the presidency of a Northerner, Martin Van Buren, and his novel is a disguised text-book of rebellion, to arouse the fire-eaters of the South.

In the same year, 1836, Tucker published *George Balcombe*, a lively novel of border life in Missouri and Virginia, which Poe praised highly.

John Esten Cooke, novelist and historian, portrayed the

early days of Virginia in seven books: *Leather Stocking in Silk* (1854), *The Virginia Comedians* (1854), *The Youth of Jefferson* (1854), *Ellie* (1855), *The Last of the Foresters* (1856), *Henry St. John* (1859), and *Fairfax* (1867). He stated that his aim was "to paint the Virginia phase of American society, to do for the Old Dominion what Cooper has done for the Indians, Simms for the Revolutionary drama in South Carolina, Irving for the Dutch Knickerbockers, and Hawthorne for the Puritan Life of New England."   Unconcerned with historical accuracy, he wrote novels of manners, of which the best is *The Virginia Comedians*, with its pictures and incidents of Williamsburg as the colonial center of drama, society, and politics. Cooke stated that "this history . . . aims at presenting in a brief and rapid manner, some view, however slight, of the various classes of individuals who formed that Virginia of 1765,"[71] and J. O. Beaty notes that "this inclusion of various classes marked a decided advance in Virginia fiction, the writers of which had seen in Colonial Virginia chiefly cavaliers and servants."[72]   Although the book is prolix and uneven, one is inclined to agree with Mr. Hubbell that it is "the best novel written by a Virginian before the Civil War." Few readers, however, have discovered its sequel, *Henry St. John, Gentleman*, which completes the reconstruction of colonial Virginia. Cooke had a post-war literary career which we shall note later.

The most prolific writer of the Old South was William Gilmore Simms of South Carolina. Besides his poetry and drama of many volumes, and the uncollected writings in newspapers and magazines, he wrote novels of over twenty titles, novelettes and stories of seven titles, and histories, biographies, and essay collections. We can discuss only some of his novels and stories, with references to some critical writings.

His first novel, *Martin Faber: The Story of a Criminal* (1833)

[71] *Virginia Comedians* (New York: 1883), II, 197.
[72] *John Esten Cooke, Virginian* (New York: 1922), p. 41.

was an elaboration of a story, "Confessions of a Murderer," published in the Charleston *Southern Literary Gazette*. With charges of plagiarism, and a quarrel with Samuel Daly Langtree, later editor of *Knickerbocker's Magazine*, Simms began his fiction career with a bad start; but the book sold and he was encouraged to write more thrillers, founded on actuality. His border romances of *Guy Rivers* (1834), *Richard Hurdis* (1838), and *Border Beagles* (1840) followed three visits to the pioneer Southwest. At the age of nineteen he made a trip to see his father, who had gone to Mississippi years before.[73] There he viewed with sharp eyes the border life of Creek and Cherokee Indians, half-breeds in the swamps, "broken-down aristocrats," wild game-eating mountaineers, flashy gamblers, rascally pettifoggers, Yankee peddlers, circuit riders, and some worthy woodsmen. The second visit was in 1830, following his father's death. H. M. Jarrell gives evidence that Simms went to Mississippi in 1834, in search of literary materials, and talked with Virgil A. Stewart, the captor of John A. Murrell, leader of a notorious gang of "land pirates."[74] *Richard Hurdis* and *Border Beagles* are based upon Simms's conversations with Stewart, also on H. R. Howard's book on Stewart, published in 1836.[75]

In *The Yemassee* Simms wrote a historical romance of the

[73] W. P. Trent, *William Gilmore Simms* (Boston: 1892), pp. 14–15.

[74] "Simms's Visit to the Southwest," *American Literature*, V, 29–35 (March, 1933).

[75] Trent scorned the border romances, stating that "they should never have been written, since they have nothing ennobling in them." (*William Gilmore Simms*, p. 328). A. H. Quinn states that "Simms did his poorest work in the 'border romances.'" See *American Fiction* (New York: 1936), p. 121. But, as has been indicated, Poe preferred the border romances. H. M. Jarrell condemns Trent for his dislike of realism in fiction, and for his inartistic stressing of the ethical, "ennobling" qualities of fiction; he regards Simms's border romances superior to the colonial romances and the romances of the Revolution. See Mr. Jarrell's unpublished dissertation, *William Gilmore Simms's Realistic Romances* (Duke University, Durham, N.C.: 1930).

early colonial days of South Carolina. The struggle against the Indians is the enveloping action; the love of Governor Charles Craven, disguised as Gabriel Harrison, for Bess Mathews, the daughter of the Puritan pastor of the colony, forms the romantic action.[76] The Yemassee Indians, whom Simms called the Yemassee, lived in the coastal region of South Carolina and Georgia. In 1715, after trouble with the traders, they organized a combination of tribes against the English. A few traders were slaughtered and there was a general massacre of settlers. After several skirmishes the Indians were defeated by troops led by Governor Craven, and were driven across the Savannah River. The Spaniards received them into Florida, where they were later enslaved and destroyed by the Seminoles.[77] Sanutee, chief of the Yemassee, is the typical Indian of romance, loving the forest which is his hunting ground, jealously viewing the steady advance of the white man; Matiwan, his squaw, is a strong defender of tradition; and Occonestoga, their degenerate son, has been ruined, body and soul, by the white man's strong drink. With a convincing knowledge of colonial South Carolina history, and a knowledge of Scott's and Cooper's novelistic technique, Simms wrote a romance which some critics believe his best fictitious creation.

Simms wrote seven novels dealing with themes of the Revolution, in which he attempted to give realistic pictures of events and personalities in the lower section of South Carolina during 1780 and 1781. *The Partisan* relates the struggle between the partisans and Tories in 1780; *Mellichampe* continues the account of guerrilla warfare in the rivalry between Ernest Mellichampe, a partisan, and Barsfield, a Tory; *Katherine Wal-*

---

[76] See *The Yemassee*, edited by Alexander Cowie (American Fiction Series; New York: 1937), for text with biographical and critical introduction.

[77] For details see V. W. Crane, *The Southern Frontier* (Durham, N.C.: 1928), and C. J. Milling, *Red Carolinians* (Chapel Hill, N.C.: 1940).

ton, is the third of the partisan-Tory trilogy; *The Kinsmen*, later republished as *The Scout*, narrates the feud of the half-brothers Conway in guerrilla fighting; *The Forayers* tells of the terrible Dog Days raid in 1781; *Eutaw* is a sequel to *The Forayers* and ends with the battle of Eutaw; *The Sword and the Distaff*, later republished as *Woodcraft*, deals with the post-war period, when Lieutenant Porgy returns from war to struggle with poverty, debt, and rascals, and to make love unsuccessfully to two women at the same time. Lieutenant Porgy, "the fat and philosophic partisan under Marion," appears in all the romances except *The Kinsmen* (*The Scout*).

Simms wrote and published at least fifty-eight stories, besides five novelettes, which indicates that he was as prolific as Poe. Most of these stories were first published in newspapers, magazines, and annuals, to be collected in volumes under seven titles. Some of the best stories, including "Grayling," which Poe praised, and "The Lazy Crow," are accessible in *The Wigwam and the Cabin*.

Simms wrote in the Scott-Cooper tradition, and to both Scott and Cooper he gave tribute. Ten years after Scott's death, and after Simms had written several of his colonial, Revolution, and border romances, he gave praise to Scott's fiction method.[78] He wrote at length in his characteristic elaborate, ornate style. Not all was praise, for Simms indicated what he considered faults in style and characterization. For example, "We have no respect for heroes placed always in subordinate positions—sent hither and thither—baffled by every breath of circumstance—creatures without will, and constantly governed by the caprices of other persons. This was the enfeebling characteristic in Scott's heroes."[79] Simms found both excellencies and defects in Cooper's early novels, but the Americanism in *The Spy*, *The Pioneers*, *The Pilot*, and *The*

[78] *Views and Reviews* (New York: 1843), pp. 215–216.
[79] *Ibid.*, p. 213.

Last of the Mohicans was an element dear to him. He said that *The Spy* was "the boldest and best attempt at the historical romance which had ever been made in America," in which Cooper "struck the vein, and convinced the people not only that there was gold in the land, but that the gold of the land was good." This tale created a demand in the foreign and native markets for fiction employing American materials, and Cooper "proceeded with proper industry to supply the demand." He writes that in the "details of Indian art and resource . . . Cooper was inimitable"; "his conception of the frontier white man, if less true than picturesque, is . . . an artistical conception of great originality and effect"; and "his scout, his trapper, his hunter, and his pilot, all live to our eyes and thoughts, the perfect ideals of moral individuality." After sketching Cooper's satirical works and the decline of his literary reputation, Simms concludes: "As we have already said, the Americanism of Mr. Cooper would move us to forgive him all his faults, were they twice as many."[80]

Thus Cooper and Simms were of the Scott school, and readers will continue to compare Simms's novels with Scott's and Cooper's in plot, characterization, and style.

X. HUMOROUS SKETCHES

In the hinterland, almost unnoticed by the literati, an authentic southern literature of considerable vigor and influence was developing. It consisted mainly of humorous sketches concerning the large middle class of small farmers with few or no slaves, of traders, merchants, professional men, and artisans, and also a larger class, the mudsill of society, the "poor whites," the mountaineers, crackers, settlers, hunters, and other frontier people, living in shacks, clothed in skins and rags, eating hog and hominy, speaking rude dialect.

Shields McIlwaine has treated the literature of these people

[80] *Ibid.*, p. 237.

in *The Southern Poor-White*. He summarizes his discussion as follows.

In the Colonial era, Byrd recorded humorously the origin of the poor-white as frontier lubber along the Virginia-North Carolina border—an indolent, shiftless wretch, bedevilled by vermin, agues, and the "country distemper" from eating un-salted pork.

From the early 1800's to the Civil War, the lubber emerged in literature as the poor-white, variously dubbed Cracker, woolhat, dirt-eater, or tacky.... The Southern novelists in the plantation tradition largely ignored him, although Caruthers in *Kentuckian in New York* (1834) pitied him and Simms used him as a villain, achieving the notable portrait of Bostwick [*The Sword and the Distaff*]. Humorists in the South, however, from Longstreet to Charles H. Smith, employed the trashy Cracker with excellent effect and produced the most important inter-pretation before the twentieth century.[81]

Among the best of the "sketch-writers" was Augustus Baldwin Longstreet (1790–1870). In 1835 he collected nine-teen of these sketches under the title of *Georgia Scenes, Char-acters, Incidents, etc., in the First Half Century of the Republic*.[82] These *Georgia Scenes*, dealing with country parties, horse-trades, fox-hunts, shooting-matches, and brutal fights, imme-diately attained wide popularity. Even the critics were favorable. W. P. Trent wrote that "If the fighting, swearing, drinking, gambling, hail-fellow-well-met Southwest had pro-duced no other literary monuments than this, it would not have broken the Ten Commandments in vain."[83]

William Tappan Thompson (1812–1882), Georgia journal-

---

[81] Shields McIlwaine, *The Southern Poor-White: From Lubberland to Tobacco Road* (Norman, Okla.: 1939), p. 241.

[82] John Donald Wade, *Augustus Baldwin Longstreet* (New York: 1934).

[83] "A Retrospect of American Humor," *Century Magazine*, XLI, 63 (November, 1901).

ist, editor, and soldier, was associated with Longstreet on the *Sentinel*, and was the editor of other Georgia newspapers. *Major Jones's Courtship* (1844), *Major Jones's Chronicles of Pineville* (1845), and *Major Jones's Sketches of Travel* (1847) were written "to depict some of the peculiar features of Georgia backwoodsmen." "Major" Joseph Jones is a simple, good-natured bumpkin whose credulity makes him the butt of the local pranksters. In a succession of letters "Major" Jones writes to "Colonel" Thompson yarns relating how he hung himself in a meal sack as a "Chrismus gift" to the blushing Mary Stallins, took his first ride on a train, which went "humming along jest like iled thunder," rode by stage-coach and by "steambote," and so on, in a series of countryman's adventures.

Joseph Glover Baldwin (1815–1864) was born in Virginia and won reputation in Mississippi and Alabama as a lawyer, office-holder, and judge, but he is known today as the author of *Flush Times in Alabama and Mississippi* (1853).

Johnson Jones Hooper (1815–1863), North Carolina and Alabama lawyer, office-holder, and newspaper editor, published *Some Adventures of Captain Simon Suggs* (1845), creating a picaresque rascal, a "sharp and vulgar, sunny and venal swashbuckler," whose motto is, "It is good to be shifty in a new country."

David Crockett (1786–1836) was a Tennessee settler, hunter, Indian fighter, Congressman, and defender of the Alamo. There are several books to which Crockett's name is attached, but he had slight part in writing them. Even *A Narrative of the Life of David Crockett . . . Written by Himself*, the most authentic of his writings, was prepared by a "ghost writer," probably Thomas Chilton.

Thomas Bangs Thorpe (1815–1878), Louisiana painter, newspaper editor, and soldier, published "The Big Bear of Arkansas," in the New York *Spirit of the Times* (1841), *The Mysteries of the Backwoods* (1846), and *The Hive of the Bee*

Hunter (1854), which contained tall tales of border life of the Southwest.

George Washington Harris (1814–1869), Tennessee silversmith, river-boat captain, and political writer, published *Sut Lovingood's Yarns* (1867), of coarse humor about primitive, illiterate, tough youths who loved corn whiskey and practical jokes.

Charles Henry Smith (1826–1903), Georgia lawyer and soldier, wrote *Bill Arp, So-Called* (1866) and *Bill Arp's Letters* (1868), in which he satirized the Union cause in the open letters to "Mr. Abe Linkhorn."[84]

Literary historians discuss this literature, based upon personal anecdotes, stories, and letters of illiterate, uncouth folk, as the literature of humor. Humor, however, defies definition and analysis because the appeal of the comic depends upon too many factors. The stories may have been humorous to the writers, and they were certainly popularly received by their readers a hundred years ago. Most of the stories, however, do not seem very funny to the readers of today, for the fashions in humorous devices have changed. For example, most of us find no humor in misspellings. Some stories are often too coarse for readers of taste and culture. Many honest people are ashamed to laugh at the misfortunes of distressed people below them in the social and economic scale.

Not as a "literature of humor" but as "folk literature" should the writings of Longstreet, Thompson, Hooper, Crockett, Thorpe, Harris, Bagby, Smith, and dozens of newspaper and magazine journalists be studied. Watterson says that these

[84] Some of the best collections of selections from these humorists are, in the order of publication, Henry Watterson, *Oddities in Southern Life and Character* (Boston: 1882), Franklin J. Meine, *Tall Tales of the Southewst* (New York: 1930), Arthur Palmer Hudson, *Humor of the Old Deep South* (New York: 1936), and Walter Blair, *Native American Humor, 1800–1900* (New York: 1937). See the last book for a complete bibliography of American humor.

Chronicles of the nether side of Southern life ... [tell about] the good old times of muster days and quarter racing, before the camp-meeting and the barbecue had lost their power and their charm; when men led simple, homely lives, doing their love-making and their law-making as they did their fighting and their plowing, in a straight furrow; when there was no national debt multiplying the dangers and magnifying the expenses of dis-tillation in the hills and hollows, and pouring in upon the log-rolling, the quilting, the corn-shucking, and the fish-fry an inquisitorial crew of tax-gatherers and detectives to spoil the sport and dull the edge of patriotic husbandry.[85]

Unquestionably the writers knew the folk whom they char-acterized. As lawyers and judges—and many were lawyers—they defended these people when accused of hog-stealings, distillings, knife-cuttings, arsons, and murders; as physicians they rode horses or mules on "slick" or rocky roads to cure their diseases or deliver their babies; as soldiers they shared leaky tents, smoky camp-fires, and wormy food with each other; as journalists they smilingly but courteously poked into men's private affairs to get newspaper items.

These recorders of folk life were giving homely pictures of rough life. The devices of humor were needed, for the writers sought to amuse the lower and middle-class readers of news-papers. And these early sketch writers have considerable re-lation to such writers of stories of local color as Cable, Thomas Nelson Page, Miss Murfree, and Joel Chandler Harris, in the last quarter of the century. They created original characters with idiosyncracies of manners and dialectal speech; they localized them, to some extent, in sections of Virginia, Georgia, Tennessee, and other states; they wove incidents into plots. But they treated their characters objectively and without sen-timentality. In many respects, therefore, the early sketch writers are more closely allied with such "literary comedians"

[85] *Oddities in Southern Life and Character* (Boston, c. 1882), p. vii.

as Artemus Ward, Josh Billings, and Mark Twain than with Cable, Page, and Harris, and in this close connection may be seen the strength of their influence upon the writers of other sections.

XI. MAGAZINES

In the South magazines were not published until the last decade of the eighteenth century, for the newspapers freely offered their columns to writers of political and religious articles, essays, fiction, and poetry. In the early national and ante-bellum periods hundreds of magazines were published in Charleston, Baltimore, Richmond, New Orleans, and other cities. We can discuss only a few of the most important ones.[86]

Charleston was indubitably a cultural and literary center, for it actually published sixty-three magazines before 1860. The first was *The Traiteur*, published in six issues in 1795–1796, frankly imitative of the *Tatler* and the *Spectator*, and the last was *Russell's Magazine*, edited and supported by able men.[87] An early distinctive Charleston magazine was the *Southern Review* (1828–1832) which was published in a somewhat peaceful economic and political period prior to nullification and secession troubles.[88] The editors were Stephen Elliott, Yale graduate, planter, banker, botanist, founder of the Literary and Philosophical Society of South Carolina; also his son, Stephen Elliott, Jr., lawyer, clergyman, later bishop in the Protestant Episcopal church; and Hugh Swinton Legaré,

---

[86] See F. L. Mott, *A History of American Magazines, 1741–1850* (New York: 1930); L. N. Richardson, *A History of Early American Magazines, 1741–1850* (New York: 1931).

[87] See Guy A. Cardwell, *Charleston Periodicals, 1795–1860: A Study in Literary Influences, with a Descriptive Check List of Seventy-Five Magazines.* (Unpublished dissertation, University of North Carolina, 1836); William Stanley Hoole, *The Literary and Cultural Background of Charleston, 1838–1860.* (Unpublished dissertation, Duke University, 1934.)

[88] Cardwell, *op. cit.*, p. 113.

lawyer, orator, and classical scholar. Many of the review articles were written by the editors themselves, and other contributors included such able men as President Thomas Cooper of the College of South Carolina, United States Senator Robert Y. Hayne, and Attorney-General James L. Petigru. Of all these men Legaré was the best equipped for essay writing, and his critical reviews are worthy of careful study. In an opening number he defended the classical culture beloved by Charleston aristocrats.[89] But Legaré was a wide reader of English literature, as later references to Milton, Pope, Wordsworth, Byron, and other authors indicate, and Edd W. Parks concludes that "Legaré, to my mind, represents the classicist tempered by romanticism."[90] The writers of the various articles stressed pride in the newly-established democracy, dislike of monarchies, of which Great Britain was an example, and nationalism in politics. The writers could not agree about nationalism in literature. An extreme attitude against a nationalistic American literature was expressed in Edward W. Johnston's review of Samuel Knapp's *Lectures on American Literature* (1829) and Samuel Kettell's *Specimens of American Poetry* (1829). With ironic scorn the reviewer quoted the worst passages from the New England writers and closed with objections to a native literature.[91] On the other hand, another writer, possibly Legaré, contended that America should develop a distinctive literature, maintaining that every beautiful literature springs naturally from the soil, and that it is "connected with the history, animated by the spirit, and in perfect harmony with the character and opinions of the people."[92]

A contemporary rival of the *Southern Review* was the *Southern Literary Gazette* (1828–1829), the first of Simms's magazine

[89] *Southern Review*, I, 20 (February, 1828).

[90] "Legaré and Grayson," in *Segments of Southern Thought* (Athens, Ga.: 1938).

[91] *Southern Review*, VI, 438–444 (August, 1831).

[92] *Southern Review*, V, 62 (February, 1830).

ventures. The contributions were critical articles, reviews, poetry, and occasional fiction, including Simms's "Oakatibbe, or the Choctaw Sampson." In a review of J. E. Heath's *Edge-Hill*, Simms pleaded for a regional literature: "This [novel] looks well; the South is not asleep, merely dozing, perhaps; we hope her nap will shortly be concluded. We like to see southern books."[93]

The *Magnolia; or Southern Appalachian* was published in Macon and Savannah, Georgia, and later in Charleston, under various titles with successive editors. After it was moved to Charleston (1842–1843), the skillful editorship of Simms gave it importance second only to the later *Russell's Magazine*. His zeal for the region inspired him to accept, or even write himself, essays and stories based upon romantic incidents in southern history, legend, and life. He encouraged Longstreet to contribute several of his "Georgia Scenes." In asserting the intellectual independence of the South he waged an unpleasant, ineffectual quarrel with the editors of the New York *Knickerbocker*. The contributors included many eminent men and women of the period, especially from South Carolina and Georgia. In the *Southern and Western Monthly Magazine and Review*, frequently called *Simms' Magazine* (January–December, 1845), Simms championed national and regional literature, restating his views in an article "Americanism in Literature."[94] The twelve monthly issues contain articles, stories, and poetry, including some of Simms's best stories.[95]

The *Southern Quarterly Review* was published intermittently from 1842 to 1857, in New Orleans, Charleston, and Columbia. Of its several editors, Simms, who guided its fortunes from 1849 to 1855, gave it the ablest direction. The contents of the

---

[93] *Southern Literary Gazette*, I, 25 (October, 1828).

[94] Reprinted in *Views and Reviews* (New York: 1845).

[95] See J. Allen Morris, "The Stories of William Gilmore Simms" *American Literature*, XIV, 10–20 (March, 1942).

successive numbers, as given by E. R. Rogers, indicate a lively interest in contemporary regional literature, economics, and politics.[96] In this magazine one can find literary articles and extensive book notices, but the interest of the writers was largely concentrated on politics. The views of Simms had changed since 1832, when, from his newspaper office, he had recklessly defied a mob of nullifiers. He had turned from unionism to secession. In successive articles slavery was defended, the South was exhorted to secession, and the North was bitterly warned.

The close connection between politics and literature in the South became more apparent. The ranks of the profession of law were filled with writers. Wirt, Kennedy, Baldwin, Legaré, Simms, and many others had received legal training. Politics and political ideas were increasingly the matter of writing during the decades preceding the war, as Southerners sought to retain the rights of states against federal encroachment, and struggled to maintain an agrarianism based on slave labor. Most of the writers of poems, fiction, and essays in the ante-bellum period were lawyers, and, as one writer states, "A list of the prominent men of the South down to 1861 would be, mainly, a roll of attorneys."

Literary historians praise *Russell's Magazine*, even ranking it next to the *Southern Literary Messenger* in excellence. Published in sixteen monthly numbers from April, 1857, to March, 1865, this magazine was the literary expression of two groups in Charleston with some common members—a coterie which centered around Simms, and a group which gathered in John Russell's bookshop on King Street. On the evenings of pleasant autumn and winter days Simms, Hayne, and other Charlestonians frequently gathered in the rear of Russell's bookshop for literary gossip. According to Hayne, who wrote a reminiscent sketch twenty-five years later, John Russell was "a man

[96] *Four Southern Magazines* [Richmond: 1902].

of quick, bright mind, of much native shrewdness, and acquired information; a clever, and occasionally even an instructive talker." He had a kind heart, and in business affairs was "generous to a fault."[97] The scholars and cultivated gentlemen of Charleston who had made his bookshop a rendezvous for fifteen years hailed Russell as "Lord John," which he genially accepted. He had told them the incident of being mistaken for Lord John Russell, the English premier, while traveling between Calais and Dover. Hayne pictured the presence of Charleston notables in Lord John's store. In an evening there might enter James L. Petigru, Mitchell King, a "large-bodied, beetle-browed old man with the Scotch accent, . . . equally noted as an able scholar and sound lawyer"; the physician Dr. Samuel Henry Dickson, "one among the most brilliant *general* scholars and artistic writers of his day"; Father Lynch, a Roman Catholic priest, with "his enameled snuff-box"; another clergyman, the Rev. James W. Miles, "a man of air and fire"; William R. Rabor, the young editor of the *Charleston Mercury*, William John Grayson, author of a biographical sketch of Petigru and of the pro-slavery poem, "The Hireling and the Slave."[98]

In Hayne's words, "A few of the scholars and cultivated gentlemen of Charleston conceived the notion, in the year 1856, of establishing a monthly literary magazine in that city. It was designed to be a representative organ, not merely of local, but of Southern intellect, taste, and opinions."[99] The excellence of the magazine rests upon Hayne, who was the editor-in-chief. A recent writer does not over-praise him in stating that "the charm of Paul Hayne's gentle nature, the sheer loveliness and nobility of his character, grips the heart. How slow he was to condemn, how ready to praise, how delicate in

[97] "Ante-Bellum Charleston," *Southern Bivouac*, N. S., I, 330 (December, 1885).
[98] *Ibid.*, I, 328–330.   [99] *Ibid.*, I, 330.

rebuke or question, how ardent in friendship, those parts of the magazine which can be traced to his pen bear abundant testimony."[100]

Although Hayne hoped to edit a literary journal, the thinking men of the South were talking about slavery and the threat of an impending conflict. In the leading article of the first number William J. Grayson defended slavery at length, and he attacked the abolitionists in later articles. The political topics of slavery, states' rights, and threatened secession could not be kept out of even a literary journal of the fifties.

Besides the verse and the criticism of poetry, there was considerable fiction, both stories and serials. Most of the fiction is sentimental and moral, written by the popular Mrs. Susan Petigru King, the daughter of James L. Petigru, under such titles as "A Marriage of Persuasion," "A Male Flirt," "The Best of Friends," and "Sylvia's World," and by Miss Essie Cheseborough, who wrote on such themes as fair damsels forced by heartless parents into loveless marriages, or neglected wives deserted by profligate husbands. Hayne contributed verse, stories, able editorials, and book notices. Simms and Timrod contributed verse and articles. All three were concerned about the production of southern literature.

By 1834 Richmond had become the literary capital of Virginia. The little city of about seventeen thousand people, of whom only half were whites, boasted the State Library and the Virginia Historical and Philosophical Society. In Richmond, Williamsburg, and other towns of the state, and at the recently established University of Virginia in Charlottesville, were men of culture and literary tastes—enough of them to justify Thomas Willis White, prosperous printer, in establishing in 1834 the *Southern Literary Messenger*.[101] In this literary ven-

---

[100] Froude Kennedy, "Russell's Magazine," *South Atlantic Quarterly*, XVIII, 137 (April, 1919).

[101] See David K. Jackson, *Poe and the Southern Literary Messenger*

ture White depended on such friends as James Ewell Heath (1792–1862), author of *Edge-Hill;* Nathaniel Beverley Tucker (1784–1851), son of St. George Tucker, and the author of *The Partisan Leader* and *George Balcombe;* and Lucian Minor (1802–1858), professor of law at William and Mary College and an able writer. Heath contributed to the first number, which he edited, an article entitled "Southern Literature."

The *Messenger* prospered under a succession of publishers and editors until 1864. The death of White in 1843 was a misfortune, for he had been the patron and guardian of the enterprise. Edgar Allan Poe brought enduring reputation to the *Messenger* as contributor and editor. Poe owed his employment as editorial assistant to the recommendation by John Pendleton Kennedy, who had been one of the judges to award him the *Baltimore Saturday Visiter* prize for his "MS Found in a Bottle." Kennedy introduced Poe to White, who accepted "Bernice—A Tale" for the March, 1835, issue, and several tales and poems for succeeding issues. Throughout the summer and fall of 1835 Poe was intermittently a member of the editorial staff.

For the 1836 issues he was the active editor, and his actual editorial connection terminated with the January, 1837, number. His thirty tales and poems and his numerous editorials and book reviews brought such literary reputation to the magazine that it became the chief vehicle for southern writers. More important than his tales and poems Poe's critical reviews gave the *Messenger* a national reputation. Imitating the "tomahawk" manner of book reviewing established by Francis Jeffrey in the *Edinburgh Review*, and William Gifford in the *Quarterly Review*, Poe proceeded to "hang, draw, and *Quar-*

(Richmond: 1934) and *The Contributors and Contributions to the Southern Literary Messenger* (Richmond: 1936); Frank L. Mott, *A History of American Magazines, 1841–1850* (New York: 1930); Jay B. Hubbell, "Southern Magazines," in *Culture in the South* (Chapel Hill, N.C.: 1933).

terly" a few victims of the *Knickerbocker* school of New York or of the "Frogpondians" of Boston. In the December, 1835, *Messenger* he flayed *Norman Leslie* by Theodore S. Fay, one of the editors of the *New York Mirror*, and "used it up," in his own phrase. Many other minor writers were tomahawked. Nor did all southern books escape censure; yet he treated gently his patron Kennedy's books and those by the lady writers. His derogatory treatment of *The Partisan* was so bitterly resented by Simms that it was not until after Poe left the *Messenger* that Simms sent contributions. Poe's best reviews and especially his later articles on critical theory were of great value to literary novices and to editors who were encouraging a regional literature. During his editorship the circulation rose from seven hundred to nearly five thousand, and Poe claimed that the annual profit was ten thousand dollars. But Poe was not all of the *Messenger*. Such later editors as Matthew F. Maury (1840–1843), Benjamin B. Minor (1843–1847), John R. Thompson (1847–1860), and George W. Bagby (1860–1864) were men of literary and editorial ability. More important than the editors were the contributors, and a file of the *Messenger* contains writings by authors of literary excellence.

The study of literary centers in the publication of magazines leads the student to Baltimore, Louisville, Atlanta, New Orleans, and other cities. Some of the magazines, however, had greater prominence after the war. It would be profitable to consider the literary material in such magazines as *De Bow's Review* (1846–1880), published in New Orleans and other cities, and the *Southern Review* (1867–1879), edited in Baltimore by Albert Taylor Bledsoe.[102]

---

[102] See Gertrude Gilmer, *Checklist of Southern Periodicals to 1861* (Boston: 1934); "Maryland Magazines—Ante Bellum, 1793–1861," *Maryland Historical Magazine*, XXIX, 120–131 (1934); "A Critique of Certain Georgia Ante-Bellum Literary Magazines Arranged

In his analysis of "Literary Nationalism in the Old South," Professor J. B. Hubbell concludes that

> The demand for a Southern literature resulted in the establishment of numerous short-lived periodicals, and it stimulated some persons to write or at least to publish what had been written with no thought of publication.... But it did not serve to make Southern literature *Southern* except in a rather superficial sense of the word.... The writings of the humorists, published for the most part in Southern newspapers and written without literary pretensions, are far more Southern than the great bulk of the material printed in Southern magazines.[103]

XII. THE PLANTATION TRADITION

The year 1870 inaugurated an era of new authors, themes, and movements in southern literature. The old era was reviewed by J. W. Davidson, who published in 1869 his *Living Writers of the South*, in which he listed alphabetically "the names of 241 writers,—116 male and 75 female. Of these, 201 have published books." With great frankness Davidson adds, "Some of the writers have talents and character, with corresponding results, which enable them to stand in the front rank of American Authorship. Some have limited abilities. And some have none." Since he listed only living writers, he could not name Calhoun, Tucker, Grayson, Wilde, Legaré, Poe, Baldwin, Hooper, Philip Cooke, Timrod, and a few others of "front rank." Among the active authors listed were John Esten Cooke, George William Bagby, Charles Gayarré, Hayne, Lanier, R. M. Johnston, Tourgée, and Henry Watterson. Three of the best Old

Chronologically, and a Checklist," *Georgia Historical Quarterly*, XVIII, 293–334 (1934); Max L. Griffin, "A Bibliography of New Orleans Magazines," *Louisiana Historical Quarterly*, XVIII, 3–66 (1935); J. C. McCloskey, "A Note on the *Portico*," *American Literature*, VIII, 300–314 (1936).

[103] *American Studies in Honor of William Kenneth Boyd* (Durham, N.C.: 1940), p. 218.

South authors, Simms, Longstreet, and Kennedy, died the next year, 1870.

Most of the new writers publishing after 1870 had been too young to enlist in the war or to send aid from home to the troops; but they were old enough to witness the horrors of war and to suffer in the black days of Reconstruction. Among these postwar authors were Joel Chandler Harris, who spent his boyhood on the Turner plantation in Georgia; George W. Cable, who was old enough to fight with the Confederate army; James Lane Allen on his father's farm in Kentucky; Mary Noailles Murfree at home on the plantation near Murfreesboro, Tennessee; Grace King, refugeeing on a plantation below New Orleans; Thomas Nelson Page, watching as a boy the destruction of the Page estate of "Rosewell"; and Walter Hines Page, listening to the war talk of wounded soldiers. These alert, gifted men and women saw gallant men enlisting to fight the hated Yankees, greeted wounded fathers and brothers as they returned from the struggle, watched the looting and burning of homes by straggling soldiers, and struggled after the war to rebuild their half-ruined lives.

In retrospect some of them visioned the old plantation life romantically and ideally. They pictured a spacious house, with massive furniture and silver plate, the savory, abundant food served by smiling, loyal slaves, and the gracious hospitality to numerous guests. Surrounding the mansion were noble oak and magnolia trees, boxwood hedges, flowers everywhere, and in the rolling distance fertile fields of abundant crops adjacent to forests full of game. Those were the good old times, the fruit of the best of all civilizations. Such was the Plantation Tradition.

In expressing the nostalgic idealization of old plantation life Dr. George William Bagby and Thomas Nelson Page delivered stirring addresses to their Virginia audiences. Bagby had acquired a considerable reputation as newspaper correspondent, magazine editor, and creator of the "Mozis Addums" papers. Active in Richmond at one period during the war, he was editor of the *Southern Literary Messenger*, and contributor to the *Whig*, the *Examiner*, and several out-of-state papers. Before members of historical societies in Richmond he delivered an address on "The Old Virginia Gentleman." This should be read in entirety because of its literary quality, for it is not adequately presented by quotations and paraphrase. Approaching an old home, well back from "the main, plain road," Colonel Tidewater is struck by a scene of exceeding beauty, as his eyes wander over "wide fields of waving grain" and "mottled tobacco," and over pastures of fat cattle and peaceful sheep. This view and that of the old mansion convinces the tired horseman that all the years of a man's life should be spent in the country. He notices the stir and bustle. There are "the young master, with his troop of little darkies," the "Young Mistiss," with "her retinue of sable attendants," some one always coming or going in gig, double buggy, carry-all, or carriage, and the mistress and servants (Virginians never say "slaves") moving about from kitchen to smoke-house to dairy. The house, the barns, the fields, and the woods seem to be bustling in activity. After Colonel Tidewater enters the habitation, for "house is too short a word to express it," he takes three pages to describe its comfort and magnificence. With rapture he sees the girls —"are there such girls nowadays?"; he greets the mistress— "words fail to tell what the Virginia lady of the best type was" —but he tries to do so, in *five* pages, for he is "carried away by recollections of the sweethearts of other days"; finally he describes the old-time Virginia gentleman—which requires only *four* pages—and produces a being "as nearly perfect as human infirmity permits man to be." According to Bagby, these men of character based upon honor, courage, and a love of liberty, had been tested "in the War of the Revolution, again in 1812, again in Mexico, again in the great rebellion, so called, and yet

again in the long torture of Reconstruction." Although ad-
mitting that his picture of the Virginia of the "spring and gourd"
period is somewhat idealized, Bagby stoutly maintains that "In
simple truth and beyond question there was in our Virginia
country life a beauty, a simplicity, a purity, an uprightness, a
cordial and lavish hospitality, warmth and grace which shine
in the lens of memory with a charm that passes all language at
my command."

By birth, temperament, and training Thomas Nelson Page
was fitted to extol the Old South. He warmly approved Bagby's
"Old Virginia Gentleman," calling it "the most beautiful
sketch of life in the South that has ever appeared." In seven
essays and addresses, printed as *The Old South: Essays Social
and Political*, Page defended and eulogized the Virginia of his
fathers. In "Social Life Before the South" he elaborates on
Bagby's sentimental and humorous picture by sketching the
joys of Christmas on the plantation. He concludes by listing
the contributions of the Old South to Christian civilization.[104]

His first story, "Marse Chan," published in 1884, is a sentimental story, entirely in Negro dialect, of a Confederate
mother's grief, and the steadfast loyalty with which the Negro
served his master. "Unc Edinburg's Drowndin" is a portrayal of the social life of the old epoch, of duelling, chivalry,
love-making, fox-hunting, Christmas celebrations, and hospitality, all related from the haze of the past in the words of the
old Negro. In these and other stories Page portrayed the
cordiality and steadfast kindliness of the race relations. The
narrators are former slaves who tell in their simple way of the
satisfactory life in an irrecoverable enchanted era. "Dem was
good ole times, Marster; de best Sam ever see!"

In *The Gentleman of the Black Stock*, Page coined a phrase
which is used as representing the aristocratic Old South gentle-

[104] "Social Life Before the War" in *The Old South* (New York:
1892), pp. 184–185.

man. In the preface to *Red Rock*, Page makes us feel that a glory has departed from the earth. "Even the moonlight was richer and mellower before the war than it is now."

Like Page of Virginia Joel Chandler Harris of Georgia viewed the success and happiness of the old plantation as owing to the slaves—the old uncle, telling legendary stories and singing quaint songs, the old mammy, cherishing or bossing the children, and the other servants, entertaining and advising the white folks. The Uncle Remus stories presented the old-time Negro on a Georgia cotton plantation, telling folk-lore stories in the best dialect ever recorded. When asked about the original of Uncle Remus, Harris replied: "He was not an invention of my own, but a human syndicate, I might say, of three or four old darkies whom I had known. I just walloped them together into one person and called him 'Uncle Remus'."[105]

Although he was not the first to use Negro dialect, for Simms had introduced Gullah dialect in several stories, Irwin Russell had written poems in dialect, and Jim Crow minstrels had pranced on the stage for decades, Harris was the first faithful recorder of Negro speech. His friend James W. Davidson—he who wrote *Living Writers of the South*—said of *Uncle Remus:* "It is the only *true* dialect I ever saw printed. It marks our era in its line—the first successful attempt to write what the Negro has actually said, and in his own peculiar way."[106] Thomas Nelson Page asserted that "No man who has ever written has known one-tenth part about the negro that Mr Harris knows, and for those who hereafter shall wish to find not merely words, but the real language of the negro of the old-time, his works will prove the best thesaurus."[107]

In the development of the plantation tradition in literature

•

[105] Julia Collier Harris, *The Life and Letters of Joel Chandler Harris* (Boston: 1918), p. 146.

[106] *Ibid.*, p. 163.

[107] *Ibid.*, p. 165.

Page and Harris are the principal names, but there are others of importance.[108]

The plantation tradition followed the ancestors of James Lane Allen from Virginia to Kentucky. For generations they had been gentleman farmers, nourishing proudly the family pride in blood, but living meagrely in genteel poverty. The father owned no Negroes, and the boy worked at the hardest farm work. His whole life was a struggle to attain money and recognition as a gentleman. Two of his stories are as much of the aristocratic tradition as are those by Bagby and Page. "Two Gentlemen of Kentucky" tells about the steadfast loyalty of an old Negro for his master, about whom "the whole vast, social system of the old regime had fallen." "King Solomon of Kentucky" tells about a worthless white man, King Solomon, who has been supported by an aged Negro woman, but in a yellow fever epidemic King Solomon shows his real quality by heroically ministering to the suffering and by burying the dead.

Probably no other novel has done more to keep alive the plantation tradition than Francis Hopkinson Smith's *Colonel Carter of Cartersville*. Readers South and North accepted his portrait of the ante-bellum Virginia Cavalier, proud of his section, his state, and his family, dispensing from the head of his table rich food and rare wines to his many guests, hopelessly careless about paying his debts, hotly challenging each fancied insult, courtly in his mannered treatment of women, and exemplifying "the beau ideal of a charming and quixotic civilization." As his Negro Chad says, "Dem was high times. We ain't neber seed no time like dat since de war."

Thus the plantation tradition was built up in literature, to be further idealized on the stage and in the moving-picture theatre. How the southern orators have loved it! Many a politician

---

[108] For the development of this theme see Francis Pendleton Gaines, *The Southern Plantation: A Study in the Development and Accuracy of a Tradition* (New York: 1925).

has elected himself to office by flowery appeals to the beauty and glory of the past. The historians and biographers sketch the times and heroes as they actually were, the economists point out the evils of the plantation system, the satirists ridicule the artificialities, and the realists plead for truth, but always attractive is the Plantation Tradition.

XIII. LOCAL COLOR

Thomas Nelson Page and Joel Chandler Harris were representatives of a group of "local colorists" or "social historians" who belonged to a new school in the writing of short stories. Fiction in novels, but especially in stories, was a literary type adapted to portraying the various racial and class groups living in well-defined sections, and maintaining folk peculiarities. During the war and in the postwar period America was discovering herself. The northern soldiers had campaigned and fought over the southern states, and in their wanderings had found peoples and customs that were new and strangely interesting. In the rapid expansion of the West and Southwest the pioneers and settlers found wild regions and a wilder society. Men and women with a literary bent began to publish tales of these new-found Americans, and in a few years every isolated section and neighborhood had a chronicler. Perhaps the literary movement began with Bret Harte and Mark Twain, whose tales of rough life in the mining camps of Nevada and California were accepted eagerly by the editors of Boston and New York.

The South, however, was the richest field for literary treatment, and scores of story writers created a real southern literature, appreciated at home, but avidly read in the North and abroad. The fiction writers localized their stories on the plantations of Virginia, the slopes and coves of the Appalachians, the cotton fields of the Deep South, the sugar plantations of Louisiana, the French quarter of New Orleans, the canebrakes of Arkansas, and in dozens of other picturesque localities. They related incidents of plantation love-making, the slave quarters, court trials, fox and 'possum hunts, "field" schools, camp-meetings, yellow fever epidemics, barbecues, mountain feuds, and moonshining. The colorful characters included runaway slaves, free Negroes, voodoo practitioners, gamblers, deserters, Creoles, cajuns, crackers, hillbillies, Ku Kluxers, and many others, speaking in dialect. There was great diversity and literary richness in incidents and characters. To the readers of one town or state the lives of the people in a distant town or state were bizarre and exotic. Even today some of these localities seem "foreign" to the visitor.

We can mention only a few of these writers, for extended treatment by able literary historians may be found in easily accessible books. George Washington Cable collected his magazine stories of Louisiana Creoles and quadroons in *Old Creole Days* (1879), *Madame Delphine* (1891), and *Strange True Stories of Louisiana* (1889). Grace King, claiming to present more authentic Creole stories, wrote tales of Louisiana in *Monsieur Motte* (1889), *Tales of a Time and Place* (1892), and *Balcony Stories* (1893). Kate Chopin wrote more Creole stories in *Bayou Folk* (1894) and *A Night in Acadie* (1897). Mary Noailles Murfree (Charles Egbert Craddock) introduced the mountaineers of the Cumberland and Great Smoky Mountains in the stories of *In the Tennessee Mountains* (1884) and the novel, *The Prophet of the Great Smoky Mountains* (1885). Sherwood Bonner published Negro and poor-white stories, usually localized in Mississippi, in *Dialect Tales* (1883) and *Suwanee River Tales* (1884). Alice French (Octave Thanet) introduced life in the canebrakes of Arkansas in *Knitters in the Sun* (1887) and *Otto the Knight and Other Trans-Mississippi Stories* (1881). James Lane Allen collected romantic stories of Kentucky in *Flute and Violin and Other Kentucky Tales and Romances* (1891) and *A Kentucky Cardinal* (1894). Harry

Stillwell Edwards collected his stories of Georgia life in *Two Runaways and Other Stories* (1889) and *His Defence and Other Stories* (1899).[109]

Unlike the sketch writers of the early period, the local colorists were in sympathy with their characters. For example, Thomas Nelson Page loved the old plantation life so deeply that Meh Lady, Marse Chan, and Unc Edinburg are idealized characters. Cable touched with kindly hand the gambler 'Sieur George, the brother-shielding Jean Marie Poquelin, and the drunken Posson Jone. Miss Murfree's fifteen summers in the Cumberland Mountains brought her enough knowledge to treat gently the outlaw Rich Pearson, the revengeful Tony Britt, and even the stern mountain preachers. Joel Chandler Harris, James Lane Allen, and other local colorists depicted all sorts and conditions of men with charity for their faults and peculiarities.

The success of these new southern writers was owing to their welcome by northern publishers and readers. The South had no publishing houses of importance, and southern people bought few books. Even in the ante-bellum period, books by southern authors were usually published in New York, Philadelphia, and Boston. Before Simms became a recognized successful literary man, he had won recognition first in New England and New York, and most of his books throughout his career were published in Boston and New York. The Boston publishing houses of Ticknor and Fields, Brown and Company, and Phillips, Sampson and Company, the Philadelphia house of Lippincott and Company, and the New York houses of D. Appleton and Company, Harper and Brothers, G. P. Putnam and Company, and Charles Scribner published most of the books by southern authors.

[109] For lists of regional authors and stories see the *Library of Southern Literature*, Volume XVI; R. C. Beale, *The Development of the Short Story in the South* (Charlottesville, Va.: 1930).

In the decades after 1870 thousands of readers in New England and the Middle States were eager to read books, articles, and stories about this southern land of diverse peoples. Each state, from Virginia to Florida and Texas, needed a guidebook, and there were no Federal Writers projects. The publishers were ready to supply this reading matter, as shown by the establishing of many new magazines and the printing of many books. The editors of *Scribner's Monthly*, *Century Magazine*, *Scribner's Magazine*, *Atlantic Monthly*, and *Harper's Monthly Magazine* eagerly sought descriptive articles and local color fiction about the South. Most of the stories mentioned in the collections by Cable, Page, and others had previously been published in these magazines.

The first magazine to exploit southern writers was *Scribner's Monthly Magazine*—not to be confused with the later *Scribner's Magazine*.[110] *Scribner's Monthly Magazine* was founded by Dr. Josiah Gilbert Holland, Roswell Smith, and Charles Scribner, and published from 1870 to 1881. Its editor was Dr. Holland, assisted by Richard Watson Gilder, a man of literary ability and fine taste. In 1881, after he had acquired most of the stock, Roswell Smith changed the name to the *Century Magazine*, and Gilder became editor. The Century Company published the magazine with great success for decades, but with later declining patronage, until its demise in 1930. The publishers and editors of *Scribner's Monthly* and the *Century Magazine* were liberal in political views, broadly national in spirit, and conciliatory toward the South. Smith sent Edward King on a twenty-five thousand mile journey by carriage, stagecoach, and saddle through all the southern states. His articles, copiously illustrated, entitled "The Great South,"

---

[110] See F. L. Mott, *A History of American Magazines, 1850–1865*, and *A History of American Magazines, 1865–1885* (Cambridge, Mass.: 1938) for facts about all these magazines, except *Scribner's Magazine*, which was founded later.

covered over four hundred and fifty pages of *Scribner's Monthly* and were later published in book form. Cable was not the only southern writer to owe his recognition to editor Gilder and the appreciative readers of his magazines, as is evidenced by the long succession of stories by various authors. Perhaps it was Gilder himself who stated in the anonymous "Topics of the Time—Southern Literature" that "Attention has recently been called to the large number of southern contributions to the magazine. No less than seven articles contributed by Southern readers appeared in a recent number of *Scribner* and we are glad to recognize the fact of a permanent productive force in literature in the Southern States." The peak of southern productivity, however, was reached in the five-year period from 1884 to 1888.

The correspondence between Gilder and Harris shows that they were personal friends and that Gilder was a shrewd literary adviser. Gilder accepted for the *Century* "At Teague Poteet's," which is a story of law-defying mountaineers; "Free Joe, and the Rest of the World," perhaps the best of Harris's stories; "Trouble on Lost Mountain," another mountain story; "Little Compton," which Gilder called "a wonderful little story"; "Azallia," about the "Tackies" of the pine woods; and "The Old Bascom Place," "A Conscript's Christmas," and "Balaam and His Master." According to a legend Gilder almost made a blunder when he held Page's "Marse Chan" in his editorial drawer for four years before publishing it in 1884, but he accepted very promptly "Meh Lady: A Story of the War." Although Grace King's first stories were not published in the *Century*, Gilder accepted all the stories later collected as *Balcony Stories*. Gilder welcomed stories by Allen, Johnston, Alice French, John Fox, Jr., Ruth McEnery Stuart, and H. S. Edwards.

Scribner's Magazine was founded by Charles Scribner's Sons in 1887, with Edward L. Burlingame as editor. The early numbers attracted a splendid list of contributors. In the first volume appeared such excellent stories by southerners as Harris's "Aunt Fountain's Prisoner," Alice French's "Half a Curse," and Page's "No Haid Pawn" (No Head Pond). Harris's eight stories in *The Chronicles of Aunt Minervy Ann* (1899) had previously been published in *Scribner's Magazine*, as were later stories by Miss French.

The *Atlantic Monthly* was an older magazine, having been founded in 1857. The early contributors were usually from New England, including such recognized writers as Lowell, Emerson, Longfellow, Holmes, and Whittier. William Dean Howells, who came to the editor's chair in 1871, was not a New Englander. He, and his successor, Thomas Bailey Aldrich, were willing that the ramparts of the Yankee citadel should be stormed by writers from the South. The story of how the *Atlantic* office discovered that Charles Egbert Craddock was not a man, but the crippled little lady, Mary Noailles Murfree, is a more interesting story than any that Miss Murfree herself wrote. All of Miss Murfree's eight stories, collected under the title of *In the Tennessee Mountains*, had appeared in the *Atlantic*.[111] By 1892 so many articles and stories dealing with southern themes had filled the pages of the *Atlantic* that the editors accepted Dr. Basil L. Gildersleeve's classic exposition and defence of the Old South.

Harper's Magazine dates from 1850. In its early years its columns were largely filled with "pirated" current literature from English periodicals, and it prospered financially. A magazine for middle-class readers, "it had no opinions, no politics, no strong opinions." Avoiding controversial issues, the editors in the fifties and sixties accepted few articles or stories with the South or the war as the background. After

---

[111] See Edd Winfield Parks, *Charles Egbert Craddock* (Chapel Hill, N.C.: c. 1941), for biography of Miss Murfree and a complete bibliography.

the Civil War the demand by readers for information about the New South could not be resisted. In 1874, inspired by the success of King's Great South series in *Scribner's Monthly*, Edwin De Leon contributed three articles on "The New South," treating of its agricultural and commercial aspects. During the eighties *Harper's Magazine* was "as jammed with Southern contributions as the *Century*."[112]

In these magazines and dozens of lesser-known ones stories of the South were being published, to be reprinted in collections and books. This was not the sectional literature which Simms and Hayne had wanted, but a provincial literature which delighted readers of the North and West, and was a part of a new national literature. This local color, regional literature was recognized by the critics. In 1887 Charles W. Coleman, Jr., wrote an article in which, after making complimentary references to the writings by Cable, Johnston, Miss Murfree, and others, he added that "Through these and yet more recent writers the profession of letters holds a secure and elevated position among other professions of the South."[113]

Ten years later Professor William Malone Baskervill of Vanderbilt University published the first volume of *Southern Writers*, which contained biographical and critical studies of Harris, Maurice Thompson, Irvin Russell, Lanier, Cable, and Charles Egbert Craddock. Trained in the classics, with a Leipzig degree in philology, having edited texts in Anglo-Saxon, Professor Baskervill became an eager reader and a penetrating, appreciative critic of the literature of the New South. His wife wrote about him: "How well I remember the advent of the new school of Southern writers. With what zest he read and reread, feeling a kind of personal pride in each

[112] Paul H. Buck, *The Road to Reunion, 1865–1900* (Boston: 1938), pp. 224–225. See especially the chapters on "The South Begins to Write," and "The North Feels the Power of the Pen."

[113] "The Recent Movement in Southern Literature," *Harper's Magazine*, LXXIV, 337, 855 (May, 1887).

new discovery. His heart and soul were in that work."[114] He
indicated how very different were the aims of the new writers
in comparison with those of the early days of deadly struggle:
"The literature of the New South had for its cardinal principles good will and sympathy. Its aims were to cement
bonds of good fellowship between the sections, to depict
the negro according to his real character, and to exhibit to the
world the true relations which existed between master and
slave."[115]

To the recently-founded *Sewanee Review* Professor John
Henneman of Hampden-Sidney College contributed a notable
article in 1903, in which he said: "Not until 1870 does the new
Southern literature begin. The movement in American letters
—a momentous one for the development of our national life
and spirit in the twenty critical years from 1870 to 1890—
cannot be understood without the clear recognition of the importance of the Southern writers and some little study of the
significance of the Southern romantic spirit."[116]

By the end of the nineteenth century the local colorists had
exhausted their material and the taste of the readers was changing. Such writers of excellent stories as Cable, Miss Murfree,
and Thomas Nelson Page never equaled their first stories,
collected in *Old Creole Days*, *The Tennessee Mountains*, and
In Ole Virginia. With the changes wrought by the Spanish-
American War and by the muck-raking of national and municipal corruption, literary taste was changing. An anonymous
critic, writing for *The Nation* in 1907, expressed a universal
complaint: "We all know to our sorrow what local color is.
The novel of today reeks with it—dialect so carefully spelled
as to be unintelligible, passages of precise description of per-

[114] Quoted by Charles Foster Smith in Baskervill's *Southern
Writers* (Nashville, Tenn.: 1887), II, 15.
[115] *Ibid.*
[116] "The National Element in Southern Literature," *Sewanee Review*, XI, 348 (July, 1903).

sons and places, meticulous attention to costumes, forms, and customs. It is realism run mad."[117]

XIV. LITERATURE IN THE NEW SOUTH

The term "New South" has been applied for over half a century to various phases of the South's economic, political, and cultural life. After the passing of the tragedy of Reconstruction there were evident the beginnings of the industrial revolution which was to replace with multiple industries the dominant agrarianism of the South. Although agriculture remains today the chief occupation of the majority of the people, manufacturing and transportation have changed the pattern of the agrarian South.

In the seventies and eighties, newspaper editors and orators were active leaders in encouraging a disheartened people to develop the rich natural resources of their fertile soil, their abundant water power, their forests of valuable timber, their mines of coal and iron, and the fisheries of their coastal waters. Some of these leaders urged the South to forget and forgive the evils of war and Reconstruction, and to turn to a future rich in economic promise. They stressed nationalism and reconciliation, especially after the Philadelphia Centennial Exposition of 1876, which turned the thoughts of the nation, both North and South, back to the time of the Revolution when all had fought together in a common cause.

Henry W. Grady, as editor of the Atlanta *Constitution* and as a popular orator, was the apostle of this spirit. In 1886 he spoke before the New England Club of New York on "The New South." Only a few sentences can be quoted from this sturdy speech of conciliation:

We have found out that in the summing up the free negro counts more than he did as a slave. We have planted the school-

[117] "The Worship of Local Color," *The Nation*, LXXXIV, 408 (December, 1903).

house on the hilltop and made it free to white and black. We have sowed towns and cities in the place of theories, and put business above politics. We have challenged your spinners in Massachusetts and your iron-makers in Pennsylvania. . . .

The old South rested everything on slavery and agriculture, unconscious that these could neither give nor maintain healthy growth. The new South presents a perfect democracy, the oligarchs leading in the popular movement—a social system compact and closely knitted, less splendid on the surface, but stronger at the core—a hundred farms for every plantation, fifty homes for every palace—and a diversified industry that meets the complex need of this complex age.[118]

A sharper critic of the South, whose pen had a "javelin-like quality," was Walter Hines Page, the editor of the Raleigh *State Chronicle* from 1883 to 1885. Page was more of a nationalist than Grady, in strongly opposing the provincialism of the South. He founded the Watauga Club, a group of young men in Raleigh, North Carolina, for the purpose of studying political questions. The club had a spirited credo:

I believe in this land—our land—whose infinite variety of beauty and riches we do not yet know. Wake up, old Land! I believe in these people—our people—whose development may be illimitable. Wake up, my People! I believe in the continuous improvement of human society, in the immortality of our democracy, in the rightmindedness of the masses. Wake up, old Commonwealth![119]

In the words of Professor R. D. W. Connor, Page saw that "A South, illiterate, unhealthy, poverty-stricken, was a national peril; therefore, the South must be encouraged and helped to build schools, establish boards of health, develop her natural resources, and make adequate provisions for the social and

[118] *The New South and Other Addresses* (New York: c. 1904), pp. 32, 37–38.
[119] Nicholas Worth [Walter Hines Page], *The Southerner*, p. 239.

spiritual welfare of the average man."[120]   Page made a plea for universal education in an address at Greensboro, North Carolina, and his "Forgotten Man" became a slogan for an educational movement to help the illiterate whites. He pointed out that there were "incalculable undeveloped resources . . . in our streams, our forests, our mines, our quarries, our soil, . . . but there is one undeveloped resource more valuable than all these, and that is the people themselves." He therefore urged "the development of forgotten and neglected man," and pleaded for taxation to support the free education of the masses. He stated his platform: "A public school system generously supported by public sentiment, and generously maintained by both State and local taxation, is the only effective means to develop the forgotten man."

But the way of the New South, "which was somehow to rise miraculously from the old," was uphill indeed. "It was expected," says Charles W. Ramsdell,

that recovery would come through agriculture, for cotton brought an abnormally high price at the end of the war. . . . The result was disappointing, for cotton growing recovered only slowly during the turmoil of reconstruction. Throughout wide areas where the federal armies had penetrated, houses, barns, gins and fences had been burned, the stock killed or driven away. The land remained, but its market value was less than half that of 1860 and it often had to be mortgaged in order to procure the means for starting anew.[121]

Further, the entire labor system had been disrupted and both planter and field hand had to adjust to a new relationship. This adjustment, together with the unfortunate credit situation, led inevitably to the most disastrous situation in the history of

[120] "Walter Hines Page: A Southern Nationalist," *Journal of Social Forces*, II, 167 (January, 1924).
[121] "The Southern Heritage," in *Culture in the South*, p. 11.

modern agriculture, the tenant farmer system, which still rides the agricultural South like a nightmare.

Not from agriculture, therefore, did a relative prosperity return to the South, but from manufacturing. Typical of this was the beginning of the tobacco industry, started on a small scale shortly after the Civil War and developed by such men as the Dukes and R. J. Reynolds. Following the example of William Gregg, who before the Civil War had preached the necessity of manufacturing for the South and had successfully operated a cotton factory in South Carolina, certain public-spirited and far-sighted men, most of them formerly of the planter class, started cotton factories, mainly in the Piedmont where water power is abundant, thus inaugurating a movement which resulted ultimately in the shifting of the cotton manufacturing center from New England to the South. The great resources of iron and coal in northern Alabama and adjacent territories were tapped, and Birmingham began to belch the smoke of its steel mills into the hitherto unsullied atmosphere above the southern hills. Towns began to grow and prosper, and railroad-building, well started before the Civil War but terribly disrupted in the conflict, picked up momentum and, aided by more or less predatory northern capital, became a power to be reckoned with in politics as in industry.

Agriculture, however, the mainstay of the Old South, languished as the farmer became more and more deeply involved in debt.

The most serious handicap of the farmer . . . was the credit situation. . . . As his land was generally unacceptable as security and he had little else to pledge except his hoped-for crop, he was driven to the pawn-shop system of crop-liens, which remained a curse to the agricultural South ever after. . . .

When the crop-lien victim gathered his harvest, it was not his own. It must go at once to the merchant. If, as was often the case, it proved insufficient to cover his indebtedness, he must renew his bondage for another year. . . .

Thus from eighty to ninety per cent of the farmers of the South remained in the toils of debt and dependence from the Civil War to the twentieth century.[122]

Other factors which operated against agriculture were the rapidly falling prices of farm products, the rapacity of the railroads in resisting taxation and state control, and a tax system which rested more heavily on the farmer than on anyone else.

In an attempt to remedy the situation, the Farmers Alliance, formed in the late eighties, went into politics; but although it gained a measure of political power for a time, its cause was overshadowed by the race issues of the nineties, and it accomplished little.

Control in the South had passed from agriculture to business, from country to town, and the members of the old planter aristocracy retained control only in so far as they allied themselves with the new order and with the rising middle class, in a racial solidarity pledged to laissez faire as a means of maintaining a hard-won supremacy.

With the turn of the century, the South began to share in a growing national prosperity; and its leaders, campaigning for improved farming methods, education, public health, highways, conservation, and development of natural resources, inaugurated movements which are today in active process. Thus the New South has been swept into the national stream—is following, to a marked degree, the national pattern, and Southerners themselves are divided as to whether this is a curse or a blessing. To many, the loss of the old way of life is a matter of eternal regret. To others, the New South seems, on the whole, better than the old. But, as Mr. Stark Young has said, "Out of any epoch in civilization there may arise things worth while, that

[122] Benjamin Burks Kendrick and Alex Mathews Arnett, *The South Looks at Its Past* (Chapel Hill, N.C.: 1935), pp. 116–117.

are the flowers of it. To abandon these, when another epoch
arrives, is only stupid, so long as there is still in them the breath
and flux of life."[123]

Some of these "things worth while" have been well sum-
marized by another writer:

While it must be acknolwedged that the popular legend of the
ante-bellum southern aristocracy contains many absurdities, no
one who has honestly tried to understand the group can escape
the conclusion that it had qualities which neither the South nor
the nation can well afford to lose. It was not necessarily a class
of great wealth, . . . but of enough means to afford travel, the
possession of books, and the leisure to read them. Its essential
character was in its way of life and its attitude toward life; and
these, the result of generations of good breeding and quiet living, were rooted deep in traditions of family honor, public
responsibility, self-respect, a contempt for lying and cowardice
—in short they were the standards of gentlemen and gentle-
women in every age and country. Not all the aristocracy, of
course, lived up to the ideals of their class, but the finer representatives of the group exercised an influence on southern life
far out of proportion to their number.[124]

Before a Southern Education Conference in Birmingham in
1904, Walter Hines Page had exclaimed, "We look forward to a
golden age that we may surely help to bring, not back to one
that never was." To look forward to a golden age in education
or religion or industry is an inspiring thought, and one well
in keeping with the theory of progress which dominated American thinking in the decades immediately preceding the World
War. Southern writers, however, continued to write fiction
and biography dealing with the colonial and ante-bellum days
of the Old South, and to some of them these periods were in-

[123] *I'll Take My Stand: The South and the Agrarian Tradition,*
by Twelve Southerners (New York: 1930), p. 328.
[124] Charles W. Ramsdell, "The Southern Heritage," in *Culture in
the South,* pp. 14–15.

deed a golden age. The literary critics, too, were well pleased with the profusion of stories and novels of local color and the plantation tradition. Baskervill's critical volume of 1897 discussed with general approval the writings of Harris, Thompson, Russell, Lanier, Cable, and Charles Egbert Craddock. The volume of 1903 included essays on Margaret Preston, Richard M. Johnston, Sherwood Bonner, Thomas Nelson Page, James Lane Allen, Mrs. Burton Harrison, Grace King, and Samuel M. Peck. In 1905 William P. Trent published his *Southern Writers*, an excellent collection of selections and bio-critical sketches. In 1907 came Mildred Lewis's *The South in History and Literature* and in 1910 Montrose J. Moses published his *Literature of the South*, with a chapter on "The New South," in which he discussed, all too briefly, forty authors.

In 1907–1913, *The Library of Southern Literature* appeared in sixteen volumes, with five thousand selections written by over three thousand authors. The editors stressed the genial, romantic aspects of a plantation aristocracy, the coarse, robust life of "poor whites," and the happy, humorous life of Negroes. The large middle class of industrial, professional, and artisan workers does not appear very often in the selections in these volumes.

In 1923 the editors issued a seventeenth volume, including the writings of "thirty-three men and women from fourteen states." This volume gave belated recognition to Walter Hines Page, with a sketch, based upon personal acquaintance, by Dr. Edwin Anderson Alderman, president of the University of Virginia. Selections from other writers, such as Irvin S. Cobb, Corra Harris, and Archibald Rutledge were abundantly justified, but most of the added authors were sentimental idealists. A World War had swept thousands of Southerners into a great conflict; training camps and military posts had been widely established in the South; German submarines had sunk American ships within sight of the Carolina coast; a president from the South had led the nation through a World War. But the southern writers represented in this volume seemed to be unaware of the march of time and the realities of the present.

According to some critics, the lowest point in southern culture was reached in the years immediately following World War I. In his caustic, envenomed style, Henry L. Mencken, then at the height of his *Smart Set* popularity, published an essay on "The Sahara of the Bozart,"[125] which infuriated most Southerners. Here are a few quotations:

> Alas for the South! Her books have grown fewer—
> She never was much given to literature.

In the lamented J. Gordon Coogler, author of these elegiac lines, there was the insight of a true poet. He was the last bard of Dixie, at least in the legitimate line. . . . For all its size and all its wealth and all the "progress" it babbles of, it is almost as sterile, artistically, intellectually, culturally, as the Sahara Desert. . . . Down to the middle of the last century there were men of delicate fancy, urbane instinct and aristocratic manner— in brief, superior men. . . . The *Ur*-Confederate had leisure. He liked to toy with ideas. He was hospitable and tolerant. He had a vague thing that we call culture. . . . The old aristocracy went down the red gullet of war; the poor white trash are now in the saddle. . . . Virginia has no art, no literature, no philosophy, no mind or aspiration of her own. . . . If one turns to such a commonwealth as Georgia the picture becomes far darker. Virginia is the best of the south today, and Georgia is perhaps the worst. . . . Between lies a vast plain of mediocrity, stupidity, lethargy, almost a dead silence.

In this essay Mencken introduced a dozen controversial issues of politics, economics, religion, and society. Although he was prejudiced and inaccurate, some of his criticisms, especially of the arts, were taken up by a few leaders who were

[125] In *Prejudices: Second Series* (New York; 1920), pp. 136–154.

trying to encourage the creation of literature, drama, and music. In Richmond a group of literary critics established a critical magazine, *The Reviewer*, edited by Emily Clark, James Branch Cabell (for three numbers), and Paul Green (for the four numbers of 1925).

In the initial article on "Richmond and Writing," Mary Johnston loyally proclaimed that the artists of Richmond will find "more to paint, more to sing, more to write of. And it will be done better and better, finer and finer."[126]

For the third number Ellen Glasgow contributed a significant article, "The Dynamic Past," in which she praised Virginia, but boldly asserted that Virginians must look forward and press towards the New South. Here are a few striking sentences:

> When Virginia was noblest, she was freest. She was creating, not copying. The supreme facts of her history are not surrender to tradition, but defiance of tradition. . . . We can take our right place in the present and the future—a place worthy of our past—only by making some fresh, some ever-green contributions to the periods in which we live. . . . We shall never write great books or paint great pictures or make great statues until we are free—for the soul of genius . . . is courage.[127]

Mencken had praised James Branch Cabell as the "single southern prose writer who can really write," and *The Reviewer* was always kindly toward him, reviewing his *Figures of Earth*

---

[126] Possibly Mencken did not consider Mary Johnston a novelist of merit, although she had published *Prisoners of Hope* (1898), *To Have and to Hold* (1900), *Audrey* (1902), *Sir Roger Mortimer* (1904), *The Long Roll* (1911), *Cease Firing* (1912), and *The Witch* (1918).

[127] How could Mencken have disregarded Ellen Glasgow? She had already published thirteen books, including some vitally important ones, such as *The Voice of the People* (1900), *The Battle-Ground* (1902), *The Romance of a Plain Man* (1913), *Virginia* (1913), and *The Builders* (1919).

(1921) with approval, and printing occasionally his stories and articles.[128]

The Reviewer made a notable discovery of an author in printing Julia M. Peterkin's "From Lang Syne Plantation," a tragic tale of Negro life. The story is that Carl Sandburg had urged her to turn from music to the writing of the little dramas of life which she knew so well on her South Carolina plantation. She followed her first story with a dozen realistic stories and sketches, which were later collected in *Green Thursday* (1924). Her first novel was *Black April* (1927), and the following one, *Scarlet Sister Mary* (1928), was awarded the Pulitzer Prize as the best American novel of the year. As Emily Clark wrote: "She has given to a modern public the half-barbaric plantation Negro in a form quite new; a creature far removed from low comedy or from conventional romance; a courageous, inarticulate, heart-tearing creature to whom propaganda or race conflict is yet unknown; a creature in conflict . . . with Fate itself."[129]

The later editors and critics of *The Reviewer* were dissatisfied with the current literature of the South because it was essentially romantic. They viewed with disgust the "words of earth-departing spinsters, shave-tail poets, ninety-day wonders, cross-roads philosophers, minute Alfred Tennysons, and nostalgic, whimpering Poes." They asked for "a truer and fresher interpretation of our environment," hoping that "some day, not very remote, the hand of the artist will gather material from the life of our newly developing industrialism, our tenant-farms, our religious intolerances and our political indecencies."[130]

---

[128] Cabell had published *The Eagle's Shadow* (1904), *The Cords of Vanity* (1909), *The Soul of Mellicent* (1913), *The Rivet in Grandfather's Neck* (1915), *The Cream of the Jest* (1915), and *Jurgen* (1919).

[129] *Innocence Abroad* (New York: 1931), p. 221.

[130] See Paul Green, "A Plain Statement about Southern Literature," *The Reviewer*, V, 71–80 (January, 1925), and Addison Hibbard, "Literature South—1924," *The Reviewer*, V, 52–63 (January, 1925).

Professor Edwin Mims recorded in *The Advancing South* (1926) the progress in commercial prosperity, education, and liberal thinking—before the debacle of the thirties. With critical appreciation he discussed Walter Hines Page as a constructive critic of the South; Ellen Glasgow and Sidney Lanier, who foresee the significance of agricultural development; Corra Harris, with her realistic stories of Georgia communities; and the essays of Gerald W. Johnson and Frances Newman, which are "prophetic of a new criticism applied to southern life and problems."

During the same decade, however, there was a literary group opposed to the New South movement. The Fugitive group of poets at Nashville became increasingly interested in historical and economic questions and drew into their numbers historians, economists, and even business men. This Agrarian group made their position clear in their symposium, *I'll Take My Stand: The South and the Agrarian Tradition.*[131] Militantly faithful to the agrarian South of the ante-bellum period and opposed to industrialism, they advocated a literature of regionalism. This twelve-bladed statement is largely an attack on economic and industrial evils, and most of the writers do not mention literature. But in "A Mirror for Artists" Donald Davidson states the critical theory of the Agrarians. Here are a few references to the New South and to southern literature:

In the South today we have artists whose work reveals richness, repose, brilliance, continuity. The performance of James Branch Cabell has a consistency that might have been more unflickering and unstable if it had originated in some less quiet region than Virginia. The novels of Ellen Glasgow have a

[131] The Twelve Southerners were John Crowe Ransom, Donald Davidson, Frank Lawrence Owsley, John Gould Fletcher, Lyle H. Lanier, Allen Tate, Herman Clarence Nixon, Andrew Nelson Lytle, Robert Penn Warren, John Donald Wade, Henry Blue Kline, and Stark Young.

strength that may come from long, slow prosecution by a mind
far from nervous. Yet these and others have not gone untainted.
Why does Mr. Cabell seem so much nearer to Paris than to
Richmond, to Anatole France than to Lee and to Jefferson?
Why does Miss Glasgow, self-styled the "social historian" of
Virginia, propagate ideas that would be more quickly approved
by Oswald Garrison Villard than by descendants of the first
families? Why are DuBose Heyward's and Paul Green's studies
of negro life so palpably tinged with latter-day abolitionism?
Why does T. S. Stribling write like a spiritual companion of
Harriet Beecher Stowe and Clarence Darrow? [132]

In the past fifteen years the Agrarians have been creatively
articulate in the writing of poems, essays, novels, and biographies, and critically active in reviewing books and editing
journals.

The able editors of metropolitan newspapers are most potent
in moulding opinion, for they often have broader, saner views
than cloister-bound collegians. In 1932 Virginius Dabney,
editor of the *Richmond Times-Despatch* published *Liberalism
in the South*,[133] in which he traced the rise of political, religious,
scientific, and literary liberalism through "The Era of Jefferson,"
"The Era of Calhoun," "Up from the Ashes," and "The New
South." The chapter on "Literature and Journalism Below
the Potomac," contains shrewd comment on writers. Although, he says, the "mellow and moon-drenched" writings
of Cable, Harris, and Thomas Nelson Page may be "properly
subject to criticism," they are not "lacking in literary distinction"; but "definitely pernicious" are such writings as *The
Leopard's Spots*, *The Clansman*, and *The Traitor*, by Thomas
Dixon, Jr., in which the author "sought to foment discord and
strife between the North and the South." On the other hand,
"the general effect of Miss Glasgow's nineteen novels upon

[132] *I'll Take My Stand*, pp. 52 and 59.
[133] Chapel Hill, N.C.: 1932.

southern habits of mind has been liberalizing." The new spirit of intelligent critical writing is apparent in the literary treatment of Negroes by such writers as DuBose Heyward, in *Porgy*, Paul Green, in *In Abraham's Bosom*, Julia Peterkin, in *Scarlet Sister Mary*, Howard W. Odum, in *Rainbow 'Round My Shoulder*, and T. S. Stribling, in *Birthright*, as well as in interpretations by George Madden Martin and Roark Bradford.

Mr. Dabney sees intellectual liberalism in such writers as Isa Glenn, Stark Young, Fielding Burke, Elizabeth Madox Roberts, Mary and Stanley Chapman, William Faulkner, Evelyn Scott, John Peale Bishop, Caroline Gordon, Thomas Wolfe, Jonathan Daniels, Erskine Caldwell, Roy Flannagan, Sara Haardt, Gerald W. Johnson, Frances Newman, and John D. Wade.

In the development of intellectual and literary culture in the recent South, the services of learned journals and literary reviews have been important. At Johns Hopkins University is *Modern Language Notes* (1886–), under such editors as A. Marshall Elliott, James W. Bright, Edwin Greenlaw, and H. C. Lancaster; at the University of the South is *The Sewanee Review* (1892–), under William Peterfield Trent, John Bell Henneman, W. B. Knickerbocker, and Allen Tate; at Trinity College, now Duke University, is *The South Atlantic Quarterly* (1902–), founded by John Spencer Bassett and continued under various editors, including Henry R. Dwire; at the University of North Carolina is *Studies in Philology* (1906–), under C. Alphonso Smith, Edwin Greenlaw, James F. Royster, and George R. Coffman; at the University of Texas was *The Texas Review* (1915–1924), founded by Stark Young, continued by Robert Adger Law, and merged into *The Southwest Review* (1924–) at Southern Methodist University under Jay B. Hubbell; in New Orleans was *The Double Dealer* (1921–1926), under Julius Friend, Basil Thompson, and John McClure; in Richmond and Chapel Hill was *The Reviewer* (1921–1925), under Emily Clark,

James Branch Cabell, and Paul Green; at Vanderbilt University
was *The Fugitive* (1922–1925), under John Crowe Ransom,
Donald Davidson, and Allen Tate; at the University of Virginia
is *The Virginia Quarterly Review* (1923–), under James Southall
Wilson, Stringfellow Barr, and Archibald Bolling Shepperson;
at Duke University is *American Literature* (1929–), under Jay
B. Hubbell; at the University of Louisiana is *The Southern Review* (1935–1942), under C. W. Pipkin.[134]

Under the stimuli of lively criticism and the increasing importance of the South in national life, a newer literature has been
produced in the past twenty years, a literature vigorous, challenging, and intelligent. Even in the historical novel a new
spirit is evident. The themes are the same, mainly the Revolution and the Civil War, but the methods are different. The
conventional southern historical romance was of a marked
type and the author's method had been set by Scott and his
successors. As Montrose Moses states: "The old-time historical method was one of proud tradition rather than one of
analytical judgment; events were measured by leaders; and
writers, whether they were dealing in biography or in fiction,
idealized their heroes for the sake of character above fact."[135]
The historical romances by John Esten Cooke illustrate this
method.

The modern historical novels differ from the earlier ones in
realistic detail; they stress common men in heroic roles, and
picture noncombatants in their lives behind the battle fronts;
they point out the economic significance of the tragic and
stirring events of war. They are less frantically sectional.
The older historical novel was usually built around some
glorious hero, who strode through the pages like a tragic
character on the Shakespearean stage. The newer historical

[134] See Jay B. Hubbell, "Southern Magazines," and Donald Davidson, "The Trend of Literature," in *Culture in the South.*
[135] *The Literature of the South,* p. 298.

novel is based upon social history, and the novelist tries to present a living picture of the period, without omitting commonplace, even sordid, details.

Ellen Glasgow was one of the first novelists to break away from the sentimental tradition in her presentation of studies of Virginia in Civil War and Reconstruction days. *The Voice of the People* (1900) is a serious study of life during the Reconstruction period. The hero, Nicholas Burr, is the son of a shiftless father of the "poor white" class and of a mother who was "one of those sallow, over-driven drudges who stare like helpless effigies from the tumble-down cabins along a country roadside." Nicholas rises to the governorship, where he brings about reforms, and he is killed by a mob bent upon lynching a Negro. *The Battle-Ground* (1902) is a series of pictures of noncombatants in Richmond, during the war, with unconventional characters solving economic and social problems. *The Deliverance* (1904) depicts the sufferings and tragic lives of people on a plantation immediately after the Civil War. *The Romance of a Plain* (1909) is the story of Richmond after the war.

James Boyd (a Pennsylvanian who had long made his home in the South, a veteran of World War I), wrote *Drums* (1925), dealing with the Revolutionary War in North Carolina and introducing simple characters who speak in the dialect of farmers of the eighteenth century. In 1927 he wrote *Marching On*, a treatment of the Civil War from the point of view of the common soldier, which conveys a strong impression of the wastefulness and inhumanity of war.

The volume of historical fiction out of and about the South increases annually, and all that can here be done is to suggest its trends; but one should at least mention Margaret Mitchell's *Gone With the Wind*, a sensation of 1936, and a novelist's, publisher's, and moving picture producer's triumph. It is a historical novel on a theme which might well have been considered

outworn, and yet it is so rooted in actuality that, without benefit of ancestral attitudes (though with considerable help from
the melodramatic), it has made the past live again, not only for
the South but for the nation as a whole.

Another large segment of prose literature which attained
scope and significance in the 1920's and 1930's consists of
stories and novels picturing, more or less realistically, various
aspects of the southern contemporary scene. The Negro has
been portrayed, with insight and sympathy, by such writers as
T. S. Stribling, in *Birthright* (1922), DuBose Heyward, in
Porgy (1925), Julia Peterkin, in *Black April* (1927) and *Scarlet
Sister Mary* (1928), and by Roark Bradford and Paul Green in
various stories and plays.

The southern "poor whites" are not only the concern of
sociologists; they are also the subject of stories and novels by
current writers. Ellen Glasgow, T. S. Stribling, Olive Tilford
Dargan, Elizabeth Madox Roberts, DuBose Heyward, Thomas
Wolfe, Erskine Caldwell, William Faulkner, Marjorie Rawlings,
James Street, and others write about the mountaineers, the mill
workers, and the tenant farmers. Ellen Glasgow, Elizabeth
Madox Roberts, and Paul Green have theories about the causes
of the distresses of their characters, and picture these characters
as struggling unsuccessfully against their environment. Most
sharply critical of their characters are Frances Newman, T. S.
Stribling, Erskine Caldwell, William Faulkner, and other
writers of the "You-Have-Seen-Their-Faces" school, who
have broken entirely with the Genteel Tradition and recognize
no taboos.

In biography, recent years have been fruitful. Among the
successful writers in this field are such men as Gerald Johnson,
George Fort Milton, Robert W. Winston, and John Donald
Wade, with the culminating point in southern biography being,
probably, Douglas Southall Freeman's *R. E. Lee* (1934).

Of recent southern biography, Mr. Donald Davidson says,

Suddenly, in the very clash and thunder of partisan views, the historic South was being rehabilitated. Ironically enough, the biographers, the seekers after fact, were setting up the identical southern tradition that some of the fiction writers had been engaged in knocking down. And biography was reinforced by the definitive studies that a distinguished group of southern historians had long had under way—such men as Ulrich B. Phillips, William E. Dodd, Walter L. Fleming, Frank Lawrence Owsley, and many more. . . . Now it was a short-sighted publisher indeed, however remote from the southern scene, who did not carry on his list, along with Stracheyan biographies and advance-guard fiction, lively or sober works from southern pens that subjected southern culture, history, heroes, scenes, places, to an intense and often an admiring scrutiny.[136]

Northern historians, too, were "taking a fresh view of the past," and reinterpreting for northern readers the era of the Civil War and Reconstruction. Thus the southern tradition, as expressed in literary prose, rounds a circle and thereby proclaims its unity and integrity. The prose of the South is the expression of a people living in a distinctive region, with a historic and highly dramatic past, in which the clash of ideas and ideals has far exceeded that of any other section of the United States. It challenges study and understanding, and it is hoped that the selections in this volume, taken, as many of them are, from the less accessible sources, and chosen for their representative nature, will arouse greater interest in an important field and stimulate thought, research, and interpretative writing.

[136] "The Trend of Literature: A Partisan View." in *Culture in the South*, pp. 194–195.

SELECTED BIBLIOGRAPHY

I. GENERAL

American Studies in Honor of William Kenneth Boyd. Edited by David Kelly Jackson. By members of the Americana Club of Duke University. Durham, N.C.: 1940. (Several of the excellent chapters are by Jay B. Hubbell, Charles Roberts Anderson, David K. Jackson, and Clarence Gohdes.)

Baskervill, William Malone. *Southern Writers: Biographical and Critical Studies.* Nashville: 1897–1903. 2 vols. (Three of the chapters in the first volume are excellent critical sketches of Harris, Cable, and Miss Murfree. The chapters in the second volume include studies by various critics of Johnston, Sherwood Bonner, T. N. Page, Allen, Mrs. Harrison, and Grace King.)

Blair, Walter. *Native American Humor (1800–1900).* New York: c. 1937. (Textbook and able treatise of American humor, including discussion of southern humorists and extensive bibliographies.)

Brevard, Caroline M. *Literature of the South.* New York: c. 1908. (Some of the prose writers discussed, rather superficially, are Audubon, Poe, Legaré, and Simms.)

The Cambridge History of American Literature. Edited by W. P. Trent, John Erskine, Stuart P. Sherman, and Carl Van Doren. New York: c. 1917–1921. 4 vols. (The treatment of southern prose writers is uneven and usually meagre. The bibliographies are still indispensable.)

Couch, William Terry (ed.). *Culture in the South.* Chapel Hill, N.C.: 1934. (Thirty-one specialists write on all phases of traditional and contemporary southern life, thus producing an indispensable book.)

Davidson, Donald. *The Attack on Leviathan: Regionalism and Nationalism in the United States.* Chapel Hill, N.C.: 1938. (Studies by a leader of the Agrarians.)

Davidson, James Wood. *The Living Writers of the South.* New York: 1869. (An attempt to discuss biographically and critically the "living" writers of the South—and the author found over two hundred of them in 1869. First-hand information, sometimes inaccurate, with lively comments.)

Dictionary of American Biography, Under the auspices of the American Council of Learned Societies. Edited by Allen Johnson and Dumas Malone. New York: 1928–1937. Reprinted in 1943. 21 vols. (The sketches of southern prose writers, especially the political writers, are usually excellent. The bibliographical references are few but well chosen.)

Eaton, Clement. *Freedom of Thought in the Old South.* Durham, N.C.: 1940. (The rise of liberal thought and action.)

Gaines, Francis Pendleton. *The Southern Plantation: A Study in the Development and the Accuracy of the Tradition.* New York: 1925. (Valuable as background material for the study of J. C. Harris, T. N. Page, and others who treated the antebellum plantation life.)

Henneman, John Bell. *Shakespearean and Other Papers.* Sewanee, Tenn.: 1911. (The reprinting of ten articles, including "James Lane Allen," "English Studies in the South," "The National Element in Southern Literature," and "Historical Studies in the South since the War.")

Henneman, John Bell, *et al. The South in the Building of the Nation.* Richmond: 1909–1913. 12 vols. (Two useful volumes are Vol. VII, *History of the Literary and Intellectual Life of the South,* with chapters by specialists, and Vol. VIII, *History of Southern Fiction,* with selections from eight writers, and an introduction by Edwin Mims.)

Holliday, Carl. *A History of Southern Literature.* New York: 1906. (A readable book, marred, however, by inaccuracy and superficiality.)

Hubbell, Jay Broadus. *Virginia Life in Fiction.* Dallas: 1922. (Sections of a Columbia University dissertation. The fiction is thoughtfully and realistically viewed in its relation to changing social and political life.)

Jenkins, W. S. *Pro-Slavery Thought in the Old South*. Chapel Hill, N.C.: 1935.

Johnson, James Gibson (comp.). *Southern Fiction Prior to 1860: An Attempt at a First-Hand Bibliography*. Charlottesville, Va.: 1909. (Refer also to Wright, Lyle Henry. *American Fiction, 1774–1850: A Contribution toward a Bibliography*. San Marino, Calif.: 1939.)

A Library of Southern Literature. Edited by Edwin Anderson Alderman, Joel Chandler Harris, Charles William Kent, and others. Atlanta: 1907–1923. 17 vols. (An indispensable collection, with biographical and critical sketches which are generally laudatory. Volume XIV contains a "Bibliography of Books and Articles on Southern Literature," and Volume XVII contains author bibliographies, helpful but often out-dated.)

Link, Samuel Albert. *Pioneers of the South*. Nashville: 1899–1900. 2 vols. (Sketches of Simms, Kennedy, Cooke, Poe, Baldwin, Hooper, Thompson, Crockett, Jefferson, Calhoun, and others. Inferior to the criticism by Baskervill.)

McIlwaine, Shields. *The Southern Poor-White from Lubberland to Tobacco Road*. Norman, Okla.: 1939. (The social story of the poor-whites, and their literary treatment from Byrd to Caldwell.)

Mims, Edwin. *The Advancing South*. Garden City, N.Y.: 1926. (A valuable book, especially encouraging before the depression hit us.)

Moses, Montrose. *The Literature of the South*. New York: 1910. (Although this is the best available literary history of the South, it is disappointing, for the essays are more social than literary, the treatment is laboriously prolix, and the minor inaccuracies are frequent. The bibliography is very helpful.)

Mott, Frank L. *A History of American Magazines*. 3 vols. Vol. I. New York: 1931. Reissued Cambridge, Mass.: 1938. Vols. II and III, Cambridge, Mass.: 1938. (These three volumes, covering the chief magazines published from 1741 to 1885, are of great service to all students and scholars. The introductory chapters give a social history of the time. The information about the magazines, of which a number are southern, is factual and critical.)

Page, Thomas Nelson. *The Old South: Essays Social and Political*. New York: 1927. (Eight essays, of which the first is on "Authorship in the South before the War.")

Parks, Edd W. *Segments of Southern Thought*. Athens, Ga.: 1938. (Critical essays, in which Legaré, Grayson, Johnston, Walter Hines Page, and other southern writers are considered.)

Parks, Edd W. *Southern Poets*. New York: 1936. (Introduction and Bibliography, pp. xvii–cxlviii.)

Parrington, Vernon Louis. *Main Currents in American Thought*. New York: 1927–1930. 3 vols. (Studies of political, economic, and religious ideas in American literature. The first chapters of Volume II are devoted to southern writings.)

Pattee, Fred Lewis. *The Development of the American Short Story*. New York: 1923.

Pattee, Fred Lewis. *A History of American Literature since 1870*. New York: 1915. (The critical interpretations of story writers and humorists are excellent.)

Quinn, Arthur Hobson. *American Fiction: An Historical and Critical Survey*. New York: 1936. (Synopses and criticism of stories and novels.)

Rogers, Edward R. *Four Southern Magazines*. Richmond: 1902. (An outline study of some value of *DeBow's Review* of New Orleans, *The Southern Review* of Charleston, *The Southern Quarterly Review* of Charleston, and *The Southern Literary Messenger* of Richmond.)

Rourke, Constance. *American Humor: A Study of the National Character*. New York: 1931. (Excellent discussion of comic types.)

Rutherford, Mildred L. *The South in History and Literature: A Hand-Book of Southern Authors from the Settlement of Jamestown, 1607, to Living Writers*. Atlanta: 1907. (Elementary, sentimental discussion of many writers, with brief selections; many questionable statements of fact and critical judgment.)

Smith, C. Alphonso. *Southern Literary Studies: A Collection of Literary, Biographical, and Other Sketches.* With a biographical study by F. Stringfellow Barr. Chapel Hill, N.C.: 1927. (Some of the prose writers discussed are Jefferson, Poe, J. C. Harris, and O. Henry.)

[Tardy, Mary T.] Ida Raymond, *pseud. Southland Writers. Biographical and Critical Sketches of the Living Female Writers of the South. With Extracts from Their Writings.* Philadelphia: 1870. 2 vols. (Arrangement by states; useful in studying Poe's reviews.)

Toulmin, Henry A. *Social Historians.* Boston: c. 1911. (Chapters on T. N. Page, Cable, Charles Egbert Craddock, Allen, and J. C. Harris. The treatment is too brief to be of much value.)

Twelve Southerners. *I'll Take My Stand: The South and the Agrarian Tradition.* New York: 1930. (The chapters are by J. C. Ranson, Donald Davidson, F. L. Owsley, J. G. Fletcher, L. H. Lanier, Allen Tate, H. C. Nixon, A. N. Lytle, R. P. Warren, J. D. Wade, H. B. Kline, and Stark Young.)

Van Doren, Carl. *The American Novel, 1789–1939,* New York: 1940. (A revision of the first edition of 1921.)

The articles in magazines and journals on the southern prose writers, biographical, critical, popular, and scholarly, are so numerous that they cannot be listed. The student is referred to bibliographical appendixes to the literary histories itemized above and to the American Literature sections of the "American Bibliography" of the *Publications of the Modern Language Association,* published each year since 1922.

II. AUTHORS

James Lane Allen

Brown, Edith Baker. "Mr. James Lane Allen," *Atlantic Monthly,* LXXIX, 104–110 (January, 1897). (Tempered praise of his realism.)

Henneman, J. B. "James Lane Allen: A Study," in Baskervill's

Southern Writers (Nashville, Tenn.: 1903), I, 152–243. Also reprinted in Henneman's *Shakespearian and Other Papers* (Sewanee, Tenn.: 1911), 114–166, and in *The South in the Building of the Nation* (Richmond, Va.: 1909), VIII, 330–358. (Sound criticism of Allen's early work, before the publication of *The Mettle of the Pasture*.)

Knight, Grant C. *James Lane Allen and the Genteel Tradition.* Chapel Hill, N.C.: 1935. (A full-length biography, with able discussion of Allen's writings. The materials for the biography were not extensive, for Allen led an uneventful life. The biographer distinguishes between an earlier romantic literary period, treated in a chapter entitled "The Feminine Principle," which is Allen's phrase, and a later realistic period, reflecting the influence of Hardy, entitled "The Masculine Principle." The use of the term "Genteel Tradition" in the title is unfortunate, for Allen had only partial allegiance to this tradition. The "Notes on Sources" and the chronological list of Allen's writings are very complete. The student can find ample references here.)

Marcosson, Isaac F. "James Lane Allen," *Library of Southern Literature*, I, 41–45. (A friend writes warm critical approval.)

Nelson, J. H. "James Lane Allen," *Dictionary of American Biography*, I, 195–197. (A very good sketch, which was written, however, before the publication of Knight's biography.)

Quinn, A. H. "James Lane Allen and the Novel of the Spirit," in *American Fiction* (New York: 1936), 472–483. (Discerning criticisms of stories and novels, which do not always agree with Knight's.)

Townsend, J. H. *Kentucky in American Letters, 1784–1912.* Cedar Rapids, Iowa: 1913. II, 4–17. (A brief sketch, with selections.)

Joseph Glover Baldwin

Bancroft, H. H. *History of California.* San Francisco: 1890. (VII, 221–222; 233–234, traces Baldwin's legal career in California. He was "an able lawyer," and "his Yankee shrewdness was toned down by the more genial southern temperament.")

Garrett, William. *Reminiscences of Public Men in Alabama, for Thirty Years.* Atlanta: 1872. (Pages 358–359 give references to Baldwin.)

Jackson, D. K. *The Contributors and Contributions to the Southern Literary Messenger (1834–1864).* Charlottesville, Va.: 1936. (Baldwin's sixteen contributions are listed on pages 111, 116, 120, 128.)

Link, S. A. "Joseph G. Baldwin," in *Pioneers of Southern Literature*, II, 486–504. (Inaccurate biographical statements, with quotations from *Flush Times*.)

Mellen, G. F. "Joseph Glover Baldwin, 1815–1864," *Library of Southern Literature*, I, 175–181.

Mellen, G. F. "Joseph G. Baldwin and the 'Flush Times,'" *Sewanee Review*, IX, 171–184 (April, 1901). (An expansion of the sketch in the *Library of Southern Literature*. This is the best biographical and critical treatment of Baldwin.)

Nelson, J. H. "Joseph Glover Baldwin," *Dictionary of American Biography*, I, 538–539.

Wetmore, T. B. "Joseph G. Baldwin," *Transactions Alabama Historical Society, 1897–1898*, II, 67–73. Reprinted from the *Choctaw Herald*, Butler, Ala., February 4 and 11, 1892. (A personal, eulogistic appraisal.)

Sherwood Bonner

Bolwell, Robert W. "Katherine Sherwood Bonner Mac-Dowell," *Dictionary of American Biography*, XII, 33–34.

Bondurant, Alexander L. "Sherwood Bonner—Her Life and Place in the Literature of the South," *Publications of the Mississippi Historical Society*, II, 43–68 (1899). (Undocumented, but the author appears to have had access to unpublished material and quotes freely from contemporary estimates. Gives a summary of *Like Unto Like*.)

Bondurant, Alexander L. "Sherwood Bonner," *Library of Southern Literature*, I, 439–462. (A shortened and revised form of the article cited above.)

Drake, B. M. "Sherwood Bonner," in Baskervill's *Southern Writers*, II, 82–119. (Undocumented, but obviously makes use of Bondurant's article, Sophia Kirk's Preface to *Suwanee River Tales*, and some unpublished letters.)

Gilligan, Dorothy L. "Life and Works of Sherwood Bonner." Unpublished master's thesis, George Washington University, Washington, D.C., September 27, 1930. (Valuable chiefly for its information as to the periodicals and newspapers in which Sherwood Bonner's stories and articles were first published. Much of this information is nowhere else available.)

Harper's Weekly, XXVII (August 11, 1883). An editorial comment at the time of Sherwood Bonner's death. (Harper and Brothers were her publishers, and this editorial gives the best available picture of her personality and a valuable contemporary estimate of her work.)

Kirk, Sophia. Preface to *Suwanee River Tales*. New York: 1884. (A short sketch by an intimate friend, stressing personality rather than biographical facts.)

William Byrd

Available Editions

The Writings of "Colonel William Byrd, of Westover in Virginia, esq." Edited by John Spencer Bassett. New York: 1901. (The best edition, with an able introduction, containing a biographical sketch.)

A Journey to the Land of Eden and Other Papers. (American Bookshelf Series.) New York: 1928. (Contains also the *History of the Dividing Line* and *A Journey to the Mines*. A good reading edition, without notes.)

William Byrd's Histories of the Dividing Line Betwixt Virginia and North Carolina. Edited by William K. Boyd. Raleigh, N.C.:1929. (The first printing of the *Secret History*, and a reprinting of the *History of the Dividing Line*, with an excellent introduction.)

The Secret Diary of William Byrd of Westover 1709–1712. Edited by Louis B. Wright and Marion Tinling. Richmond, Va.: 1941. (Transcribed from the shorthand in which it was kept. The first of three portions of the detailed journal which Byrd kept throughout most of his life.)

Another Secret Diary of William Byrd of Westover 1739–1741, With Letters and Literary Exercises, 1696–1726. Edited by Maude H. Woodfin. Richmond, Va.: 1942. (From the manuscript in the University of North Carolina library.)

Biography and Criticism

Beatty, Richmond C. *William Byrd of Westover*. Boston: 1932. (An analysis of Byrd's education, his years in England, and his Virginia activities; a limited discussion of his writings.)

Cannon, Carl L. "William Byrd II of Westover," *Colophon* III, 291–302 (Spring, 1938).

"Letters of the Byrd Family," *Virginia Magazine of History and Biography*, IX, XXXVII–XXXIX (1901, 1927–1931).

Masterson, James R. "William Byrd in Lubberland," *American Literature*, IX, 153–170 (May, 1937).

Wertenbaker, Thomas J. "William Byrd," *Dictionary of American Biography*, III, 383–384.

Wright, Louis B. "A Shorthand Diary of William Byrd of Westover," *Huntington Library Quarterly*, II, 489–496 (July, 1939).

Wright, Louis B., and Tinling, Marion. "William Byrd of Westover, an American Pepys," *South Atlantic Quarterly*, XXXIX, 259–294 (July, 1940).

George Washington Cable

Baskervill, W. M. "George W. Cable," in *Southern Writers*, I, 299–356. (Writing twenty years before Cable's death, Baskervill gives a just estimate of Cable's many-sided personality, recognizes his literary artistry, deplores his polemical —sometimes anti-Southern—writings, and ranks, with shrewd critical appraisal, his chief writings. A most valuable chapter.)

Biklé, Lucy Leffingwell Cable. *George W. Cable: His Life and Letters*. New York: 1928. (The daughter of Cable writes a "family" biography of high rank, by editing the numerous letters impartially and by attempting to harmonize the many aspects of his life. The appended "Bibliography" lists twenty books, and eighty-eight stories, articles, reviews, and open letters by Cable.)

Bishop, D. H. "A Commencement in the Eighties: George W. Cable's First Public Address," *Southwest Review*, XVIII, 108–114 (January, 1933).

Hearn, Lafcadio. "The Scenes of Cable's Romances," *Century Magazine*, n.s. V, 40–47 (November, 1883). (After visiting the streets and houses described in *Old Creole Days* and *The Grandissimes*, Hearn states that "the scenes of his stories are in no sense fanciful; and the strict perfection of his creole architecture is readily recognized by all who have resided in New Orleans.")

Kendall, Isoline Rodd (Mrs. John S.) "George Washington Cable," in *Library of Southern Literature*, II, 619–624. (Granting the incomplete information available twenty years before Cable's death, this article has considerable merit, but is marred by critical and factual restraint.)

Pattee, F. L. "George Washington Cable," *Dictionary of American Biography*, III, 392–393.

Pattee, F. L. *The Development of the American Short Story*. New York: 1923. Pages 255–259; 264–265.

Pattee, F. L. *A History of American Literature since 1870*. New York: 1915. Pages 246–253.

Tinker, E. L. "Cable and the Creoles," *American Literature*, V, 313–326 (January, 1934). (The best article on Cable, including a lively picture, an analysis of the causes of his hatred by Louisiana Creoles, and a defense of him as the "first, among Southern writers, who treated objectively and realistically the life around him, and was first to break the taboo against writing about the Negro.")

Turner, Arlin. "George Washington Cable's Literary Apprenticeship," *Louisiana Historical Quarterly*, XXIV, 169–186 (January, 1941).

Wykoff, G. S. "The Cable Family in Indiana," *American Literature*, I, 183–195 (May, 1929).

John Caldwell Calhoun

The Works of John C. Calhoun. Edited by Richard K. Crallé. New York: 1853–1855. 6 vols. Vol. I. A Disquisition on Government and a Discourse on the Constitution and Government of the United States. Vols. II–IV. Speeches Delivered in the House of Representatives and in the Senate of the United States. Vols. V–VI. Reports and Public Lectures.

Dodd, William E. "John C. Calhoun," in *Statesman of the Old South.* New York: 1911.

Holst, Hermann E. von. *John C. Calhoun.* Boston: 1882. ("censorious and homilectic"—Phillips)

Hunt, Gaillard. *John C. Calhoun.* Philadelphia: 1908. ("discriminatingly sympathetic"—Phillips)

Jenkins, John S. *The Life of John Caldwell Calhoun.* New York: [1851]. ("a perfunctory product"—Phillips)

Meigs, William M. *The Life of John Caldwell Calhoun.* New York: 1917. 2 vols. ("elaborate and painstaking"—Phillips)

Phillips, U. B. "John Caldwell Calhoun," *Dictionary of American Biography*, III, 411–419. (The best brief biography, with accurate factual and sane critical statements.)

Pinckney, Gustavus M. *Life of John C. Calhoun.* Charleston, S.C.: 1903. ("eulogistic"—Phillips)

White, Henry A. "John Caldwell Calhoun," in *Library of Southern Literature*, II, 673–679. (Factual and eulogistic.)

John Esten Cooke

Armstrong, J. L. "John Esten Cooke," *Library of Southern Literature*, III, 1031–1037. (A brief biographical and critical sketch.)

Beaty, J. O. "John Esten Cooke," *Dictionary of American Biography*, IX, 385–386.

Beaty, J. O. *John Esten Cooke, Virginian.* New York: 1922. (An able biographical and critical study, and the most complete source of information. The appended Bibliography gives a list of Cooke's books, and the titles of his articles in four magazines: *Southern Literary Messenger, Putnam's Monthly Magazine, Harper's Magazine,* and *Appleton's Journal.*)

Holliday, Carl. "John Esten Cooke as a Novelist," *Sewanee Review,* XIII, 216–220 (April, 1905). (Cooke was "the most widely known and most popular novelist the South ever had," and for future readers there are "such permanent works as *Virginia Comedians, Stories of the Old Dominion, Surry of Eagle's Nest, Henry St. John, Gentleman,* and *Hilt to Hilt.*")

Hubbell, Jay B. (ed.). "The War Diary of John Esten Cooke," *Journal of Southern History,* VII, 536–540 (November, 1941).

Link, S. A. "John Esten Cooke," in *Pioneers of Southern Literature,* I, 248–270. (A good sketch, but sentimentally appreciative.)

Wegelin, Oscar. "A Bibliography of the Separate Writings of John Esten Cooke," *Americana Collector,* I, 96–99 (December, 1925). (A listing of the imprint data of thirty-four first editions with some later editions.)

David Crockett

The biographies by J. S. C. Abbott (1874), and Edward S. Ellis (1884) were written for boys.

Davy Crockett: American Comic Legend. Edited with an introduction by Richard M. Dorson: foreword by Howard Mumford Jones. New York: 1939.

Dorson, Richard M. "Davy Crockett and the Heroic Age," *Southern Folklore Quarterly,* VI, 95–102 (June, 1942).

Foster, A. P. "David Crockett," *Tennessee Historical Magazine,* IX, 166–177 (October, 1925). (The best brief sketch.)

French, Janie P. C. and Armstrong, Zella. *Notable Southern Families: The Crockett Family and Connecting Lines.* Bristol, Tenn.: 1928. (Genealogical and biographical facts.)

Garland, Hamlin. "Introduction" to *The Autobiography of David Crockett.* Scribner's Modern Student's Library. New York: c. 1923. (A critical sketch which introduces the reprinting of Crockett's *Narrative, An Account of Col. Crockett's*

Tour, and *Col. Crockett's Exploits and Adventures in Texas,* in an available edition.)

Ghent, W. J. "David Crockett," *Dictionary of American Biography,* IV, 555–556.

Rourke, Constance. *American Humor: A Study in the National Character.* New York: 1931. (One of the comic types is the backwoodsman, as portrayed in the Crockett almanacs.)

———. "Davy Crockett: Forgotten Facts and Legends," *Southwest Review,* XIV, 149–161 (Winter, 1934). (An excellent bibliographical article.)

———. *Davy Crockett.* New York: 1934. (This recent book on Crockett seems accurate in fact and interpretation.)

Wade, J. D. "The Authorship of David Crockett's 'Autobiography,'" *Georgia Historical Quarterly,* VI, 265–268 (September, 1922). (Evidence that Augustin Smith Clayton (1783–1839) of Georgia was Crockett's spokesman in writing the books attributed to him. Certainly Clayton wrote the life of Van Buren.)

Joel Chandler Harris

Baskervill, W. M. "Joel Chandler Harris" in *Southern Writers,* I, 1–48. (An appraisal of his early stories as discerning portrayals of phases of southern life.)

Blair, Walter. *Native American Humor (1800–1900)* New York: 1937. (Pages 137–138, 143–147, and *passim;* selections on pages 503–511.) (The success of a local color writer in the field of humorous depiction.)

English, T. H. "Memorializing Pride in an Adopted Son: Emory Library Holds Famous Uncle Remus Manuscripts," *Emory Alumnus* (Emory University, Atlanta), V, 7–8 (March, 1929). (Professor English is an authority on Harris manuscripts and editions.)

Genzmer, G. H. "Joel Chandler Harris," *Dictionary of American Biography,* VIII, 312–314. (An excellent sketch.)

Harris, Julia Collier. *The Life and Letters of Joel Chandler Harris.* Boston: 1918. (Mrs. Harris, the wife of Julian Harris, the author's son, writes the standard biography.

The appended bibliography is a revision of a list prepared and published in 1907 by Mrs. Katherine H. Wootten.)

——. *Joel Chandler Harris: Editor and Essayist; Miscellaneous Literary, Political, and Social Writings.* Chapel Hill, N.C.: 1931. (An indispensable book of selections, with editorial comments, revealing Harris as an essayist of importance.

——. "Joel Chandler Harris: Constructive Realist," in *Southern Pioneers in Social Interpretation.* Edited by H. W. Odum. Chapel Hill, N.C.: 1925. Pages 143–164.

——. "Joel Chandler Harris—Fearless Editor: His Example Moulds Policy of a Georgia Newspaper," *Emory Alumnus,* V, 9–10 (March, 1929).

Jemison, Margaret. "Library Gathers Folklore of Old South: Harris Collection Becomes Nucleus for Literary Shrine," *Emory Alumnus,* V, 11–12 (March, 1929).

Miller, H. P. "Bibliography of Joel Chandler Harris: List of Author's Published Works Is Made Available," *Emory Alumnus,* V, 13–14, 22 (March, 1929).

Nelson, J. H. "Uncle Remus Arrives," in *The Negro Character in American Literature.* Lawrence, Kans.: 1926. Pages 106–119. (Excellent criticism.)

Quinn, A. H. "Joel Chandler Harris and the Fiction of Folklore," in *American Fiction,* pages 374–384.

Smith, C. Alphonso. "Joel Chandler Harris: A Discussion of the Negro as Literary Material," in *Southern Literary Studies,* Chapel Hill: 1927. Pages 128–157.

Wade, J. D. "Profits and Losses in the Life of Joel Chandler Harris," *American Review,* I, 17–35 (April, 1933).

Wiggins, Robert L. *The Life of Joel Chandler Harris from Obscurity in Boyhood to Fame in Early Manhood.* Nashville, Tenn.: 1918. (The first biography, which contains much original material.)

Thomas Jefferson

Becker, Carl L. *The Declaration of Independence.* New York: 1922. (A study of the political ideas leading up to Jefferson's culminating expression.)

Chinard, Gilbert. *Thomas Jefferson, the Apostle of American-ism.* Boston: 1929. (The best biography. See other books on Jefferson by Chinard.)

Ford, Paul Leicester (ed.). *The Writings of Thomas Jefferson.* New York: 1892–1894. 10 vols. (Carefully edited, with copious notes.)

Hirst, Francis W. *Life and Letters of Thomas Jefferson.* New York: 1926. (An Englishman's sympathetic view.)

Johnson, Allen. *Jefferson and His Colleagues.* The Chronicles of America Series. New Haven, Conn.: [1921].

Malone, Dumas. "Joel Chandler Harris" *Dictionary of American Biography*, X, 15–35.

Prescott, Frederick C. (ed.). *Alexander Hamilton and Thomas Jefferson: Representative Selections*, with Introduction, Bibliography, and Notes. New York: 1934. (Indispensable for the study of Jefferson.)

Randall, Henry S. *The Life of Thomas Jefferson.* New York: 1858. 3 vols. ("The official biography; painstaking, copious, partisan, but the most important source of information." —Prescott.)

Tucker, George. *The Life of Thomas Jefferson.* Philadelphia: 1837. 2 vols. ("The first important life; by a friend of Jefferson; drawn on local sources."—Prescott.)

Wilstach, Paul. *Jefferson and Monticello.* Garden City, N.Y.: 3rd ed. rev., 1931.

John Pendleton Kennedy

Campbell, Killis. "The Kennedy Papers," *Sewanee Review*, XXV, 1–19; 193–208; 348–360 (January, April, and July, 1917.) (Kennedy left a sealed box of papers in the Peabody Institute Library, which was not be be opened for thirty years after his death. Campbell, and later, Gwathmey, have found a few letters of importance.)

Gwathmey, E. M. *John Pendleton Kennedy.* New York: 1931. (A brief biography, with analyses of the chief writings, and considerable discussion of Kennedy's relationship with Thackeray and Poe.)

Hubbell, J. B. (ed.). *Swallow Barn*. American Authors Series. New York: 1929. (The introduction contains an excellent biographical sketch, and a discussion of the Virginia tradition in fiction.)

Leisy, E. E. (ed.). *Horse-Shoe Robinson*. American Fiction Series. New York: 1937. (The introduction is able, and the "Selected Bibliography" is the best listing of Kennedy biography and criticism.)

Link, S. A. "John Pendleton Kennedy," *Pioneers of Southern Literature*. I, 223–247. (A good biographical sketch, with praise of several books.)

Orrick, J. L. "John Pendleton Kennedy," *Library of Southern Literature*, VII, 2897–2901. (Inadequate sketch.)

Parrington, V. L. *Main Currents in American Thought*. II, 46–56. (Although inherently unsympathetic toward Kennedy's politics, Parrington recognizes merit in his novels, saying that "*Rob of the Bowl* is certainly Kennedy's best work," and *Quodlibet* is "the most vivacious criticism of Jacksonianism in our political library.")

Tuckerman, H. T. *The Life of John Pendleton Kennedy*. New York: 1871. (The most complete biography.)

Williams, Mary W. "John Pendleton Kennedy," *Dictionary of American Biography*, X, 333–334.

Wynne, James. "John P. Kennedy," *Harper's Magazine*, XXV, 335–340 (August, 1862). (Reminiscences by a fellow-townsman of Baltimore.)

Grace Elizabeth King

Beer, William. "List of Writings of Grace King." *Louisiana Historical Quarterly*, VI, 378–379 (July, 1923). A listing of ten books and pamphlets, and over thirty articles and stories. This bibliography introduces a number of articles written as tributes to Miss King by members of the Louisiana Historical Society, of which she had been secretary. The articles are "Miss King's Historical Works" by Henry P. Dart, "The Fiction of Grace King" by R. S. Cocks, "A Southern Author in Her New Orleans Home" by Louise H. Guyol, and "The Distinction of Grace King" by Katherine Pope.)

Faust, Marie Elisabeth. "In Memoriam: Grace King," *Bookman*, LXXV, 360–361 (August, 1932). (Intimate memories.)

Garnett, Edward. "A Gossip on Criticism," *Atlantic Monthly*, CXVII, 174–184 (February, 1916). (Praise of *The Pleasant Ways of St. Medard*.)

King, Grace. *Memories of a Southern Woman of Letters*. New York: 1932. (Since there is no complete biography of Miss King, this book of reminiscences is a source of original material. The intimate glimpses of many contemporary editors and men of letters show how deeply indebted she was to friends in the North.)

Kirk, Richard R. "Grace King," *Dictionary of American Biography*, X, 389–390. (A brief, inadequate sketch.)

M'Caleb, Thomas. *The Louisiana Book: Selections from the Literature of the State*. New Orleans: 1894.

McVoy, Lizzie C., and Campbell, Ruth B. *A Bibliography of Fiction by Louisianians and on Louisiana Subjects*. *Louisiana State University Studies*. No. 18. Baton Rouge: 1935.

Snyder, H. N. "Miss Grace Elizabeth King," in Baskervill's *Southern Writers*, II, 272–290. (An appreciative essay.)

Sidney Lanier

Anderson, Charles R. (ed.). *The Centennial Edition of the Works and Letters of Sidney Lanier*. 9 vols. (This definitive edition of Lanier's writings will be published by the Johns Hopkins Press.)

Baskervill, W. M. *Southern Writers*, I, 137–298. (An able general discussion of Lanier's poetry and his literary importance.)

Clark, Harry Hayden (ed.). "Sidney Lanier," *Major American Poets*. New York: c. 1936. Pages 611–649; 903–913. (The annotated Bibliography and the Notes are very helpful to the student of Lanier's prose as well as of his poetry.)

Graham, Philip. "Lanier's Reading," *University of Texas Studies in English*, No. 11 (1931), pp. 63–89. (A list of 419 titles, showing, as H. H. Clark states, "his special devotion, during different periods, to Carlyle, German romanticists,

Keats and Poe, Shakespeare and the Bible, Anglo-Saxon writings, Chaucer, Malory and the romancers, Spencer and Huxley, and Tennyson, Browning, Swinburne and Whitman.")

Lorenz, Lincoln. *The Life of Sidney Lanier.* New York: 1935. (A readable, sentimental study, which adds little to the earlier studies by Mims and Starke.)

Mims, Edwin. *Sidney Lanier.* Boston: 1905. (Drawing upon primary materials now unavailable and from a deep knowledge of the South, but confined by the limits of a volume in the American Men of Letters Series, the biographer has presented an indispensable critical interpretation.)

Mims, Edwin. "Sidney Lanier," *Dictionary of American Biography*, X, 601–605. (A comprehensive brief biography.)

Starke, Aubrey H. *Sidney Lanier: A Biographical and Critical Study.* Chapel Hill, N.C.: 1935. (A definitive biography of Lanier, in over 500 pages, with detailed life facts, analysis and criticism of all his writings, consideration of his social and economic views, and defense of his critical and aesthetic theories. The appended Bibliography is complete to date of publication. This can be supplemented by reference to the annual issues of the "American Bibliography" of the *Publications of the Modern Language Association.*)

Hugh Swinton Legaré

Hamilton, J. G. de R. "Hugh Swinton Legaré," *Dictionary of American Biography*, XI, 144–145.

[Hillard, George S., ed.] *Life, Letters, and Journals of George Ticknor.* Boston: 1876. 2 vols. (Many references to Legaré).

Preston, W. C. *Eulogy on Hugh Swinton Legaré: Delivered at the Request of the City of Charleston. . . .* Nov. 7, 1843. Charleston, S.C.: 1843. (This able South Carolina contemporary of Legaré delivered many orations, of which this is probably the best known.)

Ramage, B. J. "Hugh Swinton Legaré," *Sewanee Review*, X, 43–55; 167–180 (January and April, 1902). (Two articles on "Legaré's Youth" and "Legaré, the Statesman.")

Rhea, Linda. *Hugh Swinton Legaré: A Charleston Intellectual.* Chapel Hill, N.C.: 1934. (The most recent biography, based upon all the earlier sketches. The chapters on *The Southern Review* would profit by revision.)

Writings of Hugh Swinton Legaré. . . . Prefaced by a Memoir of His Life. [By E. W. Johnson]. Edited by His Sister [Mrs. Mary S. Legaré Bullen]. Charleston, S.C.: 1846. 2 vols. (Since the memoir is based upon letters and records, which are not available now, it includes primary source material.)

"Writings of Hugh Swinton Legaré." *Southern Quarterly Review*, IX, 321–361 (April, 1846). (A serious, learned review, based upon the recently published volumes of Legaré's writings. Any conjecture regarding the identity of the author, who affixed an "H" to the article, might be wrong.)

Augustus Baldwin Longstreet

Davidson, J. W. *Living Writers of the South.* New York: 1869. Pages 337–342. (A spirited sketch.)

Dexter, F. B. *Biographical Sketches of the Graduates of Yale College, with Annals of Church History.* 6 vols. New York: 1885–1912. VI, 580–583. (Includes a list of Longstreet's writings.)

Fitzgerald, O. P. *Library of Southern Literature*, VII, 3241–3244.

Fitzgerald, O. P. *Judge Longstreet: A Life Sketch.* Nashville, Tenn.: 1891. (A bishop of the M. E. Church South writes a eulogistic biography, which is of value because of the inclusion of letters and speeches.)

Parrington, V. L. *Main Currents in American Thought*, II, 166–172. (Although Longstreet was a mediocre man, "incapable of rigorous intellectual processes, . . . he set the style that was followed in a long series of frontier sketches, and established the tradition of frontier humor that flowered at last in Mark Twain.")

Wade, J. D. *August Baldwin Longstreet: A Study of the Development of Culture in the South.* New York: 1934. (An excellent biography in which Longstreet is projected against the southern cultural background. The chapters on "Georgia Scenes," "Georgia Scenes—One by One," and "Uncollected Scenes" are of especial literary importance.)

Wade, J. D. "Augustus Baldwin Longstreet," *Dictionary of American Biography*, XI, 390–391.

Mary Noailles Murfree
(Charles Egbert Craddock)

Adkins, M. T. "The Mountains and Mountaineers of Craddock's Fiction," *Magazine of American History*, XXIV, 305–309 (October, 1890). (A defence of her fiction, by one who knew the Tennessee mountain region.)

Baskervill, W. M. *Southern Writers*. I, 357–404. (Competent criticism of early writings.)

Backette, G. H. "Charles Egbert Craddock," *Library of Southern Literature*, XIII, 3721–3726. (A laudatory sketch.)

Lewis, C. L. "Mary Noailles Murfree," *Dictionary of American Biography*, XIII, 344–345. (A good sketch, with a few factual errors.)

Parks, Edd W. *Charles Egbert Craddock (Mary Noailles Murfree)*. Chapel Hill, N. C.: 1941. (A critical biography based upon public and family records, contemporary periodicals, and the author's many stories, articles, and books, with an extensive bibliography.)

Reichert, Alfred. *Charles Egbert Craddock und die Amerikanische Short-Story*. Leipzig: 1912. (A discussion of the theory of the short-story, and a critical appraisal of Craddock's stories, based upon only four volumes.)

Walter Hines Page

Connor, R. D. W. "Walter Hines Page: A Southern Nationalist," *Journal of Social Forces*, II, 164–168 (January, 1924). (The recognition of Page's achievements, with explanations of how he lost the southern point of view in becoming a nationalist.)

Hendrick, Burton J. *The Life and Letters of Walter H. Page.* Garden City, N.Y.: 1922, 1925. 3 vols. (Volumes I and II constitute the biography, with appendix and index. Volume III contains the letters to Woodrow Wilson.)

Hendrick, Burton J. *The Training of an American: The Earlier Life and Letters of Walter H. Page, 1855–1913.* Boston: 1928. (Hendrick writes: "The purpose of this book is to complete the biography of Walter H. Page. The materials concerning Mr. Page's work as Ambassador . . . absorbed practically all of the two volumes originally assigned for his 'Life and Letters.' The author was therefore forced . . . to compress the fifty-eight years preceding the London Embassy into the merest sketch.")

Meneely, A. Howard. "Walter Hines Page," *Dictionary of American Biography,* XIV, 142–144. (A good sketch, with stress upon Page's activities as ambassador.)

Mims, Edwin. "Walter Hines Page: Friendly Critic of the South," in *The Advancing South,* New York: 1926. The reprinting of an article, with revisions, from the *South Atlantic Quarterly,* XVIII, 97–115 (April, 1919). (Comparison of Walter Hines Page and Thomas Nelson Page; praise of Page's writings and his service to the South.)

Shaw, Albert. "Walter Hines Page—Memorial Address," *North Carolina Historical Review,* II, 3–25 (January, 1924). (Eulogistic.)

Thomas Nelson Page

Gordon, Armistead C. "Thomas Nelson Page: An Appreciation," *Scribner's Magazine,* LXXII, 75–80 (January, 1923). (His collaborator in the *Befo' de War* poems recalls personal incidents.)

Kent, Charles W. "Thomas Nelson Page," *Library of Southern Literature,* IX, 3849–3853. (Laudatory.)

Mims, Edwin. "Thomas Nelson Page," Baskervill's *Southern Writers,* II, 120–151. (Published in the middle of Page's career, this sketch gives measured criticism of his early stories and novels.)

Mims, Edwin. "Thomas Nelson Page," *Atlantic Monthly*, C, 109–115 (July, 1907).

Nelson, J. H. "Thomas Nelson Page," *Dictionary of American Biography*, XIV, 141–142.

Page, Rosewell. *Thomas Nelson Page: A Memoir of a Virginia Gentleman*. New York: 1923. (A brother writes an intimate biography which is especially valuable in sketching his early life.)

Toulmin, H. A., Jr. "Thomas Nelson Page," in *Social Historians*, Boston: [1911], pp. 1–32. (Too brief for satisfactory treatment.)

William Sydney Porter
(O. Henry)

Clarkson, Paul S. (comp.). *A Bibliography of William Sydney Porter*. Caldwell, Idaho: 1938.

Courtney, Luther W. "O. Henry's Case Reconsidered," *American Literature*, XIV, 361–371 (January, 1943).

Davis, Robert H., and Maurice, Arthur B. *The Caliph of Bagdad: Being Arabian Nights Flashes of the Life, Letters, and Work of O. Henry*. New York: 1921. (The first parts, probably written by Mr. Maurice, contain the necessary facts of O. Henry's early life, gleaned very competently from many sources; the later chapters by Mr. Davis [Bob Davis of the *World*] are pleasant anecdotes of O. Henry in New York.)

Harrell, Mary S. (ed.). *O. Henry Encore: Stories and Illustrations*. New York: 1939. (Previously published in the *Houston Post*, 1895–1896.)

Pattee, F. L. "The Age of O. Henry," in *Side-Lights on American Literature*, New York: 1922, pp. 3–55. (An excellent appraisal of his humor, which is "as indigenous to the American soil as the early Mark Twain," but with questioning approval of his short-story art.)

Rollins, Hyder E. "O. Henry's Texas," *Texas Review*, IV, 295–307 (July, 1919). ("O. Henry did not attempt to give realistic pictures of cowboys, outlaws, and Rangers; . . . few [of his stories] have real local color.")

Smith, C. Alphonso. *O. Henry Biography*. Garden City, N.Y.: 1916. (The first biography, detailing the facts of his early life, including the prison years, with high approval of his stories.)

Van Doren, Carl. "William Sydney Porter," *Dictionary of American Biography*, XV, 105–107. (Adequate facts; critically unsympathetic.)

William Gilmore Simms

Cowie, Alexander (ed.). *The Yemassee* (American Fiction Series). New York: 1937. (A reprinting of Simms's revised edition of 1853, with an introduction and annotated bibliography which are helpful and important in the study of Simms as a writer of romances.)

Erskine, John. *Leading American Novelists*. New York: 1910. (In the chapter on Simms there is judicious estimate of the merits and faults of his novels.)

Hingham, John W. "The Changing Loyalties of William Gilmore Simms," *Journal of Southern History*, IX, 210–223 (May, 1943). (From a nationalist to a secessionist.)

Hoole, William S. "A Note on Simms's Visits to the Southwest," *American Literature*, VI, 334–336 (November, 1934).

Hoole, William S. "William Gilmore Simms's Career as Editor," *Georgia Historical Quarterly*, XIX, 47–54 (March, 1935).

Jarrell, Hampton M. "Falstaff and Simms's Porgy," *American Literature*, III, 204–212 (May, 1931).

Jarrell, Hampton M. "Simms's Visits to the Southwest," *American Literature*, V, 29–35 (March, 1933). (In these articles and in his Duke University dissertation Dr. Jarrell contributes to the knowledge of Simms's fiction.)

Link, Samuel A. *Pioneers of Southern Literature*. I, 149–221.

Morris, J. Allen. "The Stories of William Gilmore Simms," *American Literature*, XIV, 20–25 (March, 1942). (Bibliographical listing and critical discussion of fifty-eight stories.)

Parrington, V. L. *Main Currents in American Thought*. II, 125–136. (Stimulating, because the critical judgments differ from those by others.)

Salley, A. S., Jr. "A Bibliography of William Gilmore Simms," *Publications of the Southern History Association*, I, 269–295 (October, 1897); XI, 343–344 (September, 1907). (As State Historian of South Carolina and as a lifelong collector of Simms items, Mr. Salley is a bibliographical authority.)

——. *Catalogue of the Salley Collection of the Works of William Gilmore Simms*. Columbia, S.C.: 1943.

Trent, William P. *William Gilmore Simms*. Boston: 1896. (A pioneer biographical and critical study, with some inaccuracies in interpretation.)

Van Doren, Carl. "William Gilmore Simms," *Dictionary of American Biography*, XVII, 171–174.

Wegelin, Oscar. *A List of the Separate Writings of William Gilmore Simms of South Carolina, 1806–1870*. New York: 1906. Revised and reprinted, under a slightly different title, in the *American Book Collector*, III, 113–116, 149–151, 216–218, 284–286 (February to May-June, 1933).

John Taylor

Beard, Charles A. *The Economic Origins of Jeffersonian Democracy*. New York: 1915. Chapter XI.

Craven, Avery O. "John Taylor," *Dictionary of American Biography*, XVIII, 331–333.

Craven, Avery O. "John Taylor and Southern Agriculture," *Journal of Southern History*, IV, 137–147 (May, 1938).

Dodd, William E. "John Taylor of Caroline, Prophet of Secession," *The John P. Branch Historical Papers of Randolph-Macon College*, II, Nos. 3 and 4, 214–252 (June, 1908). (Gives summaries and interpretations of Taylor's most important works as follows: *A Defence of the Measures of the Administration of Thomas Jefferson*, taken from the *National Intelligencer*, Washington, 1804; *Arator; being a series of Agricultural Essays, Practical and Political*, Georgetown, 1813; *An Inquiry into the Principles and Policy of the Government of the United States*, Fredericksburg, 1814; *Construction Construed and Constitutions Vindicated*, Richmond, 1820; *Tyranny Unmasked*, Washington, 1822; *New Views of the*

Constitution of the United States, Washington, 1823. In this same volume are "Letters of John Taylor," written mainly to Madison and Monroe, with a few to Jefferson and others.)

Drell, Bernard. "John Taylor of Caroline and the Preservation of an Old Social Order," *Virginia Magazine of History and Biography*, XLVI, 285–298 (October, 1938).

Mudge, Eugene T. *The Social Philosophy of John Taylor of Caroline: A Study in Jeffersonian Democracy*. New York: 1939.

Parrington, V. L. *Main Currents in American Thought*, New York: 1927. II, 14–19.

Simms, Henry H. *Life of John Taylor: The Story of a Brilliant Leader in the Early Virginia State Rights School*. Richmond: 1932.

Woodrow Wilson

Baker, Ray Stannard. *Woodrow Wilson: Life and Letters*. Garden City, N.Y.: 1927–1938. Volumes I–VII. (To be completed.) (The most important biography; distinctly favorable.)

Bolling, John R., *et al. Chronology of Woodrow Wilson*. New York: 1927. (With extracts from writings.)

Creel, George. *The War, the World and Wilson*. New York: [1920].

Daniels, Josephus. *The Life of Woodrow Wilson, 1856–1924.* Chicago: 1924. (By the Secretary of the Navy, 1913–1921.)

Dodd, William E. *Woodrow Wilson and His Work*. Garden City, N.Y.: 1920. (By the Ambassador to Germany, 1933–1937.)

Ford, Henry J. *Woodrow Wilson: The Man and His Work: A Biographical Study*. New York: 1916. (By a professor of politics at Princeton.)

Harris, H. Wilson. *President Wilson: His Problems and His Policy: An English View*. New York: 1917.

Lawrence, David. *The True Story of Woodrow Wilson*. New York: [1924]. (By a correspondent for the Associated Press.)

Princeton Univeristy Library. *Essays Towards a Bibliography of the Published Writings and Addresses of Woodrow Wilson.* 1875–1910, by Harry Clemons; 1910–1917, by George Dobbin Brown; 1917–1921, by Howard Seavoy Leach. Princeton, N. J.: 1913, 1917, 1922.

Sears, L. M. "Wilson," in *The Marcus W. Jernegan Essays in American Historiography*, edited by W. T. Hutchinson. Chicago: 1937.

Seymour, Charles. "Woodrow Wilson," *Dictionary of American Biography*, XX, 352–368. (This long sketch is followed by an extensive bibliography.)

Seymour, Charles. *Woodrow Wilson and the World War: A Chronicle of Our Own Times.* The Chronicles of America Series. New Haven, Conn.: 1921.

Tumulty, Joseph P. *Woodrow Wilson As I Know Him.* Garden City, N.Y.: 1921.

White, William Allen. *Woodrow Wilson: The Man, His Times and His Task.* Boston: 1924.

William Wirt

Abernethy, T. P. "William Wirt," *Dictionary of American Biography*, XX, 418–421. (This sketch emphasizes the achievements of Wirt as lawyer and attorney-general.)

Cauble, Frank P. *William Wirt and His Friends: A Study in Southern Culture*, 1772–1834. Chapel Hill: 1933. (This unpublished University of North Carolina dissertation supplements Kennedy's life by the inclusion of new material and the critical analyses of Wirt's writings. The bibliography lists the successive editions of Wirt's works, and itemizes all the biographical and critical studies about him and his literary associates.)

[Cruse, P. H.] "Biographical Sketch of William Wirt," a preface to *The Letters of the British Spy.* 10th ed. New York: 1832. (Cruse was a Baltimore lawyer and literary figure. Each successive reprint of *The Letters of the British Spy* after the first by Harpers was likewise labeled the *tenth* edition.)

Dobie, Armistead M. "William Wirt." *Library of Southern Literature*, XIII, 5903–5908. (A good sketch.)

Kennedy, J. P. *Memoirs of the Life of William Wirt, Attorney-General of the United States*. 2 vols. Philadelphia: 1849. (Dr. Cauble writes: "His numerous misstatements in regard to Wirt's literary efforts show that he was by no means a careful investigator. . . . Kennedy performed an invaluable service in printing a large number of Wirt's letters which would otherwise have been permanently lost, and all students of Wirt and his friends are forced to go to Kennedy's volumes for a great deal of material which cannot be found elsewhere.")

Parrington, V. L. *Main Currents in American Thought*. II, 30–35. (Shrewd criticism, which, however, repeats some of the conventional false statements about Wirt.)

*

Selections from
SOUTHERN PROSE WRITERS

*

WILLIAM BYRD

William Byrd was born in the settlement which later became Richmond, on March 28, 1674, and died at Westover, on August 26, 1744. He was the second of three men who made the name of Byrd famous in the history of colonial Virginia. The first William Byrd inherited in 1671 the Virginia estate of his uncle, Thomas Stagg. He rose rapidly in commercial and public life and in his later years he was a man of great importance in the colony, his honors being crowned by the King's appointing him "Receiver-general of his Majesty's revenues for the Colony." First living in his uncle's home at the falls of the James River, where Richmond now stands, he bought in 1688 the estate called Westover, twenty miles below, which he and his son made famous. The father built a wooden building, but his son erected the fine brick mansion which still stands. At the age of ten he was sent to England to be educated under the direction of his grandfather, Warham Horsemanden. There he entered a school conducted by Christopher Glasscock, where he made good progress. Upon the advice of his father he was sent over to Holland for a year. In 1692 he began to study law at the Middle Temple. J. S. Bassett, the able editor of his writings, states: "His course must have been a thorough one, for in the catalogue of the Byrd books are most of the great legal classics, both Roman, English and Continental." During this period, or perhaps before he went to Holland, Byrd made the acquaintance of Sir Robert Southwell, a distinguished diplomat and author and also an influential public man. Southwell became Byrd's patron, and through him, as his epitaph states, Byrd "was first introduced to the acquaintance of many of the first persons of the age for knowledge, wit, virtue, birth, or high station, and particularly contracted a most intimate and bosom friendship with the learned and illustrious Charles Boyle, Earl of Orrey." Undoubtedly it was through Southwell's influence that Byrd was elected a Fellow of the Royal Society of London in 1696. Although Byrd's only known contribution to the Society was one paper,

published in the *Transactions* for 1697, he maintained a deep
interest in the Society all his life.

Byrd returned to Virginia in 1696, after having spent twenty-
two of his most formative years abroad. As the son of a
prominent man, and himself a well-educated and polished person, he immediately plunged into public affairs. Upon his
father's death in 1704 he succeeded to an estate of over twenty-
six thousand acres. His participation in the commercial and
political affairs of Virginia was active, bringing him friends and
enemies. But we are glad to learn that Governor Spotswood
and he patched up their quarrel and became friends. At various times he was a member of the House of Burgesses, Auditor
of the Colony, and Receiver General of Quit Rents; and he
returned to England on three important missions. Byrd was
married twice, first to Lucy Parke, daughter of the colorful
General Daniel Parke. About one of their daughters, Evelyn,
there still persist legends of crossed love. The only son of the
second wife, Maria Taylor, lived an active commercial and
military life, but dissipated the family inheritance. Returning
in 1726 from his last sojourn in England, Byrd spent his remaining years at Westover, devoting himself to the many leisurely pursuits of a cultivated country gentleman. During
this period he wrote his best works, *The History of the Dividing
Line*, *The Journey to the Land of Eden*, and *The Progress to the
Mines*, which were copied by his secretary and librarian, William Proctor, and remained in manuscript for a century or
more after his death.

William Byrd accumulated at Westover a library of over
thirty-three hundred volumes, of which there is a catalogue in
the appendix of Bassett's edition of his writings. The study
of the contents of this extensive collection, the largest in the
colonial South, leads one to speculate on the liberal literary
culture of the most prominent Virginia gentleman of his time.
After the death of the third William Byrd in 1777, the library
was sold. Two unique and valuable volumes, the *Records of
the Virginia Company of London*, sometimes called the *South-
ampton Papers*, are now in the Library of Congress.

Byrd lies buried in the family plot near Westover, where
the visitor may read a record of his achievements in the fulsome praise of the tombstone inscription characteristic of the
period.

From THE SECRET HISTORY OF THE LINE

The Surveyors Enter the Dismal Swamp

March 13, 1728. In the Morning our Chaplain came to us, & with him some Men we had sent for, to relieve those who had waded thro' the Mire from Coratuck. But they beg'd they might not be reliev'd, believing they shou'd gain immortal Honour by going thro' the Dismal. Only Patillo desired to be excus'd, on the Account of his Eyes. Old Ellis Petition'd to go in the Room of his Son, and Kimball was depriv'd from that favour by Lot. That griev'd him so, that he offer'd a Crown to Hambleton to let him go in his room, which the other wou'd not Listen to for ten times the Money. When this great affair was settled, we dismist all the Men to their Quarters at Capt Wilson's, except the Nine Dismalites. Of these we sent 5 with the Surveyors who ran the Line to the Skirts of the Dismal, which began first with Dwarf Reeds, & moist uneven Grounds. We discharged our Periaugas[1] and about Noon our good Friend Capt Wilkins conducted us to his own House, & entertain'd us hospitably. We made the necessary Disposition for entering the Dismal next Morning with 9 of our Men, & 3 of Carolina, so many being necessary to attend the Surveyors, & for carrying the Bedding & Provisions. The Men were in good Spirits but poor Orion began to repent, & wish he had Slept in a whole Skin at the College, rather than become a prey to Turkey-buzzard. These reflections sunk his Courage so low, that neither Liquor nor Toast cou'd raise it. I hardly knew how to behave myself in a Bed, after having lain a week in the Open Field, & seeing the Stars twinkle over my head.

March 14, 1728. This Morning early the Men began to make up the Packs they were to carry on their Shoulders into the Dismal. They were victual'd for 8 Days, which was judg'd sufficient for the Service. Those Provisions with the Blankets & other Necessaries loaded the Men with a Burthen of 50 or 60^lb

---

[1] Superior numbers here and elsewhere refer to the Notes, 377–392.

for Each. Orion helpt most of all to make these Loads so
heavy, by taking his Bed, and several changes of Raiment, not
forgeting a Suit for Sundays along with him. This was a little
unmercifull, which with his peevish Temper made him no
Favorite. We fixt them out about ten in the Morning, & then
Meanwell, Puzzlecause, & I went along with them, resolving
to enter them fairly into this dreadful Swamp, which no body
before ever had either the Courage or Curiosity to pass. But
Firebrand & Shoebrush chose rather to toast their Noses
over a good Fire, & Spare their dear Persons. After a March of
2 Miles thro' very bad way, the Men sweating under their
Burthens, we arriv'd at the Edge of the Dismal, where the
Surveyors had left off the Night before. Here Steddy thought
proper to encourage the Men by a short harangue to this
effect. "Gentlemen, we are at last arriv'd at this dreadfull
place, which til now has been thought unpassable. Tho' I
make no doubt but you will convince every Body, that there is
no difficulty which may not be conquer'd by Spirit & constancy.
You have hitherto behaved with so much Vigour, that the
most I can desire of you, is to persevere unto the End; I protest
to You the only reason we don't Share in Your Fatigue, is, the
fear of adding to Your Burthens, (which are but too heavy
already,) while we are Sure we can add nothing to your Resolution. I shall say no more, but only pray the Almighty to
prosper your Undertaking, & grant we may meet on the other
Side in perfect Health & Safety." The Men took this Speech
very kindly, and answer'd it in the most cheerful manner, with
3 Huzzas. Immediately we enter'd the Dismal, 2 Men clearing
the way before the Surveyors, to enable them to take their
Sight. The Reeds which grew about 12 feet high, were so
thick, & so interlaced with Bamboe-Briars, that our Pioneers
were forc't to open a Passage. The Ground, if I may properly
call it so, was so Spungy, that the Prints of our Feet were instantly fill'd with Water. Amongst the Reeds here & there
stood a white Cedar, commonly mistaken for Juniper. Of
this Sort was the Soil for about half a Mile together, after
which we came to a piece of high land about 100 Yards in

Breadth. We were above 2 Hours scuffling thro' the Reeds to this Place, where we refresh't the poor Men. Then we took leave, recommending both them & the Surveyors to Providence. We furnish'd Astrolabe with Bark[2] & other Medicines, for any of the People, that might happen to be Sick, not forgetting 3 Kinds of Rattle-Snake Root made into Doses in case of Need. It was 4 a Clock before we return'd to our Quarters, where we found our Collegues under some Apprehension that we were gone with the People quite thro' the Dismal. During my Absence Firebrand was so very carefull in sending away the Baggage, that he forgot the Candles. When we had settled Accounts with our Landlord, we rode away to Cap[t] Wilson's, who treated us with Pork upon Pork. He was a great Lover of Conversation, & rather than it shou'd drop, he wou'd repeat the same Story over & over. Firebrand chose rather to litter the Floor, than lye with the Parson, & since he cou'd not have the best Bed, he sullenly wou'd have none at all. However it broil'd upon his Stomach so much, that he swore anough in the Night, to bring the Devil into the Room had not the Chaplain been there.

The Surveyors Find Game in the Piedmont

October 2, 1728. The Surveyors got out about 9 a clock, & advanc't the Line about 9 Miles. We follow'd with the Baggage at 11, & past at 3 Miles distance from our Camp, Mossamory Creek, an Indian Name signifying Paint Creek, from red Earth found upon the Banks of it, which in a fresh tinges the Water of that Colour. Three Miles farther we got over Yapatoco, or Bever Creek with some difficulty, the Bevers[3] having rais'd the Water a great way up. We proceeded 3¼ Miles beyond this, & encampt on the West Side of Ohimpamony Creek, an Indian Name which signifys Fishing Creek. By the way Firebrand had another Occasion to show his Prowess, in killing a poor little Wild Cat, which had been crippled by 2 or 3 before. Poor Puss was unhappily making a Meal on a Fox Squirrel when all these misfortunes befell her. Meanwell had like to have quarrell'd with Firebrand & his Carolina Squadron, for not halting for me on the West Side of Yapatsco, having been almost mired in crossing that Creek while they had the fortune to get over it at a better place. The Indians kill'd 2 Deer & John Evans a third, which made great plenty & consequently great content in Israel.

October 3, 1728. We hurry'd away the Surveyors by 9, who ran something more than 8½ Miles. We follow'd them at 11, & crost several Branches of Excellent Water. We went thro' a large level of very rich high-Land, near 2 Miles in Length & of an unknown Breadth. Our Indian kill'd one Deer, & William Pool another, & this last we graciously gave to the Carolina Men, who deserv'd it not, because they had declared they did not care to rely on Providence. We encampt upon Tewahominy or Tuscoruda Creek. We saw many Buffalo [4] Tracks, & abundance of their Dung, but the Noise we made drove them all from our Sight. The Carolina Commissioners with their Leader, lagg'd behind to stop the Cravings of their Appetites, nor were we ever happy with their Conversation, but only at Dinner, when they play'd their Parts more for spite than Hunger.

October 4, 1728. The Surveyors got to work a little after 9, & extended the Line near 8 Miles, notwithstanding the Ground was very uneven. We decampt after them about 11, & at 5 Miles Distance crost Blewing Creek, & 3 Miles beyond that, we forded Sugar-Tree Creek, & pitch't our Tent on the West Side of it. This Creek receiv'd its Name from many Sugar Trees, which grow in the Low-Grounds of it. By tapping the Sugar Tree in the Spring, a great Quantity of Sugar flows out of it, which may be boil'd up into good Sugar. It grows very tall, & the Wood of it is very soft & Spungy. Here we also found abundance of Spice Trees, whose Leaves are fragrant, & the Berry they bear is black when dry, & hot like Pepper. Both these Trees grow only in a very rich Soil. The Low Ground upon this Creek is very wide, sometimes on One Side, sometimes on the other, but on the Opposite Side the high land advances close to the Creek. It ought to be remember'd, that the Commissioners of Carolina, made a complement of about

2000 Acres of Land lying on this Creek to Astrolabe, without paying any Fees. Robert Hix saw 3 Buffalos, but his gun being loaden only with Shot cou'd do no Execution. Bootes shot one Deer, & the Indians kill'd 3 more, & one of the Carolina men 4 Wild Turkeys. Thus Providence was very plentifull to us, & did not disappoint us who rely'd upon it.

From THE HISTORY OF THE DIVIDING LINE

The Surveyors Enter the Dismal Swamp

March 13, 1728. Early this Morning our Chaplain repair'd to us with the Men we had left at Mr. Wilson's. We had sent for them the Evening before to relieve those who had the Labour-Oar from Corotuck-Inlet. But to our great surprise, they petition'd not to be reliev'd, hoping to gain immortal Reputation by being the first of Mankind that Ventur'd thro' the great Dismal. But the rest being equally Ambitious of the same Honour, it was but fair to decide their Pretensions by Lot. After Fortune had declar'd herself, those which she had excluded offer'd Money to the Happy Persons to go in their Stead. But Hercules would have as soon sold the Glory of Cleansing the Augean Stables, which was pretty near the same Sort of Work.

No sooner was the Controversy at an end, but we sent them unfortunate Fellows back to their Quarters, whom Chance had Condemn'd to remain upon Firm Land and Sleep in a whole Skin. In the mean while the Surveyors carry'd the Line 3 Miles, which was no Contemptible day's work, considering how cruelly they were entangled with Bryars and Gall Bushes. The Leaf of this last Shrub bespeaks it to be of the Alaternus Family.

Our Work ended within a Quarter of a Mile of the Dismal above-mention'd, where the Ground began to be already full of Sunken Holes and Slashes, which had, here and there, some few Reeds growing in them.

Tis hardly credible how little the Bordering inhabitants were acquainted with this mighty Swamp, nothwithstanding they had liv'd their whole lives within Smell of it. Yet, as great Strangers as they were to it, they pretended to be very exact in their Account of its Dimensions, and were positive it could not be above 7 or 8 Miles wide, but knew no more of the Matter than Star-gazers know of the Distance of the Fixt Stars. At the Same time, they were Simple enough to amuse our Men with Idle Stories of the Lyons, Panthers and Alligators, they were like to encounter in that dreadful Place.

In short, we saw plainly there was no Intelligence of this Terra Incognita to be got, but from our own Experience. For that Reason it was resolv'd to make the requisite Dispositions to enter it next Morning. We allotted every one of the Surveyors for this painful Enterprise, with 12 Men to attend them. Fewer than that cou'd not be employ'd in clearing the way, carrying the Chain, marking the Trees, and bearing the necessary Bedding and Provisions. Nor wou'd the Commissioners themselves have Spared their Persons on this Occasion, but for fear of adding to the poor men's Burthen, while they were certain they cou'd add nothing to their Resolution.

We quarter'd with our Friend and Fellow Traveller, William Wilkins, who had been our faithful Pilot to Coratuck, and liv'd about a mile from the Place where the Line ended. Everything lookt so very clean, and the Furniture so neat, that we were tempted to Lodge within Doors. But the Novelty of being shut up so close quite spoil'd our rest, nor did we breathe so free by abundance, as when we lay in the open Air.

March 14, 1728. Before nine of the Clock this Morning, the Provisions, Bedding and other Necessaries, were made up into Packs for the Men to carry on their Shoulders into the Dismal. They were victuall'd for 8 days at full Allowance, Nobody doubting but that wou'd be abundantly Sufficient to carry them thro' that Inhospitable Place; nor Indeed was it possible for the Poor Fellows to Stagger under more. As it was, their Loads weigh'd from 60 to 70 Pounds, in just Proportion to the Strength of those who were to bear them.

Twou'd have been unconscionable to have Saddled them with Burthens heavier than that, when they were to lugg them thro' a filthy Bogg, which was hardly practicable with no Burthen at all.

Besides this Luggage at their Backs, they were oblig'd to measure the distance, mark the Trees, and clear the way for the Surveyors every Step they went. It was really a Pleasure to see with how much Cheerfulness they undertook, and with how much Spirit they went thro' all this Drudgery. For their Greater Safety, the Commissioners took care to furnish them with Peruvian-Bark, Rhubarb and Hipocoacanah,[5] in case they might happen, in that wet Journey, to be taken with fevers or Fluxes.

Altho' there was no need for Example to inflame Persons already so cheerful, yet to enter the People with better grace, the Author and two more of the Commissioners accompanied them half a Mile into the Dismal. The Skirts of it were thinly Planted with Dwarf Reeds and Gall-Bushes, but when we got into the Dismal itself, we found the Reeds grew there much taller and closer, and, to mend the matter was so interlac'd with bamo-briars, that there was no scuffling thro' them without the help of Pioneers. At the same time, we found the Ground moist and trembling under our feet like a Quagmire, insomuch that it was an easy Matter to run a Ten-Foot-Pole up to the Head in it, without exerting any uncommon Strength to do it.

Two of the Men, whose Burthens were the least cumbersome, had orders to march before, with their Tomahawks, and clear the way, in order to make an Opening for the Surveyors. By their Assistance we made a Shift to push the Line half a Mile in 3 Hours, and then reacht a small piece of firm Land, about 100 Yards wide, Standing up above the rest like an Island. Here the people were glad to lay down their Loads and take a little refreshment, while the happy man, whose lot it was to carry the Jugg of Rum, began already, like Aesop's Bread-Carriers to find it grow a good deal lighter.

After reposing about an Hour, the Commissioners recommended Vigour and Constancy to their Fellow-Travellers, by whom they were answer'd with 3 Cheerful Huzzas, in Token of Obedience. This Ceremony was no sooner over but they took up their Burthens and attended the Motion of the Surveyers, who, tho' they workt with all their might, could reach but one Mile farther, the same obstacles still attending them which they had met with in the Morning.

However small this distance may seem so such as are us'd to travel at their Ease, yet our Poor Men, who were oblig'd to work with an unwieldy Load at their Backs, had reason to think it a long way; Especially in a Bogg where they had no firm Footing, but every Step made a deep Impression, which was instantly fill'd with Water. At the same time they were labouring with their Hands to cut down the Reeds, which were Ten-feet high, their Legs were hampered with the Bryars. Besides, the Weather happen'd to be very warm, and the tallness of the Reeds kept off every Friendly Breeze from coming to refresh them. And, indeed, it was a little provoking to hear the Wind whistling among the Branches of the White Cedars, which grew here and there amongst the Reeds, and at the same time not have the Comfort to feel the least Breath of it.

In the mean time the 3 Commissioners return'd out of the Dismal the same way they went in, and having join'd their Brethren, proceeded that Night as far as Mr. Wilson's.

This worthy Person lives within sight of the Dismal, in the Skirts whereof his Stocks range and Maintain themselves all the Winter, and yet he knew as little of it is he did of Terra Australis Incognita. He told us a Canterbury Tale of a North Briton, whose Curiosity Spurr'd him a long way into this great Desart, as he call'd it, near 20 Years ago, but he having no Compass, nor seeing the Sun for several Days Together, wander'd about till he was almost famisht; but at last he bethought himself of a Secret his Countrymen make use of to Pilot themselves in a Dark day.

He took a fat Louse out of his Collar, and expos'd it to the open day on a Piece of White Paper, which he brought along with him for his Journal. The poor Insect having no Eye-

lids, turn'd himself about till he found the Darkest Part of the
Heavens, and so made the best of his way towards the North.
By this Direction he Sterr'd himself Safe out, and gave such a
frightful account of the Monsters he saw, and the Distresses
he underwent, that no mortall Since has been hardy enough to
go upon the like dangerous Discovery.

The Surveyors Find Game in the Piedmont

October 2, 1728. So soon as the Horses cou'd be found, we
hurry'd away the Surveyors, who advanc't the Line 9 Miles and
254 Poles. About 3 Miles from the Camp they crosst a large
Creek, which the Indians call'd Massamoni, Signifying, in their
Language, Paint-Creek, because of the great Quantity of Red
ochre found in its banks. This in every Fresh tinges the Water
just as the same Mineral did formerly, and to this day continues
to tinge, the famous River Adonis, in Phoenicia, by which
there hangs a celebrated Fable.

Three Miles beyond that we past another Water with difficulty, call'd Yaypatsco, or Bever Creek. Those industrious
Animals had damm'd up the water so high, that we had much
ado to get over. Tis hardly credible how much work of this
kind they will do in the Space of one Night. They bite young
Saplings into proper Lengths with their Fore-teeth, which are
exceeding Strong and Sharp, and afterwards drag them to the
Place where they intend to Stop the Water.

Then they know how to join Timber and Earth together with
so much Skill, that their Work is able to resist the most violent
Flood that can happen. In this they are qualify'd to instruct
their Betters, it being certain their damms will stand firm when
the Strongest that are made by men will be carry'd down the
Stream.

We observed very broad low Grounds upon this Creek, with
a growth of large Trees, and all the other Signs of Fertility,
but seem'd subject to be every where overflow'd in a fresh.

The certain way to catch these Sagacious Animals is thus:
Squeeze all the Juice out of the large Pride of the Beaver, and
6 drops out of the small Pride. Powder the inward Bark of

Sassafras, and mix it with this Juice, then bait therewith a
Steel Trap, and they will eagerly come to it, and be taken.

About three Miles and a half farther we came to the Banks
of another creek, call'd in the Saponi [6] Language, Ohimpa-
moni, Signifying Jumping Creek, from the frequent Jumping
of Fish during the Spring Season.

Here we encampt, and by the time the Horses were hobbled,
our Hunters brought us no less than a Brace and a half of Deer,
which made great Plenty, and consequently great content in
our Quarters.

Some of our People had Shot a great Wild Cat, which was
that fatal moment making a comfortable Meal upon a Fox-
Squirrel, and an Ambitious Sportsman of our Company claim'd
the merit of killing this monster after it was dead.

The Wild-cat is as big again as any Household-Cat, and much
the fiercest Inhabitant of the Woods. Whenever 'tis disabled,
it will tear its own Flesh for madness. Altho' a Panther will
run away from a Man, a Wild-cat will only make a Surly Retreat, now and then facing about, if he be too closely pursued;
and will even pursue in his turn, if he observe the least Sign of
Fear or even of caution in those that pretend to follow Him.

The Flesh of this Beast, as well as of the Panther, is as white
as veal, and altogether as sweet and delicious.

October 3, 1728. We got to work early this Morning, and
carry'd the line 8 Miles and 160 Poles. We forded Several Runs
of Excellent Water, and afterwards traverst a large levil of high
land full of lofty Walnut, Poplar, and White Oak Trees, which
are certain Proofs of a fruitful Soil. This levil was near two
Miles in length, and of an unknown breadth, quite out of Danger
of being overflow'd, which is a misfortune most of the Low
Grounds are liable to in those Parts. As we marcht along we
saw many Buffalo-Tracks, and abundance of their Dung very
Fresh, but could not have the pleasure of seeing them. They
either Smelt us out, having that sense very Quick, or else were
alarm'd at the Noise that so many People must necessarily
make in marching along. At the Sight of a Man they will

Snort and Grunt, cock up their ridiculous Short Tails, and tear up the Ground with a Sort of Timorous Fury.

These wild Cattle hardly ever range alone, but herd together like those that are tame. They are Seldom seen so far North as 40° of latitude, delighting much in canes and Reeds, which grow generally more Southerly.

We quarter'd on the Banks of a Creek that the Inhabitants call Tewahominy, or Tuskarooda [7] creek, because one of that Nation had been kill'd thereabouts, and his Body thrown into the Creek.

Our People had the Fortune to kill a Brace of does, one of which we presented to the Carolina-Gentlemen, who were glad to partake of the Bounty of Providence, at the same time that they sneer'd at us for depending upon it.

October 4, 1728. We hurry'd away the Surveyors about 9 this Morning, who extended the Line 7 Miles and 160 Poles, notwithstanding the Ground was exceedingly uneven. At the Distance of five Miles we forded a stream to which we gave the Name of Blewing creek, because of the great Number of those Fowls that then frequented it.

About 2½ Miles beyond that, we came upon Sugar-Tree-Creek, so call'd from the many Trees of that kind that grow upon it. By tapping this Tree, in the first Warm weather in February, one may get from 20 to 40 Gallons of Liquor, very sweet to the tast and agreeable to the Stomach. This may be boiled into molosses first, and afterwards into very good Sugar, allowing about 10 Gallons of the Liquor to make a Pound. There's no doubt, too, that a very fine Spirit may be distill'd from the molasses, at least as good as Rum. The Sugar Tree delights only in Rich Ground, where it grows very tall, and by the Softness and Spunginess of the Wood shou'd be a quick Grower.

Near this Creek we discovered likewise Several Spice-Trees, the Leaves of which are fragrant, and the Berries they bear are black when dry, and of a hot tast, not much unlike Pepper.

The low Grounds upon the creek are very wide, sometimes on

one Side, Sometimes on the Other, tho' most commonly upon the Opposite Shore the high-land advances close to the Bank, only on the North-Side of the Line it spreads itself into a great Breadth of rich low Ground on both sides the Creek for four Miles together, as far as this Stream runs into Hico-River, whereof I shall presently make mention.

One of our Men Spy'd three Buffaloes, but his Piece being loaded only with Goose-shot, he was able to make no effectual Impression on their thick hides; however, this Disappointment was made up by a Brace of Bucks, and as many Wild Turkeys, kill'd by the rest of the company.

Thus Providence was very Bountiful to our Endeavours, never disappointing those that Faithfully rely upon it, and pray heartily for their Daily Bread.

THOMAS JEFFERSON

Thomas Jefferson was born at Shadwell, Albemarle County, Virginia, April 13, 1743, and died at Monticello, in the same county, July 4, 1826. His father was a surveyor, of Welsh descent, and his mother was of the patrician family of Randolph. He was educated at William and Mary College in the capital city of Williamsburg, graduating in 1760. After reading law under Chancellor George Wythe, and being admitted to the bar in 1767, he practised law with success. Entering the House of Burgesses in 1769 (not 1767, as sometimes stated), he served from time to time with distinction until the eve of the Revolution. In the Continental Congresses of 1775 and 1776 he succeeded John Dickinson as drafter of state papers, and wrote much of the Declaration of Independence. This notable paper is a masterpiece for its clear statement of the "natural rights" theory of government and for its rhetorical phrasing. Returning to Virginia, he served again in the House of Burgesses and as Governor, laboring successfully to democratize the state laws by abolishing the laws of entail and primogeniture and by separating the Church and State. Re-entering Congress in 1783, after the Revolution, he aided in passing important legislation. In the following year he was sent to Europe to secure treaties of commerce, and in 1785 he succeeded Franklin as minister to France, with a successful career as diplomat. Washington recalled him in 1790 to become his Secretary of State. He served with John Adams as Vice-President from 1797 to 1801, and as President from 1801 to 1809. Retiring to private life at Monticello he maintained his power in politics by voluminous correspondence and by lavish hospitality—which impoverished him. To relieve himself from pressing debts he sold his library to Congress for $23,950, and this magnificent collection formed the nucleus of the Library of Congress, which is now one of the largest libraries in the world, if not the largest. The last ten years of his life were devoted with zeal and intelligence to the founding of the University of Virginia in the adjacent town of Charlottesville, and he saw it opened on March 7, 1825. He died on July 4, 1826, on the same day as his political rival, John Adams.

Jefferson is of importance to the student of literature for his zeal for learning, expressed in many solid and gracious ways, for his theories of government, which had their origins in English and French liberal political thought, and for his shrewd observations on the American scene.

From NOTES ON VIRGINIA

Query XVIII: The particular customs and manners that may happen to be received in that State?

It is difficult to determine on the standard by which the manners of a nation may be tried, whether *catholic* or *particular*. It is more difficult for a native to bring to that standard the manners of his own nation, familiarized to him by habit. There must doubtless be an unhappy influence on the manners of our people produced by the existence of slavery among us. The whole commerce between master and slave is a perpetual exercise of the most boisterous passions, the most unremitting despotism on the one part, and degrading submissions on the other. Our children see this, and learn to imitate it; for man is an imitative animal. This quality is the germ of all education in him. From his cradle to his grave he is learning to do what he sees others do. If a parent could find no motive either in his philanthropy or his self-love, for restraining the intemperance of passion towards his slave, it should always be a sufficient one that his child is present. But generally it is not sufficient. The parent storms, the child looks on, catches the lineaments of wrath, puts on the same airs in the circle of smaller slaves, gives a loose to the worst of passions, and thus nursed, educated, and daily exercised in tyranny, cannot but be stamped by it with odious peculiarities. The man must be a prodigy who can retain his manners and morals undepraved by such circumstances. And with what execration should the statesman be loaded, who, permitting one-half the citizens thus to trample on the rights of the other, transforms those into despots, and these into enemies, destroys the morals of the one part, and the *amor patriae* of the other. For if a slave can have a country in this world, it must be any other in preference to that in which he is born to live and labor for another; in which he must lock up the faculties of his nature, contribute as far as depends on his individual endeavors to the evanishment of the human race, or entail his own miserable condition on the endless generations proceeding from him. With the morals of the people, their industry also is destroyed. For in a warm climate, no man will labor for himself who can make another labor for him. This is so true, that of the proprietors of slaves a very small proportion indeed are ever seen to labor. And can the liberties of a nation be thought secure when we have removed their only firm basis, a conviction in the minds of the people that these liberties are of the gift of God? That they are not to be violated but with His wrath? Indeed I tremble for my country when I reflect that God is just; that his justice cannot sleep forever; that considering numbers, nature and natural means only, a revolution of the wheel of fortune, an exchange of situation is among possible events; that it may become probable by supernatural interference! The Almighty has no attribute which can take side with us in such a contest. But it is impossible to be temperate and to pursue this subject through the various considerations of policy, of morals, of history natural and civil. We must be contented to hope they will force their way into every one's mind. I think a change already perceptible, since the origin of the present revolution. The spirit of the master is abating, that of the slave rising from the dust, his condition mollifying, the way I hope preparing, under the auspices of heaven, for a total emancipation, and that this is disposed, in the order of events, to be with the consent of the masters, rather than by their extirpation.

Query XXII: The Public Income and Expense?

... To this estimate of our abilities, let me add a word as to the application of them, if, when cleared of the present contest, and of the debts with which that will charge us, we come to

measure force hereafter with any European power. Such
events are devoutly to be deprecated. Young as we are, and
with such a country before us to fill with people and with happiness, we should point in that direction the whole generative
force of nature, wasting none of it in efforts of mutual destruction. It should be our endeavor to cultivate the peace and
friendship of every nation, even of that which has injured us
most, when we shall have carried our point against her. Our
interest will be to throw open the doors of commerce, and to
knock off all its shackles, giving perfect freedom to all persons
for the vent of whatever they may choose to bring into our
ports, and asking the same in theirs. Never was so much false
arithmetic employed on any subject, as that which has been
employed to persuade nations that it is their interest to go to
war. Were the money which it has cost to gain, at the close
of a long war, a little town, or a little territory, the right to cut
wood here, or to catch fish there, expended in improving what
they already possess, in making roads, opening rivers, building
ports, improving the arts, and finding employment for their
idle poor, it would render them much stronger, much wealthier
and happier. This I hope will be our wisdom. And, perhaps,
to remove as much as possible the occasions of making war, it
might be better for us to abandon the ocean altogether, that
being the element whereon we shall be principally exposed to
jostle with other nations; to leave to others to bring what we
shall want, and to carry what we can spare. This would make
us invulnerable to Europe, by offering none of our property to
their prize, and would turn all our citizens to the cultivation of
the earth; and, I repeat it again, cultivators of the earth are the
most virtuous and independent citizens. It might be time
enough to seek employment for them at sea, when the land no
longer offers it. But the actual habits of our countrymen
attach them to commerce. They will exercise it for themselves.
Wars then must sometimes be our lot; and all the wise can do,
will be to avoid that half of them which would be produced by
our own follies and our own acts of injustice; and to make for
the other half the best preparations we can. Of what nature

should these be? A land army would be useless for offence, and not the best nor safest instrument of defence. For either of these purposes, the sea is the field on which we should meet an European enemy. On that element it is necessary we should possess some power. To aim at such a navy as the greater nations of Europe possess, would be a foolish and wicked waste of the energies of our countrymen. It would be to pull on our own heads the load of military expense which makes the European laborer go supperless to bed, and moistens his bread with the sweat of his brows. It will be enough if we enable ourselves to prevent insults from those nations of Europe which are weak on the sea, because circumstances exist, which render even the stronger ones weak as to us. Providence has placed their richest and most defenceless possessions at our door; has obliged their most precious commerce to pass, as it were, in review before us. To protect this, or to assail, a small part only of their naval force will ever be risked across the Atlantic. The dangers to which the elements expose them here are too well known, and the greater dangers to which they would be exposed at home were any general calamity to involve their whole fleet. They can attack us by detachment only; and it will suffice to make ourselves equal to what they may detach. Even a smaller force than they may detach will be rendered equal or superior by the quickness with which any check may be repaired with us, while losses with them will be irreparable till too late. A small naval force then is sufficient for us, and a small one is necessary. What this should be, I will not undertake to say. I will only say, it should by no means be so great as we are able to make it. Suppose the million dollars, or three hundred thousand pounds, which Virginia could annually spare without distress, to be applied to the creating a navy. A single year's contribution would build, equip, man, and send to sea a force which should carry three hundred guns. The rest of the confederacy, exerting themselves in the same proportion, would equip in the same time fifteen hundred guns more. So that one year's contributions would set up a navy of eighteen hundred guns. The British ships of

the line average seventy-six guns; their frigates thirty-eight.
Eighteen hundred guns then would form a fleet of thirty ships,
eighteen of which might be of the line, and twelve frigates.
Allowing eight men, the British average, for every gun, their
annual expense, including subsistence, clothing, pay, and ordinary repairs, would be about $1,280 for every gun, or
$2,304,000 for the whole. I state this only as one year's pos-
sible exertion, without deciding whether more or less than a
year's exertion should be thus applied. . . .

FIRST INAUGURAL ADDRESS

Delivered March 4, 1801

Friends and fellow-citizens:

Called upon to undertake the duties of the first executive
office of our country, I avail myself of the presence of that portion of my fellow-citizens which is here assembled, to express
my grateful thanks for the favor with which they have been
pleased to look towards me, to declare a sincere consciousness
that the task is above my talents, and that I approach it with
those anxious and awful presentiments which the greatness of
the charge and the weakness of my powers so justly inspire.
A rising nation, spread over a wide and fruitful land; travers-
ing all the seas with the rich productions of their industry; engaged in commerce with nations who feel power and forget
right; advancing rapidly to destinies beyond the reach of mortal eye,—when I contemplate these transcendent objects, and
see the honor, the happiness, and the hopes of this beloved
country committed to the issue and the auspices of this day, I
shrink from the contemplation, and humble myself before the
magnitude of the undertaking.   Utterly, indeed, should I despair, did not the presence of many whom I here see remind me,
that in the other high authorities provided by our Constitution
I shall find resources of wisdom, of virtue, and of zeal, on which
to rely under all difficulties.   To you, then, gentlemen, who
are charged with the sovereign functions of legislation, and to
those associated with you, I look with encouragement for that

guidance and support which may enable us to steer with safety the vessel in which we are all embarked, amid the conflicting elements of a troubled sea.

During the contest of opinion through which we have passed, the animation of discussion and of exertions has sometimes worn an aspect which might impose on strangers, unused to think freely, and to speak and to write what they think. But, this being now decided by the voice of the nation, enounced according to the rules of the Constitution, all will, of course, arrange themselves under the will of the law, and unite in common efforts for the common good. All, too, will bear in mind this sacred principle, that, though the will of the majority is in all cases to prevail, that will, to be rightful, must be reasonable; that the minority possess their equal rights, which equal laws must protect, and to violate [which] would be oppression. Let us, then, fellow-citizens, unite with one heart and one mind; let us restore to social intercourse that harmony and affection without which liberty and even life itself are but dreary things. And let us reflect that having banished from our land that religious intolerance under which mankind so long bled and suffered, we have yet gained little if we countenance a political intolerance as despotic, as wicked, and capable of as bitter and bloody persecutions. During the throes and convulsions of the ancient world, during the agonized spasms of infuriated man, seeking through blood and slaughter his long-lost liberty, it was not wonderful that the agitation of the billows should reach even this distant and peaceful shore; that this should be more felt and feared by some and less by others, and should divide opinions as to measures of safety. But every difference of opinion is not a difference of principle. We have called by different names brethren of the same principle. We are all republicans; we are all federalists. If there be any among us who would wish to dissolve this Union, or to change its republican form, let them stand, undisturbed, as monuments of the safety with which error of opinion may be tolerated where reason is left free to combat it. I know, indeed, that some honest men have feared that a republican government cannot be strong; that this government is not strong enough. But would the honest patriot, in the full tide of successful experiment, abandon a government which has so far kept us free and firm, on the theoretic and visionary fear that this government, the world's best hope, may, by possibility, want energy to preserve itself? I trust not. I believe this, on the contrary, the strongest government on earth. I believe it is the only one where every man, at the call of the law, would fly to the standard of the law, and would meet invasions of public order as his own personal concern. Sometimes it is said that man cannot be trusted with the government of himself. Can he, then, be trusted with the government of others? Or have we found angels in the form of kings to govern him? Let history answer this question.

Let us, then, pursue with courage and confidence our own federal and republican principles, our attachment to Union and representative government. Kindly separated by nature and a wide ocean from the exterminating havoc of one quarter of the globe; too high-minded to endure the degradations of the others; possessing a chosen country, with room enough for all descendants to the hundredth and thousandth generation; entertaining a due sense of our equal right to the use of our own faculties, to the acquisitions of our industry, to honor and confidence from our fellow-citizens, resulting not from birth but from our actions, and their sense of them; enlightened by a benign religion, professed, indeed, and practiced in various forms, yet all of them inculcating honesty, truth, temperance, gratitude, and the love of man; acknowledging and adoring an overruling Providence, which, by all its dispensations, proves that it delights in the happiness of man here, and his greater happiness hereafter; with all these blessings, what more is necessary to make us a happy and a prosperous people? Still one thing more, fellow-citizens,—a wise and frugal government, which shall restrain men from injuring one another, shall leave them otherwise free to regulate their own pursuits of industry and improvement, and shall not take from the mouth of labor the bread it has earned. This is the sum of good government, and this is necessary to close the circle of our felicities.

About to enter, fellow-citizens, on the exercise of duties which comprehend everything dear and valuable to you, it is proper you should understand what I deem the essential principles of this government, and, consequently, those which ought to shape its administration. I will compress them in the narrowest compass they will bear, stating the general principle, but not all its limitations. Equal and exact justice to all men, of whatever state or persuasion, religious or political; peace, commerce, and honest friendship with all nations, entangling alliances with none; the support of the State governments in all their rights, as the most competent administrations for our domestic concerns, and the surest bulwarks against anti-republican tendencies; the preservation of the General Government in its whole constitutional vigor, as the sheet anchor of our peace at home and safety abroad; a jealous care of the right of election by the people,—a mild and safe corrective of abuses which are lopped by the sword of revolution where peaceable remedies are unprovided; absolute acquiescence in the decisions of the majority,—the vital principle of republics, from which is no appeal but to force, the vital principle and immediate parent of despotism; a well-disciplined militia,—our best reliance in peace and for the first moments of war, till regulars may relieve them; the supremacy of the civil over the military authority; economy in the public expense, that labor may be lightly burdened; the honest payment of our debts and sacred preservation of the public faith; encouragement of agriculture, and of commerce as its handmaid; the diffusion of information and arraignment of all abuses at the bar of public reason; freedom of religion; freedom of the press; and freedom of persons under the protection of the *habeas corpus;* and trial by juries impartially selected. These principles form the bright constellation which has gone before us, and guided our steps through an age of revolution and reformation. The wisdom of our sages and blood of our heroes have been devoted to their attainment. They should be the creed of our political faith, the text of civic instruction, the touchstone by which to try the services of those we trust; and should we wander from them in moments of error or alarm, let us hasten to retrace our steps, and to regain the road which alone leads to peace, liberty, and safety.

I repair, then, fellow-citizens, to the post which you have assigned me. With experience enough in subordinate stations to know the difficulties of this, the greatest of all, I have learned to expect that it will rarely fall to the lot of imperfect man to retire from this station with the reputation and the favor which bring him into it. Without pretensions to that high confidence you reposed in our first and greatest revolutionary character, whose preëminent services had entitled him to the first place in his country's love, and destined for him the fairest page in the volume of faithful history, I ask so much confidence only as may give firmness and effect to the legal administration of your affairs. I shall often go wrong, through defect of judgment. When right, I shall often be thought wrong by those whose positions will not command a view of the whole ground. I ask your indulgence for my own errors, which will never be intentional; and your support against the errors of others, who may condemn what they would not, if seen in all its parts. The approbation implied by your suffrage is a great consolation to me for the past; and my future solicitude will be to retain the good opinion of those who have bestowed it in advance, to conciliate that of others by doing them all the good in my power, and to be instrumental to the happiness and freedom of all.

Relying, then, on the patronage of your good will, I advance with obedience to the work, ready to retire from it whenever you become sensible how much better choice it is in your power to make. And may that Infinite Power which rules the destinies of the universe, lead our councils to what is best, and give them a favorable issue for your peace and prosperity.

WILLIAM WIRT

William Wirt was born on November 8, 1772, in Bladensburg, Maryland, and died on February 18, 1834, in Washington.
His father, who was of German-Swiss parentage, came to the
colonies as an indentured servant but soon became a freeman
and acquired a modest property as a tavern-keeper. The boy
attended three "classical academies," of which the best was
James Hunt's, where he received a thorough training in Latin
and some instruction in other subjects. While tutoring in the
home of Benjamin Edwards, he read widely in eighteenth-
century literature, not only the earlier writers, but also Gray,
Young, Ossian, Sterne, Burke, Mrs. Radcliffe, Mackenzie, and
others. After a year's law reading with William P. Hunt, the
son of his former schoolmaster, he studied with Thomas
Swann at Leesburg, Virginia. In 1792 he began practising law
at Fairfax, Culpeper County, Virginia. He made many friends
and rose rapidly in his profession. In 1795 he married Mildred
Gilmer, the daughter of Dr. George Gilmer, a physician and
politician of eminence. The young couple lived at "Pen Park"
plantation, until Mrs. Wirt died in 1799. A few months later
he opened a law office in Richmond. After a few years of
moderate success and fast living, Wirt removed to Williamsburg, where he went to fill the newly-created post of Chancellor
for the eastern district of Virginia, with the title of "Judge of
the High Court of Chancery." In 1802 Wirt married Elizabeth
Gamble, the daughter of Colonel Robert Gamble, an officer
of the Revolution and a successful merchant of Richmond. In
1803 he resigned his post in the judiciary because of inadequate
salary and took his wife back to Richmond. During the summer months he wrote *The Letters of the British Spy*. In 1803
there was no magazine published in Richmond, but there were
four flourishing newspapers: the *Virginia Gazette*, the *Examiner*, the *Recorder*, and the *Virginia Argus*. Samuel Pleasants, Jr., the editor of the *Argus*, accepted for publication Wirt's
letters, which were published anonymously. The ten letters
were printed irregularly in numbers of the *Argus* from August
20 to September 4, 1803, and immediately reissued by Pleas-

ants in book form. These essays treat of such subjects as the
founding of Richmond, oratory, the ill-treatment of the Indians, characterizations of Monroe, Marshall, Edmund Randolph, and John Wickham, a blind preacher's eloquence,
praises of the *Spectator*, and the popularity of Edmund Burke.
The genre of pseudo-letters, in which a pretended foreigner
pictures and satirizes the country he visits, was a well-developed
literary form in Italian, English, and French literature. Well-
known examples are Montesquieu's *Les Lettres Persanes* (1721)
and Goldsmith's *Chinese Letters* (1760–1761). In writing his
letters Wirt was not an "old-fashioned gentleman," as literary
historians have persisted in calling him, but a "meek and harmless young man," in his own phrase, thirty years of age, and
widely read in contemporary English literature. There is no
evidence of "cultural lag" in the literary Richmond of the time.

In August, 1804, Wirt and his friends started a collaborative
series of essays called *The Rainbow*, published in the *Richmond
Enquirer*. Out of the remains of the *Examiner*, which had
ceased publication in 1803, Judge Spencer Roone established
the *Enquirer*, which rose to national prominence under the editorship of Thomas Ritchie. The ten essays which Wirt and his
friends called *The Rainbow*, ran from August 11, 1804, to October 20, 1804. Wirt was the probable author of "On the Utility
of Miscellaneous Essays," "On the Building of Towns," "Truth
and Eloquence: An Allegory," and "On the Establishment of
Charity Schools." *The Rainbow: First Series* was published by
Ritchie in book form in 1804. The nine essays of *The Rainbow:
Second Series* were published in the *Enquirer* from October 7,
1804, to April 6, 1805, but not in book form. Wirt probably
wrote "On Forensic Eloquence," "On Celibacy," "On Public
Schools," and "A Moral Picture." Only one number of *The
Rainbow: Third Series* was published, that in the *Enquirer* of
April 19, 1805.

In 1807 Wirt gained a national reputation for his legal adroit-
ness and his four-hour speech in the prosecution of Aaron
Burr. In the next year he was elected to the Virginia legislature
and took an active part in politics.

During 1810–1811 Wirt was the dictator of a literary group
in Richmond who stimulated each other in essay writing. Under the title of *The Old Bachelor* twenty-eight essays, written
by Wirt and six of his friends, were published in the *Enquirer*,

and five more essays were added to the volume published in 1814. Wirt wrote at least eighteen of these essays and parts of several others. The essayists imitated very closely many of the devices employed in the *Spectator*, but they also show an awareness of current Virginia life.

The year 1817 marks the "consummation of the two major phases in Wirt's career." For twelve years he and his friends had studied the career of Patrick Henry, and with deep satisfaction he produced *Sketches of the Life and Character of Patrick Henry*. Wirt's picture of Henry was intentionally partial, and the romantic rhapsody created the Patrick Henry legend which still persists. In the same year President Monroe appointed him Attorney General of the United States. He served also through the administration of John Quincy Adams, but resigned when Jackson was elected, because he was not in sympathy with his politics. In 1832 he protestingly allowed himself to be nominated on an Anti-Masonic ticket, vainly hoping that many would support him in their dislike of Jackson. During these years he attained considerable reputation as an orator and as a lawyer. In 1829 he took up his residence in Baltimore, and resumed private practice. He deepened his acquaintance with John Pendleton Kennedy, who dedicated *Swallow Barn* (1832) to him, and after Kennedy's death wrote his biography.

From DISCOURSE ON THE LIVES AND CHARACTERS OF THOMAS JEFFERSON AND JOHN ADAMS

Jefferson at Monticello

Let us now turn for a moment to the patriot of the South. The Roman moralist, in that great work which he has left for the government of man in all the offices of life, has descended even to prescribe the kind of habitation in which an honored and distinguished man should dwell. It should not, he says, be small, and mean, and sordid: nor, on the other hand, extended with profuse and wanton extravagance. It should be large enough to receive and accommodate the visiters which such a man never fails to attract, and suited in its ornaments, as well as its dimensions, to the character and fortune of the individual. Monticello has now lost its great charm. Those of you who have not already visited it, will not be very apt to visit it, hereafter: and, from the feelings which you cherish for its departed owner, I persuade myself that you will not be displeased with a brief and rapid sketch of that abode of domestic bliss, that temple of science. Nor is it, indeed, foreign to the express purpose of this meeting, which, in looking to "his life and character," naturally embraces his home and his domestic habits. Can any thing be indifferent to us, which was so dear to him, and which was a subject of such just admiration to the hundreds and thousands that were continually resorting to it, as to an object of pious pilgrimage?

The Mansion House at Monticello was built and furnished in the days of his prosperity. In its dimensions, its architecture, its arrangements, and ornaments, it is such a one as became the character and fortune of the man. It stands upon an elliptic plain, formed by cutting down the apex of a mountain; and, on the West, stretching away to the North and the South, it commands a view of the Blue Ridge for a hundred and fifty miles, and brings under the eye one of the boldest and most beautiful horizons in the world: while, on the East, it presents an extent of prospect, bounded only by the spherical form of the earth, in which nature seems to sleep in repose, as if to form one of her finest contrasts with the rude and rolling grandeur on the West. In the wide prospect, and scattered to the North and South, are several detached mountains, which contribute to animate and diversify this enchanting landscape; and among them, to the South, Williss' Mountain, which is so interestingly depicted in his Notes. From this summit, the Philosopher was wont to enjoy that spectacle, among the sublimest of Nature's operations, the looming of the distant mountains; and to watch the motions of the planets, and the greater revolution of the celestial sphere. From this summit, too, the patriot could look down, with uninterrupted vision, upon the wide expanse of the world around, for which he considered himself born; and upward, to the open and vaulted Heavens which he seemed to approach, as if to keep him continually in mind of his high responsibility. It is indeed a prospect in which you see and feel, at once, that nothing mean or little could live. It is a scene fit to nourish those great and high-souled principles which formed the elements of his character, and was a most noble and appropriate post, for such a sentinel, over the rights and liberties of man.

Approaching the house on the East, the visiter instinctively paused, to cast around one thrilling glance at this magnificent panorama: and then passed to the vestibule, where, if he had not been previously informed, he would immediately perceive that he was entering the house of no common man. In the spacious and lofty hall which opens before him, he marks no tawdry and unmeaning ornaments: but before, on the right, on the left, all around, the eye is struck and gratified with objects of science and taste, so classed and arranged as to produce their finest effect. On one side, specimens of sculpture set out, in such order, as to exhibit at a *coup d' œil*, the historical progress of that art; from the first rude attempts of the aborigines of our country, up to that exquisite and finished bust of the great patriot himself, from the master hand of Caracci. On the other side, the visiter sees displayed a vast collection of specimens of Indian art, their paintings, weapons, ornaments, and manufactures; on another, an array of the fossil productions of our country, mineral and animal; the polished remains of those colossal monsters that once trod our forests, and are no more; and a variegated display of the branching honors of those "monarchs of the waste," that still people the wilds of the American Continent.

From this hall he was ushered into a noble saloon, from which the glorious landscape of the West again bursts upon his view; and which, within, is hung thick around with the finest productions of the pencil—historical paintings of the most striking subjects from all countries, and all ages; the portraits of distinguished men and patriots, both of Europe and America, and medallions and engravings in endless profusion.

While the visiter was yet lost in the contemplation of these treasures of the arts and sciences, he was startled by the approach of a strong and sprightly step, and turning with instinctive reverence to the door of entrance, he was met by the tall, and animated, and stately figure of the patriot himself— his countenance beaming with intelligence and benignity, and his outstretched hand, with its strong and cordial pressure, confirming the courteous welcome of his lips. And then came that charm of manner and conversation that passes all description—so cheerful—so unassuming—so free, and easy, and frank, and kind, and gay—that even the young, and over-awed, and embarrassed visiter at once forgot his fears, and felt himself by the side of an old and familiar friend. There was no effort, no ambition in the conversation of the philosopher. It was as simple and unpretending as nature itself. And while in this easy manner he was pouring out instruction, like light from an inexhaustible solar fountain, he seemed continually to be asking, instead of giving information. The visiter felt himself lifted by the contact, into a new and nobler region of thought, and became surprised at his own buoyance and vigor. He could not, indeed, help being astounded, now and then, at those transcendant leaps of the mind, which he saw made without the slightest exertion, and the ease with which this wonderful man played with subjects which he had been in the habit of considering among the *argumenta crucis* of the intellect. And then there seemed to be no end to his knowledge. He was a thorough master of every subject that was touched. From the details of the humblest mechanic art, up to the highest summit of science, he was perfectly at his ease, and every where at home. There seemed to be no longer any *terra incognita* of the human understanding: for, what the visiter had thought so, he now found reduced to a familiar garden walk; and all this carried off so lightly, so playfully, so gracefully, so engagingly, that he won every heart that approached him, as certainly as he astonished every mind.

Mr. Jefferson was wont to remark, that he never left the conversation of Dr. Franklin without carrying away with him something new and useful. How often, and how truly, has the same remark been made of him. Nor is this wonderful, when we reflect, that, that mind of matchless vigor and versatility had been, all his life, intensely engaged in conversing with the illustrious dead, or following the march of science in every land, or bearing away, on its own steady and powerful wing, into new and unexplored regions of thought.

From THE LIFE OF PATRICK HENRY

On Monday, the 20th of March, 1775, the convention of delegates, from the several counties and corporations of Virginia, met for the second time. This assembly was held in the old church in the town of Richmond. Mr. Henry was a member of that body also. The reader will bear in mind the tone of the instructions given by the convention of the preceding year to their deputies in congress. He will remember that, while they recite with great feeling the series of grievances under which the colonies had laboured, and insist with firmness on their constitutional rights, they give, nevertheless, the most explicit and solemn pledge of their faith and true allegiance to his majesty King George III., and avow their determination to support him with their lives and fortunes, in the legal exercise of all his just rights and prerogatives. He will remember, that these instructions contain also, an expression of their sincere approbation of a connexion with Great Britain, and their ardent wishes for a return of that friendly intercourse from which this country had derived so much prosperity and happiness. These sentiments still influenced many of the leading members of the convention of 1775. They could not part with the fond hope that those peaceful days would again return which had shed so much light and warmth over the land; and the report of the king's gracious reception of the petition from congress tended to cherish and foster that hope, and to render them averse to any means of violence. But Mr. Henry saw things with a steadier eye and a deeper insight. His judgment was too solid to be duped by appearances; and his heart too firm and manly to be amused by false and flattering hopes.

He had long since read the true character of the British court,
and saw that no alternative remained for his country but abject submission or heroic resistance. It was not for a soul like
Henry's to hesitate between these courses. He had offered
upon the altar of liberty no divided heart. The gulf of war
which yawned before him was indeed fiery and fearful; but
he saw that the awful plunge was inevitable. The body of
the convention, however, hesitated. They cast around "a
longing, lingering look" on those flowery fields on which
peace, and ease, and joy, were still sporting; and it required all
the energies of a Mentor like Henry to push them from the
precipice, and conduct them over the stormy sea of the revolution, to liberty and glory.

The convention being formed and organized for business,
proceeded, in the first place, to express their unqualified approbation of the measures of congress, and to declare that they considered "this whole continent as under the highest obligations
to that respectable body, for the wisdom of their counsels, and
their unremitted endeavors to maintain and preserve inviolate
the just rights and liberties of his majesty's dutiful and loyal
subjects in America."

They next resolve, that "the warmest thanks of the convention, and of all the inhabitants of this colony, were due, and
that this just tribute of applause be presented to the worthy
delegates, deputed by a former convention to represent this
colony in general congress, for their cheerful undertaking and
faithful discharge of the very important trust reposed in them."

The morning of the 23d of March was opened, by reading
a petition and memorial from the assembly of Jamaica, to the
king's most excellent majesty: whereupon it was—"Resolved,
That the unfeigned thanks and most grateful acknowledg-
ments of the convention be presented to that very respectable
assembly, for the exceeding generous and affectionate part they
have so nobly taken, in the unhappy contest between Great
Britain and her colonies; and for their truly patriotic endeavours
to fix the just claims of the colonists upon the most permanent
constitutional principles:—that the assembly be assured, that

it is the most ardent wish of this colony, [and they were persuaded of the whole continent of North America,] to see a
speedy return of those halcyon days, when we lived a free and
happy people."

These proceedings were not adapted to the taste of Mr.
Henry; on the contrary, they were "gall and wormwood" to
him. The house required to be wrought up to a bolder tone.
He rose, therefore, and moved the following manly resolutions:—

"Resolved, That a well-regulated militia, composed of gentlemen and yeomen, is the natural strength and only security
of a free government; that such a militia in this colony would
for ever render it unnecessary for the mother-country to keep
among us, for the purpose of our defence, any standing army
of mercenary soldiers, always subversive of the quiet, and
dangerous to the liberties of the people, and would obviate
the pretext of taxing us for their support.

"That the establishment of such militia is, *at this time*,
peculiarly necessary, by the state of our laws, for the protection and defence of the country, some of which are already ex-
pired, and others will shortly be so: and that the known
remissness of government in calling us together in legislative
capacity, renders it too insecure, in this time of danger and distress, to rely that opportunity will be given of renewing them,
in general assembly, *or making any provision to secure our inestimable rights and liberties, from those further violations with
which they are threatened.*

"Resolved, therefore, *That this colony be immediately put
into a state of defence, and that
be a committee to prepare a plan for imbodying, arming, and dis-
ciplining such a number of men, as may be sufficient for that
purpose.*"

The alarm which such a proposition must have given to those
who had contemplated no resistance of a character more serious
than petition, non-importation, and passive fortitude, and who
still hung with suppliant tenderness on the skirts of Britain,
will be readily conceived by the reflecting reader. The shock

was painful. It was almost general. The resolutions were opposed as not only rash in policy, but as harsh and well nigh impious in point of feeling. Some of the warmest patriots of the convention opposed them. Richard Bland, Benjamin Harrison, and Edmund Pendleton, who had so lately drunk of the fountain of patriotism in the continental congress, and Robert C. Nicholas, one of the best as well as ablest men and patriots in the state, resisted them with all their influence and abilities.

They urged the late gracious reception of the congressional petition by the throne. They insisted that national comity, and much more filial respect, demanded the exercise of a more dignified patience. That the sympathies of the parent-country were now on our side. That the friends of American liberty in parliament were still with us, and had, as yet, had no cause to blush for our indiscretion. That the manufacturing interests of Great Britain, already smarting under the effects of our non-importation, co-operated powerfully toward our relief. That the sovereign himself had relented, and showed that he looked upon our sufferings with an eye of pity. "Was this a moment," they asked, "to disgust our friends, to extinguish all the conspiring sympathies which were working in our favour, to turn their friendship into hatred, their pity into revenge? And what was there, they asked, in the situation of the colony, to tempt us to this? Were we a great military people? Were we ready for war? Where were our stores—where were our arms—where our soldiers—where our generals—where our money, the sinews of war? They were nowhere to be found. In truth, we were poor—we were naked—we were defenceless. And yet we talk of assuming the front of war! of assuming it, too, against a nation, one of the most formidable in the world! A nation ready and armed at all points! Her navies riding triumphant in every sea; her armies never marching but to certain victory! What was to be the issue of the struggle we were called upon to court? What *could* be the issue, in the comparative circumstances of the two countries, but to yield up *this country* an easy prey to Great Britain, and to convert the illegitimate right which the British parliament now claimed, into a firm and indubitable right, *by conquest?* The measure might be brave; but it was the bravery of madmen. It had no pretension to the character of prudence; and as little to the grace of genuine courage. It would be time enough to resort to measures of *despair*, when every well-founded *hope* had entirely vanished."

To this strong view of the subject, supported as it was by the stubborn fact of the well-known helpless condition of the colony, the opponents of those resolutions superadded every topic of persuasion which belonged to the cause.

"The strength and lustre which we have derived from our connexion with Great Britain—the domestic comforts which we had drawn from the same source, and whose value we were now able to estimate by their loss—that ray of reconciliation which was dawning upon us from the east, and which promised so fair and happy a day:—with this they contrasted the clouds and storms which the measure now proposed was so well calculated to raise—and in which we should not have even the poor consolation of being pitied by the world, since we should have so needlessly and rashly drawn them upon ourselves."

These arguments and topics of persuasion were so well justified by the appearance of things, and were moreover so entirely in unison with that love of ease and quiet which is natural to man, and that disposition to hope for happier times, even under the most forbidding circumstances, that an ordinary man, in Mr. Henry's situation, would have been glad to compound with the displeasure of the house, by being permitted to withdraw his resolutions in silence.

Not so Mr. Henry. His was a spirit fitted to raise the whirlwind, as well as to ride in and direct it. His was that comprehensive view, that unerring prescience, that perfect command over the actions of men, which qualified him not merely to guide, but almost to create the destinies of nations.

He rose at this time with a majesty unusual to him in an exordium, and with all that self-possession by which he was so invariable distinguished. "No man," he said, "thought more

highly than he did of the patriotism, as well as abilities, of the
very worthy gentlemen who had just addressed the house. But
different men often saw the same subject in different lights;
and, therefore, he hoped it would not be thought disrespectful
to those gentlemen, if, entertaining as he did, opinions of a
character very opposite to theirs, he should speak forth *his*
sentiments freely, and without reserve. This," he said, "was
no time for ceremony. The question before this house was one
of awful moment to the country. For his own part, he considered it as nothing less than a question of freedom or slavery.
And in proportion to the magnitude of the subject, ought to be
the freedom of the debate. It was only in this way that they
could hope to arrive at truth, and fulfil the great responsibility
which they held to God and their country. Should he keep
back his opinions at such a time, through fear of giving offence,
he should consider himself as guilty of treason toward his
country, and of an act of disloyalty toward the majesty of
heaven, which he revered above all earthly kings."

"Mr. President," said he, "it is natural to man to indulge in
the illusions of hope. We are apt to shut our eyes against a
painful truth—and listen to the song of that siren, till she
transforms us into beasts. Is this," he asked, "the part of
wise men, engaged in a great and arduous struggle for liberty?
Were we disposed to be of the number of those, who having
eyes, see not, and having ears, hear not, the things which so
nearly concern their temporal salvation? For his part, whatever
anguish of spirit it might cost, *he* was willing to know the
whole truth; to know the worst, and to provide for it."

"He had," he said, "but one lamp by which his feet were
guided; and that was the lamp of experience. He knew of no
way of judging of the future but by the past. And judging by
the past, he wished to know what there had been in the conduct
of the British ministry for the last ten years to justify those
hopes with which gentlemen had been pleased to solace themselves and the house? Is it that insidious smile with which our
petition has been lately received? Trust it not, sir; it will prove
a snare to your feet. Suffer not yourselves to be betrayed with

a kiss. Ask yourselves how this gracious reception of our petition comports with those warlike preparations which cover our waters and darken our land. Are fleets and armies necessary to a work of love and reconciliation? Have we shown ourselves so unwilling to be reconciled, that force must be called in to win back our love? Let us not deceive ourselves, sir. These are the implements of war and subjugation—the last arguments to which kings resort. I ask gentlemen, sir, what means this martial array, if its purpose be not to force us to submission? Can gentlemen assign any other possible motive for it? Has Great Britain any enemy in this quarter of the world, to call for all this accumulation of navies and armies? No, sir, she has none. They are meant for us: they can be meant for no other. They are sent over to bind and rivet upon us those chains which the British ministry have been so long forging. And what have we [to] oppose to them? Shall we try argument? Sir, we have been trying that for the last ten years. Have we any thing new to offer upon the subject? Nothing. We have held the subject up in every light of which it is capable; but it has been all in vain. Shall we resort to entreaty and humble supplication? What terms shall we find, which have not been already exhausted? Let us not, I beseech you, sir, deceive ourselves longer. Sir, we have done every thing that could be done, to avert the storm which is now coming on. We have petitioned—we have remonstrated—we have supplicated—we have prostrated ourselves before the throne, and have implored its interposition to arrest the tyrannical hands of the ministry and parliament. Our petitions have been slighted; our remonstrances have produced additional violence and insult; our supplications have been disregarded; and we have been spurned, with contempt, from the foot of the throne. In vain, after these things, may we indulge the fond hope of peace and reconciliation. *There is no longer any room for hope.* If we wish to be free—if we mean to preserve inviolate those inestimable privileges for which we have been so long contending—if we mean not basely to abandon the noble struggle in which we have been so long engaged, and which we have

pledged ourselves never to abandon, until the glorious object
of our contest shall be obtained—we must fight!—I repeat
it, sir, we must fight! ! An appeal to arms and to the God of
hosts, is all that is left us!"

"They tell us, sir," continued Mr. Henry, "that we are weak
—unable to cope with so formidable an adversary. But when
shall we be stronger [?] Will it be the next week or the next
year? Will it be when we are totally disarmed, and when a
British guard shall be stationed in every house? Shall we
gather strength by irresolution and inaction? Shall we acquire the means of effectual resistance by lying supinely on our
backs, and hugging the delusive phantom of hope, until our
enemies shall have bound us hand and foot? Sir, we are not
weak, if we make a proper use of those means which the God
of nature hath placed in our power. Three millions of people
armed in the holy cause of liberty and in such a country as that
which we possess, are invincible by any force which our enemy
can send against us. Besides, sir, we shall not fight our battles
alone. There is a just God who presides over the destinies of
nations, and who will raise up friends to fight our battles for
us. The battle, sir, is not to the strong alone; it is to the
vigilant, the active, the brave. Besides, sir, we have no election. If we were base enough to desire it, it is now too late
to retire from the contest. There is no retreat but in submission and slavery! Our chains are forged. Their clanking
may be heard on the plains of Boston! The war is inevitable
—and let it come! ! I repeat it, sir, let it come! ! !

"It is vain, sir, to extenuate the matter. Gentlemen may cry,
peace, peace—but there is no peace. The war is actually begun! The next gale that sweeps from the north will bring to
our ears the clash of resounding arms! Our brethren are
already in the field! Why stand we here idle? What is it that
gentlemen wish? What would they have? Is life so dear, or
peace so sweet, as to be purchased at the price of chains and
slavery? Forbid it, Almighty God!—I know not what course
others may take; but as for me," cried he, with both his arms
extended aloft, his brows knit, every feature marked with the

resolute purpose of his soul, and his voice swelled to its boldest note of exclamation—"give me liberty, or give me death!"

He took his seat. No murmur of applause was heard. The effect was too deep. After the trance of a moment, several members started from their seats. The cry, "to arms!" seemed to quiver on every lip, and gleam from every eye! Richard H. Lee arose and supported Mr. Henry, with his usual spirit and elegance. But his melody was lost amid the agitations of that ocean, which the master-spirit of the storm had lifted up on high. That supernatural voice still sounded in their ears, and shivered along their arteries. They heard, in every pause, the cry of liberty or death. They became impatient of speech—their souls were on fire for action.

The resolutions were adopted; and Patrick Henry, Richard H. Lee, Robert C. Nicholas, Benjamin Harrison, Lemuel Riddick, George Washington, Adam Stevens, Andrew Lewis, William Christian, Edmund Pendleton, Thomas Jefferson, and Isaac Zane, esquires, were appointed a committee to prepare the plan called for by the last resolution. . . .

JOHN TAYLOR

John Taylor, commonly known as John Taylor of Caroline (Caroline County, Virginia), was born in 1753, in either Orange or Caroline County, and died at his plantation home, "Hazelwood," in 1824. When he was three years old, his father died, and he passed into the care of his kinsman, Edmund Pendleton. Private tutors, a private school, William and Mary College, and the law office of Edmund Pendleton constituted his education. His career as lawyer was barely started when the American Revolution began, and he immediately entered the army, serving, mainly in Virginia, New York, and Pennsylvania, and reaching the rank of major. Later he entered the Virginia militia as lieutenant colonel and fought with Lafayette against the Hessians.

In 1779 he entered the Virginia legislature, serving (with the exception of the year 1782) until 1785, and again from 1796 to 1800. Meantime, in 1783 he had married Lucy Penn, a cousin, the daughter of wealthy John Penn, who by the gift of a number of slaves to his son-in-law probably started him on his successful career as planter. Within a few years he owned three large plantations in Caroline County, each well-manned with slaves. He lived mainly at "Hazelwood," with a family that ultimately numbered eight, six sons and two daughters. His portrait shows him to have been a man of strong and attractive personality. He is said to have been tall and slender and red-haired.

Beginning in 1783, for a period of ten years, Taylor actively practiced law before the Virginia bar, making a fortune in the process, and winning distinction even in competition with such men as John Marshall, Patrick Henry, and Alexander Campbell. He first entered the United States Senate in 1792, serving until 1794, when he resigned. Back in the Virginia legislature, with the prestige of his Senate experience, he played an influential part in opposing the encroachments of special privilege and the growing dominance of the Federal government, itself increasingly dominated by the financial interests of the Northeast. He also enunciated his belief in the strengthening of states' rights as the only means of preventing "scission." In

1803 and in 1822 he again served briefly in the United States Senate, each time to fill out an incompleted term.

Taylor's thinking was both conditioned and stimulated by three potent factors: the time, the place, and the people. The time was the period leading up to the Revolution and the first decades of the young Republic, with its seething discussions, both practical and theoretical, of the problems of government, and with life-and-death decisions daily facing its leaders. The place was Virginia, wealthy colony, Revolutionary battle-ground, home of statesmen. The people were such men as Jefferson, Madison, Monroe, Marshall, Mason—with all of whom Taylor had intimate association. As Taylor himself says in his Preface to *An Inquiry into the Principles and Policy of the Government of the United States* (1814): "Having arrived at manhood just before the commencement of the Revolutionary war, the ardour of that controversy, a considerable intercourse with many of the chiefs who managed it, a service of three years in the continental army, of twelve in legislative bodies, and an experience of our policy both in poverty and affluence, inspired him [Taylor] with the opinions he has endeavoured to sustain."

With his power of incisive thinking and his gift for clear, vigorous, often brilliant expression, his greatest influence, even in his own day, lay in his writings. Of these, perhaps the most powerful is the *Inquiry*, mentioned above, written in reply to John Adams's *A Defense of the Constitutions of Government of the United States of America against the Attacks of Mr. Turgot* (1787), in which Taylor, as he said, attempted "an antidote against sliding into the English policy upon the skates of legislation." Whether or not Taylor misunderstood, as Adams claimed, the scope and application of the *Defence*, Taylor's *Inquiry*, in and of itself, in the opinion of Charles A. Beard, "deserves to rank among the two or three really historic contributions to political science which have been produced in the United States." The fact that it took Taylor over a quarter of a century to reply to Adams may account for this, as well as for Taylor's broadening the application of Adams's work beyond its author's intention.

Taylor's interests as a Virginia planter are embodied in *The Arator*, a series of essays, as he says, "originally offered to the publick in a newspaper, without foreseeing that they would appear in a book." The newspaper publication occurred in 1803. The essays appeared in book form in 1813. They consist mainly of descriptions of methods whereby the deplorable state of agriculture in Virginia might be improved, together with statements concerning the relations of agriculture to government. In them Taylor "predicted the ruin of the South under the operation of slavery and lamented the ruthless destruction of invaluable forests and naturally fertile soil." The following titles of essays show that Taylor did more than deplore agricultural conditions: "Inclosing," "Manuring," "Ploughing," "Sheep," "Hogs" (Taylor was much interested in hogs), "Live Fences," "Draining," "Tobacco." Taylor was an important agricultural authority in his day, and his *Arator* essays were highly praised by such men as John Adams, Jefferson, Edmund Ruffin, and Madison. To him the agricultural way of life was the good life. One cannot, however, channel him exclusively as an agrarian, unless one believes that the "moral principles" which he regarded as the essential foundation of good government are exclusively rural, or that democracy and agrarianism are completely and exclusively synonymous. In a letter to Thomas Jefferson [Richmond, 1798] he wrote, "It would be happy indeed for us if agriculture and farming still continued to be interesting subjects—but alas! Can we, when our house is on fire, be solicitous to save the kittens?"

THE ARATOR

Number 2: The Present State of Agriculture

A patient must know that he is sick, before he will take physick. A collection of a few facts, to ascertain the ill health of agriculture, is necessary to invigorate our efforts towards a cure. One, apparent to the most superficial observer, is, that our land has diminished in fertility.—Arts improve the work of nature—when they injure it, they are not arts, but barbarous customs. It is the office of agriculture, as an art, not to impoverish, but to fertilize the soil and make it more useful than in its natural state. Such is the effect of every species of agriculture, which can aspire to the character of an art.—Its object being to furnish man with articles of the first necessity, whatever defeats that object, is a crime of the first magnitude. Had men a power to obscure or brighten the light of the sun, by obscuring it, they would imitate the morality of diminishing the fertility of the earth. Is not one as criminal as the other? Yet it is a fact, that lands in their natural state, are more valuable, than those which have undergone our habit of agriculture, of which emigrations are complete proofs.

The decay of a multitude of small towns, so situated as to depend for support on unalterable districts, is another proof of the impoverishment of the soil. It is true, that a few large towns have grown up, but this is owing, not to an increased product, but to an increased pasture; whereas, in every case, where the pasture is limited, or isolated by local circumstances, small towns have sprung up, whilst the lands were fresh, and decayed, as they were worn out. I have no facts to ascertain certainly the products of agriculture at different periods relative to the number of people; such would furnish a demonstration of its state. But I have understood, that sixty-thousand hogsheads of tobacco were exported from Virginia, when it contained about one-fourth of its present population. If so, had the fertility of the country remained undiminished, Virginia ought now to export two hundred and forty thousand hogsheads, or an equivalent. In this estimate, every species of export except tobacco, is excluded at one epoch, and exports of every kind included at the other; yet the latter would fall far short of exhibiting the equivalent necessary to bring itself on a footing, as to agriculture, with the former. Two hundred and forty thousand hogsheads of tobacco, which, or an equivalent, Virginia would now export, if the state of agriculture had been as flourishing as it was sixty or seventy years past, at the present value, by which all our exports are rated, would be worth above seventeen millions of dollars; and supposing Virginia to furnish one seventh part of the native agricultural exports of the United States, these ought now to amount to one hundred and twenty millions of dollars, had the products of agriculture kept pace with the increase of population. If this statement is not exactly correct, enough of it certainly is so, to demonstrate a rapid impoverishment of the soil of the United States.

The decay of the culture of tobacco is testimony to this unwelcome fact. It is deserted because the lands are exhausted. To conceal from ourselves a disagreeable truth, we resort to the delusion, that tobacco requires new or fresh land; whereas every one acquainted with the plant knows, that its quantity and quality, as is the case with most or all plants, are both greatly improved by manured land, or land, the fertility of which has been artificially increased. Whole counties, comprising large districts of country, which once grew tobacco in great quantities, are now too sterile to grow any of moment; and the wheat crops substituted for tobacco, have already sunk to an average below profit.

From the mass of facts, to prove that the fertility of our country has been long declining, and that our agriculture is in a miserable state, I shall only select one more. The average of our native exports, is about forty millions of dollars annually. Some portion of this amount consists of manufactures, the materials for which are not furnished by agriculture; another, as is extensively the fact in the case of flour, has passed through the hands of the manufacturer. Of the first portion he receives the whole price, of the second a proportion. And a third portion of our products is obtained from the sea. Of the forty millions exported, agriculture, therefore, receives about thirty-five. The taxes of every kind, state and federal, may be estimated at twenty millions of dollars, of which agriculture pays at least fifteen, leaving twenty millions of her exports for her own use. Counting all the slaves, who ought to be counted both as sources of product and expense, in estimating the state of agriculture, the people of the United States may probably amount to about seven millions, and it may be fairly assumed, that the interest or occupation of six millions of these seven, is agricultural. Of the whole surplus product of agriculture exported, after deducting the taxes it pays, there remains for each individual a few cents above three dollars. Out of this mass of profit, he is to pay for the manufactures, luxuries and necessaries he consumes, not raised by himself; and the only remaining article to be carried to the credit of agriculture, is the small gain it derives from its domestick sales, not to itself, or from sales by one of its members to another, for that does not enrich it, but to other classes, such as manufacturers and soldiers. Against the former, agriculture is to be debited with the bounties she is made by law to pay them; against the latter, she has been already debited by deducting her taxes from her exports. Neither can be a source of much wealth or profit to her, because in one case she furnishes the money by taxation, and in the other by bounties, with which her products are purchased. It is, therefore, nearly true, that the income of agriculture is only three dollars per poll, and that this income is her whole fund for supplying her wants and extending her improvements. This estimate is infinitely more correct, than one drawn from individual wealth or poverty. To infer from the first, that every body might become rich, as a defence of our agricultural regimen, would be a conclusion as fallacious, as to infer from the second, that every body must become poor, as a proof of its badness. Extraordinary talents or industry will produce extraordinary effects. Instances of happiness or wealth under a despotism, do not prove that its regimen is calculated for general wealth or happiness. A system, commercial, political or agricultural, so wretched as not to exhibit cases of individual prosperity, has never appeared, because an universal scourge would be universally abhorred. It is not from partial, but general facts, that we can draw a correct knowledge of our agriculture. Even a personal view of the country, might deceive the thoughtless, because neither the shortness of life, nor the gradual impoverishment of land, are calculated to establish a visible standard for comparison. A man must be old and possess a turn for observation from his youth, to be able to judge correctly from this source. I have known many farms for above forty years, and though I think that all of them have been greatly impoverished, yet I rely more upon the general facts I have stated, for agreeing with Strickland in opinion, "that the agriculture of the United States affords only a bare subsistence—that the fertility of our lands is gradually declining—and that the agriculture of Virginia has arrived to the lowest state of degradation."

Number 3: The Political State of Agriculture

In collecting the causes which have contributed to the miserable agricultural state of the country, as it is a national calamity of the highest magnitude, we should be careful not to be blinded by partiality for our customs or institutions, nor corrupted by a disposition to flatter ourselves or others. I shall begin with those of a political nature. These are a secondary providence, which govern unseen the great interests of society; and if agriculture is bad and languishing in a country and climate, where it may be good and prosperous, no doubt remains with me, that political institutions have chiefly perpetrated the evil; just as they decide the fate of commerce.

The device of subjecting it to the payment of bounties to manufacturing, is an institution of this kind. This device is one item in every system for rendering governments too strong for nations. Such an object never was and never can be effected, except by factions legally created at the publick expense. The wealth transferred from the nation to such factions, devotes them to the will of the government, by which it is bestowed. They must render the service for which it was given, or it would be taken away. It is unexceptionably given to support a government against a nation, or one faction against another. Armies, loaning, banking, and an intricate treasury system, endowing a government with the absolute power of applying publick money, under the cover of nominal checks, are other devices of this kind. Whatever strength or wealth a government and its legal factions acquire by law, is taken from a nation; and whatever is taken from a nation, weakens and impoverishes that interest, which composes the majority. There, political oppression in every form must finally fall, however it may oscillate during the period of transit from a good to a bad government, so as sometimes to scratch factions. Agriculture being the interest covering a great majority of the people of the

United States, every device for getting money or power, hatched by a fellow-feeling or common interest, between a government and its legal creatures, must of course weaken and impoverish it.—Desertion, for the sake of reaping without labour, a share in the harvest of wealth and power, bestowed by laws at its expense, thins its ranks; an annual tribute to these legal factions, empties its purse; and poverty debilitates both its soil and understanding.

The device of protecting duties, under the pretext of encouraging manufactures, operates like its kindred, by creating a capitalist interest, which instantly seizes upon the bounty taken by law from agriculture; and instead of doing any good to the actual workers in wood, metals, cotton or other substances, it helps to rear up an aristocratical order, at the expense of the workers in earth, to unite with governments in oppressing every species of useful industry.

The products of agriculture and manufacturing, unshackled by law, would seek each for themselves, the best markets through commercial channels, but these markets would hardly ever be the same; protecting duties tie travellers together, whose business and interest lie in different directions. This ligature upon nature, will, like all unnatural ligatures, weaken or kill. The best markets of our agriculture lie in foreign countries, whilst the best markets of our manufactures are at home.— Our agriculture has to cross the ocean, and encounter a competition with foreign agriculture on its own ground. Our manufactures meet at home a competition with foreign manufactures. The disadvantages of the first competition, suffice to excite all the efforts of agriculture to save her life; the advantages of the second suffice gradually to bestow a sound constitution on manufacturing. But the manufacture of an aristocratical interest, under the pretext of encouraging work of a very different nature, may reduce both manufacturers and husbandmen, as Strickland says, is already effected in the case of the latter, to the "lowest state of degradation."

This degradation could never have been seen by a friend to either, who could afterwards approve of protecting duties. Let us take the article of wheat to unfold an idea of the disadvantages which have produced it. If wheat is worth 16s. sterling in England the 70 lb. the farmers sell it here at about 6s. sterling.—American agriculture then meets English agriculture in a competition, compelling her to sell at little more than one third of the price obtained by her rival. But American manufactures take the field against English on very different terms. These competitors meet in the United States. The American manufactures receive first, a bounty equal to the freight, commission and English taxes, upon their English rivals; and secondly, a bounty equal to our own necessary imposts. Without protecting duties, therefore, the American manufacturer gets for the same article, about 25 per cent. more, and the American agriculturalist about 180 per cent. less, than their English rivals. Protecting duties added to these inequalities, may raise up an order of masters for actual manufacturers, to intercept advantages too enormous to escape the vigilance of capital, impoverish husbandmen, and aid in changing a fair to a fraudulent government; but they will never make either of these intrinsically valuable classes richer, wiser or freer.

Number 60: The Rights of Agriculture

It is lamentable to confess, that this, to be a true, must be almost a negative number.—This most useful and virtuous interest, enjoys no rights, except in the United States; and there it enjoys no exclusive rights, whilst the few in which it shares are daily contracted by the various arts of ambition and avarice. Every where else, agriculture is a slave; here she is only a dupe. Abroad she is condemned by avowed force to feed voluptuousness, avarice and ambition; here, she is deluded by flattery and craft, during fits of joy or of fury, to squander her property, to mortgage her labourers, and to shackle her freedom. Abroad, she suffers contempt, and is sensible of her degradation; here, she is a blind Quixote, mounted on a wooden horse, and persuaded by the acclamations of her foes, that she is soaring to the stars, whilst she is ready to tumble into the dust.

Privileges are rearing by laws all around at her expense, and whilst she is taught to believe that they will only take from her a few inconsiderable slips, they will at length draw a spacious circumvallation, within which will gradually grow up a power, beyond her control. Tricks, as well as inventions, are daily fortified with legal bulwarks, called charters, to transfer her wealth, and to secure frauds against her efforts. Capital in every form, save that of agriculture, is fed by taxes and by bounties, which she must pay; whilst not a single bounty is paid to her by capital in any form; and instead of being favoured with some prizes in the lottery of society, she pays most, and is rewarded herself by the blanks of underwriting the projects of statesmen, and bearing the burdens of government.

The use of society, is to secure the fruits of his own industry and talents to each associator. Its abuse consists in artifice or force, for transferring those fruits from some partners to others. Of this abuse, that interest covering the majority of partners is the victim. And the difficulty of discriminating laws, transferring such fruits for the benefit of society, from those having in view the gratification of avarice and ambition, produces a sympathy and combination between these distinct kinds of law. As the members of the government, and members of legal frauds, both extract power and income from the majority, they are apt to coalesce; and each party to favour the designs of its ally, in their operations upon the common enemy. Hence governments love to create exclusive rights, and exclusive rights cling to governments. The ligament of parent and child, binds them together, and the power creating these abuses, must make them props for its support, or instruments for its subversion. Its election between these alternatives is certain, and society is thus unavoidably thrown into two divisions. One containing all those who pay, and the other those who receive contributions, required either for publick use, or to foster private avarice or ambition. Good government is graduated by this latter kind of contribution thus unfortunately allied to the former. The highest amount constitutes the worst, and the lowest, the best possible species of government. But as both are drawn from the majority of every society, whenever the agricultural interest covers that majority, this interest is the victim of the coalition; and as it almost universally does cover this majority, the agricultural interest is almost universally its slaves.

The consequences to agriculture will be demonstrated by converting this coalition between government and its creatures, or of all who receive tolls given by law, into a political pope, and placing in his mouth an address to agriculture, in a parody of Ernulphus's form of excommunication.

"May you be taxed in your land, your slaves, your houses, your carriages, your horses, your clothing, your liquors, your coffee, your tea, and your salt. May you be taxed by banks, by protecting duties, by embargoes, and by charters of a thousand different forms. May the exemption of your exports from taxation be removed, and may you then be taxed through your wheat, your corn, your tobacco, your cotton, your rice, your indigo, your sugar, your hemp, your live stock, your beef, your pork, your tar, pitch and turpentine, your onions, your cheese, and your potatoes. May you be taxed for the support of government, or to enrich exclusive or chartered interests, through every article you import, and through every article you export, by duties called protecting, but intended to take away your constitutional protection against taxation for the benefit of capitalists. May you be taxed through every article produced by your labour or necessary to your subsistence, comfort and pleasure, by exercises [excises]. And whilst every species of your products, and of your consumptions are thus taxed, may your capital, being visible, be moreover taxed in various modes. May all these taxes whether plain or intricate, (after deducting the small sum necessary to produce the genuine end of society) be employed in enriching capitalists, and buying soldiers, placemen and contractors, to make you submissive to usurpations, and as quiet under your burthens, as a martyr tied to the stake, under the flames. After you have been taxed as far as you can pay, may you by the bounty of God Almighty be moreover mortgaged up to your value or credit, for the benefit of the said coalition of capitalists. And finally, may none of this good and useful coalition, to whom is given the wealth of this world, as the kingdom of heaven is to the pope and his clergy, be taxed in their stock or principal held under any law or charter whatsoever; nor in their capital employed in any manufacture or speculation, nor in any profit drawn from such principal stock or capital; nor thro' any of their sinecures, salaries, contracts or incomes; but on the contrary, may such stock, principal, capital, profits, salaries, contracts, and sinecures, be constantly fostered by bounties in various injurious forms, to be paid by you, you damned dirty working, productive bitch, agriculture." Throughout the world, agriculture, like one of Ernulphus's contrite excommunicants, responds, amen, to this pious invocation.

Throughout the world, agriculture has enjoyed, and in England, continues to enjoy, one of the rights in which she has a share in the United States; that of a voice in elections.—And throughout the world, this right has been unable to shield her against an anathema, which prescribes for her as perfect a hell, as the formula of Ernulphus prescribes for his heretick. Let the agricultural interest of the United States, pause here and look around. Is a blind confidence in a right so universally ineffectual, a sufficient safeguard for its freedom and happiness? To me it seems, that an interest can never be long free, which blindly confides in a coalition, whose object it is to draw from that interest, power and wealth. That the major interest must be as cunning, as wise and as watchful, as the minor, or that the minor interest will enslave it. And that agriculture must as attentively keep her eyes upon the coalition, to avoid its operations upon her, as the coalition does upon agriculture, for the purpose of transfering to its members portions of her power and wealth, whenever she slumbers.

Hence have arisen the political suggestions to be found in these essays. I cannot discern much good in an improvement of agriculture, to get luxury, voluptuousness and tyranny for a few, and wretchedness for a multitude.—The best cultivated country in the world, abounds most in paupers and thieves. Agriculture must be a politician to avoid this fate;

and those who ridicule her pretensions to knowledge in this science, intend by persuading her to repose in a blind confidence, built upon the frail right of election, to expose her to it. How can she even judiciously elect, if she cannot or will not judge of publick measures, by the light of her own interest?

The moral consequence of this supineness or ignorance, is, that social happiness gradually becomes the dependant of a minority, and of course it is provided for, by continually subtracting from the happines of a majority. The visible immorality of this, demonstrates the virtue, as well as wisdom of suggestions designed to obstruct it.

The remaining right in which agriculture participates, in common with all other interests, having any thing to export, is bestowed by the constitutional prohibition of duties upon exports. This right originated in state jealousies, and not from a disposition to favour agriculture, but yet it is her best security, for the preservation of that portion of our government, which will longest be sensible of her elective influence; and its relinquishment will be the most fatal wound which can be inflicted on her. The coalition I have described will try every art in her most unguarded moments, to snatch it from her, and it will be the last relinquishment it will need. To determine whether her elective influence can bear further wounds, let agriculture re-survey the legislation of our whole term of independence, and compare the catalogues she may select, of laws for creating or fostering privileges and exclusive interests, with those for fostering herself; and let this comparison form the criterion for ascertaining her legislative influence. Thus only can she judiciously increase this influence, if it has settled too low, or diminish it, if it has raised too high. There is no fair mode of judging, except by these legislative acts. To infer, that the agricultural interest influences legislatures, because it chiefly elects them, would be like inferring, that the French nation influences the tribunate, because they wholly elect it. Let agriculture therefore hold fast the solitary security she enjoys in common with her industrious associates, against the ambitions of usurpers, and the avarice of capitalists, nor be deluded into the absurd notion, that it is wise to relinquish the only peculium of industry, for the sake of some temporary operation upon foreign nations, inevitably resulting upon herself in the form of retaliation, whilst the protection of exports against taxation, will be gone forever.

A NOTE:

Political Morality

Society is unavoidably made up of two interests only, in one of which all special and particular modifications of interest are included; namely, one subsisting by industry; the other, by law. Government is instituted for the happiness of the first interest, but belonging itself to the second, it is perpetually drawn towards that by the strongest cords. Therefore, unless the first is able very accurately to distinguish between laws calculated to do it a benefit or an injury, it must be gradually sacrificed to the appetites of the second, because government, a member of the second, legislates. All men enjoying honour, power or wealth by law, or striving to acquire either through that channel, are like coin struck with the same dies. The engravers, avarice and ambition, constantly mark the same etching, and the aqua fortis, self-interest, indeliably [indelibly] imprints it on the human mind. From this fact, the preference of a republican government is deduced, as being calculated for checking the natural disposition of legislatures or the government, to favour the minor class, composed of legal or factitious interests, at the expense of the major class, composed of natural interests; including all who subsist, not by means of legal donations, but by useful talents in every form, such as those employed in agriculture, manufacturing, tuition, physick, and all trades and scientifick professions. The propensity of law to sacrifice the great or natural interest of nations, to the class of little or factitious interests, arises from two causes; one, the government being the matrix of the latter, views her progeny with the eyes of an owl, and considers them as beautiful; the other, that although law can enable the small class to live on the great one, it cannot enable the great class to live upon the small one; uniting to produce this propensity in a degree so violent, that mankind have pronounced it irresistible, except by a countervailing union between strong republican fetters upon government, and a degree of political knowledge in the major class, sufficient to prevent these fetters from being broken by laws. The remedy is so rare, that many honest men doubt of its existence; and have concluded in despair, that the major class or general interest of a nation, must inevitably become the slave of the minor or factitious interest in some mode. Others believe, that by exciting the general interest to watch, to think, and to judge for itself, its intellect will be brightened, and its rights preserved. But all agree that neither any individual nor any interest dictated to by another, can prosper; and that political ignorance universally implies political slavery. Election has no power beyond a charter or a commission, to prevent the elected from being transferred by his election from the great class of general interest, to the little class of factitious or legal interest; on the contrary, the structure of republican government is raised upon the principle, that it necessarily transfers him from one to the other, at least in most instances. This is unanimously admitted by the elected themselves. They separate into two parties, called inns and outs. The inns say that the outs are influenced by a desire to get in, and the outs, that the inns are influenced by a desire to keep in. Agreeing that both belong to the minor class, and neither to the major class, which can neither get in nor keep in; these two members of the minor class vote in constant opposition, because they stand in each other's way, which could not possibly happen if they were genuine members of the general interest class. How then can the major class expect happiness from this species of political gambling for a rich stake which it pays, and the gamblers alternately win, if it has no skill in the game?

Agriculture is the most powerful member of the class constituting the general interest, but if her sons are too ignorant to use this power with discretion (like a body of elephants thrown into confusion in a battle) they rush in every direction, trampling down friends and foes for a short time, and inevitably become an easy prey to their enemies. As the most powerful individual constituting the major class of general interest, the political ignorance of agriculture, would of course destroy the rights of the whole class. If she divides herself between any of the members of the inferiour class, each of her moieties enlist under an aristocratical or monarchical power, whether it be called executive, legislative, credit or charter, and the member obtaining the victory by her aid, becomes her master. Just as in a division of her forces between a king and a nobility, the king or the nobility and not agriculture, gains a victory, both over her, and over all her weaker associates in the class of the general interest.

As there are two classes of interest only in society, there are also only two political codes, each appropriated by nature to one class. The code of the minor class is constituted of intrigues and stratagems to beguile the major class, and to advance the separate interests of the individuals, parties and legal combinations, of which the minor class is compounded.—The code of the major class consists of good moral principles, by which the national rights and happiness can only be preserved. The guilt of offensive war, and the virtue of defensive, are the essential qualities of the respective codes. One is compounded of the best, and the other of the worst qualities of human nature; and the members of the general or natural interest of society, can never avoid oppression nor sustain a just and free government unless they are skilled in both.

As the extension of comfort and happiness is the only good motive for writing an agricultural book, whatever would defeat the end belongs to the subject; and as a legal profusion in overstocking a nation with members of the minor class, is the solitary process for enslaving it, unless the major class understands the sublime branch of ethicks, namely, political morality, it cannot counteract this process. Thus only can it distinguish between laws and projects calculated for benefitting or injuring the nation. This science only can prevent the liberty, the virtue, the happiness, the bravery and the talents of the nation from being extinguished. The treasury of the United States has been cited as a proper subject for its application. If the agricultural and other members of the major class should discern that the president had become a king of the treasury, surrounded with nominal checks and balances appointed by himself; if they should discern that the representatives of the people were convinced of a great waste of publick money, and yet ignorant of the modes by which it was effected; if they should recollect the consequences of such an errour in the English form of government; and if they knew that nations were enslaved by a corrupting application of their own treasure, would not the correction of the evil be founded in genuine political morality, and be plainly adverse to the erroneous and flagitious political code of the minor class. . . .

JOHN CALDWELL CALHOUN

John Caldwell Calhoun was born March 18, 1782, at Calhoun Creek, near Little River, Abbeville District, South Carolina, and died March 31, 1850, in Washington. He was of Scotch-Irish ancestry, the fourth son of Patrick Calhoun and Martha Caldwell. Although slaves were few in the region, Patrick Calhoun was prosperous enough to own a score or more. When John was thirteen years old, he entered the school, in Columbus County, Georgia, of Dr. Moses Waddel, who had married Catherine Calhoun, the boy's sister. Within a year his father died, and he was summoned home, where he managed the plantation successfully for several years. After Dr. Waddel had established a new academy in the district, young Calhoun studied Latin and mathematics under him, in preparation for collegiate and legal education. Entering the junior class of Yale College in 1802, he was graduated in 1804. He studied law in Tapping Reeve's school at Litchfield, Connecticut, and in a law office at Charleston, being admitted to the bar in 1807.

In 1811 Calhoun married his cousin, Floride Calhoun; they had nine children. In 1825 he established a plantation named Fort Hill, in the Pendleton district, where Clemson College is now located.

His fine mind and character had early impressed his neighbors at Abbeville, and after his admission to the bar in 1807 he was promptly sent to the state legislature for two years. Elected to Congress in 1810, he joined with Clay and other political leaders of the new generation in forcing Madison into the War of 1812. His legislative efforts were so vigorous in the prosecution of the war that he was called "the young Hercules who carried the war on his shoulders." In the years following the war he advocated an increased navy and standing army, internal improvements, such as public roads and canals, the encouragement of manufacturing by a protective tariff, a national bank, and various other measures that tended to strengthen the national government, "thus occupying," says U. B. Phillips, "a position from which he afterwards retreated." Appointed Secretary of War by Monroe in 1817, he served for over seven years with distinction, improving the efficiency of the army and reorganizing the bureaus under the war department. From 1822 until his death he was actually or potentially a candidate for the presidency. In the political scramble of 1824 he was elected Vice-President under John Quincy Adams, and in 1829 he was re-elected, serving under Jackson. His hope had been to succeed to the presidency in 1828, but a quarrel with Jackson, who had a large following, made even the nomination impossible. During his vice-presidency he altered his views about the tariff, and in 1827 he defeated a higher-tariff bill by his casting vote. At the request of W. C. Preston and other South Carolinians, he wrote the "South Carolina Exposition," in which he asserted the unconstitutionality of a federal tariff law and maintained the power of a state "to estop the enforcement of an unconstitutional act." After South Carolina passed the ordinance of nullification in November, 1832, he resigned the vice-presidency in order to be appointed to the Senate where he might do effective work for his state. He opposed Webster in powerful debate and joined with Clay in securing a compromise tariff act. In 1843 he retired from the Senate, served for a year (1844–1845) as Secretary of State under Tyler, and returned to the Senate in 1845, where he continued until his death. His views on the slavery issue were modified during his career in Washington. After the settling of the Missouri question in 1820 he was hopeful of the prospect "that a question which has so deeply agitated this country will be settled forever." Soon, however, he became convinced that slavery was a permanent institution in the South and that each new state in the West should be open to slavery. The powerful expression of his theories of government are in the *Discourse on Government* and *Discourse on the Constitution of the United States*, which were published posthumously. Calhoun's last address in the Senate, which was read by Senator Mason of Virginia, was a vigorous reply to Clay's Omnibus Bill. Three days after hearing Webster's great speech of compromise, he still thought it "difficult to see how two peoples so different and hostile can exist together in one common Union." Ten years later came the war.

From A DISCOURSE ON GOVERNMENT

To perfect society, it is necessary to develope the faculties, intellectual and moral, with which man is endowed. But the main spring to their development, and, through this, to progress, improvement and civilization, with all their blessings, is the desire of individuals to better their condition. For, this purpose, liberty and security are indispensable. Liberty leaves each free to pursue the course he may deem best to promote his interest and happiness, as far as it may be compatible with the primary end for which government is ordained;—while security gives assurance to each, that he shall not be deprived of the fruits of his exertions to better his condition. These combined, give to this desire the strongest impulse of which it is susceptible. For, to extend liberty beyond the limits assigned, would be to weaken the government and to render it incompetent to fulfil its primary end,—the protection of society against dangers, internal and external. The effect of this would be, insecurity; and, of insecurity,—to weaken the impulse of individuals to better their condition, and thereby retard progress and improvement. On the other hand, to extend the powers of the government, so as to contract the sphere assigned to liberty, would have the same effect, by disabling individuals in their efforts to better their condition.

Herein is to be found the principle which assigns to power and liberty their proper spheres, and reconciles each to the other under all circumstances. For, if power be necessary to secure to liberty the fruits of its exertions, liberty, in turn, repays power with interest, by increasing population, wealth, and other advantages, which progress and improvement bestow on the community. By thus assigning to each its appropriate sphere, all conflicts between them cease; and each is made to co-operate with and assist the other, in fulfilling the great ends for which government is ordained.

But the principle, applied to different communities, will assign to them different limits. It will assign a larger sphere to power and a more contracted one to liberty, or the reverse, according to circumstances. To the former, there must ever be allotted, under all circumstances, a sphere sufficiently large to protect the community against danger from without and violence and anarchy within. The residuum belongs to liberty. More cannot be safely or rightly allotted to it.

But some communities require a far greater amount of power than others to protect them against anarchy and external dangers; and, of course, the sphere of liberty in such, must be proportionally contracted. The causes calculated to enlarge the one and contract the other, are numerous and various. Some are physical;—such as open and exposed frontiers, surrounded by powerful and hostile neighbors. Others are moral;—such as the different degrees of intelligence, patriotism, and virtue among the mass of the community, and their experience and proficiency in the art of self-government. Of these, the moral are, by far, the most influential. A community may possess all the necessary moral qualifications, in so high a degree, as to be capable of self-government under the most adverse circumstances; while, on the other hand, another may be so sunk in ignorance and vice, as to be incapable of forming a conception of liberty, or of living, even when most favored by circumstances, under any other than an absolute and despotic government.

The principle, in all communities, according to these numerous and various causes, assigns to power and liberty their proper spheres. To allow to liberty, in any case, a sphere of action more extended than this assigns, would lead to anarchy; and this, probably, in the end, to a contraction instead of an enlargement of its sphere. Liberty, then, when forced on a people unfit for it, would, instead of a blessing, be a curse; as it would, in its reaction, lead directly to anarchy,—the greatest of all curses. No people, indeed, can long enjoy more liberty than that to which their situation and advanced intelligence and morals fairly entitle them. If more than this be allowed, they must soon fall into confusion and disorder,—to be followed, if not by anarchy and despotism, by a change to a form of government more simple and absolute; and, therefore, better suited to their condition. And hence, although it may be true, that a people may not have as much liberty as they are fairly entitled to, and are capable of enjoying,—yet the reverse is unquestionably true,—that no people can long possess more than they are fairly entitled to.

Liberty, indeed, though among the greatest of blessings, is not so great as that of protection; inasmuch, as the end of the former is the progress and improvement of the race,—while that of the latter is its preservation and perpetuation. And hence, when the two come into conflict, liberty must, and ever ought, to yield to protection; as the existence of the race is of greater moment than its improvement.

It follows, from what has been stated, that it is a great and dangerous error to suppose that all people are equally entitled to liberty. It is a reward to be earned, not a blessing to be gratuitously lavished on all alike;—a reward reserved for the intelligent, the patriotic, the virtuous and deserving;—and not a boon to be bestowed on a people too ignorant, degraded and vicious, to be capable either of appreciating or of enjoying it. Nor is it any disparagement to liberty, that such is, and ought to be the case. On the contrary, its greatest praise,—its proudest distinction is, that an all-wise Providence has reserved it, as the noblest and highest reward for the development of our faculties, moral and intellectual. A reward more appropriate than liberty could not be conferred on the deserving;—nor a punishment inflicted on the undeserving more just, than to be subject to lawless and despotic rule. This dispensation seems to be the result of some fixed law;—and every effort to disturb or defeat it, by attempting to elevate a people in the scale of liberty, above the point to which they are entitled to rise, must ever prove abortive, and end in disappointment. The progress of a people rising from a lower to a higher point in the scale of liberty, is necessarily slow;—and by attempting to precipitate, we either retard, or permanently defeat it.

There is another error, not less great and dangerous, usually associated with the one which has just been considered. I refer to the opinion, that liberty and equality are so intimately united, that liberty cannot be perfect without perfect equality.

That they are united to a certain extent,—and that equality of citizens, in the eyes of the law, is essential to liberty in a popular government, is conceded. But to go further, and make equality of *condition* essential to liberty, would be to destroy both liberty and progress. The reason is, that inequality of condition, while it is a necessary consequence of liberty is, at the same time, indispensable to progress. In order to understand why this is so, it is necessary to bear in mind, that the main spring to progress is, the desire of individuals to better their condition; and that the strongest impulse which can be given to it is, to leave individuals free to exert themselves in the manner they may deem best for that purpose, as far at least as it can be done consistently with the ends for which government is ordained,—and to secure to all the fruits of their exertions. Now, as individuals differ greatly from each other, in intelligence, sagacity, energy, perseverance, skill, habits of industry and economy, physical power, position and opportunity,—the necessary effect of leaving all free to exert themselves to better their condition, must be a corresponding inequality between those who may possess these qualities and advantages in a high degree, and those who may be deficient in them. The only means by which this result can be prevented are, either to impose such restrictions on the exertions of those who may possess them in a high degree, as will place them on a level with those who do not; or to deprive them of the fruits of their exertions. But to impose such restrictions on them would be destructive of liberty,—while, to deprive them of the fruits of their exertions, would be to destroy the desire of bettering their condition. It is, indeed, this inequality of condition between the front and rear ranks, in the march of progress, which gives so strong an impulse to the former to maintain their position, and to the latter to press forward into their files. This gives to progress its greatest impulse. To force the front rank back to the rear, or attempt to push forward the rear into line with the front, by the interposition of the government, would put an end to the impulse, and effectually arrest the march of progress.

These great and dangerous errors have their origin in the prevalent opinion that all men are born free and equal;—than which nothing can be more unfounded and false. It rests upon the assumption of a fact, which is contrary to universal observation, in whatever light it may be regarded. It is, indeed, difficult to explain how an opinion so destitute of all sound reason, ever could have been so extensively entertained, unless we regard it as being confounded with another, which has some semblance of truth;—but which, when properly understood, is not less false and dangerous. I refer to the assertion, that all men are equal in the state of nature; meaning, by a state of nature, a state of individuality, supposed to have existed prior to the social and political state; and in which men lived apart and independent of each other. If such a state ever did exist, all men would have been, indeed, free and equal in it; that is, free to do as they pleased, and exempt from the authority or control of others—as, by supposition, it existed anterior to society and government. But such a state is purely hypothetical. It never did, nor can exist; as it is inconsistent with the preservation and perpetuation of the race. It is, therefore, a great misnomer to call it *the state of nature*. Instead of being the natural state of man, it is, of all conceivable states, the most opposed to his nature—most repugnant to his feelings, and most incompatible with his wants. His natural state is, the social and political—the one for which his Creator made him, and the only one in which he can preserve and perfect his race. As, then, there never was such a state as the, so called, state of nature, and never can be, it follows, that men, instead of being born in it, are born in the social and political state; and of course, instead of being born free and equal, are born subject, not only to parental authority, but to the laws and institutions of the country where born, and under whose protection they draw their first breath. With these remarks, I return from this digression, to resume the thread of the discourse.

It follows, from all that has been said, that the more perfectly a government combines power and liberty,—that is, the greater its power and the more enlarged and secure the liberty of individuals, the more perfectly it fulfils the ends for which government is ordained. To show, then, that the government of the concurrent majority is better calculated to fulfil them than that of the numerical, it is only necessary to explain why the former is better suited to combine a higher degree of power, and a wider scope of liberty than the latter. I shall begin with the former.

The concurrent majority, then, is better suited to enlarge and secure the bounds of liberty, because it is better suited to prevent government from passing beyond its proper limits, and to restrict it to its primary end,—the protection of the community. But in doing this, it leaves, necessarily, all beyond it open and free to individual exertions; and thus enlarges and secures the sphere of liberty to the greatest extent which the condition of the community will admit, as has been explained. The tendency of government to pass beyond its proper limits is what exposes liberty to danger, and renders it insecure; and it is the strong counteraction of governments of the concurrent majority to this tendency which makes them so favorable to liberty. On the contrary, those of the numerical, instead of opposing and counteracting this tendency, add to it increased strength, in consequence of the violent party struggles incident to them, as has been fully explained. And hence their encroachments on liberty, and the danger to which it is exposed under such governments.

So great, indeed, is the difference between the two in this respect, that liberty is little more than a name under all governments of the absolute form, including that of the numerical majority; and can only have a secure and durable existence under those of the concurrent or constitutional form. The latter, by giving to each portion of the community which may be unequally affected by its action, a negative on the others, prevents all partial or local legislation, and restricts its action to such measures as are designed for the protection and the good of the whole. In doing this, it secures, at the same time, the rights and liberty of the people, regarded individually; as each portion consists of those who, whatever may be the diversity of interests among themselves, have the same interest in reference to the action of the government.

Such being the case, the interest of each individual may be safely confided to the majority, or voice of his portion, against that of all others, and, of course, the government itself. It is only through an organism which vests each with a negative, in some one form or another, that those who have like interests in preventing the government from passing beyond its proper sphere, and encroaching on the rights and liberty of individuals, can co-operate peaceably and effectually in resisting the encroachments of power, and thereby preserve their rights and liberty. Individual resistance is too feeble, and the difficulty of concert and co-operation too great unaided by such an organism, to oppose, successfully, the organized power of government, with all the means of the community at its disposal; especially in populous countries of great extent; where concert and co-operation are almost impossible. Even when the oppression of the government comes to be too great to be borne, and force is resorted to in order to overthrow it, the result is rarely ever followed by the establishment of liberty. The force sufficient to overthrow an oppressive government is usually sufficient to establish one equally, or more, oppressive in its place. And hence, in no governments, except those that rest on the principle of the concurrent or constitutional majority, can the people guard their liberty against power; and hence, also, when lost, the great difficulty and uncertainty of regaining it by force.

It may be further affirmed that, being more favorable to the enlargement and security of liberty, governments of the concurrent, must necessarily be more favorable to progress, development, improvement, and civilization,—and, of course, to the increase of power which results from, and depends on these, than those of the numerical majority. That it is liberty which gives to them their greatest inpulse, has already been shown; and it now remains to show, that these, in turn, contribute greatly to the increase of power.

In the earlier stages of society, numbers and individual prowess constituted the principal elements of power. In a more advanced stage, when communities had passed from the barbarous to the civilized state, discipline, strategy, weapons of increased power, and money,—as the means of meeting increased expense,—became additional and important elements. In this stage, the effects of progress and improvement on the increase of power, began to be disclosed; but still numbers and personal prowess were sufficient, for a long period, to enable barbarous nations to contend successfully with the civilized,— and, in the end, to overpower them,—as the pages of history abundantly testify. But a more advanced progress, with its numerous inventions and improvements, has furnished new and far more powerful and destructive implements of offence and defence, and greatly increased the intelligence and wealth, necessary to engage the skill and meet the increased expense required for their construction and application to purposes of war. The discovery of gunpowder, and the use of steam as an impelling force, and their application to military purposes, have for ever settled the question of ascendency between civilized and barbarous communities, in favor of the former. Indeed, these, with other improvements, belonging to the present state of progress, have given to communities the most advanced, a superiority over those the least so, almost as great as that of the latter over the brute creation. And among the civilized, the same causes have decided the question of superiority, where other circumstances are nearly equal, in favor of those whose governments have given the greatest impulse to development, progress, and improvement; that is, to those whose liberty is the largest and best secured. Among these, England and the United States afford striking examples, not only of the effects of liberty in increasing power, but of the more perfect adaptation of governments founded on the principle of the concurrent, or constitutional majority, to enlarge and secure liberty. They are both governments of this description, as will be shown hereafter.

But in estimating the power of a community, moral, as well

as physical causes, must be taken into the calculation; and in estimating the effects of liberty on power, it must not be over-looked, that it is, in itself, an important agent in augmenting the force of moral, as well as of physical power. It bestows on a people elevation, self-reliance, energy, and enthusiasm; and these combined, give to physical power a vastly augmented and almost irresistible impetus.

These, however, are not the only elements of moral power. There are others, and among them harmony, unanimity, de-votion to country, and a disposition to elevate to places of trust and power, those who are distinguished for wisdom and experience. These, when the occasion requires it, will, without compulsion, and from their very nature, unite and put forth the entire force of the community in the most efficient manner, without hazard to its institutions or its liberty.

All these causes combined, give to a community its maximum of power. Either of them, without the other, would leave it comparatively feeble. But it cannot be necessary, after what has been stated, to enter into any further explanation or argu-ment in order to establish the superiority of governments of the concurrent majority over the numerical, in developing the great elements of moral power. So vast is this superiority, that the one, by its operation, necessarily leads to their develop-ment, while the other as necessarily prevents it,—as has been fully shown.

From the SPEECH ON THE SLAVERY QUESTION,
DELIVERED IN THE SENATE
MARCH 4TH, 1850

I have, Senators, believed from the first that the agitation of the subject of slavery would, if not prevented by some timely and effective measure, end in disunion. Entertaining this opinion, I have, on all proper occasions, endeavored to call the attention of both the two great parties which divide the country to adopt some measure to prevent so great a disaster, but without success. The agitation has been permitted to proceed, with almost no attempt to resist it, until it has reached a point when it can no longer be disguised or denied that the Union is in danger. You have thus had forced upon you the greatest and gravest question that can ever come under your consideration—How can the Union be preserved? . . .

There is but one way by which it can with any certainty; and that is, by a full and final settlement, on the principle of justice, of all the questions at issue between the two sections. The South asks for justice, simple justice, and less she ought not to take. She has no compromise to offer but the constitution; and no concession or surrender to make. She has already surrendered so much that she has little left to surrender. Such a settlement would go to the root of the evil, and remove all cause of discontent; by satisfying the South she could remain honorably and safely in the Union, and thereby restore the harmony and fraternal feelings between the sections, which existed anterior to the Missouri agitation. Nothing else can, with any certainty, finally and forever settle the questions at issue, terminate agitation, and save the Union.

But can this be done? Yes, easily; not by the weaker party, for it can of itself do nothing—not even protect itself—but by the stronger. The North has only to will it to accomplish it —to do justice by conceding to the South an equal right in the acquired territory, and to do her duty by causing the stipulations relative to fugitive slaves to be faithfully fulfilled—to cease the agitation of the slave question, and to provide for the insertion of a provision in the constitution, by an amendment, which will restore to the South, in substance, the power she possessed of protecting herself, before the equilibrium between the sections was destroyed by the action of this Government. There will be no difficulty in devising such a provision—one that will protect the South, and which, at the same time, will improve and strengthen the Government, instead of impairing and weakening it.

But will the North agree to this? It is for her to answer the question. But, I will say, she cannot refuse, if she has half the love of the Union which she professes to have, or without justly exposing herself to the charge that her love of power and aggrandizement is far greater than her love of the Union. At all events, the responsibility of saving the Union rests on the North, and not on the South. The South cannot save it by any act of hers, and the North may save it without any sacrifice whatever, unless to do justice, and to perform her duty under the Constitution, should be regarded by her as a sacrifice.

It is time, Senators, that there should be an open and manly avowal on all sides, as to what is intended to be done. If the question is not now settled, it is uncertain whether it ever can hereafter be; and we, as the representatives of the States of this Union, regarded as governments, should come to a distinct understanding as to our respective views, in order to ascertain whether the great questions at issue can be settled or not. If you, who represent the stronger portion, cannot agree to settle them on the broad principle of justice and duty, say so; and let the States we both represent agree to separate and part in peace. If you are unwilling we should part in peace, tell us so, and we shall know what to do, when you reduce the question to submission or resistance. If you remain silent, you will compel us to infer by your acts what you intend. In that case, California will become the test question. If you admit her, under all the difficulties that oppose her admission, you compel us to infer that you intend to exclude us from the whole of the acquired territories, with the intention of destroying, irretrievably, the equilibrium between the two sections. We would be blind not to perceive in that case, that your real objects are power and aggrandizement, and infatuated not to act accordingly.

I have now, Senators, done my duty in expressing my opinions fully, freely, and candidly, on this solemn occasion. In doing so, I have been governed by the motives which have governed me in all the stages of the agitation of the slavery question since its commencement. I have exerted myself, during the whole period, to arrest it, with the intention of saving the Union, if it could be done; and if it could not, to save the section where it has pleased Providence to cast my lot, and which I sincerely believe has justice and the constitution on its side. Having faithfully done my duty to the best of my ability, both to the Union and my section, throughout this agitation, I shall have the consolation, let what will come, that I am free from all responsibility.

HUGH SWINTON LEGARÉ

Hugh Swinton Legaré was born on John's Island in the Ashley River near Charleston, January 2, 1797, and died in Boston, June 20, 1843. His father was of Huguenot descent, and his mother was Scotch. His father died when he was two years old, leaving the task of the plantation and family to his mother. His older sister, Mary, was closely associated with Legaré all his life. In his fourth year he was poisoned by an inoculation of smallpox, which "wasted and stunted" him, leaving him with crippled limbs. His biographers, however, speak of his well-developed body and of his fine head and face. His infirmity centered his attention upon reading and study and led to his development as a remarkable classical and legal scholar, but it also fostered sensitiveness and seclusion. From the ages of ten to thirteen he studied under Mitchell King, head of the Charleston High School, which later became the College of Charleston. His mother sent him, against his wishes, to the famous Willington Academy, established by Dr. Moses Waddel. She may have agreed with a character in Longstreet's *Master William Mitten:* "That school fills my notion of what a boy's school ought to be. Plain dressing, plain eating, hard working, close studying, close watching, and when needful good whipping." But young Legaré spent an unhappy year there, disliking the order of routine, although he recognized the thorough classical training he was receiving. John C. Calhoun (*q.v.*) had attended Waddel's school and had approved of the Spartan system, which encouraged "emulation to excel," but Legaré never liked Calhoun or his later politics. James L. Petigru, another of Waddel's famous students, became the lifelong friend of Legaré. Augustus Baldwin Longstreet (*q.v.*), a later student, was always enthusiastically approving of Dr. Waddel. In 1811–1814 Legaré attended South-Carolina College, at Columbia, now the University of South Carolina, where he studied classical literature, philosophy, and oratory, read Shakespeare and Milton, and "masterid" French, Italian, Spanish, and Portuguese. His vanity was satisfied by his being chosen valedictorian of his class.

In 1818–1820 he made the "grand tour," spending some time in Paris, studying civil law with a fellow-Charlestonian, William C. Preston, and meeting a Bostonian, George Ticknor, at the University of Edinburgh. Returning to Charleston he began an active legal and political life. In 1820–1822 he was a legislator in the lower house in the General Assembly; in 1830 he served as Attorney General of South Carolina. In 1832–1836 he was chargé d'affaires in Belgium, where he enjoyed the occasional diplomatic duties, the frequent trips to adjoining countries, and the renewal of his friendship with Ticknor. After his return to Charleston, he served as member of Congress (1837–1839), but his opposition to the Jackson and Van Buren administrations brought about his defeat for re-election. Appointed Attorney General of the United States by President Harrison, he served with distinction from 1841 until his death; and after Webster's resignation as Secretary of State in May, 1843, he served a few weeks as Secretary *ad interim*. In his early political life he was known as a firm believer in states' rights, but later he joined the Union party and opposed Calhoun's extreme position. He was also an opponent of the protective tariff system. In the presidential campaign of 1840 he actively supported the Whigs, not because of their principles and election practices, but because he disliked, and had opposed vehemently, the administrations by Jackson and Van Buren.

As a man of letters Legaré is of importance because of his notable addresses, and for his able reviews published in magazines. The first formal address made by Legaré was made before the members of the '76 Association, of Charleston, on July 4, 1823. Another public address, which met with approval, was on the occasion of the Centennial celebration of Washington's Birthday, February 22, 1832. In 1828–1832 he was associated with Stephen Elliott, Sr. and Stephen Elliott, Jr. in the editing of the Charleston *Southern Review*. For the quarterly numbers Legaré wrote at least twenty long review articles, each giving evidence of scholarly knowledge and critical judgment. His love of the classics is found in such reviews as "Classical Learning" (February, 1828), "Roman Literature" (May, 1828), "Cicero de Republica" (August, 1829), and "The Public Economy of Athens" (February, 1832). As a reader of English literature he wrote such significant review-essays as "Sir Philip Sidney's Miscellanies" (May, 1830), "Lord Byron's

Character and Writings" (May, 1830), and "Byron's Letters
and Journals" (May, 1831). Unfortunately for our interest in
southern literature, he could not write essays on the writings of
Simms, Kennedy, Baldwin, and Longstreet, for their books
had not been published before 1832. He wrote a devastating,
savagely just review of the poetry of his fellow-townsman,
William Craft. His review of Hall's *Travels in North America*
(November, 1829) gave him an opportunity to express his
ideas about education. Hugh Swinton Legaré was a richly-
educated man, a scholar of wide knowledge and rich acquisitions, and he died in the home of a great New England scholar,
George Ticknor. After his death his sister Mary edited his
letters, addresses, and reviews in two volumes. These volumes
do not, however, contain all his published writings, and the
canon of Legaré's publications is yet to be established.

From FOURTH OF JULY, 1823, ORATION, *DELIV-
ERED BEFORE THE '76 ASSOCIATION,
CHARLESTON*

But *another* most fortunate and striking peculiarity of the
Revolution we are celebrating is that it occurred in a NEW
WORLD.

The importance that ought to be attached to this circumstance will be obvious to every one who will reflect, for a moment, upon the miracles which are exhibiting in the settlement
of this country and the increase of its population. Behold
how the pomœrium of the republic advances in the wilderness
of the West! See how empires are starting up into being, in
periods of time, shorter even than the interval between infancy
and manhood in the span allotted to the individuals that com-
pose them! Contemplate the peaceful triumphs of industry
—the rapid progress of cultivation—the diffusion of knowledge—the growth of populous cities, with all the arts that em-
bellish life, and soften while they exalt the character of man—
and think of the countless multitudes that are springing up to
inherit these blessings! The three millions by whom our independence was achieved, less than half a century ago, are al-

ready grown to *ten,* which in the course of another half century will have swelled up to *fifty;* and so on, with a continually
accelerated progress, until, at no distant day, the language of
MILTON shall be spoken from shore to shore, over the vastest
portion of the earth's surface that was ever inhabited by a race
worthy of speaking a language consecrated to Liberty. . . .

With respect to ourselves, who have been so systematically
vilified by British critics—if any answer were expected to be
given to their shallow and vulgar sophistry, and there was not
a sufficient practical refutation of it, in the undoubted success
of some of the artists and writers that are springing up in our
own times—we should be perfectly safe, in resting, upon the
operation of general causes and the whole analogy of history,
our anticipation of the proudest success, in all the pursuits of a
high and honorable ambition.   That living, as we do, in the
midst of a forest, we have been principally engaged in felling
and improving it—and that those arts, which suppose wealth
and leisure and a crowded population, are not yet so flourishing
amongst us as they will be in the course of a century or two, is
so much a matter of course, that instead of exciting wonder and
disgust, one is only surprised how it should even have attracted
notice—but the question, whether we are destitute of genius
and sensibility and loftiness of character, and all the aspirings
that prompt to illustrious achievements, and all the elements of
national greatness and glory, is quite a distinct thing—and we
may appeal, with confidence, to what we have done and to what
we are, to the Revolution we are this day celebrating, to the
career we have since run, to our recent exploits upon the flood
and in the field, to the skill of our diplomacy, to the comprehensive views and undoubted abilities of our statesmen, to the
virtues and prosperity of our people, to the exhibition on every
occasion of all the talent called for by its exigencies and admitted by its nature—nay, to the very hatred—the vehement
and irrepressible hatred, with which these revilers themselves
have so abundantly honored us—to shew that nothing can be
more preposterous than the *contempt,* with which they have
sometimes *affected* to speak of us.

And, were there no *other* argument, as there are many, to prove that the character of the nation is altogether worthy of its high destinies, would it not be enough to say that we live under a form of government and in a state of society, to which the world has never yet exhibited a parallel? Is it then *nothing* to be *free?* How many nations, in the whole annals of human kind, have proved themselves worthy of being so? Is it nothing that we are Republicans? Were all men as enlightened, as brave, as *proud* as they ought to be, would they suffer themselves to be insulted with any other title? Is it nothing, that so many independent sovereignties should be held together in such a confederacy as ours? What does history teach us of the difficulty of instituting and maintaining such a polity, and of the glory that, of consequence, ought to be given to those who enjoy its advantages in so much perfection, and on so grand a scale? For, can any thing be more striking and sublime, that the idea of an IMPERIAL REPUBLIC—spreading over an extent of territory, more immense than the empire of the Cæsars, in the accumulated conquests of a thousand years—without præfects or proconsuls or publicans—founded in the maxims of common sense—employing within itself no arms, but those of reason—and known to its subjects only by the blessings it bestows or perpetuates—yet, capable of directing, against a foreign foe, all the energies of a military despotism—a Republic, in which men are completely insignificant, and *principles* and *laws* exercise, throughout its vast dominion, a peaceful and irresistible sway—blending in one divine harmony such various habits and conflicting opinions—and mingling in our institutions the light of philosophy with all that is dazzling in the associations of heroic achievement and extended domination, and deep seated and formidable power!

To conclude: Our institutions have sprung up naturally in the progress of society. They will flourish and decay with those improvements of which they were the fruit—they will grow with the growth of knowledge—they will strengthen with the strength of reason—their influence will be extended by every advance of *true* civilization—every thing that has a

tendency to make man wiser and better, will confirm and improve and adorn them. If humanity was not endowed, in vain,
with such noble faculties, many ages of glory and freedom are
before us—many nations shall learn, from our example, how to
be free and great. The fortunes of the species are thus, in some
degree, identified with those of THE REPUBLIC—and if our experiment fail, there is no hope for man on this side of the grave.

And now, my friends! Let us be proud that we are free—
let us exult in a distinction as singular as it is honorable. Our
country exhibits the last specimen of that form of government,
which has done so much for the dignity and happiness of man.
It stands alone—it is surrounded with ruins. In the language
of BYRON—

> "The name of Commonwealth, is past and gone
> O'er the three fractions of the groaning globe."

But, painful as is that reflection, we may be allowed to repeat, with honest triumph, the lines which follow—to proclaim to the world, that

> "Still one great clime,
> Whose vigorous offspring by dividing ocean
> Are kept apart, and nursed in the devotion
> Of freedom, which their fathers fought for and
> Bequeathed—a heritage of heart and hand,
> And proud distinction from each other land—
> Still ONE GREAT CLIME, in full and free defence
> Yet rears her crest—unconquered and sublime—
> Above the far Atlantic."

From the REVIEW OF CAPTAIN BASIL HALL'S TRAVELS IN NORTH–AMERICA IN THE YEARS 1827 AND 1828

A very striking instance of Captain Hall's prejudice is to be
found in his remarks upon the state of education in this country. He admits, that what he calls elementary, that is popular,
education is successfully cultivated and universally diffused;

but he affirms, that the attainments of young men, who go regularly through the grammar school and the college, are lamentably superficial. This he considers as an undoubted effect of our levelling principles—an opinion altogether irreconcilable with the facts of the case, and even with the account of this matter which Captain Hall has himself given in a passage hereafter to be submitted to our readers. Now we do not pretend to repel the imputation: we have too often said as much on previous occasions, not to consider ourselves fairly estopped on this subject. There are very few men of science and still fewer scholars among us—we speak, of course, in reference to the European standard. But how many were there under the Provincial Governments, with all "appliances and means to boot" furnished by the right of primogeniture! A dozen or two young gentlemen from Carolina, not so many from Virginia, and still fewer (if any at all) from the North of the Potomac, were sent to English schools and universities.[8] The *élite* of these became accomplished scholars up to a certain point. The late General Thomas Pinckney, for instance, was, we have no doubt, the very best Hellenist (of a young man) that any part of America has ever had to boast of[9]; though we do not know that he became extensively read in Greek learning. Just before the breaking out of the Revolution, a cluster of accomplished young men, contemporaries of the distinguished person just mentioned, returned to Carolina from their studies in England, and, true to the spirit imbibed in the writings of the ancients, contributed greatly to the independence of their country. We are far, very far, from disputing their merit—they were an honour and blessing to the State, and they formed a society far superior, in some interesting respects, to anything that has succeeded it in any part of the Union. But the system was essentially aristocratic and exclusive, as the improvements it led to were altogether *exotic*. Those who were born to large fortunes were thus educated in England; but what was done for learning at home? What was done to prepare the soil here for future cultivation and productiveness? What seats, what seminaries of science were endowed in the Provinces—we mean the Southern more particularly. No means at all of acquiring knowledge, or next to none, were provided by the government for people of moderate fortunes. When, therefore, the separation from the mother country, and the abolition of the right of primogeniture put an end to the practice of educating young men at English grammar schools, there was an end to all scholarship, for the simple reason, that there were no grammar schools on this side of the ocean, at which more than a smattering of Greek and Latin could be acquired. The people of the South now began to send their children to Northern colleges, where the standard of classical learning had never been high, even under the old *régime*, because the fortunes of the people did not admit of their giving their youth a foreign education, and where until, very recently, it continued to be exceedingly low. Here is an explanation of the whole affair. Following mechanically the old system, we have confined our boys almost exclusively, during their whole elementary course, to the very studies which it was impossible they should cultivate successfully. We have insisted on making them classical scholars, and nothing but classical scholars, when there was no such thing as a classical teacher to be had in the whole country for love or money. The first fifteen or sixteen years of life were thus thrown away almost entirely— childhood, and a good part of youth were struck out of existence, for all purposes of solid improvement; for, a young gentleman was sent to college, as a matter of course, ignorant of every thing but a few grammar rules, which he did not know how to apply, and a few scraps of Greek and Latin (hideously mispronounced) which he did not know how to construe. Of the four years allotted to the college course, a very considerable portion was thrown away upon the same mockery of classical studies; but it would be injustice to deny that something more was acquired at the same time. Before the young man was admitted to his first degree, he had a fair chance of picking up a little geometry, a little chemistry, a little school-logic, and quite as much as was desirable of Scotch metaphysics. These various attainments, surmounted with a suitable stock of self-sufficiency, and a lofty contempt of prejudice and authority, fitted him to enter with advantage upon the duties of active life. The truth is, however, that the root of this execrable system is not to be sought in the discipline of the college, which, as things go, is a mere hospital of incurables. We must begin at the beginning. A boy, when he is matriculated at a university, ought to be already an accomplished scholar, in the highest sense of the word. He ought to be critically versed in Latin and Greek as well as in English, that is to say, he ought to be able to *write* them all with correctness, and have his mind deeply imbued with the beauties which a knowledge of them reveals to the adept. But if he have acquired nothing, before he go to a college, what can the most assiduous and learned teacher make of him there in a few years, but a smatterer and a *charlatan?* Such is the true historical explanation of the fact; and now we ask, what has *democracy* to do with it? We venture to say, that if by any magic, three such schools as Eton, Westminster and Winchester, or the Charter-House, could be established in the three great divisions of the Atlantic States, in the course of ten years, at the outside, a total change would have taken place in the state of literature all over the country. We speak advisedly, from the wonderful progress which, without such a help, we have made in the same period just elapsed. But we need not tell a Scotchman how difficult it has been found to get up a good grammar school, even under a monarchial government, and in the "modern Athens," itself. Indeed, it is strange enough, but not so strange as ridiculous, to hear the objection to our want of classical learning coming from such a quarter. We should like to be informed how many scholars could be found, on the most accurate survey, between Johnny Groat's House and the Tweed!

In education as in other things, the beginning is half the work. If we are still behind hand in this important concern, it is owing to causes growing out of the situation of the country, not of the form of government. The people considered either in their individual or collective capacity, have been anything but indifferent to education and letters. It is almost superfluous to cite examples to shew this. What can be more magnificent, than the liberality which Harvard has experienced from the opulent merchants of Boston? And where can any society be found more entirely devoted to liberal pursuits, than that of the city just mentioned? The same spirit has prevailed in every part of the country—even where circumstances have been far less favorable to its development. This State, for instance, appropriates annually much more than a tithe [10] of its whole revenue to the instruction of its people. She has founded at great expense a college which has been justly complimented by Captain Hall, and furnished it with a most excellent library. She annually appropriates to the support of it, about $15,000. By this means, the advantage of attending the lectures of some of the most learned men in America, is extended to all who can afford a small annual advance out of their own funds. To the education of the poor, in free schools, we give nearly $40,000 per annum. All this for a population of only 240,000 whites. This is only one out of many other equally shining examples in the Atlantic States, while in the West, whole townships of land in those rising commonwealths, have been consecrated to letters, and the education of youth provided for by a solemn covenant, and placed beyond the reach of chance or change, among "the canon laws of their foundation."

JOHN PENDLETON KENNEDY

John Pendleton Kennedy was born in Baltimore, October 25, 1795, died in Newport, Rhode Island, August 18, 1870, and was buried in Baltimore. His father was a prosperous Scotch-Irish merchant, and his mother was Nancy Pendleton of Martinsburg, Virginia (now West Virginia). After his father's business failure in 1809, the family returned to Virginia, where the boy's horseback rides furnished pictures used later by the novelist. He was educated at Sinclair's Academy and Baltimore College, graduating in 1812. In the War of 1812 he participated bloodlessly in the skirmishes at Bladensburg and North Point. After reading law in the offices of his uncle, Edmund Pendleton, and of Walter Dorsey, he was admitted to the bar in 1816. After several years of law practice, which he disliked, he was relieved by a legacy from his uncle. In 1824 he married Mary Tennant, who died within a year, and in 1829 he married Elizabeth Gray, who survived him.

In his active political life Kennedy was a Whig. In 1820–1823 he served in the Maryland legislature; in 1838 he filled out an unexpired term in Congress, and was re-elected in 1840 and 1842; in 1846 he returned to the Maryland House of Delegates, and was elected Speaker; in 1852–1853 he served with distinction as Secretary of the Navy under Fillmore, organizing four important naval expeditions, including the one sent to Japan under Matthew C. Perry, the naval hero of the War of 1812. He strongly opposed the annexation of Texas, and he supported the Union cause in the Civil War.

In Baltimore he became a leading, respected citizen. He served as provost of the University of Maryland and as president of the board of trustees of Peabody Institute. As the leader of the literati in Baltimore he wrote many essays, novels, and biographies, and he was the patron of various literary enterprises and persons—especially Edgar Allan Poe.

In 1860 J. P. Lippincott reprinted his writings in five volumes: *Swallow Barn, Horse-Shoe Robinson, Rob of the Bowl, Quodlibet,* and *Memoirs of the Life of William Wirt. Swallow Barn, or a Sojourn in the Old Dominion* (1832) had been published in two volumes under the pseudonym of "Mark Little-

ton." These incidents and pictures of ante-bellum Virginia
are bound loosely together by two plots: first, the boundary
line dispute between the owners of the estates of "Swallow
Barn" and "The Brakes," Frank Meriwether and Isaac Tracy,
and, second, the love affair of Ned Hazard and Bel Tracy. The
characterization and incidents are reminiscent of Irving and
Thackeray. *Horse-Shoe Robinson; A Tale of the Tory Ascendency* (1835) is an exciting story of the Revolution in the Carolinas, founded upon the actual exploits of a blacksmith, one
Galbraith Robinson, introducing gallant soldiers and lovely
ladies, and culminating with the battle of King's Mountain.
Poe and Simms differed in their critical judgments of the romance.

Rob of the Bowl: a Legend of St. Inigoe's (1838) is a historical
romance of late seventeenth-century Maryland, with the place
setting in the capital, the town of St. Mary's, near the southern
extremity of the peninsula formed by the Chesapeake Bay and
the Potomac River. Its thirty-four chapters include incidents
of pirates, concealed identity, thwarted love, wealthy aristocrats, and lowly commoners. *Quodlibet: Containing Some
Annals Thereof . . . By Solomon Secondthought, Schoolmaster*
(1840) is a humorous satire on Jacksonian Democracy, published in the year of the famous presidential campaign of Harrison and Tyler against Van Buren. The title is whimsical, for
quodlibet is defined as "what you please, anything you please,
anything at all." *Memoirs of the Life of William Wirt, Attorney General of the United States* (1849) is a faithful biography
of Kennedy's old friend and political leader.

In his will Kennedy left five thousand dollars towards the
publication of his complete works after his death. His literary
executors and the publishing house of Putnam and Sons issued
in 1871 his works in ten volumes, including the life by Tuckerman.

From SWALLOW BARN, OR A SOJOURN
IN THE OLD DOMINION

Chapter I. Swallow Barn

Swallow Barn is an aristocratic old edifice which sits, like a
brooding hen, on the southern bank of the James River. It

looks down upon a shady pocket or nook, formed by an inden-
tation of the shore, from a gentle acclivity thinly sprinkled
with oaks whose magnificent branches afford habitation to sundry friendly colonies of squirrels and woodpeckers.

This time-honored mansion was the residence of the family of
Hazards. But in the present generation, the spells of love and
mortgage have translated the possession to Frank Meriwether,
who having married Lucretia, the eldest daughter of my late
Uncle Walter Hazard, and lifted some gentlemanlike incum-
brances which had been sleeping for years upon the domain,
was thus inducted into the proprietary rights. The adjacency
of his own estate gave a territorial feature to this alliance, of
which the fruits were no less discernible in the multiplication
of negroes, cattle, and poultry, than in a flourishing clan of
Meriwethers.

The main building is more than a century old. It is built
with thick brick walls, but one story in height, and surmounted
by a double-faced or hipped roof, which gives the idea of a
ship bottom upwards. Later buildings have been added to this,
as the wants or ambition of the family have expanded. These
are all constructed of wood, and seem to have been built in
defiance of all laws of congruity, just as convenience required.
But they form altogether an agreeable picture of habitation,
suggesting the idea of comfort in the ample space they fill, and
in their conspicuous adaptation to domestic uses.

The hall door is an ancient piece of walnut, which has grown
too heavy for its hinges, and by its daily travel has furrowed the
floor in a quadrant, over which it has an uneasy journey. It is
shaded by a narrow porch, with a carved pediment upheld by
massive columns of wood, somewhat split by the sun. An
ample court-yard, inclosed by a semi-circular paling, extends in
front of the whole pile, and is traversed by a gravel road
leading from a rather ostentatious iron gate, which is swung
between two pillars of brick surmounted by globes of cut
stone. Between the gate and the house a large willow spreads
its arched and pendent drapery over the grass. A bridle rack
stands within the inclosure, and near it a ragged horse-nibbled

plum-tree—the current belief being that a plum-tree thrives on ill usage—casts its skeleton shadow on the dust.

Some Lombardy poplars, springing above a mass of shrubbery, partially screen various supernumerary buildings at a short distance in the rear of the mansion. Amongst these is to be seen the gable end of a stable, with the date of its erection stiffly emblazoned in black bricks near the upper angle, in figures set in after the fashion of the work on a girl's sampler. In the same quarter a pigeon-box, reared on a post and resembling a huge tee-totum, is visible, and about its several doors and windows a family of pragmatical pigeons are generally strutting, bridling, and bragging at each other from sunrise until dark.

Appendant to this homestead is an extensive tract of land which stretches some three or four miles along the river, presenting alternately abrupt promontories mantled with pine and dwarf oak, and small inlets terminating in swamps. Some sparse portions of forest vary the landscape, which, for the most part, exhibits a succession of fields clothed with Indian corn, some small patches of cotton or tobacco plants, with the usual variety of stubble and fallow grounds. These are inclosed by worm fences of shrunken chestnut, where lizards and ground-squirrels are perpetually running races along the rails.

A few hundred steps from the mansion, a brook glides at a snail's pace towards the river, holding its course through a wilderness of laurel and alder, and creeping around islets covered with green mosses. Across this stream is thrown a rough bridge, which it would delight a painter to see; and not far below it an aged sycamore twists its roots into a grotesque framework to the pure mirror of a spring, which wells up its cool waters from a bed of gravel and runs gurgling to the brook. There it aids in furnishing a cruising ground to a squadron of ducks who, in defiance of all nautical propriety, are incessantly turning up their sterns to the skies. On the grass which skirts the margin of the spring, I observe the family linen is usually spread out by some three or four negro women, who chant shrill music over their wash-tubs, and seem to live in ceaseless warfare with sundry little besmirched and bow-legged blacks, who are never tired of making somersets, and mischievously pushing each other on the clothes laid down to dry.

Beyond the bridge, at some distance, stands a prominent object in the perspective of this picture,—the most venerable appendage to the establishment—a huge barn with an immense roof hanging almost to the ground, and thatched a foot thick with sunburnt straw, which reaches below the eaves in ragged flakes. It has a singularly drowsy and decrepit aspect. The yard around it is strewed knee-deep with litter, from the midst of which arises a long rack resembling a chevaux de frise, which is ordinarily filled with fodder. This is the customary lounge of half a score of oxen and as many cows, who sustain an imperturbable companionship with a sickly wagon, whose parched tongue and drooping swingle-trees, as it stands in the sun, give it a most forlorn and invalid character; whilst some sociable carts under the sheds, with their shafts perched against the walls, suggest the idea of a set of gossiping cronies taking their ease in a tavern porch. Now and then a clownish hobble-de-hoy colt, with long fetlocks and disordered mane, and a thousand burs in his tail, stalks through this company. But as it is forbidden ground to all his tribe, he is likely very soon to encounter a shower of corn-cobs from some of the negro men; upon which contingency he makes a rapid retreat across the bars which imperfectly guard the entrance to the yard, and with an uncouth display of his heels bounds away towards the brook, where he stops and looks back with a saucy defiance; and after affecting to drink for a moment, gallops away with a braggart whinny to the fields.

Chapter VII. Traces of the Feudal System

Virginia has the sentiments and opinions of an independent nation. She enjoyed in the colonial state a high degree of the favor of the mother country; and the blandishments of her climate, together with the report of her fertile soil and her hidden territorial resources, from the first attracted the regard of the British emigrants. Her early population, therefore, consisted of gentlemen of good name and condition, who brought within her confines a solid fund of respectability and wealth. This race of men grew vigorous in her genial atmosphere; her cloudless skies quickened and enlivened their tempers, and, in two centuries, gradually matured the sober and thinking Englishman into that spirited, imaginative being who now inhabits the lowlands of this state. When the Revolution broke out, she was among the first of its champions, ardent in the assertion of the principles upon which it turned, and brave in the support of them. Since that period, her annals have been singularly brilliant with the fame of orators and statesmen. Four Presidents have been given to the Union from her nursery. The first, the brightest figure of history; the others also master-spirits, worthy to be ranked amongst the greatest of their day. In the light of these men and of their gallant contemporaries, she has found a glory to stimulate her ambition, and to minister to her pride. It is not wonderful that in these circumstances she should deem herself a predominant star in the Union. It is a feature in her education and policy to hold all other interests subordinate to her own.

Her wealth is territorial; her institutions all savor of the soil; her population consists of landholders, of many descents, unmixed with foreign alloy. She has no large towns where men may meet and devise improvements or changes in the arts of life. She may be called a nation without a capital. From this cause she has been less disturbed by popular commotions, less influenced by popular fervors, than other communities. Her laws and habits, in consequence, have a certain fixedness, which even reject many of the valuable improvements of the day. In policy and government she is, according to the simplest and purest form, a republic: in temper and opinion, in the usages of life, and in the qualities of her moral nature, she is aristocratic.

The gentlemen of Virginia live apart from each other. They are surrounded by their bondsmen and dependents; and the customary intercourse of society familiarizes their minds to the relation of high and low degree. They frequently meet in the interchange of a large and thriftless hospitality, in which the forms of society are foregone for its comforts, and the business of life thrown aside for the enjoyment of its pleasures. The halls are large, and their boards ample; and surrounding the great family hearth, with its immense burthen of blazing wood casting a broad and merry glare over the congregated household and the numerous retainers, a social winter party in Virginia affords a tolerable picture of feudal munificence.

Frank Meriwether is a good specimen of the class I have described. He seeks companionship with men of ability, and is a zealous disseminator of the personal fame of individuals who have won any portion of renown in the state. Sometimes, I even think he exaggerates a little, when descanting upon the prodigies of genius that have been reared in the Old Dominion; and he manifestly seems to consider that a young man who has astonished a whole village in Virginia by the splendor of his talents, must, of course, be known throughout the United States;—for he frequently opens his eyes at me with an air of astonishment when I happen to ask him who is the marvel he is speaking of.

I observe, moreover, that he has a constitutional fondness for paradoxes, and does not scruple to adopt and republish any apothegm that is calculated to startle one by its novelty. He has a correspondence with several old friends, who were with him at college, and who have now risen into an extensive political notoriety in the state:—these gentlemen furnish him with many new currents of thought, along which he glides with a happy velocity. He is essentially meditative in his character, and somewhat given to declamation; and these traits have communicated a certain measured and deliberate gesticulation to his discourse. I have frequently seen him after dinner stride backward and forward across the room, for some moments, wrapped in thought, and then fling himself upon the sofa, and come out with some weighty doubt, expressed with a solemn emphasis. In this form he lately began a conversation, or rather a speech, that for a moment quite disconcerted me. "After all," said he, as if he had been talking to me before,

although these were the first words he uttered—then making a
parenthesis, so as to qualify what he was going to say—"I
don't deny that the steamboat is destined to produce valuable
results—but after all, I much question—(and here he bit his
upper lip, and paused an instant)—if we are not better without
it. I declare, I think, it strikes deeper at the supremacy of the
states than most persons are willing to allow. This annihilation
of space, sir, is not to be desired. Our protection against the
evils of consolidation consists in the very obstacles to our intercourse. Splatterwaite Dubbs of Dinwiddie—(or some such
name,—Frank is famous for quoting the opinions of his contemporaries. This Splatterwaite, I take it, was some old college chum who had got into the legislature, and I dare say made
pungent speeches,)—Dubbs of Dinwiddie made a good remark—That the home material of Virginia was never so good
as when the roads were at their worst." And so Frank went
on with quite a harangue, to which none of the company replied a word, for fear we might get into a dispute. Every body
seems to understand the advantage of silence when Meriwether
is inclined to be expatiatory.

This strain of philosophizing has a pretty marked influence
in the neighborhood, for I perceive that Frank's opinions are
very much quoted. There is a set of under-talkers about these
large country establishments, who are very glad to pick up
the crumbs of wisdom which fall from a rich man's table;
secondhand philosophers, who trade upon other people's stock.
Some of these have a natural bias to this venting of upper
opinions, by reason of certain dependencies in the way of trade
and favor: others have it from affinity of blood, which works
like a charm over a whole county. Frank stands related, by
some tie of marriage or mixture of kin, to an infinite train of
connections, spread over the state; and it is curious to learn
what a decided hue this gives to the opinions of the district.
We had a notable example of this one morning, not long after
my arrival at Swallow Barn. Meriwether had given several
indications, immediately after breakfast, of a design to pour
out upon us the gathered ruminations of the last twenty-four

hours, but we had evaded the storm with some caution, when the arrival of two or three neighbors,—plain, homespun farmers,—who had ridden to Swallow Barn to execute some papers before Frank as a magistrate, furnished him with an occasion that was not to be lost. After dispatching their business, he detained them, ostensibly to inquire about their crops, and other matters of their vocation,—but, in reality, to give them that very flood of politics which we had escaped. We, of course, listened without concern, since we were assured of an auditory that would not flinch. In the course of this disquisition, he made use of a figure of speech which savored of some previous study, or, at least, was highly in the oratorical vein. "Mark me, gentlemen," said he, contracting his brow over his fine thoughtful eye, and pointing the forefinger of his left hand directly at the face of the person he addressed, "Mark me, gentlemen,—you and I may not live to see it, but our children will see it, and wail over it—the sovereignty of this Union will be as the rod of Aaron;—it will turn into a serpent, and swallow up all that struggle with it." Mr. Chub was present at this solemn denunciation, and was very much affected by it. He rubbed his hands with some briskness, and uttered his applause in a short but vehement panegyric, in which were heard only the detached words—"Mr. Burke—Cicero."

The next day Ned and myself were walking by the schoolhouse, and were hailed by Rip, from one of the windows, who, in a sly under tone, as he beckoned us to come close to him, told us, "if we wanted to hear a regular preach, to stand fast." We could look into the schoolroom unobserved, and there was our patriotic pedagogue haranguing the boys with a violence of action that drove an additional supply of blood into his face. It was apparent that the old gentleman had got much beyond the depth of his hearers, and was pouring out his rhetoric more from oratorical vanity than from any hope of enlightening his audience. At the most animated part of his strain, he brought himself, by a kind of climax, to the identical sentiment uttered by Meriwether the day before. He warned his young hearers— the oldest of them was not above fourteen—"to keep a lynx-eyed gaze upon that serpent-like ambition which would convert the government at Washington into Aaron's rod, to swallow up the independence of their native state."

This conceit immediately ran through all the lower circles at Swallow Barn. Mr. Tongue, the overseer, repeated it at the blacksmith's shop, in the presence of the blacksmith and Mr. Absalom Bulrush, a spare, ague-and-feverish husbandman who occupies a muddy strip of marsh land, on one of the river bottoms, which is now under mortgage to Meriwether; and from these it was spread far and wide, though a good deal diluted, until in its circuit it has reached our veteran groom Carey, who considers the sentiment as importing something of an awful nature. With the smallest encouragement, Carey will put on a tragi-comic face, shake his head very slowly, turn up his eyeballs, and open out his broad, scaly hands, while he repeats with labored voice, "Look out, Master Ned! Aaron's rod a black snake in Old Virginny!" Upon which, as we fall into a roar of laughter, Carey stares with astonishment at our irreverence. But having been set to acting this scene for us once or twice, he now suspects us of some joke, and asks "if there isn't a copper for an old negro," which if he succeeds in getting, he runs off, telling us "he is too 'cute to make a fool of himself."

Meriwether does not dislike this trait in the society around him. I happened to hear two carpenters, one day, who were making some repairs at the stable, in high conversation. One of them was expounding to the other some oracular opinion of Frank's touching the political aspect of the country, and just at the moment when the speaker was most animated, Meriwether himself came up. He no sooner became aware of the topic in discussion than he walked off in another direction,— affecting not to hear it, although I knew he heard every word. He told me afterwards that there was "a wholesome tone of feeling amongst the people in that part of the country."

From ROB OF THE BOWL

Chapter XII

[*Rob of the Bowl and Kate of Warrington at home*]

The shore of the Chesapeake between Cape St. Michael—as the northern headland at the mouth of the Potomac was denominated by the early settlers—and the Patuxent, is generally flat, and distinguished by a clear pebbly beach or strand. The shore, comprising about twenty miles, is intersected by a single creek, that of St. Jerome, which enters the bay some five or six miles north of the Potomac. The line of beach, which I have referred to, is here and there relieved by small elevations which in any other region would scarce deserve the name, but which are sufficiently prominent in this locality to attract remark. From the general level of the country they rise high enough to afford a clear prospect over the wide waters, and no less to distinguish the landward perspective to the mariner whose eye eagerly seeks the varieties of landscape as he holds his course up the bay. At a few points these small hills terminate immediately upon the tide in the abrupt form of a cliff, and, at others, take the shape of a knoll sinking away by a rapid, but grass-covered, declivity to the strand. This latter feature is observable in the vicinity of St. Jerome's, where the slope falls somewhat abruptly to the level of the tide, leaving something above fifty paces in width of low ground between its base and the ordinary water-mark. It was upon this flat that, in ancient times, stood the dwelling-house of Paul Kelpy the fisherman—a long, low building of deal boards, constructed somewhat in the shape of a warehouse or magazine. Some quarter of a mile farther up the beach, so sheltered under the brow of the slope as scarcely to be seen amongst the natural shrubbery that shaded it, stood a cottage or hut of very humble pretensions. It was so low that a man of ordinary height, while standing at the door, might lay his hand upon the eaves of the roof, and, correspondent to its elevation, it was so scanty in space as to afford but two apartments, of which the largest was not above ten feet square. It was strongly built of hewn logs, and the door, strengthened by nails thickly studded over its surface, was further fortified by a heavy padlock, which rendered it sufficiently impregnable against a sharper assault than might be counted on from such as ordinarily should find motive to molest the proprietor of such a dwelling.

A small enclosure surrounded the hut and furnished ground for some common garden plants which were not neglected in their culture. A few acres, on the higher plain above the bank, exhibited signs of husbandry; and the small nets and other fishing tackle disposed about the curtilage, together with a skiff drawn up on the sand, gave evidence of the ostensible thrift by which the occupant of the hut obtained a livelihood.

To this spot I propose to introduce my reader, the day preceding that at which my story has been opened. It was about an hour before sunset, and a light drizzling rain, with a steady wind from the north-east, infused a chilly gloom into the air, and heightened the tone of solitude which prevailed over the scene. A thin curl of smoke which rose from the clumsy chimney of the hut gave a sign of habitation to the premises, and this was further confirmed by the presence of a large and cross-visaged mastiff-bitch, whose heavy head might be discerned thrust forth from beneath the sill of the gable,—a sullen warder of this sullen place of strength. The waves, now propelled upon a flood tide, rolled in upon the shore, and broke almost at the door of the hut, with a hoarse and harsh and ceaseless plash. Far out over the bay, the white caps of the wind-driven surge floated like changing snow-drifts upon the surface of the waters. The water fowl rose in squadrons above this murky waste and struggled to windward, in a flight so low as frequently to shield them from the sight in the spray. An old bald eagle perched on the loftiest branch of a lightning-riven tree, immediately upon the bank above the hut, kept anxious watch upon her nest which, built in the highest fork, rocked to and fro in the breeze, whilst her screams of warning to her young seemed to answer to the din of the waters.

In the larger apartment of the hut a few fagots blazed upon

the hearth, supplying heat to a pot that simmered above them, the care of which, together with other culinary operations, engaged the attention of a brown, haggard and weather-beaten woman, who plied this household duty with a silent and mechanical thrift. She was not the only tenant of the dwelling. Remote from the hearth, and immediately below a small window, sat, apparently upon the floor, a figure eminently calculated to challenge observation. His features were those of a man of seventy, sharp, shrewd and imprinted with a deep trace of care. His frame indicated the possession, at an earlier period of his life, of the highest degree of strength; it was broad in the shoulders, ample in chest, and still muscular, although deprived of its roundness by age. His dress, of coarse green serge, made into a doublet with skirts that fell both front and rear, secured by a leathern belt, was so contrived as to conceal, in his present posture, his lower extremities. A broad ruff received his locks of iron gray, which fell over his back in crisp wiry curls: a thick grizzly beard, of the same hue, gave an elongation to his countenance which imparted to the observer the unpleasant impression of a head disproportionably large for the body, at least as seen in its present aspect. His eyes, dark and unusually clear, were sunk deep in their sockets, whilst a shaggy and matted brow, overhanging them like a porch, gave sometimes an almost preternatural brilliancy to their quick and changeful glances—like the sparkling of water when agitated in a well. It was observable from the dropping in of the upper jaw that he had lost his teeth, and this had given a tendency of the strong furrowed lines and seams, with which his features were marked, to converge towards the mouth.

His girdle sustained a long knife or dagger, which apparently constituted a part of his ordinary equipment; and the oblique flash of his eye, and tremulous motion of his thin lip, betrayed a temperament, from which one might infer that this weapon of offence was not worn merely as an ornament of the person.

The individual described in this summary was familiar to report, throughout the province, as The Cripple. His true name was supposed to be Robert Swale,—but this was almost lost in the pervading popular designation of Rob of the Bowl, or Trencher Rob—an appellative which he had borne ever since his arrival in the province, now some fifteen years gone by. Of his history but little was known, and that little was duly mystified, in the public repute, by the common tendency in the vulgar mind to make the most of any circumstance of suspicion. The story went that he had been shipwrecked, on a winter voyage, upon this coast, and, after suffering incredible hardships, had saved his life only at the expense of the loss of both legs by frost. In this maimed condition he had reached the shore of the province, and some time afterwards built the hut in which he now dwelt, near the mouth of St. Jerome's. Here he had passed many years, without attracting other notice than such as the stinted charity of the world affords when it is exercised upon the fate or fortunes of an obscure recluse. This observation began to find a broader scope as soon as it became obvious that the hermit was not altogether an object for almsgiving; and the little world of this part of the province discovering, in process of time, that he was not absolutely penniless, were fain to take offence at the mystery of his means of earning his frugal subsistence. Before many years, some few of the traders and country people round had found out that Rob was occasionally possessed of good merchantable commodities much in request by the inhabitants of the port, and dark whispers were sometimes circulated touching the manner in which he came by them. These surmises were not made topics of public discussion for two reasons;—first, because it was not inconvenient or unprofitable to the traders in the secret to deal with Rob;—and secondly, Rob was not a man to allow this indulgence of idle speculation; he was of an irascible temper, free to strike when crossed, and, what was still more to be feared, had friends who were not unwilling to take up his quarrel. The loss of his legs was supplied by a wooden bowl or trencher, of an elliptical shape, to which his thighs were attached by a strap, and this rude contrivance was swayed forward, when the owner chose, by the aid of two short crutches, which enabled him to lift himself from the ground and assume a progressive motion. It was to the exercise which this mode of locomotion imposed upon his upper limbs, that the unusual breadth and squareness of his figure about the shoulders, as well as the visible manifestations of strength of arm for which he was remarkable, were in part, perhaps, to be attributed. Use had made him expert in the management of his bowl, and he could keep pace pretty fairly with an ordinary walker. The Cripple was a man of unsocial habits and ascetic life, although there were times in which his severe temper relaxed into an approach to companionable enjoyment, and then his intercourse with the few who had access to him was marked by a sarcastic humor and keen ridicule of human action which showed some grudge against the world, and, at the same time, denoted conversancy with mankind and by no means a deficiency of education. But, in general, his vein was peevish, and apt to vent itself in indiscriminate petulance or stern reproof.

A small painting of St. Romuald at his devotions, by the hand of Salvator himself, hung over a dressing table in the back room of the hut in which the bed of The Cripple was placed; and this exquisite gem of art, which the possessor seemed duly to appreciate, was surmounted by a crucifix, indicating the religious faith in which he worshipped. This might be gathered also from a curious, antique pix, of heavy gilded metal, a ponderous missal with silver clasps, a few old volumes of the lives of the saints, and other furniture of the like nature, all of which denoted that the ingredient of a religious devotee formed an element in his singular compound of character.

The superiority of his mind and attainments over those of the mass of the inhabitants of the province had contributed to render The Cripple an object of some interest as well as of distrust amongst them, and this sentiment was heightened into one approaching to vulgar awe, by the reputation of the person who had always been somewhat in his confidence, and now attended him as his servitress and only domestic. This person was the ungainly and repulsive beldam whom I have already noticed as ministering in the household concerns of the hut.

She was a woman who had long maintained a most unenviable fame as The Woman of Warrington, in the small hamlet of that name on the Cliffs of Patuxent, from whence she had been recently transplanted to perform the domestic drudgery in which we have found her. Her habitation was a rude hovel some few hundred paces distant from the hut of The Cripple, on the margin of St. Jerome's creek, and within gun shot of the rear of the Black Chapel. To this hovel, after her daily work was done, she retired to pass the night, leaving her master or patron to that solitude which he seemed to prefer to any society. The surly mastiff-bitch, we have noticed, alternately kept guard at the hut of the master and domestic,—roving between the two in nightly patrol, with a gruff and unsocial fidelity,—no unsuitable go-between to so strange a pair. It will not be wondered at, that, in a superstitious age, such an association as this of The Cripple and the crone, in the vicinity of such a spot, desecrated, as the fisherman's lodge had been, by the acting of a horrible tragedy, should excite, far and wide amongst the people, a sentiment of terror sufficiently potent to turn the steps of the wayfarer, as the shades of evening fell around him, aside from the path that led to St. Jerome's.

The Cripple, at the time when I have chosen to present him to my reader, was seated, as I have said, immediately beneath the window. A pair of spectacles assisted his vision as he perused a packet of papers, several of which lay scattered around him. The dim light for a while perplexed his labor, and he had directed the door to be thrown wide open that he might take advantage of the last moment before the approaching twilight should arrest his occupation. . . .

Chapter XXVIII

[*Richard Cocklescraft and his pirate followers entertain Rob of the Bowl*]

. . . When night came on, and the rain fell, and the moon was quenched, and the murky, cheerless atmosphere, so congenial with the unlawful complexion of his designs, admonished him how little likely it was that prying feet or watchful eyes should be abroad, a revel was held in the Wizard's Chapel. Amidst the lumber that lay piled in confusion over the floor of the rude but spacious building, room was found for a rough table, around which empty casks, broken boxes and other appropriate furniture of a smuggler's den, supplied seats sufficient for the accommodation of twelve or fifteen persons. Here were assembled the crew of the Escalfador, with an abundant supply of strong liquors and tobacco. A fire blazed on the ample hearth, furnishing to such as desired it the means of cooking, in a simple fashion, some substantial elements of the evening meal; an opportunity which was not neglected, as was apparent from the bones and scraps of broken victuals which lay scattered about the fire-place, and from the strong fumes of roasted meat which sent their savor into every corner of the apartment.

The men who constituted this company, numbering without their leader full sixteen, were robust, swarthy seamen,—the greater portion of them distinguished by the dark olive complexions and curling black hair which denoted their origin in Portugal or other parts of the south of Europe. Several wore rings in the ears and on the fingers, and were bedizened with strange and outlandish jewelry. The thick moustache and shaggy brow gave a peculiar ferocity to more than one of the company, whilst the close and braided seaman's jacket, gaudy woollen caps and white breeches—the common costume of the crew—imparted a foreign air to the whole group. Some wore rich girdles with ornamented pistols and daggers; and the plainest amongst them showed a knife secured under a leathern belt. Their only attendant was Kate of Warrington, who grudgingly answered the frequent call for fresh potations, as the revellers washed down their coarse mirth with draughts of brandy and usquebaugh.

Cocklescraft sat, somewhat elevated above the rest, at the head of the board, where, without carousing as deeply as his sailors, he stimulated their noisy jollity by clamorous applause. A witness, rather than a partaker of this uncouth wassail, was

The Cripple, who, having matters of account to settle with several of the crew before they took their departure, had now swung himself into a corner where, with a lighted fagot stuck in a crevice of the wall, he alternately gave his attention to a pouch containing his papers of business, and to the revelry of the moment; chiding the prodigal laughter of the crew, one moment with querulous reproof, and the next with a satirical merriment.

"Bowse it, lads!" exclaimed Cocklescraft, as he brandished a cup in his hand; "drain dry to the Escalfador!—our merry little frigate shall dance to-morrow on the green wave,—so, do honor to the last night we spend ashore. Remember, we have a reckoning to settle before we depart, with the good folks of St. Mary's. Are you all ready to follow me in an exploit of rare devilry?—Speak, boys!"

"Ay, ready, Master Captain!" was the response in a general shout.

This outburst roused The Cripple, who, lifting his head from the paper, which at that moment he was perusing, and looking from under his spectacles upon the crew, was heard to mutter when the shout subsided—"As ready as wolves to suck the blood of lambs. How can they be else under thy nursing, Dickon?"

"Ha, old dry bones, art thou awake? By St. Iago! I thought that thy leaden eyelids, Rob, had been sealed before this. Ho, lads, bring Master Robert Swale forward—we shall treat him as becomes a man of worship:—upon the table with him, boys."

The face of The Cripple grew instantly red, as a sudden flash of passion broke across it. He dropped the paper from his hand and drew his dagger;—then, with a compressed lip and kindling eye, spoke out—"By St. Romuald! the man that dares to lay hand on me to move me where it is not my pleasure to go, shall leave as deep a blood stain on this floor as flowed from the veins of Paul Kelpy. Who are you, Dickon Cocklescraft, that you venture to bait me with your bullies?"

"How now, Master Rob?" exclaimed the skipper, as he rose

from his seat and approached The Cripple. "Would'st quarrel with friends? 'Twas but in honest reverence, and not as against your will, that I would have had thee brought to the table. Come, old comrade, we will not be ruffled when we are to part so soon. What would you have, good Rob?"

"These bills shall be first paid by your drinking roysters before they go to sea," replied The Cripple, somewhat appeased by the skipper's manner. "Here are items of sundry comforts supplied—meat and drink and lodging;—and here are services of Mistress Kate both in making and mending;—here for trampling down my corn, and for killing—"

"Pshaw—a fig's end for your trampings and killings, and all this rigmarole of washing and mending!" interrupted Cocklescraft. "I would be sworn your conscience has undercharged your commodity:—so, there is enough to content you for the whole, with good usury to the back of it," he said, putting a well-stored purse of gold into Rob's hand. "You have ever been too modest in your dealings, friend Robert of the Trencher:—when you get older you will know how to increase your gear by lawful gain."

"A hang-dog—a scape-grace—a kill-cow—a devil's babe in swaddling bands of iniquity, thou art, Child Dickon!" said Rob, laughing with that bitter salt laugh that gave to his countenance the expression of extreme old age. "Thou dost not lack, with all thy wickedness, an open hand. I have ever found thee ready with thy gold. It comes over the devil's back—Dickon, ha, ha! —over the devil's back, youngster,— and it goes—you know the proverb. This closes accounts, so now for your humor, lads, I will pledge you in a cup."

"To the table with him, boys," said Cocklescraft, nodding his head to those who sat near him; and, in a moment, The Cripple was lifted up in his bowl and set, like a huge dish, in the middle of the board,—a ghastly grin of acquiescence playing all the time upon his sallow features.

"Fill me a glass of that wine of Portugal," said Rob, as soon as he found himself in the centre of the company. "Here, boys," he added when the wine was put in his hand, "here is

success to your next venture, and a merry meeting to count
your gains."

"Amen to that!" shouted Cocklescraft. "Our next venture
will be a stoop upon the doves of St. Mary's."

"And a merry meeting will it be when you count your gains,"
interposed the harsh voice of Kate of Warrington. "Robert
Swale will keep the reckoning of it."

"Peace, old woman," said Cocklescraft, sharply; "your ac-
cursed croaking is ever loudest when least welcome."

"Fill for me," cried out Roche del Carmine, in his Portuguese accent. "I will pledge the captain and our company,
with 'His Lordship's Secretary,'—we owe him a debt which
shall be paid in the coin of the Costa Rica."

"Bravo,—A la savanna, perros!—Huzza, boys,—shout to
that!" clamored Cocklescraft, at the top of his voice. "Drink
deep to it, in token of a deep vengeance! I thank you, Master
Roche, for this remembrance. Now, comrades, you have but
half an hour left before you must depart to bring down the
brigantine to the mouth of the creek. A pipe and a glass more
—and then away; so, to it roundly, and make profit of your
time!—Tobacco, Mistress Kate,—fill Master Swale's pipe first,
and then mine:—make the bottle stir, my merry men all!"

Having thus given a new spur to the revelry of the board,
the skipper, unasked, broke forth with a smoking song familiar
to the tavern haunters of that era.

> "Tobacco's a musician,
>   And in a pipe delighteth;
> It descends in a close
> Through the organ of the nose,
>   With a relish that inviteth.
> This makes me sing, So, ho, ho! so, ho, ho, boys.
> Ho, boys, sound I loudly,
>   Earth never did breed
>   Such a jovial weed
> Whereof to boast so proudly."

"The cackle of a wild goose, the screech of a kingfisher in
foul weather, hath more music in it, Dickon Cocklescraft, than

this thou call'st singing," said Rob. "I would counsel thee stick to thy vocation—thy vocation, Master Shark, of drinking and throat-cutting, and leave this gentle craft of music-making to such as have no heart to admire thy virtues. Ha, ha!"—he paused a moment to indulge his laugh. "When a galliard of your kidney, dashed with such poisonous juices as went into the milk that fed you, has a conceit to be merry, the fire-crackling of roof trees and the clashing of steel are the fittest melody for his mirth. Dickon, try no more ditties, thou wilt never make a living by the art."

"By St. James! I have sung at more honorable feasts than it ever fell to your lot to partake of. Ay, and lady-songs, too,—and been applauded for my voice, old goblin of the Bowl! Have I not sung at the back of Sir Harry Morgan's chair, in the great hall of the Governor of Chagres, in the Castle St. Lawrence, when we made feast there after the sack of the place?"

"Truly," replied The Cripple; "whilst the hall streamed with blood, and the dead corpse of the Governor was flung like rubbish into a corner, to give more zest to your banquet—and the women—"

"You have a license, Rob of the Trencher," interrupted Cocklescraft, "to snarl at those you cannot excel. So e'en take your own sweep! When you can better sing a better song, then I will hearken to you."

"On my conscience, can I now, at this very speaking, Dickon Cocklescraft," said The Cripple, "a better song than ever trilled through thy pipes.

'All dainty meats, I do defy,
Which feed men fat as swine,' "—

he sung, by way of proof of his skill, with a tremulous cadence and melancholy whine, as he flourished his pipe in a line with his eyes, and nodded his head to mark the time.

"The man has gone clean mad," ejaculated Kate of Warrington, who had for some time past been quietly seated on a stool near the fire, and who now arose and stepped up to the table to satisfy herself that it was actually The Cripple whose voice had aroused her. "You had better be telling your beads and repenting of your sins upon your shrivelled hams, than tinkling your cracked and worn-out voice at midnight, to be laughed at by guzzling fools—barked at by sea-dogs! It is time, Robert Swale, your old bones were stretched on your bed."

"Faith, thou say'st true, Mistress Nightshade," replied Rob; "thou speak'st most truly: I am over easy to be persuaded into unwholesome merriment—it has been the sin of my life. So, put me on the floor—and now my crutches—my sticks, Kate. There—thy lantern, Kate."

"Away, lads, to the brigantine," said Cocklescraft, rising from his seat. "When you get her at anchor off the Chapel, come ashore and pipe me up with the boatswain's whistle. We have some boxes here to put on board; and then, good fellows, we will make a flight into the city, and ruffle the sleep of some of the burghers, by way of a farewell. Rob, I will go with you to your cabin: I shall catch an hour's sleep in my cloak."

"As thou wilt—as thou wilt, Dickon," returned The Cripple as he set forth, with a brisk fling, on his journey, lighted by the lantern of the beldam.

"Leave the lamp burning," said Cocklescraft to the last of the crew, as the man was about to follow his companions who had already left the room; "it will serve to steer by when the brigantine comes out of the creek."

In the next moment the Wizard's Chapel was deserted by all its late noisy tenants, and the skipper was on his way, in the track of The Cripple, towards the hut.

JOSEPH GLOVER BALDWIN

Joseph Glover Baldwin was born at Friendly Grove Factory, near Winchester, Virginia, in January (day unknown), 1815, and died in San Francisco, September 30, 1864. His ancestors were of English and New England stock, and his grandparents and parents were of considerable prominence in the Shenandoah Valley. His father established the first woolen and cotton factory in the region. The boy, however, was given little education and was put to work at the age of twelve. Later he served as clerk in the district court, and at the age of seventeen edited a newspaper. After having read law with his uncle, Briscoe E. Baldwin, he decided to practise in the newly opened Southwest, where slave-holders and land-speculators engaged in much litigation. He tells in *Flush Times* how he mounted his pony, with his belongings in saddlebags, and made a long, leisurely journey to Mississippi, in 1836. The next eighteen years were successful years in the "flush times" of Mississippi and Alabama. First he practised law at De Kalb, Kemper County, Mississippi, where he was fortunate, in his first case, in making a favorable impression on the court and in winning the admiration of an older colleague, General Reuben Davis. After two years he moved to Gainesville, Sumpter County, Alabama, a prosperous town chiefly settled by Virginians and a rich harvest field for able lawyers. As Baldwin wrote: "It was a merry time for us craftsmen; and we brightened up mightily, and shook our quills joyously, like goslings in the midst of a shower. We look back to that good time 'now past and gone,' with the pious gratitude and serene satisfaction with which wreckers near the Florida Keys contemplate the last fine storm." In 1839 he married Miss Sidney White, daughter of Judge John White. Like most of the other prominent Virginians in Alabama at the time, Baldwin was a Whig, and he was rewarded by election in 1844 to the legislature; but in 1849 he was defeated in his candidacy for Congress. Garrett says that "his Democratic rival had the advantage of knocking down an abolition member on the floor of Congress in a general *melee*, and this gave him much prestige." In 1850 he removed to Livingston, and in 1853 to Mobile, to become the partner of a noted lawyer, Philip Phillips. In 1854 he migrated to California, "partly out of disappointment over political defeat, and partly out of response to the call of a newer country." Rising rapidly in legal and political prominence, he served from 1858 to 1862 as associate justice of the supreme court of California. He died from lockjaw.

Baldwin's sketches, which were published in book form as *Flush Times of Alabama and Mississippi* (1853), were contributed to the Richmond *Southern Literary Messenger*. The editor of the *Messenger* from 1847 to 1860 was John Reuben Thompson, who accepted readily the sketches by a fellow Virginian. Thompson published three *Flush Times* sketches in 1852, and eleven more in 1853. The volume published by D. Appleton and Company of New York in 1853 contains twenty-six sketches and tales. The last nine sketches, covering about fifty pages, had not been published in the *Messenger*, and are of inferior quality. Considerable personal and autobiographical material is given in "The Bench and the Bar" and "How the Times Served the Virginians." To the February, 1854, number of the *Messenger* Baldwin contributed "Old Uncle John Rosser and the Billy Goat." Thompson printed two serious articles by Baldwin: "Representative Men: Andrew Jackson and Henry Clay" (September, 1853), and "The Genius and Character of Alexander Hamilton" (May, 1856); and Appleton and Company published for him *Party Leaders: Sketches of Thomas Jefferson, Alexander Hamilton, Andrew Jackson, Henry Clay, John Randolph* (1855). But his literary reputation lives through *Flush Times in Alabama and Mississippi*. In the words of Garrett: "This work of Mr. Baldwin was an admirable hit, containing a variety of transactions in detail, with scenes in court and elsewhere, rich in originality and characters, and rarely surpassed in the humor of the narrative."

From FLUSH TIMES OF ALABAMA AND MISSISSIPPI

The Bench and the Bar

In the month of March, A.D., 1836, the writer of these faithful chronicles of law-doings in the South West, duly equipped for forensic warfare, having perused nearly the whole of Sir William Blackstone's Commentaries on the Laws of England, left behind him the red hills of his native village, in the valley of the Shenandoah, to seek his fortune. He turned his horse's head to the setting sun. His loyalty to the Old Dominion extorts the explanation that his was no voluntary expatriation. He went under the compulsion which produced the author's book—"Urged by hunger and request of friends." The gentle momentum of a female slipper, too, it might as well be confessed, added its moral suasion to the more pressing urgencies of breakfast, dinner and supper. To the South West he started because magnificent accounts came from that sunny land of most cheering and exhilarating prospects of fussing, quarreling, murdering, violation of contracts, and the whole catalogue of *crimen falsi*— in fine, of a flush tide of litigation in all of its departments, civil and criminal. It was extolled as a legal Utopia, peopled by a race of eager litigants, only waiting for the lawyers to come on and divide out to them the shells of a bountiful system of squabbling: a California of Law, whose surface strife only indicated the vast *placers* of legal dispute waiting in untold profusion, the presence of a few craftsmen to bring out the crude suits to some forum, or into chancery for trial or essay.

He resigned prospects of great brilliancy at home. His family connections were numerous, though those of influence were lawyers themselves, which made this fact only contingently beneficial—to wit, the contingency of their dying before him—which was a sort of *remotissima potentia*, seeing they were in the enjoyment of excellent health, the profession being remarkably salubrious in that village; and seeing further, that, after their death, their influence might be gone. Not counting, therefore, too much on this advantage, it was a well-ascertained fact that no man of *real* talent and energy—and, of course, every lawyerling has both at the start—had ever come to that bar, who did not, in the course of five or six years, with any thing like moderate luck, make expenses, and, surviving that short probation on board wages, lay up money, ranging from $250 to $500, according to merit and good fortune, *per*

annum. In evidence of the correctness of this calculation, it
may be added that seven young gentlemen, all of fine promise,
were enjoying *high* life—in upper stories—cultivating the cardinal virtues of Faith and Hope in themselves, and the greater
virtue of Charity in their friends—the only briefs as yet known
to them being brief of money and brief of credit; their barrenness of fruition in the daytime relieved by oriental dreams of
fairy clients, with fifteen shilling fees in each hand, and glorious
ten dollar contingents in the perspective, beckoning them on to
Fame and Fortune. But Poverty, the rugged mother of the
wind-sellers of all times and countries, as poor Peter Peebles
so irreverently calls our honorable craft,—the Necessity which
knows no Law, yet teaches so much of it, tore him from scenes
and prospects of such allurement: with the heroism of old
Regulus, he turned his back upon his country and put all to
hazard—*videlicet*, a pony valued at $35, a pair of saddle-bags
and contents, a new razor not much needed at that early day,
and $75 in Virginia bank bills.

Passing leisurely along through East Tennessee, he was
struck with the sturdy independence of the natives, of the ener-
vating refinements of artificial society and its concomitants;
not less than with the patriotic encouragement they extended to
their own productions and manufactures: the writer frequently
saw pretty farmers' daughters working barefooted in the field,
and his attention was often drawn to the number of the distil-
leries and to evident symptoms of a liberal patronage of their
products. He stopped at a seat of Justice for half a day, while
court was in session, to witness the manner in which the natives
did up judicature; but with the exception of a few cases under a
statute of universal authority and delicacy, he saw nothing of
special interest; and these did not seem to excite much attention
beyond the domestic circle.

The transition from East Tennessee to South Western Alabama and East Mississippi was something marked. It was
somewhat like a sudden change from "Sleepy Hollow" to the
Strand. A man, retailing onions by the dozen in Weathersfield,
and the same man suddenly turned into a real estate broker in

San Francisco, would realize the contrast between the picayune standard of the one region, and the wild spendthriftism, the impetuous rush and the magnificent scale of operations in the other.

The writer pitched his tabernacle on the thither side of the state line of Alabama, in the charming village of P., one of the loveliest hamlets of the plain, or rather it would be, did it not stand on a hill. Gamblers, then a numerous class, included, the village boasted a population of some five hundred souls; about a third of whom were single gentlemen who had come out on the vague errand of seeking their fortune, or the more definite one of seeking somebody else's; philosophers who mingled the spirit of Anacreon with the enterprise of Astor, and who enjoyed the present as well as laid projects for the future, to be worked out for their own profit upon the safe plan of some other person's risk. . . .

How the Times Served the Virginians

The disposition to be proud and vain of one's country, and to boast of it, is a natural feeling, indulged or not in respect to the pride, vanity, and boasting, according to the character of the native: but, with a Virginian, it is a passion. It inheres in him even as the flavor of a York river oyster in that bivalve, and no distance of deportation, and no trimmings of a gracious prosperity, and no pickling in the sharp acids of adversity, can destroy it. It is a part of the Virginia character—just as the flavor is a distinctive part of the oyster—"which cannot, save by annihilating, die." It is no use talking about it—the thing may be right, or wrong:—like Falstaff's victims at Gadshill, it is past praying for: it is a sort of cocoa grass that has got into the soil, and has so matted over it, and so *fibred* through it, as to have become a part of it; at least, there is no telling which is the grass and which is the soil; and certainly it is useless labor to try to root it out. You may destroy the soil, but you can't root out the grass.

Patriotism with a Virginian is a noun personal. It is the Virginian himself and something over. He loves Virginia *per se* and *propter se:* he loves her for herself and for himself—because *she is* Virginia and—every thing else beside. He loves to talk about her: out of the abundance of the heart the mouth speaketh. It makes no odds where he goes, he carries Virginia with him; not in the entirety always—but the little spot he came from is Virginia—as Swedenborg says the smallest part of the brain is an abridgment of all of it. *"Cœlum non animum mutant qui trans mare currunt,"* was made for a Virginian. He never gets acclimated elsewhere; he never loses citizenship to the old Home. The right of expatriation is a pure abstraction to him. He may breathe in Alabama, but he lives in Virginia. His treasure is there, and his heart also. If he looks at the Delta of the Mississippi, it reminds him of James River "low grounds"; if he sees the vast prairies of Texas, it is a memorial of the meadows of the Valley. Richmond is the centre of attraction, the *depot* of all that is grand, great, good and glorious. "It is the Kentucky of a place," which the preacher described Heaven to be to the Kentucky congregation.

Those who came many years ago from the borough towns, especially from the vicinity of Williamsburg, exceed, in attachment to their birthplace, if possible, the *emigrés* from the metropolis. It is refreshing in these costermonger times, to hear them speak of it:—they remember it when the old burg was the seat of fashion, taste, refinement, hospitality, wealth, wit, and all social graces; when genius threw its spell over the public assemblages and illumined the halls of justice, and when beauty brightened the social hour with her unmatched and matchless brilliancy.

Then the spirited and gifted youths of the College of old William and Mary, some of them just giving out the first scintillations of the genius that afterwards shone refulgent in the forum and the senate, added to the attractions of a society gay, cultivated and refined beyond example—*even* in the Old Dominion. A hallowed charm seems to rest upon the venerable city, clothing its very dilapidation in a drapery of romance and of serene and classic interest: as if all the sweet and softened splendor which invests the "Midsummer Night's Dream" were poured in a flood of mellow and poetic radiance over the now quiet and half "deserted village." There is something in the shadow from the old college walls, cast by the moon upon the grass and sleeping on the sward, that throws a like shadow soft, sad and melancholy upon the heart of the returning pilgrim who saunters out to view again, by moonlight, his old *Alma Mater*—the nursing mother of such a list and such a line of statesmen and heroes.

There is nothing presumptuously forward in this Virginianism. The Virginian does not make broad his phylacteries and crow over the poor Carolinian and Tennesseeian. He does not reproach him with his misfortune of birthplace. No, he thinks the affliction is enough without the triumph. The franchise of having been born in Virginia, and the prerogative founded thereon, are too patent of honor and distinction to be arrogantly pretended. The bare mention is enough. He finds occasion to let the fact be known, and then the fact is fully able to protect and take care of itself. Like a ducal title, there is no need of saying more than to name it: modesty then is a becoming and expected virtue; forbearance to boast is true dignity.

The Virginian is a magnanimous man. He never throws up to a Yankee the fact of his birthplace. He feels on the subject as a man of delicacy feels in alluding to a rope in the presence of a person, one of whose brothers "stood upon nothing and kicked at the U.S.," or to a female indiscretion, where there had been scandal concerning the family. So far do they carry this refinement, that I have known one of my countrymen, on occasion of a Bostonian owning where he was born, generously protest that he had never heard of it before. As if honest confession half obliterated the shame of the fact. Yet he does not lack the grace to acknowledge worth or merit in another, wherever the native place of that other: for it is a common thing to hear them say of a neighbor, "he is a clever fellow, *though* he *did* come from New Jersey or even Connecticut." . . .

Many were the instances of suffering; of pitiable misfortune, involving and crushing whole families; of pride abased; of honorable sensibilities wounded; of the provision for old age destroyed; of the hopes of manhood overcast; of independence dissipated, and the poor victim without help, or hope, or sympathy, forced to petty shifts for a bare subsistence, and a ground-scuffle, for what in happier days, he threw away. But there were too many examples of this sort for the expenditure of a useless compassion; just as the surgeon after a battle, grows case-hardened, from an excess of objects of pity.

My memory, however, fixes itself on one honored exception, the noblest of the noble, the best of the good. Old Major Willis Wormley had come in long before the *new era*. He belonged to the old school of Virginians. Nothing could have torn him from the Virginia he loved, as Jacopi Foscari, Venice, but the marrying of his eldest daughter, Mary, to a gentleman of Alabama. The Major was something between, or made of about equal parts, of Uncle Toby and Mr. Pickwick, with a slight flavor of Mr. Micawber. He was the soul of kindness, disinterestedness and hospitality. Love to every thing that had life in it, burned like a flame in his large and benignant soul; it flowed over in his countenance, and glowed through every feature, and moved every muscle in the frame it animated. The Major lived freely, was rather corpulent, and had not a lean thing on his plantations; the negroes; the dogs; the horses; the cattle; the very chickens, wore an air of corpulent complacency, and bustled about with a good-humored rotundity. There was more laughing, singing and whistling at "Hollywood," than would have set up a dozen Irish fairs. The Major's wife had, from a long life of affection, and the practice of the same pursuits, and the indulgence of the same feelings and tastes, got so much like him, that she seemed a feminine and modest edition of himself. Four daughters were all that remained in the family—two had been married off—and they had no son. The girls ranged from sixteen to twenty-two, fine, hearty, whole-souled, wholesome, cheerful lasses, with constitutions to last, and a flow of spirits like mountain springs—not beauties, but good housewife girls, whose open countenances, and neat figures, and rosy cheeks, and laughing eyes, and frank and cordial manners, made them, at home, abroad, on horseback or on foot, at the piano or discoursing on the old English books, or Washington Irving's Sketch Book, a favorite in the family ever since it was written, as entertaining and as well calculated to fix solid impressions on the heart, as any four girls in the country. The only difficulty was, they were so much alike, that you were put to fault which to fall in love with. They were all good housewives, or women, rather. But Mrs. Wormley, or Aunt Wormley, as we called her, was as far ahead of any other woman in that way, as could be found this side of the Virginia border. If there was any thing good in the culinary line that she couldn't make, I should like to know it. The Major lived on the main stage road, and if any decently dressed man ever passed the house after sundown, he escaped by sheer accident. The house was greatly visited. The Major knew every body, and every body near him knew the Major. The stage coach couldn't stop long, but in the hot summer days, about noon, as the driver tooted his horn at the top of the red hill, two negro boys stood opposite the door, with trays of the finest fruit, and a pitcher of cider for the refreshment of the wayfarers. The Major himself being on the look-out, with his hands over his eyes, bowing—as he only could bow— vaguely into the coach, and looking wistfully, to find among the passengers an acquaintance whom he could prevail upon to get out and stay a week with him. There wasn't a poor neighbor to whom the Major had not been as good as an insurer, without premium, for his stock, or for his crop; and from the way he rendered the service, you would think he was the party obliged—as he was.

This is not, in any country I have ever been in, a money-making business; and the Major, though he always made good crops, must have broke at it long ago, but for the fortunate death of a few Aunts, after whom the girls were named, who, paying their several debts of nature, left the Major the means to pay his less serious, but still weighty obligations.

The Major—for a wonder, being a Virginian—had no partisan politics. He could not have. His heart could not hold any thing that implied a warfare upon the thoughts or feelings of others. He voted all the time for his friend, that is, the candidate living nearest to him, regretting, generally, that he did not have another vote for the other man.

It would have done a Comanche Indian's heart good to see all the family together—grand-children and all—of a winter evening, with a guest or two, to excite sociability a little—not company enough to embarrass the manifestations of affection. Such a concordance—as if all hearts were attuned to the same feeling—the old lady knitting in the corner—the old man smoking his pipe opposite—both of their fine faces radiating in the pauses of the laugh, the jest, or the caress, the infinite satisfaction within.

It was enough to convert an abolitionist, to see the old Major when he came home from a long journey of two days to the county town; the negroes running in a string to the buggy; this one to hold the horse, that one to help the old man out, and the others to inquire how he was; and to observe the benignity with which—the kissing of the girls and the old lady hardly over—he distributed a piece of calico here, a plug of tobacco there, or a card of *town* ginger-bread to the little snow-balls that grinned around him; what was given being but a small part of the gift, divested of the kind, cheerful, rollicking way the old fellow had of giving it.

The Major had given out his autograph (as had almost every body else) as endorser on three several bills of exchange, of even tenor and date, and all maturing at or about the same time. His friend's friend failed to pay as he or his firm agreed, the friend himself did no better, and the Major, before he knew any thing at all of his danger, found a writ served upon him, and was told by his friend that he was dead broke, and all he could give him was his sympathy; the which, the Major as gratefully received as if it was a legal tender and would pay the debt. The Major's friends advised him he could get clear of it; that notice of protest not having been sent to the Major's post-office, released him; but the Major wouldn't hear of such a defence; he said *his* understanding was, that he was to pay the debt if his friend didn't; and to slip out of it by a quibble, was little better than pleading the gambling act. Besides, what would the lawyers say? And what would be said by his old friends in Virginia, when it reached their ears, that he had plead want of notice, to get clear of a debt, when every body knew it was the same thing as if he had got notice. And if this defence were good at law, it would not be in equity; and if they took it into chancery, it mattered not what became of the case, the property would all go, and he never could expect to see the last of it. No, no; he would pay it, and had as well set about it at once.

The rumor of the Major's condition spread far and wide. It reached old N. D., "an angel," whom the Major had "entertained," and one of the few that ever travelled that road. He came, post haste, to see into the affair; saw the creditor; made him, upon threat of defence, agree to take half the amount, and discharge the Major; advanced the money, and took the Major's negroes—except the house-servants—and put them on his Mississippi plantation to work out the debt.

The Major's heart pained him at the thought of the negroes going off; he couldn't witness it; though he consoled himself with the idea of the discipline and exercise being good for the health of sundry of them who had contracted sedentary diseases.

The Major turned his house into a tavern—that is, changed its name—put up a sign, and three weeks afterwards, you couldn't have told that any thing had happened. The family were as happy as ever—the Major never having put on airs of arrogance in prosperity, felt no humiliation in adversity; the girls were as cheerful, as bustling, and as light-hearted as ever, and seemed to think of the duties of hostesses as mere bagatelles, to enliven the time. The old Major was as profluent of anecdotes as ever, and never grew tired of telling the same ones to every new guest; and yet, the Major's anecdotes were all of Virginia growth, and not one of them under the legal age of twenty-one. If the Major had worked his negroes as he had those anecdotes, he would have been able to pay off the bills of exchange without any difficulty.

The old lady and the girls laughed at the anecdotes, though

they must have heard them at least a thousand times, and knew them by heart; for the Major told them without the variations; and the other friends of the Major laughed too; indeed, with such an air of thorough benevolence, and in such a truly social spirit did the old fellow proceed "the tale to unfold," that a Cassius like rascal that wouldn't laugh, whether he saw any thing to laugh at or not, ought to have been sent to the Penitentiary for life—half of the time to be spent in solitary confinement.

Jonathan and the Constable

Now, brother Jonathan was a distinguished member of the fraternity, and had maintained a leading position in the profession for many years, ever since, indeed, he had migrated from the land of steady habits. His masculine sense, acuteness and shrewdness, were relieved and mellowed by fine social habits and an original and genial humor, more grateful because coming from an exterior something rigid and inflexible. He had —and we hope we may be able to say so for thirty years yet— a remarkably acute and quick sense of the ridiculous, and is not fonder than other humorists of exposing a full front to the batteries of others than turning them on his friends. Some fifty-five years has passed over his head, but he is one of those evergreen or never-green plants upon which time makes but little impression. He has his whims and prejudices, and being an elder of the Presbyterian church, he is especially annoyed by a drunken man.

It so happened that a certain Ned Ellett was pretty high, as well in office as in liquor, one drizzly winter evening—during the session of the S. Circuit Court. He had taken in charge one Nash, a horse-thief, and also a tickler of rye whiskey; and this double duty coming upon him somewhat unexpectedly, was more than he could well sustain himself under. The task of discharging the prisoner over, Ned was sitting by the fire in the hall of the Choctaw House, in deep meditation upon the mutations in human affairs, when he received a summons from Jonathan, to come to his room, for the purpose of receiving a

letter to be carried to a client in the part of the county in which
Ned resided. It was about ten o'clock at night. Jonathan and
I occupied the same room and bed on the ground floor of the
building, and I had retired for the night.

Presently Ned came in, and took his seat by the fire. The
spirits, by this time, began to produce their usual effects. Ned
was habited in a green blanket over-coat, into which the rain
had soaked, and the action of the fire on it raised a considerable fog. Ned was a raw-boned, rough-looking customer,
about six feet high and weighing about two hundred net—
clothes, liquor, beard and all, about three hundred. After
Jonathan had given him the letter, and Ned had critically examined the superscription, remarking something about the
hand-writing, which, sooth to say, was not copy-plate—he
put it in his hat, and Jonathan asked him some question about
his errand to L.

"Why, Squire," said Ned, "you see I had to take Nash—
Nash had been stealing of hosses, and I had a warrant for him
and took him.—Blass, Nash is the smartest feller you ever
see. He knows about most every thing and every body. He
knows all the lawyers, Blass—I tell you he does, and no mistake. He was the merriest, jovialest feller you ever see, and
can sing more chronicle songs than one of these show fellers
that comes round with the suckus. He didn't seem to mind
bein' took than a pet sheep. I tell you he didn't, Blass—and
when I tell you a thing, Blass, you better had believe it, you
had. Blass, did you ever hear of my telling a lie? No, not by
a jug-full. Blass, aint I an hones' man? (Yes, said B., I guess
you are.)—"Guess—Guess—*I* say guess. Well, as I was a
saying, about Nash—I asked Nash, what he was doin perusin
about the country, and Nash said he was just perusin about the
country to see the climit? But I know'd Harvey Thompson
wouldn't like me to be bringin a prisoner in loose, so I put the
strings on Nash, and then his feathers drapped, and then Blass,
he got to crying—and, Blass, he told me—(blubbering) he
told me about his——old mother in Tennessee, and how her
heart would be broke, and all that—and, Blass, I'm a hard

man and my feelins aint easy teched—but (here Ned boohood right out,) Blass, I'll be——if I can bar to see a man exhausted."

Ned drew his coat-sleeve over his eyes, blew his nose, and snapped his fingers ʹover the fire and proceeded: "Blass, he asked about you and Lewis Scott, and what for a lawyer you was, and I'll tell you jest what I told him, Blass, says I, old Blass, when it comes to hard law, Nash, knows about all the law they is—but whether he kin norate it from the stump or not, that's the question. Blass, show me down some of these pairs of stairs." [They were on the ground-floor, but Ned, no doubt, was entitled to think himself high.]—B. showed him out.

All this time I was possuming sleep in the bed as innocent as a lamb. Blass came to the bedside and looked inquisitively on for a moment, and went to disrobing himself. All I could hear was a short soliloquy—"Well, doesn't that beat all? It's one comfort, J. didn't hear that—I never would have heard the last of it. It's most too good to be lost. I believe I'll lay it on him."

I got up in the morning, and as I was drawing on my left boot, muttered as if to myself, "but whither he kin norate it from the stump—*that's* the question." B. turned his head so suddenly—he was shaving, sitting on a trunk—that he came near cutting his nose off.

"You doosn't mean to say you eaves-dropped and heard that drunken fool—do you? Remember, young man, that what you hear said to a lawyer in conference is confidential, and don't get to making an ass of yourself, by blabbing this thing all over town." I told him "I thought I should have to norate it a little."

AUGUSTUS BALDWIN LONGSTREET

Augustus Baldwin Longstreet was born in Augusta, Georgia, September 22, 1790, and died in Oxford, Mississippi, July 9, 1870. His father, William Longstreet, was a skilful inventor, who claimed to have anticipated Robert Fulton in a successful trial of his steamboat. After receiving poor instruction in several schools, the son attended, in 1808–1810, the famous academy of Dr. Moses Waddel, at Willington, South Carolina. Longstreet has described the dominant personality and rigorous methods of Dr. Waddel in his classical academy in *Master William Mitten*. The preparation for college must have been thorough, for Longstreet entered Yale College in 1811, graduating in 1813. In attending Dr. Waddel's academy and Yale College he had paralleled the educational career of John C. Calhoun, and again he followed the great South Carolinian in attending Reeve's Law School at Litchfield, Connecticut. Returning to Georgia in 1814, he was admitted to the bar and took up his residence in Greensboro, Georgia. There he married, in 1817, Frances Eliza Parke, of a wealthy family.

Entering politics, he had a brief but successful active career, for he served in the state legislature in 1821 and was judge of the superior court in 1822–1823, and throughout his life he continued to speak and write on political matters. As editor of the Augusta *State Rights Sentinel*, which he established and edited, 1834–1836, he was an ardent advocate of nullification. But upon the eve of conflict, as John D. Wade writes, "he had no longer any courage in his belief, and went about appealing frantically on all sides that something be done at once to hold off the terrible destroyer. From then on till the war's end he was a strenuous but sadly dismayed patriot."

A cause of his turning from active participation in politics was his conversion to Methodism. In 1838 he was licensed as a Methodist minister, and in 1839–1848 he was president of the recently-founded Methodist institution, Emory College, then located at Oxford, Georgia. He served as president of Centenary College, Jackson, Louisiana, in 1849, of the University of Mississippi, in 1849–1856, and of the University of South

Carolina in 1857–1861. This last institution was closed in November, 1861, against the entreaties of its president, when the students left in a body and enlisted in the Confederate army. During the war Longstreet served briefly as a chaplain, and "refugeed" among friends. His last years were spent in retirement on his plantation near Oxford, Mississippi, where he wrote articles in defence of religious truth and of the southern cause. Lucius Q. C. Lamar was his son-in-law, and General James Longstreet was his nephew.

Longstreet is of literary importance chiefly for his humorous sketches in *Georgia Scenes*, which were first published in Georgia newspapers. In 1833–1835 Longstreet published twenty sketches in local Georgia newspapers, chiefly in the Milledgeville *Southern Recorder* and in his own newspaper, the Augusta *State Rights Sentinel*. In 1835 he published nineteen of these sketches in a paper-bound volume on the *Sentinel* press, under the title of *Georgia Scenes, Characters, Incidents, Etc., in the First Half Century of the Republic. By a Native Georgian.* The authorship was generally known by local readers. These *Georgia Scenes* appealed to all classes of readers, and "immediately attained wide popularity." Even the critics were favorable, Poe, for example, stating that "if this book were printed in England it would make the fortune of its author." In 1840 Harper and Brothers issued a second edition with the curious pen-and-ink drawings by E. H. Hyde.

Interest in Dr. Waddel's school leads one to read Longstreet's moral, educational novel, *Master William Mitten, A Youth of Brilliant Talents Who Was Ruined by Bad Luck* (1864). Some of Dr. Waddel's boys, besides Gus Longstreet, were John C. Calhoun, William H. Crawford, Hugh S. Legaré, George R. Gilmer, and James L. Petigru.

From GEORGIA SCENES

Georgia Theatrics

If my memory fail me not, the 10th of June, 1809, found me, at about eleven o'clock in the forenoon, ascending a long and gentle slope in what was called "The Dark Corner" of Lincoln. I believe it took its name from the moral darkness which reigned over that portion of the county at the time of which I am speaking. If in this point of view it was but a shade darker than the rest of the county, it was inconceivably dark. If any man can name a trick or sin which had not been committed at the time of which I am speaking, in the very focus of all the county's illumination (Lincolnton), he must himself be the most inventive of the tricky, and the very Judas of sinners. Since that time, however (all humor aside), Lincoln has become a living proof "that light shineth in darkness." Could I venture to mingle the solemn with the ludicrous, even for the purpose of honorable contrast, I could adduce from this county instances of the most numerous and wonderful transitions from vice and folly to virtue and holiness which have ever, perhaps, been witnessed since the days of the apostolic ministry. So much, lest it should be thought by some that what I am about to relate is characteristic of the county in which it occurred.

Whatever may be said of the *moral* condition of the Dark Corner at the time just mentioned, its *natural* condition was anything but dark. It smiled in all the charms of spring; and spring borrowed a new charm from its undulating grounds, its luxuriant woodlands, its sportive streams, its vocal birds, and its blushing flowers.

Rapt with the enchantment of the season and the scenery around me, I was slowly rising the slope, when I was startled by loud, profane, and boisterous voices, which seemed to proceed from a thick covert of undergrowth about two hundred yards in the advance of me and about one hundred to the right of my road.

"You kin, kin you?"

"Yes, I kin, and am able to do it! Boo-oo-oo! Oh, wake snakes, and walk your chalks! Brimstone and—fire! Don't hold me, Nick Stoval! The fight's made up, and let's go at it.—my soul if I don't jump down his throat, and gallop every chitterling out of him before you can say 'quit'!"

"Now, Nick, don't hold him! Jist let the wild-cat come, and I'll tame him. Ned'll see me a fair fight, won't you, Ned?"

"Oh, yes; I'll see you a fair fight, blast my old shoes if I don't!"

"That's sufficient, as Tom Haynes said when he saw the elephant. Now let him come!"

Thus they went on, with countless oaths interspersed, which I dare not even hint at, and with much that I could not distinctly hear.

In mercy's name! thought I, what band of ruffians has selected this holy season and this heavenly retreat for such pandemoniac riots! I quickened my gait, and had come nearly opposite to the thick grove whence the noise proceeded, when my eye caught, instinctively and at intervals, through the foliage of the dwarf-oaks and hickories which intervened, glimpses of a man, or men, who seemed to be in a violent struggle; and I could occasionally catch those deep-drawn, emphatic oaths which men in conflict utter when they deal blows. I dismounted, and hurried to the spot with all speed. I had overcome about half the space which separated it from me, when I saw the combatants come to the ground, and, after a short struggle, I saw the uppermost one (for I could not see the other) make a heavy plunge with both his thumbs, and at the same instant I heard a cry in the accent of keenest torture, "Enough! My eye's out!"

I was so completely horror-struck, that I stood transfixed for a moment to the spot where the cry met me. The accomplices in the hellish deed which had been perpetrated had all fled at my approach—at least, I supposed so, for they were not to be seen.

"Now, blast your corn-shucking soul," said the victor (a youth about eighteen years old) as he rose from the ground— "come cutt'n your shines 'bout me agin, next time I come to the court-house, will you! Get your owl-eye in agin if you can!"

At this moment he saw me for the first time. He looked excessively embarrassed, and was moving off, when I called to him, in a tone emboldened by the sacredness of my office and the iniquity of his crime, "Come back, you brute! and assist me in relieving your fellow-mortal, whom you have ruined for ever!"

My rudeness subdued his embarrassment in an instant; and, with a taunting curl of the nose, he replied, "You needn't kick before you're spurr'd. There a'nt nobody there, nor ha'nt been nother. I was jist seein' how I could 'a' *fout*." So saying, he bounded to his plough, which stood in the corner of the fence about fifty yards beyond the battle-ground.

And, would you believe it, gentle reader? his report was true. All that I had heard and seen was nothing more nor less than a Lincoln rehearsal, in which the youth who had just left me had played all the parts of all the characters in a court-house fight.

I went to the ground from which he had risen, and there were the prints of his two thumbs, plunged up to the balls in the mellow earth, about the distance of a man's eyes apart; and the ground around was broken up as if two stags had been engaged upon it.

From MASTER WILLIAM MITTEN

Dr. Waddel's School

. . . In the meantime the trunks took their places, the final kisses were disposed of, and a minute more found the Captain and William on their way. Nothing of special interest occurred on the journey. The Captain gave William much encouragement and good advice, and fretted a little at having to travel a half hour in the night to make his first stage, but, as no accident occurred, he was easily reconciled to it. Four o'clock the next day (Saturday,) found them at the public house, or rather boarding house, of Mr. Nelson Newby, Abbeville District, South Carolina. It was a rude log-house, with two rooms, about sixteen feet square each, and an entry nearly as large, between them. In the rear of it was another building of the same material, somewhat shorter and narrower than the first. This was the dining room. Six or seven small edifices of the same kind scattered around, with little order, served as students' lodges. A rail fence (or rather the remains of one,) three feet high, enclosed the whole. About twenty boys of various sizes, were busily engaged in cutting, splitting, and piling wood, at the doors of their respective tenements—the roughest looking set of students that ever repeated the notes of Homer and Virgil since the world began. The prospect looked gloomy, even to the Captain, and terrific to William.

"Uncle," whispered he, "these can't be big people's sons!"

"Well—don't know—they're pretty rough looking fellows—but—they seem to be very industrious boys." Poor comfort to William. The Captain and his landlord, of course, soon became acquainted; and the first expressing a wish to see Mr. Waddel, the last kindly offered to escort him to the teacher's residence.

"It is not far out of the way to go by the Academy; would you like to see it?" said Mr. Newby.

"Very much," replied the Captain.

They set forward, and at the distance of about two hundred and fifty yards from Mr. Newby's premises, they entered a street, shaded by majestic oaks, and composed entirely of log huts, varying in size from six to sixteen feet square. The truth of history demands that we should say, that there was but one of the smallest size just indicated, and that was the whimsical structure of a very whimsical fellow, by the name of Dredzel Pace. It was endangered from fire once, and *four* stout students took it up by the corners, and removed it to a place of safety.

The street was about forty yards wide, and its length was perhaps double its width; and yet the houses on either side did not number more than ten or twelve; of course, therefore they stood generally in very open order. They were all built by the students themselves, or by architects of their hiring. They served for study-houses in cold or rainy weather, though the students were allowed to study where they pleased within convenient reach of the monitors. The common price of a building, on *front row*, water proof, and easily chinked, was five dollars—the chinking was generally removed in summer for ventilation. In the suburbs, were several other buildings of the same kind, erected by literary recluses, we suppose, who could not endure the din of the city at play-time—at *play-time* we say, for there was no din in it in study hours. At the head of the street, eastward, stood the Academy, differing in nothing from the other buildings but in size and the number of its rooms. It had two; the smaller devoted to a primary school of a few boys and girls, over which Moses Waddel Dobbins, a nephew of the Rector, presided. These soon left, and Mr. Dobbins became assistant-general to his uncle. The larger, was the recitation room of Mr. Waddel himself, the prayer room, court room, (see *infra*) and general convocation room for all matters concerning the school. It was without seats, and just large enough to contain one hundred and fifty boys standing erect, close pressed, and leave a circle of six feet diameter at the door, for jigs and cotillons at the teacher's regular *soirees*, every Monday morning.

A delightful spring gushed from the foot of the hill on which the school-house stood; and at the distance of but a few paces, poured its waters into a lovely brook, which wound through a narrow plain, covered with stately beeches. . . .

. . . As they entered the road, a messenger called for Mr. Newby to return home on some special business. He gave the Captain directions to Mr. Waddel's, and returned. The directions were simply to keep the road to the next house. A walk of a quarter of a mile, or a little over, brought the Captain and his charge to the residence of the renowned teacher. It was a comfortable, framed building, two stories high, neatly, but plainly paled in—very rare things in that vicinity.

Some six or eight more boys, like the Newbyites, were differently employed about the premises.

"Do you know, my son," said the Captain, addressing one of them, "whether Mr. Waddel is at home?"

"Yes sir," said the youth, springing to the door, and opening it, "Walk in, take seats, and I will call him."

He disappeared, and in a moment returned with Mr. Waddel.

"Mr. Waddel, I presume," said the Captain.

"Yes, sir."

"Thompson, sir, is my name, and this is my nephew, William Mitten, whom I have brought to place under your instruction."

"It is rather chilly, here," said the teacher, shaking their hands cordially, "walk into my study, where I have a good fire. Won't you go in, David?" added he to the guide, who was about retiring.

"No, I thank you, sir," said David.

"That's a sprightly youth," said the Captain, as he moved towards the study, "and he is a namesake of mine."

"Yes," said the teacher, "he is a clever boy—the son of the celebrated Doctor Ramsay."

"What! Doctor Ramsay, the patriot, statesman, and historian—who married the accomplished daughter of the renowned Henry Laurens, President of the first Congress of the United States, Minister to Holland, and father of the gallant John Laurens, the beloved of Washington?"

This was a clear *splurge* for William's benefit.

"The same," said Mr. Waddel.

"Well, I feel myself honored in bearing the boy's name."

Before this conversation ended, all were seated in the teacher's study. It was crowded with books—partly the teacher's private library—partly, books laid in for the students which he furnished at cost and charges on Philadelphia prices.

"Have you studied Latin, William?" enquired Mr. Waddel.

"Yes, sir."

"How far have you gone?"

"I was reading Virgil, when I quit school."

"Well, I have a large Virgil class, which will be divided on Monday. I have found that some of them are keeping others back; and I have ordered them to get as long a lesson as they can for Monday morning. Those who get the most and recite the best, will be put in one class and the rest in another. Now, you can take either division of this class that you may be found qualified for, or you may enter the *Selectæ* class, which will commence Virgil in two or three months. Meet me at the Academy on Monday morning, and we will see what will be best."

"How many pupils have you, Mr. Waddel?" inquired the Captain.

"About one hundred and fifty."

"Where do they board?"

"Just where they please, among the neighbors around. They all take boarders, and reside at different distances from the academy, varying from a few hundred yards to three miles."

"Have the students to cut and haul their own firewood, and make their own fires?"

"Not always. At some of the boarding houses the land-lords have these things done for them, and at all, they may hire servants to perform them, if they will, or, rather, if they can; but, as at every house there is at least a *truck-wagon* and horse at the service of the students, and wood is convenient and abundant, and to be had without stint or charge, they generally supply themselves, and make their own fires."

During this conversation, which from the beginning to end, was of the most alarming interest to William, his eyes wide open, were fixed on Mr. Waddel, who was an object of still more alarming interest to him. He had never seen—we have never seen—a man of sterner features than Mr. Waddel bore. From the time that William entered the house to the time that he left it, "shadows, clouds, and darkness" were gathering and deepening upon his mind; relieved only by one faint gleam of light from young Ramsay, whom he regarded as the concentrated extract of all that was august, and great, and gifted, and good in the United States, if not in the world; and an ample verification *per se* of all that his uncle had told him about "big men's sons."

William was entered in due form a student of Mr. Waddel's school; and the Captain having enquired of the post office at which the students received their letters, and pressed Mr. Waddel to give him early information of William's conduct, standing, and progress, he left with his charge for Mr. New-by's. . . .

Monday morning came, and William moved sadly to the Academy. Soon the students of every size began to pour in from every quarter; and soon the whole school was in commotion. George Cary had got a thousand lines in Virgil! He was to leave [lead] his class, of course; for such a lesson had never been heard of before, even in Dr. Waddel's school, where the students seemed to take in Latin and Greek by absorption. As his classmates came in, they compared notes, and not one of them had got more than three hundred lines. "I didn't get but two hundred and ten," said one; "I didn't get but two hundred," said another. "Well, I'm at the foot of all," said a third, "I didn't get but a hundred and fifty; so I'm double distanced, and left, of course."

William heard these reports with overwhelming amazement. The largest lesson he had ever recited was thirty-five lines, and the largest he had ever heard of being recited was one hundred. He had been led to believe that his native village was the very focus of intellectual illumination and mental vigor, and that he himself was the centre-beam of the focus. He did not suppose that Latin and Greek were made for country folks at all, much less for poor folks; and behold, there stood before him homespun, Gilbo-shod, potato-fed chaps, even smaller than himself, who had mastered one hundred and fifty lines in Virgil, acknowledging themselves the fag-end of their class, and "double distanced!" His mind was immediately made up to take the *selectæ* class, mortifying as it was to a gentleman of his calibre to have it known at home that he had retrograded; but could he keep up with this class? He had little hope of doing so; but so shocking was the idea of falling two classes below his home stand, that he resolved to try it all at events. He had one consolation, at least, and that was, that none of the school-boys knew of his advancement before he came hither. Withal, he concluded that there must be a something about Doctor Waddel's school that made all the boys who came to it smart, and whatever that something might be, he surely would catch it in a short time. The Doctor soon made his appearance; and William signified to him his choice of classes. . . .

From a weakly, puny, cowering, retiring, say-nothing boy, he became a muscular, active, sprightly, vigorous youth, who was nearly a match for any of his age, in running, jumping, wrestling, and the active sports of the school; and for loud clamoring at bull-pen, and town-ball, he had no superior. There was but one South Carolinian in the school who could throw him down, and that one was Andrew Govan; there was not one in the school who could match him in running. From fifty lips the exclamation would come: "Did you ever see a fellow come out of the kinks as Bill Mitten has?" By the time it came his turn to make fires in the Academy, (one of the duties of every student,) he was as prompt and skillful in this work as most of his associates. Sweeping out the Academy (another duty) of course was easy. Beyond all this, there was nothing remarkable in his history until the annual examination and exhibition came on. These exercises continued for several days, and they were attended by multitudes—more, by many, than usually attend our College Commencements in these days. The order was as follows: First, the examination of all the classes; which was invariably conducted by the visitors, except when they declined the task, and this rarely occurred. Then speaking, for which prizes were awarded. And lastly, the performance of one or two dramatic pieces, usually a comedy and farce: but these were discontinued after the first and only public exhibition in which William Mitten took part, and the reading of compositions was substituted for them. The speakers were divided into three classes, according to their age and advancement; the first class being composed generally of the oldest students in the school; the second, of those next in years; and the third, of the youngest, excluding those in the elementary studies. This arrangement was not always observed, however. Sometimes the larger and less advanced were put in the first class, and the smaller and more advanced, in the second class. William's age flung him in the lowest, though his advancement would have entitled him to a place in the second. The examination approached, and William wrote pressingly to his mother and uncle to attend. They did so, and reached Newby's the day before the exercises commenced. William recognized them at the fence, and ran out to meet them. Neither of them knew him, till he greeted them, any more than if they had never seen him. His fine face was there, a little tanned, but that was all of William Mitten that was left. He had grown like a weed, and developed as we have said. The Captain looked at him in triumph—the mother in tears. . . .

On the third day the speaking commenced.

A stage of rough plank was erected adjoining the school-house. On this sat the Judges, of whom William H. Crawford, John C. Calhoun, and William W. Bibb were three. These hardly ever failed to attend the public exercises of Dr. Waddel's school. The two first had been his pupils, and the reader will excuse the digression, to learn that the first wife of the Doctor was the sister of the second.

In front of the stage, large logs were laid parallel to each other on which planks were placed at convenient distances apart, for seats. The whole was covered over with a bush-arbor. It was but a scant provision for the throng that attended upon this occasion; but what provision could accommodate all, when the number fell little, if any, short of two thousand people? The ladies, several hundreds in number, occupied all the seats.

Without going through the details of the exercises, suffice it to say that Mitten took the premium in his class by the award of the judges, approved of by every man, woman and *student* present at the exhibition. He had a part in both the dramatic pieces; and here he acquitted himself, if possible, with more credit than in declamation. When Mr. Calhoun, with a few complimentary words, presented him the prize, the whole assembly applauded loudly and cordially. One pretty little girl, beautifully dressed, quite forgot herself, and kept on clapping after everybody else had done, till her mother, laughing most heartily, stopped her. "Mitten, Mitten, Mitten!" was on every lip. All the ladies, old and young, wanted to kiss him; all the little girls fell in love with him. A thousand compliments saluted the ear of Mrs. Mitten from lips that she knew not. Through Captain Thompson, she had been made acquainted with Doctor Waddel, before the exercises commenced, and through him, with most of the gentlemen who sat as judges, and her acquaintance was still farther extended by the sojourners at Mr. Newby's; but now everybody sought an introduction to her, and everybody congratulated her upon the performance of her son.

Most of the judges waited upon her, and all of them had something flattering to say of William, or to him in her presence, for he was always at her side.

"Master Mitten," said Mr. Crawford, "I am proud to claim you as a Georgian. Cultivate your brilliant talents as a duty and an honor to the State that gave you birth."

"Master Mitten," said Mr. Calhoun, "the United States have an interest in you; and should I live to see you in the prime of life, I shall be sorely disappointed if I do not see you the admiration of them all." . . .

DAVID CROCKETT

David Crockett was born near what is now Limestone, in Washington County, Tennessee, on August 17, 1786, and was killed at the Alamo, within the present limits of San Antonio, Texas, on March 6, 1836. His father, of Irish parentage, had farmed in Pennsylvania and North Carolina, and had kept a tavern in Tennessee. His mother was, in Crockett's words, "an American woman, born in the state of Maryland." The boy's adventurous, roving life began early. At the age of twelve his father bound him out to a Virginia cattle drover, and later he ran away with another drover. After these exploits he worked for a Quaker, John Kennedy, four days a week and attended a school two days a week taught by Kennedy's son. Throughout his life he was contemptuous of schooling. In 1806 he married an Irish girl, Polly Finley. In 1809 he moved to Lincoln County in Middle Tennessee, and a year later to Franklin County, where he gained local renown as a hunter. After the Creek Indians went on the war-path in 1813, Crockett volunteered as a scout; later he served under General Andrew Jackson; but he returned home before Jackson defeated the Indians at Horseshoe Bend. About 1815 his wife died, leaving him with three children. He married a widow, Mrs. Elizabeth Patton, and soon removed to Lawrence County in the western part of the state. When a temporary government was set up by the settlers, he was elected justice of peace and later major of the militia. Although he was ignorant of legal procedure, his popularity on the frontier brought his election to the state legislatures of 1821–1822 and 1823–1824. About his first, hurly-burly campaign "in which stump speeches, dances, barbecues, squirrel hunts and shooting matches figured conspicuously," he said that "It now became necessary that I should tell the people something about the government, and eternal sight of other things that I knowed nothing more about than I did about Latin, and law, and such things as that. . . . A public document I had never seen, nor did I know there were such things." During the legislative session of 1823 he broke politically with Jackson. He voted for Colonel John Williams, who unsuccessfully opposed Jackson for United States Senator, because he "thought the Colonel had honestly discharged his duty, and even the mighty name of Jackson couldn't make me vote against him."

In 1825 he was defeated by two votes in a campaign for Congress, but in 1827 he was elected by a big majority. He served the two terms in Congress from 1827 to 1831. His opposition to Jackson's Indian bill in 1830 caused his defeat, but he was re-elected in 1833.

In 1834 he made his celebrated triumphal "tour of the north," visiting Baltimore, Philadelphia, New York, and Boston. His popularity on this tour made his defeat for re-election very bitter. Disheartened, he left his family and friends in Tennessee and went to Texas to fight with the patriots for their independence. He took part in the heroic defense of the Alamo, and fell March 6, 1836. Accounts differ regarding the manner of his death. Some historians claim that he was killed in the fort, bullet-ridden, valiantly fighting: others say that he was killed as a prisoner before Santa Anna.

Of more importance to students of literature than Crockett's political and military exploits, are the writings by and about him and the legends which grew up around his name.

As a coonskin "man from the cane," who shot 105 bears in one season, as a camp story-teller, who convulsed his comrades with "tall tales," as a whirlwind stump-orator, and as a backwoods oracle, he entered the folk legends of the Southwest. "Gentlemen, I'm the darling branch of old Kentuck that can eat up a painter, hold a buffalo up to drink, and put a rifle ball through the moon." As a baby giant he had drunk wild buffaloes' milk, and as a boy he had tied together the tails of two buffaloes. He could make fire by rubbing a flint with his knuckles. Once he escaped a tornado by leaping astride the lightning. Another time he escaped up Niagara Falls on an alligator. "The alligator walked up the great hill of water as slick as a wildcat up a white-oak." "Now I tell you what," people would say of some strange happening, "it's nothing to Crockett."

AUTOBIOGRAPHY

Preface

Fashion is a thing I care mighty little about, *except* when it happens to run just exactly according to my own notion; and I was mighty nigh sending out my book without any preface at all, until a notion struck me that perhaps it was necessary to explain a little the reason why and wherefore I had written it.

Most of authors seek fame, but I seek for justice—a holier impulse than ever entered into the ambitious struggles of the votaries of that *fickle, flirting* goddess. . . .

In the following pages I have endeavored to give the reader a plain, honest, homespun account of my state in life, and some few of the difficulties which have attended me along its journey, down to this time. I am perfectly aware, that I have related many small and, as I fear, uninteresting circumstances; but if so, my apology is, that it was rendered necessary by a desire to link the different periods of my life together, as they have passed, from my childhood onward, and thereby to enable the reader to select such parts of it as he may relish most, if, indeed, there is any thing in it which may suit his palate.

I have also been operated on by another consideration. It is this:—I know, that obscure as I am, my name is making a considerable deal of fuss in the world. I can't tell why it is, nor in what it is to end. Go where I will, everybody seems anxious to get a peep at me; and it would be hard to tell which would have the advantage, if I, and the "Government," and "Black Hawk," and a great eternal big caravan of *wild varments* were all to be showed at the same time in four different parts of any of the big cities in the nation. I am not so sure that I shouldn't get the most custom of any of the crew. There must therefore be something in me, or about me, that attracts attention, which is even mysterious to myself. I can't understand it, and I therefore put all the facts down, leaving the reader free to take his choice of them.

On the subject of my style, it is bad enough, in all con-

science, to please critics, if that is what they are after. They are
a sort of vermin, though, that I sha'n't even so much as stop
to brush off. If they want to work on my book, just let them
go ahead; and after they are done, they had better blot out all
their criticisms, than to know what opinion I would express
of *them*, and by what sort of a curious name I would call *them*,
if I was standing near them, and looking over their shoulders.
They will, at most, have only their trouble for their pay. But
I rather expect I shall have them on my side.

But I don't know of any thing in my book to be criticised
on by honourable men. Is it on my spelling?—that's not my
trade. Is it on my grammar?—I hadn't time to learn it, and
make no pretensions to it. Is it on the order and arrangement
of my book?—I never wrote one before, and never read very
many; and, of course, know mighty little about that. Will it
be on the authorship of the book?—this I claim, and I'll hang
on to it, like a wax plaster. The whole book is my own, and
every sentiment and sentence in it. I would not be such a
fool, or knave either, as to deny that I have had it hastily run
over by a friend or so, and that some little alterations have been
made in the spelling and grammar; and I am not so sure that it
is not the worse of even that, for I despise this way of spelling
contrary to nature. And as for grammar, it's pretty much a
thing of nothing at last, after all the fuss that's made about it.
In some places, I wouldn't suffer either the spelling, or grammar, or any thing else to be touch'd; and therefore it will be
found in my own way.

But if any body complains that I have had it looked over, I
can only say to him, her, or them—as the case may be—that
while critics were learning grammar, and learning to spell, I,
and "Doctor Jackson, L.L.D." were fighting in the wars; and
if our books, and messages, and proclamations, and cabinet
writings, and so forth, and so on, should need a little looking
over, and a little correcting of the spelling and the grammar to
make them fit for use, it's just nobody's business. Big men
have more important matters to attend to than crossing their
t's—, and dotting their i's—, and such like small things. But

the "Government's" name is to the proclamation, and my name's to the book; and if I didn't write the book, the "Government" didn't write the proclamation, which no man *dares to deny!*

But just read for yourself, and my ears for a heel tap, if before you get through you don't say, with many a good-natured smile and hearty laugh, "This is truly the very thing itself—the exact image of its Author,

DAVID CROCKETT."

As a Magistrate

I was appointed one of the magistrates; and when a man owed a debt, and wouldn't pay it, I and my constable ordered our warrant, and then he would take the man, and bring him before me for trial. I would give judgment against him, and then an order of an execution would easily scare the debt out of him. If any one was charged with marking his neighbor's hogs, or with stealing any thing, which happened pretty often in those days,—I would have him taken, and if there was tolerable grounds for the charge, I would have him well whip'd and cleared. We kept this up till our Legislature added us to the white settlements in Giles county; and appointed magistrates by law, to organize matters in the parts where I lived. They appointed nearly every man a magistrate who had belonged to our corporation. I was then, of course, made a squire according to law; though now the honour rested more heavily on me than before. For, at first, whenever I told my constable, says I— "Catch that fellow, and bring him up for trial"—away he went, and the fellow must come, dead or alive; for we considered this a good warrant, though it was only in verbal writings. But after I was appointed by the assembly, they told me, my warrants must be in real writing, and signed; and that I must keep a book, and write my proceedings in it. This was a hard business on me, for I could just barely write my own name; but to do this, and write the warrants too, was at least a huckleberry over my persimmon. I had a pretty well informed constable, however; and he aided me very much in this business.

Indeed I had so much confidence in him, that I told him, when
we should happen to be out anywhere, and see that a warrant
was necessary, and would have a good effect he needn't take
the trouble to come all the way to me to get one, but he could
just fill out one; and then on the trial I could correct the whole
business if he had committed any error. In this way I got on
pretty well, till by care and attention I improved my hand-
writing in such manner as to be able to prepare my warrants,
and keep my record book, without much difficulty. My judgments were never appealed from, and if they had been they
would have stuck like wax, as I gave my decisions on the principles of common justice and honesty between man and man,
and relied on natural born sense, and not on law learning to
guide me; for I had never read a page of a law book in all my
life. . . .

A Bear Story

In the morning I left my son at the camp, and we started on
towards the harricane; and when we had went about a mile,
we started a very large bear, but we got along mighty slow on
account of the cracks in the earth occasioned by the earthquakes. We, however, made out to keep in hearing of the dogs
for about three miles, and then we come to the harricane. Here
we had to quit our horses, as old Nick himself couldn't have
got through it without sneaking along in the form that he put
on, to make a fool of our old grandmother Eve. By this time
several of my dogs had got tired and come back; but we went
ahead on foot for some little time in the harricane, when we
met a bear coming straight to us, and not more than twenty or
thirty yards off. I started my tired dogs after him, and McDaniel pursued them, and I went on to where my other dogs were.
I had seen the track of the bear they were after, and I knowed
he was a screamer. I followed on to about the middle of the
harricane, but my dogs pursued him so close that they made
him climb an old stump about twenty feet high. I got in shooting distance of him and fired, but I was all over in such a flutter from fatigue and running, that I couldn't hold steady; but,

however, I broke his shoulder, and he fell. I run up and loaded my gun as quick as possible, and shot him again and killed him. When I went to take out my knife to butcher him, I found I had lost it in coming through the harricane. The vines and briers was so thick that I would sometimes have to get down and crawl like a varment to get through at all; and a vine had, as I supposed, caught in the handle and pulled it out. While I was standing and studying what to do, my friend came to me. He had followed my trail through the harricane, and had found my knife, which was mighty good news to me; as a hunter hates the worst in the world to lose a good dog, or any part of his hunting-tools. I now left McDaniel to butcher the bear, and I went after our horses, and brought them as near as the nature of case would allow. I then took our bags, and went back to where he was; and when we had skin'd the bear, we fleeced off the fat and carried it to our horses at several loads. We then packed it up on our horses, and had a heavy pack of it on each one. We now started and went on till about sunset, when I concluded we must be near our camp; so I hollered and my son answered me, and we moved on in the direction to the camp. We had gone but a little way when I heard my dogs make a warm start again; and I jumped down from my horse and gave him up to my friend, and told him I would follow them. He went on to the camp, and I went ahead after my dogs with all my might for a considerable distance, till at last night came on. The woods were very rough and hilly, and all covered over with cane.

I now was compel'd to move on more slowly; and was frequently falling over logs, and into the cracks made by the earthquakes, so that I was very much afraid I would break my gun. However I went on about three miles, when I came to a good big creek, which I waded. It was very cold, and the creek was about knee-deep; but I felt no great inconvenience from it just then, as I was all over wet with sweat from running, and I felt hot enough. After I got over the creek and out of the cane, which was very thick on all our creeks, I listened for my dogs. I found they had either treed or brought the bear to a stop, as they continued barking in the same place. I pushed on as near in the direction to the noise as I could, till I found the hill was too steep for me to climb, and so I backed and went down the creek some distance till I came to a hollow, and then took up that, till I come to a place where I could climb up the hill. It was mighty dark, and was difficult to see my way or any thing else. When I got up the hill, I found I had passed the dogs; and so I turned and went to them. I found, when I got there, they had treed the bear in a large forked poplar, and it was setting in the fork.

I could see the lump, but not plain enough to shoot with any certainty, as there was no moonlight; and so I set in to hunting for some dry brush to make me a light; but I could find none, though I could find that the ground was torn mightily to pieces by the cracks.

At last I thought I could shoot by guess, and kill him; so I pointed as near the lump as I could, and fired away. But the bear didn't come; he only clomb up higher, and got out on a limb, which helped me to see him better. I now loaded up again and fired, but this time he didn't move at all. I commenced loading for a third fire, but the first thing I knowed, the bear was down among my dogs, and they were fighting all around me. I had my big butcher in my belt, and I had a pair of dressed buckskin breeches on. So I took out my knife, and stood, determined, if he should get hold of me, to defend myself in the best way I could. I stood there for some time, and could now and then see a white dog I had, but the rest of them, and the bear, which were dark coloured, I couldn't see at all, it was so miserable dark. They still fought around me, and sometimes within three feet of me; but, at last, the bear got down into one of the cracks, that the earthquakes had made in the ground, about four feet deep, and I could tell the biting end of him by the hollering of my dogs. So I took my gun and pushed the muzzle of it about, till I thought I had it against the main part of his body, and fired; but it happened to be only the fleshy part of his foreleg. With this, he jumped out of the crack, and he and the dogs had another hard fight around me, as before. At last, however, they forced him back into the crack again, as he was when I had shot.

I had laid down my gun in the dark, and I now began to hunt for it; and, while hunting, I got hold of a pole, and I concluded I would punch him awhile with that. I did so, and when I would punch him, the dogs would jump in on him, when he would bite them badly, and they would jump out again. I concluded, as he would take punching so patiently, it might be that he would lie still enough for me to get down in the crack, and feel slowly along till I could find the right place to give him a dig with my butcher. So I got down, and my dogs got in before him and kept his head towards them, till I got along easily up to him; and placing my hand on his rump, felt for his shoulder, just behind which I intended to stick him. I made a lounge with my long knife, and fortunately stuck him right through the heart; at which he just sank down, and I crawled out in a hurry. In a little time my dogs all come out too, and seemed satisfied, which was the way they always had of telling me that they had finished him.

I suffered very much that night with cold, as my leather breeches, and every thing else I had on, was wet and frozen. But I managed to get my bear out of this crack after several hard trials, and so I butchered him, and laid down to try to sleep. But my fire was very bad, and I couldn't find any thing that would burn well to make it any better; and I concluded I should freeze, if I didn't warm myself in some way by exercise. So I got up, and hollered a while, and then I would just jump up and down with all my might, and throw myself into all sorts of motions. But all this wouldn't do; for my blood was now getting cold, and the chills coming all over me. I was so tired, too, that I could hardly walk; but I thought I would do the best I could to save my life, and then, if I died, nobody would be to blame. So I went to a tree about two feet through, and not a limb on it for thirty feet, and I would climb up it to the limbs, and then lock my arms together around it, and slide down to the bottom again. This would make the insides of my legs and arms feel mighty warm and good. I continued this till daylight in the morning, and how often I clomb up my tree and slid down I don't know, but I reckon at least a hundred times.

In the morning I got my bear hung up so as to be safe, and then set out to hunt for my camp. I found it after a while, and McDaniel and my son were very much rejoiced to see me get back, for they were about to give me up for lost. We got our breakfasts, and then secured our meat by building a high scaffold, and covering it over. We had no fear of its spoiling, for the weather was so cold that it couldn't. . . .

Crockett Goes to Congress

I have, heretofore, informed the reader that I had determined to run this race to see what effect *the price of cotton* could have again on it. I now had Col. Alexander to run against once more, and also General William Arnold.

I had difficulties enough to fight against this time, as every one will suppose; for I had no money, and a very bad prospect, so far as I know'd, of getting any to help me along. I had, however, a good friend, who sent for me to come and see him. I went, and he was good enough to offer me some money to help me out. I borrowed as much as I thought I needed at the start, and went ahead. My friend also had a good deal of business about over the district at the different courts; and if he now and then slip'd in a good word for me, it is nobody's business. We frequently met at different places, and, as he thought I needed, he would occasionally hand me a little more cash; so I was able to buy a little of "the *creature*," to put my friends in a good humour, as well as the other gentlemen, for they all treat in that country; not to get elected, of course— for that would be against the law; but just, as I before said, to make themselves and their friends feel their keeping a little.

Nobody ever did know how I got money to get along on, till after the election was over, and I had beat my competitors twenty-seven hundred and forty-eight votes. Even the price of cotton couldn't save my friend Aleck this time. My rich friend, who had been so good to me in the way of money, now sent for me, and loaned me a hundred dollars, and told me to go ahead; that that amount would bear my expenses to Congress, and I must then shift for myself. I came on to Washington, and draw'd two hundred and fifty dollars, and purchased with it a check on the bank at Nashville, and enclosed it to my friend; and I may say, in truth, I sent this money with a mighty good will, for I reckon nobody in this world loves a friend better than me, or remembers a kindness longer.

I have now given the close of the election, but I have skip'd entirely over the canvass, of which I will say a very few things in this place; as I know very well how to tell the truth, but not much about placing them in book order, so as to please critics.

Col. Alexander was a very clever fellow, and principal surveyor at that time; so much for one of the men I had to run against. My other competitor was a major-general in the militia, and an attorney-general at the law, and quite a smart, clever man also; and so it will be seen I had war work as well as law trick, to stand up under. Taking both together, they make a pretty considerable of a load for any one man to carry. But for war claims, I consider myself behind no man except "the government," and mighty little, if any, behind him; but this the people will have to determine hereafter, as I reckon it won't do to quit the work of "reform and retrenchment" yet for a spell.

But my two competitors seemed some little afraid of the influence of each other, but not to think me in their way at all. They, therefore, were generally working against each other, while I was going ahead for myself, and mixing among the people in the best way I could. I was as cunning as a little red fox, and wouldn't risk my tail in a "committal" trap.

I found the sign was good, almost everywhere I went. On one occasion, while we were in the eastern counties of the district, it happened that we all had to make a speech, and it fell on me to make the first one. I did so after my manner, and it turned pretty much on the old saying, "A short horse is soon curried," as I spoke not very long. Colonel Alexander followed me, and then General Arnold come on.

The general took much pains to reply to Alexander, but didn't so much as let on that there was any such candidate as myself at all. He had been speaking for a considerable time, when a large flock of guinea-fowls came very near to where he was, and set up the most unmerciful chattering that ever was heard, for they are a noisy little brute any way. They so confused the general, that he made a stop, and requested that they might be driven away. I let him finish his speech, and then walking up to him, said aloud, "Well, colonel, you are the first man I ever saw that understood the language of fowls." I told him that he had not had the politeness to name me in his speech, and that when my little friends, the guinea-fowls, had come up and began to holler "Crockett, Crockett, Crockett," he had been ungenerous enough to stop, and drive *them* all away. This raised a universal shout among the people for me, and the general seemed mighty bad plagued. But he got more plagued than this at the polls in August, as I have stated before. . . .

After all this, the reader will perceive that I am now here in Congress, this 28th day of January, in the year of our Lord one thousand eight hundred and thirty-four; and that, what is more agreeable to my feelings as a freeman, I am at liberty to vote as my conscience and judgment dictates to be right, without the yoke of any party on me, or the driver at my heels, with his whip in hand, commanding me to ge-wo-haw, just at his pleasure. Look at my arms, you will find no party handcuff on them! Look at my neck, you will not find there any collar, with the engraving

MY DOG.
Andrew Jackson.

But you will find me standing up to my rack, as the people's faithful representative, and the public's most obedient, very humble servant,

David Crockett.

WILLIAM GILMORE SIMMS

William Gilmore Simms was born in Charleston, South
Carolina, April 17, 1806, and died in Charleston, June 11, 1870.
When the boy was two years old, his mother died, and his
father's mercantile concern went into bankruptcy. Leaving
the boy in the care of relatives, the father went to the border
states of the Southwest, where he served under Andrew Jackson
in the Indian wars. After attending the common schools,
about which he wrote later as "worthless and scoundrelly,"
the boy first served a partial apprenticeship to a druggist and
later studied law. In 1824 or 1825 he visited his father on the
border for a leisurely sojourn which he later used richly in
writing his border romances. The period from 1825 to 1832
was marked by some minor successes, moderate literary recognition, and disheartening failures. His first publication, a
Monody on General Cotesworth Pinckney (1825), was followed
by other volumes of poems. In 1826 he married Anna Malcolm
Giles, who died in 1832. He practised law with moderate
success. With E. S. Duryea he bought a daily newspaper, the
Charleston *City Gazette*, and became involved in political
strife over nullification. According to a colorful legend he defied a mob furiously bent on destroying the printing-press.
After the deaths of his father and his wife, and because of the
discouragement caused by his publishing failures, he decided to
go north. In New York he made friends with publishers,
actors, and literati, and in New Haven he settled down for
writing. His first prose work, *Martin Faber*, was published in
1838 by Harper and Brothers. Other novels were produced
rapidly, sometimes two a year, bringing moderate financial rewards and literary recognition. In 1835 he produced two of
his best tales, *The Yemassee: A Romance of Carolina*, and *The
Partisan: A Tale of the Revolution.*

The years from 1836 to the Civil War were happy and successful in Simms's life. In 1836 he married Chevillette Roach,
the daughter of a well-to-do gentleman. They lived on the
estate "Woodlands," half-way between Charleston and Augusta,
where Simms built up a library of ten thousand volumes, wrote

many novels, poems, and reviews, and entertained his friends in amiable hospitality. He rode almost daily to Charleston, where he edited newspapers and magazines, and met Hayne, Timrod, and other writers in Russell's bookshop.

In the ante-bellum political controversies, Simms used his pen trenchantly in the defense of slavery and in advocacy of secession. During the war each southern victory was cheering to him, and successive northern victories and invasions grieved and infuriated him. He never recovered in spirit from Appomattox and its aftermath. In 1862 "Woodlands" burst into flames, from an unknown cause, and only his library and manuscripts were saved. His wife died in 1863. During the last decade of his life Simms was an unhappy, often frantic man, prematurely aged, losing relatives, property, and health, but not friends, and writing very little of importance.

Simms was a very prolific writer, as even the incomplete bibliographies of his writings indicate. Besides his several volumes of poetry and his uncollected writings in newspapers and magazines, he wrote about thirty-five books of novels, novelettes, and stories, and about ten volumes of history and biography.

Simms wrote "the epic of the Revolution" in seven romances. He followed *The Partisan* (1835) with *Mellichampe* (1836), *The Kinsmen* (1841), which was later published as *The Scout*, *Katherine Walton* (1851), *The Sword and the Distaff* (1853), which was later published as *Woodcraft*, *The Forayers* (1855), and *Eutaw* (1856). H. M. Jarrell, however, does not include *Woodcraft* as one of the Revolutionary romances, because it deals with events following the Revolution. The author's favorite character, Lieutenant Porgy, "the fat and philosophic partisan under Marion," appears in all the romances except *The Scout*, and is the central figure in *Woodcraft*. The border novels, following *Guy Rivers*, were *Richard Hurdis: A Tale of Alabama* (1838), *Border Beagles: A Tale of Mississippi* (1840), *Beauchampe, or the Kentucky Tragedy* (1842) and *Charlemont* (1852). A few years later he returned to colonial history and Indian warfare in *The Cassique of Kiawah* (1859).

Simms wrote and published at least fifty-eight stories, besides five novelettes. Many of these were collected in the following volumes: *The Book of My Lady* (1833), containing fifteen stories; *Martin Faber and Other Tales* (1838), eight stories and a novelette; *Carl Werner* (1838), eight stories; *The Wigwam and the Cabin* (1845), thirteen stories; *Wigwam and Cabin: Life in America* (1848), containing the *Wigwam and Cabin* stories, and two additional stories; *The Lily and the Totem* (1850), five stories; *Southward Ho!* (1854), fourteen stories. J. Allen Morris states: "In publishing his collections Simms felt that he was making a contribution toward the development of southern literature. Studies of the best stories in these seven collections indicate that he was right in his belief. His stories of Negroes, Indians and frontier characters are worthwhile contributions to American literature."

Simms was editorially connected with nine newspapers and magazines, of which all except *The Columbia Phoenix* were published in Charleston. *The Southern Literary Gazette* (1828–1829) suffered from the competition of Legaré's *Southern Review*. In a review of James E. Heath's *Edge-Hill*, a romance of Virginia, Simms pleaded for a southern regional literature. *The City Gazette* (1830–1832) has been mentioned. *The Cosmopolitan* (1833), which appeared in two numbers, included several of Simms's stories. *The Magnolia* (1842–1843) had been published in Macon and Savannah, Georgia, before its removal to Charleston. In various reviews Simms stressed regionalism in literature. Guy A. Cardwell, Jr., to whose dissertation on Charleston periodicals I am indebted, states that *"Russell's Magazine* is, perhaps, the only Charleston periodical of its own *genre* which surpasses it [*The Magnolia*] in interest, merit, and ambition." In a quarrel with the New York *Knickerbocker* Simms asserted the literary independence of the South. In *The Southern and Western Magazine and Review*, also called *Simms' Magazine* (1845), he was a pronounced champion of a native literature. *The Southern Quarterly Review* came from New Orleans to Charleston in 1849 and was published until 1855; Simms was the editor most of the time. He was associate editor with Henry Timrod of *The Daily South Carolinian* (1865–1866). With *The Courier* he formed a connection in 1866. As contributor and reviewer Simms aided several other newspapers and magazines, of which the last was *The XIX Century*, published in Charleston in 1869–1871.

To know southern literature before 1870, the student must read widely in the writings of this versatile champion of the South.

From THE LAZY CROW: A STORY OF THE CORNFIELD

Chapter I

We were on the Savannah river when the corn was coming up; at the residence of one of those planters of the middle country, the staid, sterling, old-time gentlemen of the last century, the stock of which is so rapidly diminishing. The season was advanced and beautiful; the flowers every where in odour, and all things promised well for the crops of the planter. Hopes and seed, however, set out in March and April, have a long time to go before ripening, and when I congratulated Mr. Carrington on the prospect before him, he would shake his head, and smile and say, in a quizzical inquiring humour, "wet or dry, cold or warm, which shall it be? what season shall we have? Tell me that, and I will hearken with more confidence to your congratulations. We can do no more than plant the seed, scuffle with the grass, say our prayers, and leave the rest to Him without whose blessing no labour can avail."

"There is something more to be done, and of scarcely less importance it would seem, if I may judge from the movements of Scipio—kill or keep off the crows."

Mr. Carrington turned as I spoke these words; we had just left the breakfast table, where we had enjoyed all the warm comforts of hot rice-waffles, journey-cake, and glowing biscuit, not to speak of hominy and hoe-cake, without paying that passing acknowledgment to dyspeptic dangers upon which modern physicians so earnestly insist. Scipio, a sleek, well-fed negro, with a round, good-humoured face, was busy in a corner of the apartment; one hand employed in grasping a goodly fragment of bread, half concealed in a similar slice of fried bacon, which he had just received from his young mistress;—while the other carefully selected from the corner, one of half a dozen double-barrelled guns, which he was about to raise to his shoulder, when my remark turned the eye of his master upon him.

"How now, Scipio, what are you going to shoot?" was the inquiry of Mr. Carrington.

"Crow, sa; dere's a dratted ugly crow dat's a-troublin me, and my heart's set for kill 'um."

"One only? why, Scip, you're well off if you hav'n't a hundred. Do they trouble you very much in the pine land field?"

"Dare's a plenty, sa; but dis one I guine kill, sa, he's wuss more nor all de rest. You hab good load in bote barrel, mossa?" . . .

"But, Scip, you surprise me. You don't mean to say that it is one crow in particular that annoys you in this manner?"

"De same one ebbery day, mossa; de same one"; was the reply.

"How long has this been?"

"Mos' a week now, massa; ebber sence las' Friday."

"Indeed! but what makes you think this troublesome crow always the same one, Scipio? Do you think the crows never change their spies?"

"Enty, I know um, mossa; dis da same crow been trouble me, ebber since las' Friday. He's a crow by hese'f, mossa. I nebber see him wid t'oder crows he no hab complexion ob t'oder crow, yet he's crow, all de same."

"Is he not black like all his tribe?"

"Yes, he black, but he ain't black like de t'oder ones. Dere's someting like a grey dirt 'pon he wing. He's black, but he no pot black—no jet;—he hab dirt, I tell you, mossa, on he wing, jis' by de skirt ob he jacket—jis yer"; and he lifted the lappel [lapel] of his master's coat as he concluded his description of the bird that troubled him.

"A strange sort of crow, indeed, Scipio, if he answers your description. Should you kill him, be sure and bring him to me. I can scarcely think him a crow."

"How, no crow, mossa? Enty, I know crow as good as anybody! He's a crow, mossa,—a dirty, black nigger ob a crow, and I'll shoot um t'rough he head, sure as a gun. He trouble me too much; look hard 'pon me as ef you bin gib um wages for obersee. Nobody ax um for watch me, see wha' I do! Who mak' him obersheer?" . . .

"Well, well, Scipio, kill your crow, but be sure and bring him in when you do so. You may go now."

"I hab um to-night for you, mossa, ef God spare me. Look ya, young missis, you hab any coffee lef' in de pot; I tanks you." . . .

. . . at evening, returning from his labors in the cornfield, who should make his appearance but Scipio. He came to place the gun in the corner from which he had taken it; but he brought with him no trophies of victory. . . .

"What, Scipio! no crow?" demanded his master.

"I no shoot, sa," replied the negro, moving off as he spoke, as if willing that the examination should rest there. But Mr. Carrington, who was something of a quiz, and saw that the poor fellow laboured under a feeling of mortified self-conceit, was not unwilling to worry him a little further.

"Ah, Scip, I always thought you a poor shot, in spite of your bragging; now I'm sure of it. A crow comes and stares you out of countenance, walks round you, and scarcely flies when you pelt him, and yet, when the gun is in your hands, you do nothing. How's that?" . . .

"Dis same crow, mossa; I tell you, mossa, 'tis dis same dirty nigger ob a crow I bin looking arter, ebber since I get over de task. He's a ting da's too sassy and aggrabates me berry much. I follow um tel de sun shut he eye, and nebber can git shot. Ef I bin git shot, I nebber miss um, mossa, I tell you."

"But why did you not get a shot? You must have bungled monstrously, Scipio, not to succeed in getting a shot at a bird that is always about you. Does he bother you less than he did before, now that you have the gun?"

"I spec' he mus' know, mossa, da's de reason; but he bodder me jis' de same. He nebber leff me all day I bin in de cornfield, but he nebber come so close for be shoot. He say to he sef, dat gun good at sixty yard, in Scip hand; I stan' sixty, I stan' a hundred; ef he shoot so far, I laugh at 'em. Da's wha' he say."

"Well, even at seventy or eighty yards, you should have

tried him, Scipio. The gun that tells at sixty, will be very apt to tell at seventy or eighty yards, if the nerves be good that hold it and the eye close. Try him even at a hundred, Scipio, rather than lose your crow; but put in your biggest shot."

Chapter III

. . . Not a day passed that the negro failed to shoot at him; always, however, by his own account, at disadvantage, and never, it appears, with any success. The consequence of all this was, that Scipio fell sick. What with the constant annoyance of the thing, and a too excitable imagination, Scipio, a stout fellow nearly six feet high, and half as many broad, laid himself at length in his cabin, at the end of the week, and was placed on the sick-list accordingly. . . .

Dr. C——, a very clever and well-read man, soon made his appearance, and was regularly introduced to the patient. His replies to the physician were as little satisfactory as those which he had made to us; and, after a long and tedious cross examination by doctor and master, the conclusion was still the same. Some few things, however, transpired in the inquiry, which led us all to the same inference with the doctor, who ascribed Scipio's condition to some mental hallucination. While the conversation had been going on in his cabin—a dwelling like most negro houses, made with poles, and the chinks stopped with clay—he turned abruptly from the physician to a negro girl that brought him soup, and asked the following question.

"Who bin tell Gullah Sam for to come in yesserday?"

The girl looked confused, and made no answer.

"Answer him," said the master.

"Da's him—why you no talk, nigger?" said the patient authoritatively. "I ax you who bin tell Gullah Sam for come in yer yesserday?"

"He bin come?" responded the girl with another inquiry.

"Sure he bin come—enty I see um wid he dirty gray jacket, like dirt on a crow wing. He tink I no see um—he 'tan dere in dis corner, close de chimney, and look wha's a cook in de pot.

Oh, how my ear bu'n—somebody's a talking bad tings 'bout Scipio now."

There was a good deal in this speech to interest Mr. Carrington and myself; we could trace something of his illness to his strife with the crow; but who was Gullah Sam? This was a question put by both the doctor and myself, at the same moment.

"You no know Gullah Sam, enty? Ha! better you don't know 'um—he's a nigger da's more dan nigger—wish he min' he own bis'ness."

With these words the patient turned his face to the wall of his habitation, and seemed unwilling to vouchsafe us any farther speech. It was thought unnecessary to annoy him with farther inquiries, and, leaving the cabin we obtained the desired information from his master.

"Gullah Sam," said he, "is a native born African from the Gold Coast, who belongs to my neighbor, Mr. Jamison, and was bought by his father out of a Rhode Island slaver, some time before the Revolution. He is now, as you may suppose, rather an old man; and, to all appearances, would seem a simple and silly one enough; but the negroes all around conceive him to be a great conjurer, and look upon his powers as a wizard, with a degree of dread, only to be accounted for by the notorious superstition of ignorance. . . . He believes himself to be bewitched by Gullah Sam, and, whether the African possesses any power such as he pretends to or not, is still the same to Scipio, if his mind has a full conviction that he does, and that he has become its victim. A superstitious negro might as well be bewitched, as to fancy that he is so." . . .

Chapter IV

That evening, we all returned to the cabin of Scipio. We found him more composed—sane, perhaps, would be the proper word—than in the morning, and, accordingly, perfectly silent on the subject of Gullah Sam. His master took the opportunity of speaking to him in plain language.

"Scipio, why do you try to keep the truth from me? Have

you ever found me a bad master, that you should fear to tell me the truth?"

"Nebber say sich ting! Who tell you, mossa, I say you bad?" replied the negro with a lofty air of indignation, rising on his arm in the bed.

"Why should you keep the truth from me?" was the reply.

"Wha' trut' I keep from you, mossa?"

"The cause of your sickness, Scipio. Why did you not tell me that Gullah Sam had bewitched you?"

The negro was confounded.

"How you know, mossa?" was his demand.

"It matters not," replied the master, "but how come Gullah Sam to bewitch you?"

"He kin 'witch den, mossa?" was the rather triumphant demand of the negro, who saw, in his master's remark, a concession to his faith, which had always been withheld before. Mr. Carrington extricated himself from the dilemma with sufficient promptness and ingenuity.

"The devil has power, Scipio, over all that believe in him. If you believe that Gullah Sam can do with you what he pleases, in spite of God and the Saviour, there is no doubt that he can; and God and the Saviour will alike give you up to his power, since, when you believe in the devil, you refuse to believe in them. They have told you, and the preacher has told you, and I have told you, that Gullah Sam can do you no sort of harm, if you will refuse to believe in what he tells you. Why then do you believe in that miserable and ignorant old African, sooner than in God and the preacher, and myself?"

"I can't help it mossa—de ting's de ting, and you can't change 'um. Dis Gullah Sam—he wus more nor ten debble— I jis' laugh at 'um t'oder day—tree week 'go, when he tumble in de hoss pond, and he shake he finger at me, and ebber since he put he bad mout' pon me. Ebber sence dat time, dat ugly crow bin stand in my eyes, whichebber way I tu'n. He hab gray dirt on he wing, and enty dere's a gray pitch on Gullah Sam jacket? Gullah Sam hab close 'quaintan' wid dat same lazy crow da's walk roun' me in de cornfield, mossa. I bin tink so from de fuss; and when he 'tan and le' me shoot at 'um, and no 'fraid, den I sartain."

"Well, Scipio," said the master, "I will soon put an end to Sam's power, I will see Mr. Jamison, and will have Sam well flogged for his witchcraft. I think you ought to be convinced that a wizard who suffers himself to be flogged, is but a poor devil after all."

The answer of the negro was full of consternation.

"For Chris' sake, mossa, I beg you do no sich ting. You lick Gullah Sam, den you lose Scipio for eber and eber, amen. Gullah Sam nebber guine take off de bad mout' he put on Scip, once you lick em. De pains will keep in de bones—de leg will dead, fuss de right leg, den de lef, one arter t'oder, and you nigger will dead, up and up, till noting lef for dead but he head. He head will hab life, when you kin put he body in de hole, and cubber um up wid du't. You mus' try n'oder tings, mossa, for get you nigger cure—you lick Gullah Sam, 'tis kill um for ebber." . . .

"Well, Scipio, it seems nothing will please you. What would you have? what course shall I take to dispossess the devil, and send Gullah Sam about his business?"

After a brief pause, in which the negro twisted from side to side of his bed, he answered as follows:

"Ef you kin trow way money on Scip, mossa, dere's a way I tink 'pon, dat'll do um help, if dere's any ting kin help um now, widout go to Gullah Sam. But it's a berry 'spensive way, mossa."

"How much will it cost?" demanded the master. "I am not unwilling to pay money for you, either to cure you when you are sick, as you ought to know by my sending for the doctor, or by putting more sense into your head than you seem to have at present. How much money do you think it will take to send the devil out of you?"

"Ha! mossa, you no speak 'spectful 'nough. Dis Gullah Sam hard to move; more dan de lazy crow dat walk in de corn-field. He will take money 'nough; mos' a bag ob cotton in dese hard times."

"Pshaw—speak out and tell me what you mean!" said the now thoroughly impatient master.

"Dere's an old nigger, mossa, dat's an Ebo,—he lib ober on St. Matt'ew's, by de bluff, place of Major Thompson. He's mighty great hand for cure bad mout'. He's named 'Tuselah, and he's a witch he sef, worse more nor Gullah Sam. Gullah Sam fear'd um—berry fear'd um. You send for 'Tuselah, mossa, he cos' you more nor twenty dollars. Scipio get well for sartin, and you neber yerry any more 'bout dat sassy crow in de cornfield."

"If I thought so," replied Mr. Carrington, looking round upon us, as if himself half ashamed to give in to the suggestion of the negro; "if I thought so, I would certainly send for Methuselah. But really, there s something very ridiculous in all this."

"I think not," was my reply. "Your own theory will sustain you, since, if Scipio's fancy makes one devil, he is equally assured, by the same fancy, of the counter power of the other."

"Besides," said the doctor, "you are sustained by the proverb, 'set a thief to catch a thief.' The thing is really curious. I shall be anxious to see how the St. Matthew's wizard overcomes him of Santee; though to speak truth, a sort of sectional interest in my own district, would almost tempt me to hope that he may be defeated. This should certainly be my prayer, were it not that I have some commiseration for Scipio. I should be sorry to see him dying by inches."

"By feet rather," replied his master with a laugh. "First the right leg, then the left, up and up, until life remains to him in his head only. But you shall have your wish, Scipio. I will send a man to-morrow by daylight to St. Matthew's for Methuselah, and if he can overcome Gullah Sam at his own weapons, I shall not begrudge him the twenty dollars."

"Tenks, mossa, tousand tenks," was the reply of the invalid; his countenance suddenly brightening for the first time for a week, as if already assured of the happy termination of his affliction. Meanwhile, we left him to his cogitations, each of us musing to himself, as well on the singular mental infirmities of a negro, at once sober, honest, and generally sensible, and that strange sort of issue which was about to be made up, between the respective followers of the rival principles of African witchcraft, the Gullah and the Ebo fetishes.

Chapter V

The indulgent master that night addressed a letter to the owner of Methuselah, stating all the circumstances of the case, and soliciting permission for the wizard, of whom such high expectations were formed, or fancied, to return with the messenger, who took with him an extra horse that the journey might be made with sufficient despatch. To this application a ready assent was given, and the messenger returned on the day after his departure, attended by the sage personage in question.

Methuselah was an African, about sixty-five years of age, with a head round as an owl's, and a countenance quite as grave and contemplative. His features indicated all the marked characteristics of his race, low forehead, high cheek bone, small eyes, flat nose, thick lips, and a chin sharp and retreating. He was not more than five feet high, and with legs so bowed that —to use Scipio's expression, when he was so far recovered as to be able again to laugh at his neighbor,—a yearling calf might easily run between them without grazing the *calf*. There was nothing promising in such a person but his sententiousness and gravity, and Methuselah possessed these characteristics in remarkable degree. When asked—

"Can you cure this fellow?" his answer, almost insolently expressed, was—

"I come for dat."

"You can cure people who are bewitched?"

"He no dead?"

"No."

"Belly [berry] well; I cure 'em; can't cure dead nigger."

There was but little to be got out of such a character by examination, direct or cross; and attending him to Scipio's wigwam, we tacitly resolved to look as closely into his proceedings as we could, assured, that in no other way could we possibly hope to arrive at any knowledge of his *modus operandi* in so curious a case.

Scipio was very glad to see the wizard of St. Matthew's and pointing to a chair, the only one in the chamber, he left us to the rude stools, of which there happened to be a sufficient supply.

"Well, brudder," said the African abruptly, "wha's matter?"

"Ha, Mr. 'Tuselah, I bin hab berry bad mout' put 'pon me."

"I know dat—you eyes run water—you ears hot—you hab knee shake—you trimble in de joint."

"You hit um; 'tis jis' dem same ting. I hab ears bu'n berry much," and thus encouraged to detail his symptoms, the garrulous Scipio would have prolonged his chronicle to the crack of doom, but that the wizard valued his time too much, to suffer any unnecessary eloquence on the part of his patient.

"You see two tings at a time?" asked the African.

"How! I no see," replied Scipio, not comprehending the question, which simply meant, do you ever see double? To this, when explained, he answered in a decided negative.

"'Tis a man den, put he bad mout' 'pon you," said the African.

"Gor-a-mighty, how you know dat?" exclaimed Scipio.

"Hush, my brudder—wha' beas' he look like?"

"He's a d—n black nigger ob a crow—a dirty crow, da's lazy for true."

"Ha! he lazy—you sure he ain't lame?"

"He no lame."

Scipio then gave a close description of the crow which had pestered him, precisely as he had given it to his master, as recorded in our previous pages. The African heard him with patience, then proceeded with oracular gravity.

"'Tis old man wha's trouble you!"

"Da's a trute!"

"Hush, my brudder. Whay you bin see dis crow?"

"Crow in de cornfiel', Mr. 'Tuselah; he can't come in de house."

"Who bin wid you all de time?"

"Jenny—de gal—he 'tan up in de corner now."

The magician turned and looked upon the person indicated by Scipio's finger—a little negro girl, probably ten years old. Then turning again to Scipio, he asked,

"You bin sick two, three, seben day, brudder—how long you bin on you bed?"

"Since Saturday night—da's six day to-day."

"And you hab nobody come for look 'pon you, since you bin on de bed, but dis gal, and de buckrah?"

Scipio confessed to several of the field negroes, servants of his own master, all of whom he proceeded to describe in compliance with the requisitions of the wizard, who, as if still unsatisfied, bade him, in stern accents, remember if nobody else had been in the cabin, or in his own language, had "set he eye 'pon you."

The patient hesitated for awhile, but the question being repeated, he confessed that in a half-sleep or stupor, he had fancied seeing Gullah Sam looking in upon him through the half-opened door; and at another time had caught glimpses, in his sleep, of the same features, through a chink between the logs, where the clay had fallen.

"Ha! ha! " said the wizard, with a half-savage grin of mingled delight and sagacity—"I hab nose,—I smell. Well, brudder, I mus' gib you physic,—you mus' hab good sweat to-night, and smood skin to-morrow."

Thus ended the conference with Scipio. The man of mystery arose and left the hovel, bidding us follow, and carefully fastening the door after him.

This done, he anointed some clay, which he gathered in the neighborhood, with his spittle, and plastered it over the lintel. He retired with us a little distance, and when we were about to separate, he for the woods, and we for the dwelling-house, he said, in tones more respectful than those which he employed to Mr. Carrington on his first coming,

"You hab niggers, mossa—women is de bes'—dat lub for talk too much?"

"Yes, a dozen of them."

"You sen' one to de plantation where dis Gullah Sam lib, but don't sen' um to Gullah Sam; sen' um to he mossa or he missis; and borrow someting—any ting—old pot or kettle— no matter if you don't want 'em, you beg um for lend you. Da's 'nough."

Mr. Carrington would have had the wizard's reasons for this wish, but finding him reluctant to declare them, he promised his consent, concluding, as was perhaps the case, that the only object was to let Gullah Sam know that a formidable enemy had taken the field against him, and in defence of his victim. This would seem to account for his desire that the messenger should be a woman, and one "wha' lub for talk too much." He then obtained directions for the nearest path to the swamp, and when we looked that night into the wigwam of Scipio, we found him returned with a peck of roots of sundry sorts, none of which we knew, prepared to make a decoction, in which his patient was to be immersed from head to heels. Leaving Scipio with the contemplation of this steaming prospect before him, we retired for the night, not a little anxious for those coming events which cast no shadow before us, or one so impenetrably thick, that we failed utterly to see through it.

Chapter VI

In the morning, strange to say, we found Scipio considerably better, and in singularly good spirits. The medicaments of the African, or more likely the pliant imagination of the patient himself, had wrought a charm in his behalf; and instead of groaning at every syllable, as he had done for several days before, he now scarcely uttered a word that was not accompanied by a grin. . . . His [Methuselah's] spells and fomentations had worked equally well, and Scipio was not only more confident in mind, but more sleek and strong in body. With his own hands, it appears, that the wizard had rubbed down the back and shoulders of his patient with cornshucks steeped in the decoction he had made, and, what was a more strange specific still, he had actually subjected Scipio to a smarter punishment, with a stout hickory, than his master had given him for many a year.

This, the poor fellow not only bore with Christian fortitude, but actually rejoiced in, imploring additional strokes when the other ceased. We could very well understand that Scipio deserved a whipping for laughing at an aged man, because he fell into the water, but we failed to ascertain from the taciturn wizard, that this was the rationale of an application which a negro ordinarily is never found to approve. This over, Scipio was again put to bed, a green twig hung over the door of his cabin within, while the unctuous plaster was renewed freshly on the outside. The African then repeated certain uncouth sounds over the patient, bade him shut his eyes and go to sleep, in order to be in readiness and go into the fields by the time the sun was turning for the west.

"What!" exclaimed Mr. Carrington, "do you think him able to go into the field to-day? He is very weak; he has taken little nourishment for several days."

"He mus' able," returned the imperative African; "he 'trong 'nough. He mus' able—he hab for carry gun."

With these words, the wizard left us without deigning any explanation of his future purposes, and taking his way towards the swamp, he was soon lost to our eyes in the mighty depth of its shrouding recesses.

When he returned, which was not till noon, he came at once to the mansion-house, without seeking his patient, and entering the hall where the family was all assembled, he challenged our attention as well by his appearance as by his words. He had, it would seem, employed himself in arranging his own appearance while in the swamp; perhaps taking one of its thousand lakes or ponds for his mirror. His woolly hair, which was very long, was plaited carefully up, so that the ends stuck out from his brow, as pertly and pointedly as the tails of pigs, suddenly aroused to a show of delightful consciousness on discovering a forgotten corn-heap. Perhaps that sort of tobacco, known by the attractive and characteristic title of "pigtail," would be the most fitting to convey to the mind of the reader the peculiar form of plait which the wizard had adopted for his hair. This mode of disposing of his matted mop, served to display the tattooed and strange figures upon his temples,—the certain signs, as he assured us, of his princely rank in his native country. He carried a long wand in his hand, freshly cut and peeled, at one end of which he had tied a small hempen cord. The skin of the wand was plaited round his own neck. In a large leaf he brought with him a small portion of some stuff which he seemed to preserve very carefully, but which appeared to us to be nothing more than coarse sand or gravel. To this he added a small portion of salt, which he obtained from the mistress of the house, and which he stirred together in our presence until the salt had been lost to the eye in the sand or gravel, or whatever might have been the article which he had brought with him. This done, he drew the shot from both barrels of the gun, and in its place, deposited the mixture which he had thus prepared.

"Buckrah will come 'long now. Scipio guine looka for de crow."

Such were his words, which he did not wait to hear answered or disputed, but taking the gun, he led the way towards the wigwam of Scipio. Our anxiety to see the conclusion of the adventure, did not suffer us to lose any time in following him. To our surprise we found Scipio dressed and up; ready, and it would seem perfectly able, to undertake what the African assigned him. The gun was placed in his hands, and he was told to take his way to the cornfield as usual, and proceed to work. He was also informed by the wizard, with a confidence that surprised us, that the lazy crow would be sure to be there as usual; and he was desired to get as close as he could, and take as good aim at his head in shooting him.

"You sure for hit um, brudder," said the African; "so don't 'tan too long for look. Jis' you get close, take you sight, and gib um bot' barrel. But fuss, 'fore you go, I mus' do someting wid you eye."

The plaster was taken from the door, as Scipio passed through it, re-softened with the saliva of the wizard, who, with his finger, described an arched line over each of the patient's eyes.

"You go 'long by you'sef now, brudder, and shoot de crow when you see um. He's a waiting for you now, I 'spec'."

We were about to follow Scipio to the field, but our African kept us back; and leading the way to a little copse that divided it from the swamp, he took us to its shelter, and required us to remain with him out of sight of the field, until some report from Scipio or his gun, should justify us in going forth.

Chapter VII

Here we remained in no little anxiety for the space of nearly two hours, in which time, however, the African showed no sort of impatience, and none of that feverish anxiety which made us restless in body and eager, to the last degree in mind. We tried to fathom his mysteries, but in vain. He contented himself with assuring us that the witchcraft which he used, and that which he professed himself able to cure, was one that never could affect the white man in any way. He insisted that the respective gods of the two races were essentially very different; as different as the races themselves. He also admitted that the god of the superior race was necessarily equal to the task of governing both, while the inferior god could only govern the one—that of taking charge of his, was one of those small businesses, with which it was not often that the former would soil his hands. To use his own phrase, "there is a god for de big house, and another for de kitchen."

While we talked over these topics, and strove, with a waste of industry, to shake the faith of the African in his own peculiar deities and demons, we heard the sound of Scipio's gun—a sound that made us forget all nicer matters of theology, and set off with full speed towards the quarter whence it came. The wizard followed us slowly, waving his wand in circles all the way, and pulling the withes from his neck, and casting them around him as he came. During this time, his mouth was in constant motion, and I could hear at moments, strange, uncouth sounds breaking from his lips. When we reached Scipio, the fellow was in a state little short of delirium. He had fired both barrels, and had cast the gun down upon the ground after the discharge. He was wringing his hands above his head in a sort of frenzy of joy, and at our approach he threw himself down upon the earth, laughing with the delight of one who has lost his wits in a dream of pleasure.

"Where's the crow?" demanded his master.

"I shoot um—I shoot um in he head—enty I tell you, mossa, I will hit um in he head? Soon he poke he nose ober de ground, I gib it to um. Hope he bin large shot. He gone t'rough he head,—t'rough and t'rough. Ha! ha! ha! If dat crow be Gullah Sam! if Gullah Sam be git in crow jacket, ho, mossa! he nebber git out crow jacket 'till somebody skin um. Ha! ha! ho! ho! ho! ki! ki! ki! ki! la! ki! Oh, mossa, wonder how Gullah Sam feel in crow jacket!"

It was in this strain of incoherent exclamation that the invalid gave vent to his joyful paroxysm at the thought of having put a handful of duck shot into the hide of his mortal enemy. The unchristian character of his exultation received a severe reproof from his master, which sobered the fellow sufficiently to enable us to get from him a more sane description of his doings. He told us that the crow had come to bedevil him as usual, only—and the fact became subsequently of considerable importance,—that he had now lost the gray dirt from his wing, which had so peculiarly distinguished it before, and was now as black as the most legitimate suit ever worn by crow, priest, lawyer, or physician. This change in the outer aspect of the bird had somewhat confounded the negro, and made him loth [loath] to expend his shot, for fear of wasting the charmed charge upon other than the genuine Simon Pure. But the deportment of the other—lazy, lounging, swaggering, as usual—convinced Scipio, in spite of his eyes, that his old enemy stood in fact before him; and without wasting time, he gave him both barrels at the same moment.

"But where's the crow?" demanded the master.

"I knock um ober, mossa; I see um tumble; 'speck you find um t'oder side de cornhill."

Nothing could exceed the consternation of Scipio, when, on reaching the designated spot, we found no sign of the supposed victim. The poor fellow rubbed his eyes, in doubt of their visual capacities, and looked round aghast, for an explanation, to the wizard who was now approaching, waving his wand in long sweeping circles as he came, and muttering, as before, those strange uncouth sounds, which we relished as little as we understood. He did not seem at all astonished at the result of Scipio's shot, but abruptly asked of him—"Whay's de fus' water, brudder Scip?"

"De water in de bay', Mass 'Tuselah," was the reply; the speaker pointing as he spoke to a little spot of drowned land on the very corner of the field, which, covered with thick shoots of the small sweet bay tree,—the magnolia glauca,— receives its common name among the people from its almost peculiar growth.

"Push for de bay! push for de bay!" exclaimed the African, "and see wha' you see. Run, Scip; run, nigger—see wha' lay in de bay!"

These words, scarcely understood by us, set Scipio in motion. At full speed he set out, and, conjecturing from his movement, rather than from the words of the African, his expectations, off we set also at full speed after him. Before we reached the spot to our great surprise, Scipio emerged from the bay, dragging behind him the reluctant and trembling form of the aged negro, Gullah Sam. He had found him washing his face, which was covered with little pimples and scratches, as if he had suddenly fallen into a nest of briars. It was with the utmost difficulty we could prevent Scipio from pummelling the dreaded wizard to death.

"What's the matter with your face, Sam?" demanded Mr. Carrington.

"Hab humour, Mass Carrington; bin trouble berry mosh wid break out in de skin."

"Da shot, mossa—da shot. I hit um in crow jacket: but whay's de gray di't? Ha! mossa, look yer; dis de black coat ob Mass Jim'son dat Gullah Sam hab on. He no wear he jacket with gray patch. Da's make de diff'rence."

The magician from St. Matthew's now came up, and our

surprise was increased when we saw him extend his hand, with an appearance of the utmost good feeling and amity, to the rival he had just overcome.

"Well, brudder Sam, how you come on?"

The other looked at him doubtfully, and with a countenance in which we saw, or fancied, a mingling expression of fear and hostility; the latter being evidently restrained by the other. He gave his hand, however, to the grasp of Methuselah, but said nothing.

"I will come take supper wid you to-night, brudder Sam," continued the wizard of St. Matthew's, with as much civility as if he spoke to the most esteemed friend under the sun. "Scip, boy, you kin go to you mossa work—you quite well ob dis bus'ness."

Scipio seemed loth to leave the company while there appeared something yet to be done, and muttered half aloud,

"You no ax Gullah Sam, wha' da' he bin do in de bay."

"Psha, boy, go 'long to you cornfiel'—enty I know," replied Methuselah. "Gullah Sam bin 'bout he own bus'ness, I s'pose. Brudder, you kin go home now, and get you tings ready for supper. I will come see you to-night."

It was in this manner that the wizard of St. Matthew's was disposed to dismiss both the patient and his persecutor; but here the master of Scipio interposed.

"Not so fast, Methuselah. If this fellow, Sam, has been playing any of his tricks upon my people, as you seem to have taken for granted, and as, indeed, very clearly appears, he must not be let off so easily. I must punish him before he goes."

"You kin punish um more dan me?" was the abrupt, almost stern inquiry of the wizard.

There was something so amusing as well as strange in the whole business, something so ludicrous in the wo-begone visage of Sam, that we pleaded with Mr. Carrington that the whole case should be left to Methuselah; satisfied that as he had done so well hitherto, there was no good reason, nor was it right, that he should be interfered with. We saw the two shake hands and part, and ascertained from Scipio that he himself was the guest of Gullah Sam, at the invitation of Methuselah, to a very good supper that night of pig and 'possum. Scipio described the affair as having gone off very well, but he chuckled mightily as he dwelt upon the face of Sam, which, as he said, by night, was completely raw from the inveterate scratching to which he had been compelled to subject it during the whole day. Methuselah the next morning departed, having received, as his reward, twenty dollars from the master, and a small pocket Bible from the young mistress of the negro; and to this day, there is not a negro in the surrounding country— and many of the whites are of the same way of thinking—who does not believe that Scipio was bewitched by Gullah Sam, and that the latter was shot in the face, while in the shape of a common crow in the cornfield, by the enchanted shot provided by the wizard of St. Matthew's for the hands of the other. . . .

From a REVIEW OF AMERICANISM IN LITERATURE

Americanism in Literature: An Oration before the Phi Kappa and Demosthenean Societies of the University of Georgia, at Athens, August 8, 1844. By Alexander B. Meek, of Alabama. Charleston: Burges & James. 1844.

This is the right title. It indicates the becoming object of our aim. Americanism in our Literature is scarcely implied by the usual phraseology. American Literature seems to be a thing, certainly,—but it is not the thing exactly. To put Americanism in our letters, is to do a something much more important. The phrase has a peculiar signification which is worth our consideration. By a liberal extension of the courtesies of criticism, we are already in possession of a due amount of American authorship; but of such as is individual, and properly peculiar to ourselves, we cannot be said to enjoy much. Our writers are numerous—quite as many, perhaps, in proportion to our years, our circumstances and necessities, as might be looked for among any people. But, with very few exceptions, their writings might as well be European. They are European.

The writers think after European models, draw their stimulus and provocation from European books, fashion themselves to European tastes, and look chiefly to the awards of European criticism. This is to denationalize the American mind. This is to enslave the national heart—to place ourselves at the mercy of the foreigner, and to yield all that is individual, in our character and hope, to the paralyzing influence of his will, and frequently hostile purposes. . . .

We take it for granted, that we are not—in the scornful language of the European press,—a mere nation of shopkeepers: —that we have qualities of soul and genius, which if not yet developed in our moral constitution, are struggling to make themselves heard and felt;—that we have a pride of character,— growing stronger (as we trust) with the progress of each succeeding day,—which makes us anxious to realize for ourselves that position of independence, in all other departments, which we have secured by arms and in politics. Mere political security—the fact that we drink freely of the air around us, and at our own choosing partake of the fruits of the earth—is not enough,—constitutes but a small portion of the triumphs, and the objects of a rational nature. Nay, even political security is temporary, always inferior if not wholly uncertain, unless it be firmly based upon the certain and constant vigilance of the intellectual moral. A nation, properly to boast itself, and to take and maintain its position with other States, must prove itself in possession of self-evolving attributes. Its character must be as individual as that of the noblest citizen that dwells within its limits. It must do its own thinking as well as its own fighting, for, as truly as all history has shown that the people who rely for their defense in battle upon foreign mercenaries inevitably become their prey, so the nation falls a victim to that genius of another, to which she passively defers. She must make, and not borrow or beg, her laws. Her institutions must grow out of her own condition and necessities, and not be arbitrarily framed upon those of other countries. Her poets and artists, to feel her wants, her hopes, her triumphs, must be born of the soil, and ardently devoted to its claims. To live, in fact, and secure the freedom of her children, a nation must live through them, in them, and by them,—by the strength of their arms, the purity of their morals, the vigour of their industry, and the wisdom of their minds. These are the essentials of a great nation, and no one of these qualities is perfectly available without the co-operation of the rest. And, as we adapt our warfare to the peculiarities of the country, and our industry to our climate, our resources and our soil, so the operations of the national mind must be suited to our characteristics. The genius of our people is required to declare itself after a fashion of its own—must be influenced by its skies, and by those natural objects which familiarly address themselves to the senses from boyhood, and colour the fancies, and urge the thoughts, and shape the growing affections of the child to a something kindred with the things which he beholds. His whole soul must be imbued with sympathies caught from surrounding aspects within his infant horizon. The heart must be moulded to an intense appreciation of our woods and streams, our dense forests and deep swamps, our vast immeasurable mountains, our voluminous and tumbling waters. It must receive its higher moral tone from the exigencies of society, its traditions and its histories. Tutored at the knee of the granddame, the boy must grasp, as subjects of familiar and frequent consideration, the broken chronicles of senility, and shape them, as he grows older, into coherence and effect. He must learn to dwell often upon the narratives of the brave fathers who first broke ground in the wilderness, who fought or treated with the red men, and who, finally, girded themselves up for the great conflict with the imperious mother who had sent them forth. These histories, making vivid impressions upon the pliant fancies of childhood, are the source of those vigorous shoots, of thought and imagination, which make a nation proud of its sons in turn, and which save her from becoming a by-word and reproach to other nations. In this, and from such impressions, the simplest records of a domestic history, expand into the most ravishing treasures of romance.

JOHN ESTEN COOKE

John Esten Cooke was born in Winchester, Virginia, in 1830, and died at "The Briars," near Millwood, Virginia, in 1886. He was the son of John Rogers Cooke, a leading lawyer in transmontane Virginia, and the brother of Philip Pendleton Cooke, a poet and story-writer. He should not be confused with his uncle, Dr. John Esten Cooke (1783–1853), a physician, theologian, and writer. After a boyhood in the Shenandoah Valley, he removed with his family to Richmond in 1840. Here he attended academies, but did not go to college. After studying law in his father's office, he practised until the Civil War. He served throughout the war, and was an ardent admirer of Stuart, Jackson, and Lee. After the war he married Mary Francis Page, and lived on a Page estate and farm in Clarke County until his death. Several early poems, stories, and articles were accepted for the *Southern Literary Messenger*, and in 1852 Harper and Brothers paid him ten dollars for a story. Later he became "the best paid southern man of letters before 1870," and his output included over thirty novels, biographies, and histories, besides many contributions to periodicals.

His first novel, *Leather Stocking and Silk*, deals with the border life in the Valley, and his second novel, *The Virginia Comedians*, treats of the Colonial Virginia of Williamsburg. During the fifties he wrote five other works portraying the Colonial life of the Old Dominion: *The Youth of Jefferson* (1854), *Ellie* (1855), *The Last of the Foresters* (1856), *Henry St. John* (1859), and *Fairfax* (1868). This last novel had been published as a serial, entitled "Greenway Court; or, The Bloody Ground," in the *Southern Literary Messenger*, April to December, 1859. Cooke based seven books on his experiences in the Civil War: *The Life of Stonewall Jackson* (1863), which was incorporated into *Stonewall Jackson: A Military Biography* (1866), *Surry of Eagle's Nest* (1866), *The Wearing of the Gray* (1867), *Hilt to Hilt* (1869), *Mohun* (1869), *Hammer and Rapier* (1870), and *A Life of Gen. Robert E. Lee* (1871). In the eight years after 1870 "Cooke produced a half-score of books which, in their setting and time, varied from the seventeenth century England of *Her Majesty the Queen* to the contemporary America of *Pretty Mrs. Gaston*." Of these *The Heir of Gaymount* (1870) is important as a record of Cooke's adjustment to economic and social environment in the decades following the war, and in its theme of "intensive farming as the salvation of post-war South." *The Virginia Bohemians* (1880) deals with contemporary life in Piedmont Virginia, and "for true local color . . . holds primacy among Cooke's novels." The last pages of Professor Beaty's biography contain an excellent summary of Cooke's achievements, with the conclusion that he "will be remembered chiefly for *The Virginia Comedians*, *Surry of Eagle's Nest*, and *Mohun* . . . he will continue to be known as a social historian of late Colonial Virginia, and as a romantic Confederate captain, who used his military experience as a basis of fiction."

From THE VIRGINIA COMEDIANS

Author's Preface to This Edition, 1883

In the autumn of 1752 the "Virginia Company of Comedians" played, at the Theatre near the Capitol in Williamsburg, Virginia, "The Merchant of Venice," the first dramatic representation in America.

It was the period of the culmination of the old social *régime*. A splendid society had burst into flower, and was enjoying itself in the sunshine and under the blue skies of the most beautiful of lands. The chill winds of the Revolution were about to blow, but no one suspected it. Life was easy, and full of laughter—of cordial greetings, grand assemblies, and the zest of existence which springs from the absence of care. Social intercourse was the joy of the epoch, and crowds flocked to the race-course, where the good horses were running for the cup, or to the cock-fight, where the favorite spangles fought to the death. The violins seemed to be ever playing—at the Raleigh Tavern, in Williamsburg, where young Jefferson "danced with Belinda in the Apollo," and was happy; or in the great manor-houses of the planters clustering along the Lowland rivers. In town and country life was a pageant. His Excellency the royal Governor went in his coach-and-six to open the Burgesses. The youths in embroidered waistcoats made love to the little beauties in curls and roses. The "Apollo" rang with music, the theatre on Gloucester Street with thunders of applause; and the houses of the planters were as full of rejoicing. At Christmas—at every season, indeed—the hospitable old "nabob" entertained throngs of guests; and, if we choose to go back in fancy, we may see those Virginians of the old age amid their most characteristic surroundings. The broad board is spread with plenty; the wood-fires roar in the wide fire-places; the canary sparkles; the wax-lights flame, lighting up the Louis Quatorze chairs, the old portraits, the curious *bric-à-brac*, and the rich dresses of fair dames and gallant men. Care stands out of the sunshine of this brilliant throng, who roll in their chariots, dance the minuet, exchange compliments, and snatch the charm of the flying hours with no thought, one would say, but enjoyment, and to make the best of the little life we live below.

This is what may be seen on the surface of society under the old Virginia *régime;* but that social organization had reached a stage when the elements of disintegration had already begun their work. A vague unrest pervaded the atmosphere, and gave warning of the approaching cataclysm. Class distinctions had been immemorially looked upon as a part of the order of nature; but certain curious and restive minds began to ask if that was just, and to glance sidewise at the wealthy nabob in his fine coach. The English Church was the church of the gentry; it was not the church of the people. The "New Light" ministers began to talk about "sinegogues of Satan," and to tell the multitudes, who thronged to hear them preach in the fields, that the reverend parsons were no better than they should be. New ideas were on the march. The spirit of change was under the calm surface. The political agitation soon to burst forth was preceded by the social. The hour was near when the merry violins were to stop playing; when the "Apollo room" at the Raleigh would become the meeting-place of political conspirators; and the Virginians, waking from their dreams of enjoyment, were to be confronted by the hard realities of the new time. . . .

Chapter I. *An Interior with Portraits*

On a splendid October afternoon, in the year of our Lord 1763, two persons who will appear frequently in this history were seated in the great dining-room of Effingham Hall.

But let us first say a few words of this old mansion. Effingham Hall was a stately edifice not far from Williamsburg, which, as every body knows, was at that period the capital city of the colony of Virginia. The hall was constructed of elegant brick brought over from England: and from the great portico in front of the building a beautiful rolling country of hills and valleys, field and forest, spread itself pleasantly before the eye, bounded far off along the circling belt of woods by the bright waters of the noble river.

Entering the large hall of the old house, you had before you, walls covered with deers' antlers, fishing-rods, and guns: portraits of cavaliers, and dames and children: even carefully painted pictures of celebrated race-horses, on whose speed and bottom many thousands of pounds had been staked and lost and won in their day and generation.

On one side of the hall a broad staircase with oaken balustrade led to the numerous apartments above: and on the opposite side, a door gave entrance into the great dining-room.

The dining-room was decorated with great elegance:—the carved oak wainscot extending above the mantelpiece in an unbroken expanse of fruits and flowers, hideous laughing faces, and long foamy surges to the cornice. The furniture was in the Louis Quatorze style, which the reader is familiar with, from its reproduction in our own day; and the chairs were the same low-seated affairs, with high carved backs, which are now seen. There were Chelsea figures, and a side-board full of plate, and a Japan cabinet, and a Kidderminster carpet, and huge andirons. On the andirons crackled a few twigs lost in the great country fireplace.

On the wall hung a dozen pictures of gay gallants, brave warriors, and dames, whose eyes outshone their diamonds:— and more than one ancestor looked grimly down, clad in cuirass and armlets, and holding in his mailed hand the sword which had done bloody service in its time. The lady portraits, as an invariable rule, were decorated with sunset clouds of yellow lace—the bright locks were powdered, and many little black patches set off the dazzling fairness of the rounded chins. Lapdogs nestled on the satin laps: and not one of the gay dames but seemed to be smiling, with her head bent sidewise fascinatingly on the courtly or warlike figures ranged with them in a long glittering line.

These portraits are worth looking up to, but those which we promised the reader are real.

In one of the carved chairs, if any thing more uncomfortable than all the rest, sits, or rather lounges, a young man of about twenty-five. He is very richly clad, and in a costume which would be apt to attract a large share of attention in our own day, when dress seems to have become a mere covering, and the prosaic tendencies of the age are to despise every thing but what ministers to actual material pleasure.

The gentleman before us lives fortunately one hundred years before our day: and suffers from an opposite tendency in costume. His head is covered with a long flowing peruke, heavy with powder, and the drop curls hang down on his cheeks ambrosially: his cheeks are delicately rouged, and two patches, arranged with matchless art, complete the distinguished *tout ensemble* of the handsome face. At breast, a cloud of lace reposes on the rich embroidery of his figured satin waistcoat, reaching to his knees:—this lace is *point de Venise* and white, that fashion having come in just one month since. The sleeves of his rich doublet are turned back to his elbows, and are as large as a bushel—the opening being filled up, however, with long ruffles, which reach down over the delicate jewelled hand. He wears silk stockings of spotless white, and his feet are cased in slippers of Spanish leather, adorned with diamond buckles. Add velvet garters below the knee:—a little muff of leopard-skin reposing near at hand upon a chair—not omitting a snuff-box peeping from the pocket, and Mr. Champ Effingham, just from Oxford and his grand tour, is before you with his various surroundings.

He is reading the work which some time since attained to such extreme popularity, Mr. Joseph Addison's serial, "The Spectator,"—collected now for its great merits, into bound volumes. Mr. Effingham reads with a languid air, just as he sits, and turns over the leaves with an ivory paper cutter, which he brought from Venice with the plate glass yonder on the sideboard near the silver baskets and pitchers. This languor is too perfect to be wholly affected, and when he yawns, as he does frequently, Mr. Effingham applies himself to that task very earnestly. . . .

Chapter II. Squire Effingham

. . . The squire is a gentleman of fifty-five or sixty, with an open frank face, clear, honest eyes, and his carriage is bold, free, and somewhat pompous. He is clad much more simply than his eldest son, his coat having upon it not a particle of embroidery, and his long plain waistcoat buttoning up to the chin: below which a white cravat and an indication only of frill are visible. His limbs are cased in thick, strong and comfortable cloth, and woollen, and he wears boots, very large and serviceable, to which strong spurs are attached. His broad, fine brow, full of intelligence and grace, is covered by an old cocked hat, which, having lost the loops which held it in the three-cornered shape, is now rolled up upon each side; and his manner in walking, speaking, arguing, reading, is much after the description of his costume—plain, straightforward, and though somewhat pompous, destitute of finery and ornament. He is the head of a princely establishment, he has thousands of acres, and hundreds of negroes, he is a justice, and has sat often in the House of Burgesses: he is rich, a dignitary, every body knows it,—why should he strive to ape elegancies, and trouble himself about the impression he produces? He is simple and plain, as he conceives, because he is a great proprietor and can afford to wear rough clothes, and talk plainly.

His pomposity is not obtrusive, and it is tempered with so much good breeding and benevolence that it does not detract from the pleasant impression produced by his honest face. As he enters now that face is brown and red with exercise upon his plantation—and he comes in with cheerful smiles; his rotund person, and long queue gathered by a ribbon smiling no less than his eyes. . . .

Chapter VII. The Old Theatre near the Capitol

The "old Theatre near the Capitol," discoursed of in the manifesto issued by Mr. Manager Hallam, was so far *old*, that the walls were well-browned by time, and the shutters to the windows of a pleasant neutral tint between rust and dust color. The building had no doubt been used for the present purpose in bygone times, before the days of the "Virginia Gazette," which is our authority for many of the facts here stated, and in relation to the "Virginia Company of Comedians"—but of the former companies of "players," as my lord Hamlet calls them, and their successes or misfortunes, printed words tell us nothing, as far as the researches of the present Chronicle extend. That there had been such companies before, however, we repeat, there is some reason to believe; else why that addition "old" applied to the "Theatre near the Capitol." The question is submitted to the future social historians of the Old Dominion.

Within, the play-house presented a somewhat more attractive appearance. There was "box," "pit," and "gallery," as in our own day; and the relative prices were arranged in much the same manner. The common mortals—gentlemen and ladies—were forced to occupy the boxes raised slightly above the level of the stage, and hemmed in by velvet-cushioned railings—in front, a flower-decorated panel, extending all around the house,—and for this position were moreover compelled to pay an admission fee of seven shillings and sixpence. The demigods—so to speak—occupied a more eligible position in the "pit," from which they could procure a highly excellent view of the actors' feet and ankles, just on a level with their noses: to conciliate the demigods, this superior advantage had been offered, and the price for them was, further still, reduced to five shillings. But "the gods" in truth were the real favorites of the manager. To attract them, he arranged the high upper "gallery"—and left it untouched, unincumbered by railing or velvet cushions, or any other device: all was free space, and liberal as the air: there were no troublesome seats for "the gods," and three shillings and nine pence was all that the managers would demand. The honor of their presence was enough.

From the boxes a stairway led down to the stage, and some rude scenes, visible at the edges of the green curtain, completed the outline.

When Mr. Lee and his daughters entered the box which had been reserved for them, next to the stage, the house was nearly full, and the neatness of the edifice was lost sight of in the sea of brilliant ladies' faces, and strong forms of cavaliers, which extended—like a line of glistening foam—around the semicircle of the boxes. The pit was occupied by well-dressed men of the lower class, as the times had it, and from the gallery proceeded hoarse murmurs and the unforgotten slang of London.

Many smiles and bows were interchanged between the parties in the different boxes; and the young gallants, following the fashion of the day, gathered at each end of the stage, and often walked across, to exchange some polite speech with the smiling dames in the boxes nearest.

Mr. Champ Effingham was, upon the whole, much the most notable fop present; and his elegant, languid, *petit maître* air, as he strolled across the stage, attracted many remarks, not invariably favorable. It was observed, however, that when the Virginia-bred youths, with honest plainness, called him "ridiculous," the young ladies, their companions, took Mr. Effingham's part, and defended him with great enthusiasm. Only when they returned home, Mr. Effingham was more unmercifully criticised than he would otherwise have been.

A little bell rang, and the orchestra, represented by three or four foreign-looking gentlemen, bearded and moustached, entered with trumpet and violin. The trumpets made the roof shake, indifferently, in honor of the *Prince of Morocco*, or *King Richard*, or any other worthy whose entrance was marked in the play-book "with a flourish." But before the orchestra ravished the ears of every one, the manager came forward, in the costume of *Bassanio*, and made a low bow. Mr. Hallam was a fat little man, of fifty or fifty-five, with a rubicund and somewhat sensual face, and he expressed extraordinary delight at meeting so many of the "noble aristocracy of the great and noble colony of Virginia," assembled to witness his very humble representation. It would be the chief end and sole ambition of his life, he said, to please the gentry, who so kindly patronized their servants—himself and his associates—and then the smiling worthy concluded by bowing lower than before. Much applause from the pit and gallery, and murmurs of approbation from the well-bred boxes, greeted this address, and, the orchestra having struck up, the curtain slowly rolled aloft. The young gallants scattered to the corners of the stage— seating themselves on stools or chairs, or standing, and the "Merchant of Venice" commenced. *Bassanio* having assumed a dignified and lofty port, criticised *Gratiano* with courteous and lordly wit: his friend *Antonio* offered him his fortune with grand magnanimity, in a loud singing voice, worthy the utmost commendation, and the first act proceeded on its way in triumph. . . .

Chapter X. Actor and Gentleman

The unknown lady was no gentle Virginia maiden, no "lady," as she had said, with perfect calmness, at their meeting in the wood—only one of the company of Comedians. Her singular expression when she uttered the words, "I think you will see me again," occurred to the young man, and he wondered that this easy solution of the riddle had not occurred to him at once.

What was her name? Mr. Effingham drew forth his bill, and saw opposite the name of Portia, *Miss Beatrice Hallam.*

"Ah, yes," he said, carelessly, "the same we were speculating upon, this morning. Let us see how Portia looks, and what change the foot-lights work in her face."

He sat down in the corner of the stage upon a wicker chair, and scanned Portia critically. Her costume was faultless. It consisted of a gown and underskirt of fawn-colored silk, trimmed with silver, and a single band of gold encircled each wrist, clearly relieved against the white, finely-rounded arm. Her hair, which was a beautiful chestnut, had been carried back from the temples and powdered, after the fashion of the time, and around her beautiful, swan-like neck, the young woman wore a necklace of pearls of rare brilliance. Thus the costume of the character defied criticism, and Mr. Effingham passed on to the face and figure. These we have already described. The countenance of Beatrice Hallam wore the same simple, yet firm and collected expression, which Mr. Effingham had observed in their first interview, and her figure had the same indefinable grace and beauty. Every movement which she made might have suited a royal palace, and in her large brilliant eyes Mr. Effingham in vain sought the least trace of confusion. She surveyed the audience, while the Prince of Morocco was uttering his speech, with perfect simplicity, but her eyes not for a single moment rested on the young men collected at the corners of the stage. For her they seemed to have no existence, and she turned to the Prince again. That gentleman having uttered his prescribed number of lines, Portia advanced graciously toward him, and addressed him. Her carelessness was gone; she no longer displayed either indifference or coldness. She was the actress, with her rôle to sustain. She commenced in a voice of noble and queenlike courtesy, a voice of pure music, and clear utterance, so to speak, such as few lips possess the power of giving forth. Every word rang and told; there was no hurry, no slurring, no hesitation; it was not an actress delivering a set speech, but the noble Portia doing the honors of her beautiful palace of Belmont. The scene ended with great applause—the young woman had evidently produced a most favorable impression on the audience. But she seemed wholly unconscious of this compliment, and made her exit quite calmly.

A buzz ran through the theatre: the audience were discussing the merits of Portia. On the stage, too, she was the subject of many comments; and this continued until Lancelot made his appearance and went through his speech. Then Portia's re-appearance with the Prince was greeted with great applause.

Mr. Effingham leaned forward and touched the young woman's sleeve.

"Come," he said, with easy carelessness, and scarcely moderating his voice, "come, fair Portia, while that tiresome fellow is making his speech, talk to me a little. We are old acquaintances—and you are indebted to me for directing you home."

"Yes, sir," said Beatrice, turning her head slightly, "but pardon me—I have my part to attend to."

"I don't care."

"Excuse me, sir—but I do."

"Really, madam, you are very stiff for an actress. Is it so very unusual a thing to ask a moment's conversation?"

"I know that it is the fashion in London and elsewhere, sir, but I dislike it. It destroys my conception of the character," she said, calmly.

Mr. Effingham laughed.

"Come here and talk to me," he said, "did you not say we should meet again?"

"Yes, sir. And I also said that I was not a lady."

"Well—what is the meaning of that addition?"

"It means, sir, that being an actress, I am not at liberty to amuse myself here as I might were I a lady in a drawing-room. Pardon me, sir," she added calmly, "I am neglecting what I have engaged to do, play Portia."

And the young woman quietly disengaging her sleeve from Mr. Effingham's fingers, moved away to another portion of the stage. . . .

GEORGE WASHINGTON CABLE

George Washington Cable was born in New Orleans on October 12, 1844, and died in St. Petersburg, Florida, on January 31, 1925. In Virginia his grandfather owned slaves. His father freed the slaves, and removed to Pennsylvania and later to Indiana, where he married Rebecca Boardman, whose ancestors had come from New England. In 1837 the Cables came to New Orleans, where the father prospered for a time, suffered failure, and died in 1859, leaving the family "completely without resources." The boy of fourteen left school to clerk in custom warehouses and in a commission merchant store. At nineteen he enlisted in the 4th Mississippi Cavalry, and served until the end of the war, being wounded twice. After the war he returned to New Orleans, where he obtained jobs as bookkeeper and surveyor and as clerk for a firm of cotton-factors from 1871 to 1879. In 1869 he married Louise Bartlett of New Orleans. "After his marriage he met his added expenses by doing a Sunday column for the *Picayune*, signed with the sanguinary pseudonym of 'Drop Shot,'" as E. L. Tinker states, but this newspaper career ended abruptly when he refused to report a theatrical performance which he considered as ungodly. During these years he had been writing sketches of the Creoles and the tales that he heard about them. He showed his manuscripts to Edward King, who was in New Orleans collecting material for his serial "The Great South," which was to be published in *Scribner's Monthly* (not to be confused with the later *Scribner's Magazine*). The appreciative King sent several stories to his editor, Dr. J. G. Holland, who turned them over to his assistant, Richard Watson Gilder. The first story to be published was " 'Sieur George," in October, 1873, which is the story of a strange old character in New Orleans who squandered all his earnings on lottery tickets. Other stories were accepted by the editors of *Scribner's Monthly*, the *Century Magazine*, and *Appleton's Magazine*. In 1879 seven of these stories were collected in *Old Creole Days*. The novelette "Madame Delphine," published in *Scribner's Monthly*, May, 1881, was included as an eighth story in later editions of

Old Creole Days. The reader observes that the time settings of these stories are not contemporary, but before the Civil War, and some are placed in the first decades of the nineteenth century. In 1879–1880 *Scribner's Monthly* serialized "The Grandissimes," and in 1880 the novel was published. These tales of exotic, foreign life were hailed with enthusiasm by northern readers as excellent local color fiction, but they stirred up a storm in the South. The proud Creoles of Louisiana felt insulted at Cable's fictional treatment of them, with suggestions of illiterate speech and mixed blood. The major assault was made by Charles Gayarré, able Louisiana historian, who lectured and wrote against Cable. Although the matter of Cable's faithfulness in the portrayal of Creoles is still a subject of controversy, Cable claimed to be a well-read student of their history, and he published articles and books about them.

Cable stirred up another controversy which still continues. His article on "The Freedman's Case in Equity" in the January, 1885, issue of the *Century Magazine*, was included in his book *The Silent South* (1885). A succession of heated replies flamed in the magazines, of which the most important was Henry W. Grady's "In Plain Black and White: A Reply to Mr. Cable." At last Cable became something of an exile, for he removed in 1886 to Northampton, Massachusetts, where he lived forty years in almost feverish activity, delivering addresses and writing many books, articles, and reviews. He was a popular lecturer, or reader, for a time, and toured the country with Mark Twain. The Home-Culture Clubs, which he organized with altruistic fervor, increased to seventy-eight in thirteen states. Nearly every other year he put out a new book, which his best critics say did not enhance his reputation. Yet students of southern literature can read profitably such books as *Dr. Sevier* (1884), a good character study, with ante-bellum New Orleans setting, *Bonaventure* (1889), the tale of a Creole among the Acadians, *John March, Southerner* (1894), a romance of Reconstruction days, *Kincaid's Battery* (1908), a romantic war novel, and *The Flower of the Chapdelaines* (1918), another New Orleans romance.

From OLD CREOLE DAYS
Jean-Ah Poquelin

In the first decade of the present century, when the newly established American Government was the most hateful thing in Louisiana—when the Creoles were still kicking at such vile innovations as the trial by jury, American dances, anti-smuggling laws, and the printing of the Governor's proclamation in English—when the Anglo-American flood that was presently to burst in a crevasse of immigration upon the delta had thus far been felt only as slippery seepage which made the Creole tremble for his footing—there stood, a short distance above what is now Canal Street, and considerably back from the line of villas which fringed the river bank on Tchoupitoulas Road, an old colonial plantation-house half in ruin.

It stood aloof from civilization, the tracts that had once been its indigo fields given over to their first noxious wildness, and grown up into one of the horridest marshes within a circuit of fifty miles.

The house was of heavy cypress, lifted up on pillars, grim, solid, and spiritless, its massive build a strong reminder of days still earlier, when every man had been his own peace officer and the insurrection of the blacks a daily contingency. Its dark, weather-beaten roof and sides were hoisted up above the jungly plain in a distracted way, like a gigantic ammunition-wagon stuck in the mud and abandoned by some retreating army. Around it was a dense growth of low water willows, with half a hundred sorts of thorny or fetid bushes, savage strangers alike to the "language of flowers" and to the botanist's Greek. They were hung with countless strands of discolored and prickly smilax, and the impassable mud below bristled with *chevaux de frise* of the dwarf palmetto. Two lone forest-trees, dead cypresses, stood in the centre of the marsh, dotted with roosting vultures. The shallow strips of water were hid by myriads of aquatic plants, under whose coarse and spiritless flowers, could one have seen it, was a harbor of reptiles, great and small, to make one shudder to the end of his days.

The house was on a slightly raised spot, the levee of a draining canal. The waters of this canal did not run; they crawled, and were full of big, ravening fish and alligators, that held it against all comers.

Such was the home of old Jean Marie Poquelin, once an opulent indigo planter, standing high in the esteem of his small, proud circle of exclusively male acquaintances in the old city; now a hermit, alike shunned by and shunning all who had ever known him. "The last of his line," said the gossips. "His father lies under the floor of the St. Louis Cathedral, with the wife of his youth on one side, and the wife of his old age on the other. Old Jean visits the spot daily. His half-brother"—alas! there was a mystery; no one knew what had become of the gentle, young half-brother, more than thirty years his junior, whom once he seemed so fondly to love, but who, seven years ago, had disappeared suddenly, once for all, and left no clew of his fate.

They had seemed to live so happily in each other's love. No father, mother, wife to either, no kindred upon earth. The elder a bold, frank, impetuous, chivalric adventurer; the younger a gentle, studious, book-loving recluse; they lived upon the ancestral estate like mated birds, one always on the wing, the other always in the nest.

There was no trait in Jean Marie Poquelin, said the old gossips, for which he was so well known among his few friends as his apparent fondness for his "little brother." "Jacques said this," and "Jacques said that"; he "would leave this or that, or anything to Jacques," for "Jacques was a scholar," and "Jacques was good," or "wise," or "just," or "far-sighted," as the nature of the case required; and "he should ask Jacques as soon as he got home," since Jacques was never elsewhere to be seen.

It was between the roving character of the one brother, and the bookishness of the other, that the estate fell into decay. Jean Marie, generous gentleman, gambled the slaves away one by one, until none was left, man or woman, but one old African mute.

The indigo-fields and vats of Louisiana had been generally abandoned as unremunerative. Certain enterprising men had substituted the culture of sugar; but while the recluse was too apathetic to take so active a course, the other saw larger, and, at that time, equally respectable profits, first in smuggling, and later in the African slave-trade. What harm could he see in it? The whole people said it was vitally necessary, and to minister to a vital public necessity,—good enough certainly, and so he laid up many a doubloon, that made him none the worse in the public regard.

One day old Jean Marie was about to start upon a voyage that was to be longer, much longer, than any that he had yet made. Jacques had begged him hard for many days not to go, but he laughed him off, and finally said, kissing him:

"*Adieu, 'tit frère.*"

"No," said Jacques, "I shall go with you."

They left the old hulk of a house in the sole care of the African mute, and went away to the Guinea Coast together.

Two years after, old Poquelin came home without his vessel. He must have arrived at his house by night. No one saw him come. No one saw "his little brother"; rumor whispered that he, too, had returned, but he had never been seen again.

A dark suspicion fell upon the old slave-trader. No matter that the few kept the many reminded of the tenderness that had ever marked his bearing to the missing man. The many shook their heads. "You know he has a quick and fearful temper"; and "why does he cover his loss with mystery?" "Grief would out with the truth."

"But," said the charitable few, "look in his face; see that expression of true humanity." The many did look in his face, and, as he looked in theirs, he read the silent question: "Where is thy brother Abel?" The few were silenced, his former friends died off, and the name of Jean Marie Poquelin became a symbol of witchery, devilish crime, and hideous nursery fictions.

The man and his house were alike shunned. The snipe and duck hunters forsook the marsh, and the wood-cutters abandoned the canal. Sometimes the hardier boys who ventured out there snake-shooting heard a slow thumping of oar-locks on the canal. They would look at each other for a moment half in consternation, half in glee, then rush from their sport in wanton haste to assail with their gibes the unoffending, withered old man who, in rusty attire, sat in the stern of a skiff, rowed homeward by his white-headed African mute.

"O Jean-ah Poquelin! O Jean-ah! Jean-ah Poquelin!"

It was not necessary to utter more than that. No hint of wickedness, deformity, or any physical or moral demerit; merely the name and the tone of mockery: "Oh, Jean-ah Poquelin!" and while they tumbled one over another in their needless haste to fly, he would rise carefully from his seat, while the aged mute, with downcast face, went on rowing, and rolling up his brown fist and extending it toward the urchins, would pour forth such an unholy broadside of French imprecation and invective as would all but craze them with delight.

Among both blacks and whites the house was the object of a thousand superstitions. Every midnight, they affirmed, the *feu follet* came out of the marsh and ran in and out of the rooms, flashing from window to window. The story of some lads, whose words in ordinary statements were worthless, was generally credited, that the night they camped in the woods, rather than pass the place after dark, they saw, about sunset, every window blood-red, and on each of the four chimneys an owl sitting, which turned his head three times round, and moaned and laughed with a human voice. There was a bottomless well, everybody professed to know, beneath the sill of the big front door under the rotten veranda; whoever set his foot upon that threshold disappeared forever in the depth below.

What wonder the marsh grew as wild as Africa! Take all the Faubourg Ste. Marie, and half the ancient city, you would not find one graceless dare-devil reckless enough to pass within a hundred yards of the house after nightfall.

The alien races pouring into old New Orleans began to find the few streets named for the Bourbon princes too strait for them. The wheel of fortune, beginning to whirl, threw them off beyond the ancient corporation lines, and sowed civilization and even trade upon the lands of the Graviers and Girods. Fields became roads, roads streets. Everywhere the leveller was peering through his glass, rodsmen were whacking their way through willow-brakes and rose-hedges, and the sweating Irishmen tossed the blue clay up with their long-handled shovels.

"Ha! that is all very well," quoth the Jean-Baptistes, feeling the reproach of an enterprise that asked neither co-operation nor advice of them, "but wait till they come yonder to Jean Poquelin's marsh; ha! ha! ha!" The supposed predicament so delighted them, that they put on a mock terror and whirled about in an assumed stampede, then caught their clasped hands between their knees in excess of mirth, and laughed till the tears ran; for whether the street-makers mired in the marsh, or contrived to cut through old "Jean-ah's" property, either event would be joyful. Meantime a line of tiny rods, with bits of white paper in their split tops, gradually extended its way straight through the haunted ground, and across the canal diagonally.

"We shall fill that ditch," said the men in mud boots, and brushed close along the chained and padlocked gate of the haunted mansion. Ah, Jean-ah Poquelin, those were not Creole boys, to be stampeded with a little hard swearing.

He went to the Governor. That official scanned the odd figure with no slight interest. Jean Poquelin was of short, broad frame, with a bronzed leonine face. His brow was ample and deeply furrowed. His eye, large and black, was bold and open like that of a war-horse, and his jaws shut together with the firmness of iron. He was dressed in a suit of Attakapas cottonade, and his shirt, unbuttoned and thrown back from the throat and bosom, sailor-wise, showed a herculean breast, hard and grizzled. There was no fierceness or defiance in his look, no harsh ungentleness, no symptom of his unlawful life or violent temper; but rather a peaceful and peaceable fearlessness. Across the whole face, not marked in one or another feature, but as it were laid softly upon the countenance like an almost imperceptible veil, was the imprint of some great grief. A careless eye might easily overlook it, but, once seen, there it hung—faint, but unmistakable.

The Governor bowed.

"*Parlez-vous français?*" asked the figure.

"I would rather talk English, if you can do so," said the Governor.

"My name, Jean Poquelin."

"How can I serve you, Mr. Poquelin?"

"My 'ouse is yond'; *dans le marais là-bas.*"

The Governor bowed.

"Dat *marais* billong to me."

"Yes, sir."

"To me; Jean Poquelin; I hown 'im meself."

"Well, sir?"

"He don't billong to you; I get him from me father."

"That is perfectly true, Mr. Poquelin, as far as I am aware."

"You want to make strit pass yond'?"

"I do not know, sir; it is quite probable; but the city will indemnify you for any loss you may suffer—you will get paid, you understand."

"Strit can't pass dare."

"You will have to see the municipal authorities about that, Mr. Poquelin."

A bitter smile came upon the old man's face:

"*Pardon, Monsieur,* you is not *le Gouverneur?*"

"Yes."

"*Mais,* yes. You har *le Gouverneur*—yes. Veh-well. I come to you. I tell you, strit can't pass at me 'ouse."

"But you will have to see"—

"I come to you. You is *le Gouverneur.* I know not the new laws. I ham a Fr-r-rench-a-man! Fr-rench-a-man have some-thing *aller au contraire*—he come at his *Gouverneur.* I come at you. If me not had been bought from me king like *bossals* in the hold time, ze king gof—France would-a-show *Monsieur le Gouverneur* to take care his men to make strit in right places.

Mais, I know; we billong to *Monsieur le Président*. I want you to do somesin for me, eh?"

"What is it?" asked the patient Governor.

"I want you to tell *Monsieur le Président*, strit—can't—pass—at—me—'ouse."

"Have a chair, Mr. Poquelin"; but the old man did not stir. The Governor took a quill and wrote a line to a city official, introducing Mr. Poquelin, and asking for him every possible courtesy. He handed it to him, instructing him where to present it.

"Mr. Poquelin," he said with a conciliatory smile, "tell me, is it your house that our Creole citizens tell such odd stories about?"

The old man glared sternly upon the speaker, and with immovable features said:

"You don't see me trade some Guinea nigga'?"

"Oh, no."

"You don't see me make some smugglin'?"

"No, sir; not at all."

"But, I am Jean Marie Poquelin. I mine me hown bizniss. Dat all right? Adieu."

He put his hat on and withdrew. By and by he stood, letter in hand, before the person to whom it was addressed. This person employed an interpreter.

"He says," said the interpreter to the officer, "he come to make you the fair warning how you muz not make the street pas' at his 'ouse."

The officer remarked that "such impudence was refreshing"; but the experienced interpreter translated freely.

"He says: 'Why you don't want?' " said the interpreter.

The old slave-trader answered at some length.

"He says," said the interpreter, again turning to the officer, "the marass is a too unhealth' for peopl' to live."

"But we expect to drain his old marsh; it's not going to be a marsh."

"*Il dit*"—The interpreter explained in French.

The old man answered tersely.

"He says the canal is a private," said the interpreter.

"Oh! *that* old ditch; that's to be filled up.   Tell the old man we're going to fix him up nicely."

Translation being duly made, the man in power was amused to see a thunder-cloud gathering on the old man's face.

"Tell him," he added, "by the time we finish, there'll not be a ghost left in his shanty."

The interpreter began to translate, but—

"*J' comprends, J' comprends,*" said the old man, with an impatient gesture, and burst forth, pouring curses upon the United States, the President, the Territory of Orleans, Congress, the Governor and all his subordinates, striding out of the apartment as he cursed, while the object of his maledictions roared with merriment and rammed the floor with his foot.

"Why, it will make his old place worth ten dollars to one," said the official to the interpreter.

"'Tis not for de worse of de property," said the interpreter.

"I should guess not," said the other, whittling his chair,— "seems to me as if some of these old Creoles would liever live in a crawfish hole than to have a neighbor."

"You know what make old Jean Poquelin make like that?   I will tell you.   You know"—

The interpreter was rolling a cigarette, and paused to light his tinder; then, as the smoke poured in a thick double stream from his nostrils, he said, in a solemn whisper:

"He is a witch."

"Ho, ho, ho!" laughed the other.

"You don't believe it?   What you want to bet?" cried the interpreter, jerking himself half up and thrusting out one arm while he bared it of its coat-sleeve with the hand of the other. "What you want to bet?"

"How do you know?" asked the official.

"Dass what I goin' to tell you.   You know, one evening I was shooting some *grosbec*.   I killed three; but I had trouble to fine them, it was becoming so dark.   When I have them I start' to come home; then I got to pas' at Jean Poquelin's house."

"Ho, ho, ho!" laughed the other, throwing his leg over the arm of his chair.

"Wait," said the interpreter. "I come along slow, not making some noises; still, still"—

"And scared," said the smiling one.

"*Mais*, wait. I get all pas' the 'ouse. 'Ah!' I say; 'all right!' Then I see two thing' before! Hah! I get as cold and humide, and shake like a leaf. You think it was nothing? There I see, so plain as can be (though it was making nearly dark), I see Jean—Marie—Po-que-lin walkin' right in front, and right there beside of him was something like a man—but not a man —white like paint!—I dropp' on the grass from scared— they pass'; so sure as I live 'twas the ghos' of Jacques Poquelin, his brother!"

"Pooh!" said the listener.

"I'll put my han' in the fire," said the interpreter.

"But did you never think," asked the other, "that that might be Jack Poquelin, as you call him, alive and well, and for some cause hid away by his brother?"

"But there har' no cause!" said the other, and the entrance of third parties changed the subject.

Some months passed and the street was opened. A canal was first dug through the marsh, the small one which passed so close to Jean Poquelin's house was filled, and the street, or rather a sunny road, just touched a corner of the old mansion's dooryard. The morass ran dry. Its venomous denizens slipped away through the bulrushes; the cattle roaming freely upon its hardened surface trampled the superabundant under- growth. The bellowing frogs croaked to westward. Lilies and the flower-de-luce sprang up in the place of reeds; smilax and poison-oak gave way to the purple-plumed iron-weed and pink spiderwort; the bindweeds ran everywhere blooming as they ran, and on one of the dead cypresses a giant creeper hung its green burden of foliage and lifted its scarlet trumpets. Sparrows and red-birds flitted through the bushes, and dew- berries grew ripe beneath. Over all these came a sweet, dry smell of salubrity which the place had not known since the sediments of the Mississippi first lifted it from the sea.

But its owner did not build. Over the willow-brakes, and

down the vista of the open street, bright new houses, some singly, some by ranks, were prying in upon the old man's privacy. They even settled down toward his southern side. First a wood-cutter's hut or two, then a market gardener's shanty, then a painted cottage, and all at once the faubourg had flanked and half surrounded him and his dried-up marsh.

Ah! then the common people began to hate him. "The old tyrant!" "You don't mean an old *tyrant?*" "Well, then, why don't he build when the public need demands it? What does he live in that unneighborly way for?" "The old pirate!" "The old kidnapper!" How easily even the most ultra Louisianians put on the imported virtues of the North when they could be brought to bear against the hermit. "There he goes, with the boys after him! Ah! ha! ha! Jean-ah Poquelin! Ah! Jean-ah! Aha! aha! Jean-ah Marie! Jean-ah Poquelin! The old villain!" How merrily the swarming Américains echo the spirit of persecution! "The old fraud," they say—"pretends to live in a haunted house, does he? We'll tar and feather him some day. Guess we can fix him."

He cannot be rowed home along the old canal now; he walks. He has broken sadly of late, and the street urchins are ever at his heels. It is like the days when they cried: "Go up, thou bald-head," and the old man now and then turns and delivers ineffectual curses.

To the Creoles—to the incoming lower class of superstitious Germans, Irish, Sicilians, and others—he became an omen and embodiment of public and private ill-fortune. Upon him all the vagaries of their superstitions gathered and grew. If a house caught fire, it was imputed to his machinations. Did a woman go off in a fit, he had bewitched her. Did a child stray off for an hour, the mother shivered with the apprehension that Jean Poquelin had offered him to strange gods. The house was the subject of every bad boy's invention who loved to contrive ghostly lies. "As long as that house stands we shall have bad luck. Do you not see our pease and beans dying, our cabbages and lettuce going to seed and our gardens turning to dust, while every day you can see it raining in the woods? The rain will never pass old Poquelin's house. He keeps a fetich. He has conjured the whole Faubourg St. Marie. And why, the old wretch? Simply because our playful and innocent children call after him as he passes."

A "Building and Improvement Company," which had not yet got its charter, "but was going to," and which had not, indeed, any tangible capital yet, but "was going to have some," joined the "Jean-ah Poquelin" war. The haunted property would be such a capital site for a market-house! They sent a deputation to the old mansion to ask its occupant to sell. The deputation never got beyond the chained gate and a very barren interview with the African mute. The President of the Board was then empowered (for he had studied French in Pennsylvania and was considered qualified) to call and persuade M. Poquelin to subscribe to the company's stock; but—

"Fact is, gentlemen," he said at the next meeting, "it would take us at least twelve months to make Mr. Pokaleen understand the rather original features of our system, and he wouldn't subscribe when we'd done; besides, the only way to see him is to stop him on the street."

There was a great laugh from the Board; they couldn't help it. "Better meet a bear robbed of her whelps," said one.

"You're mistaken as to that," said the President. "I did meet him, and stopped him, and found him quite polite. But I could get no satisfaction from him; the fellow wouldn't talk in French, and when I spoke in English he hoisted his old shoulders up, and gave the same answer to everything I said."

"And that was—?" asked one or two, impatient of the cause.

"That it 'don't worse w'ile.' "

One of the Board said: "Mr. President, this market-house project, as I take it, is not altogether a selfish one; the community is to be benefited by it. We may feel that we are working in the public interest [the Board smiled knowingly], if we employ all possible means to oust this old nuisance from among us. You may know that at the time the street was cut through, this old Poquelann did all he could to prevent it. It was owing to a certain connection which I had with that affair that I heard a

ghost story [smiles, followed by a sudden dignified check]—
ghost story, which, of course, I am not going to relate; but I
may say that my profound conviction, arising from a prolonged
study of that story, is, that this old villain, John Poquelann, has
his brother locked up in that old house. Now, if this is so, and
we can fix it on him, I merely *suggest* that we can make the
matter highly useful. I din't know," he added, beginning to
sit down, "but that it is an action we owe to the community—
hem!"

"How do you propose to handle the subject?" asked the
President.

"I was thinking," said the speaker, "that, as a Board of
Directors, it would be unadvisable for us to authorize any action
involving trespass; but if you, for instance, Mr. President,
should, as it were, for mere curiosity, *request* some one, as, for
instance, our excellent Secretary, simply as a personal favor, to
look into the matter—this is merely a suggestion."

The Secretary smiled sufficiently to be understood that, while
he certainly did not consider such preposterous service a part of
his duties as secretary, he might, notwithstanding, accede to the
President's request; and the Board adjourned.

Little White, as the Secretary was called, was a mild, kind-
hearted little man, who, nevertheless, had no fear of anything,
unless it was the fear of being unkind.

"I tell you frankly," he privately said to the President, "I go
into this purely for reasons of my own."

The next day, a little after nightfall, one might have descried
this little man slipping along the rear fence of the Poquelin
place, preparatory to vaulting over into the rank, grass-grown
yard, and bearing himself altogether more after the manner of a
collector of rare chickens than according to the usage of secre-
taries.

The picture presented to his eye was not calculated to enliven
his mind. The old mansion stood out against the western sky,
black and silent. One long, lurid pencil-stroke along a sky of
slate was all that was left of daylight. No sign of life was
apparent; no light at any window, unless it might have been on

the side of the house hidden from view. No owls were on the chimneys, no dogs were in the yard.

He entered the place, and ventured up behind a small cabin which stood apart from the house. Through one of its many crannies he easily detected the African mute crouched before a flickering pine-knot, his head on his knees, fast asleep.

He concluded to enter the mansion, and, with that view, stood and scanned it. The broad rear steps of the veranda would not serve him; he might meet some one midway. He was measuring, with his eye, the proportions of one of the pillars which supported it, and estimating the practicability of climbing it, when he heard a footstep. Some one dragged a chair out toward the railing, then seemed to change his mind and began to pace the veranda, his footfalls resounding on the dry boards with singular loudness. Little White drew a step backward, got the figure between himself and the sky, and at once recognized the short, broad-shouldered form of old Jean Poquelin.

He sat down upon a billet of wood, and, to escape the stings of a whining cloud of mosquitoes, shrouded his face and neck in his handkerchief, leaving his eyes uncovered.

He sat there but a moment when he noticed a strange, sickening odor, faint, as if coming from a distance, but loathsome and horrid.

Whence could it come? Not from the cabin; not from the marsh, for it was as dry as powder. It was not in the air; it seemed to come from the ground.

Rising up, he noticed, for the first time, a few steps before him a narrow footpath leading toward the house. He glanced down it—ha! right there was some one coming—ghostly white!

Quick as thought, and as noiselessly, he lay down at full length against the cabin. It was bold strategy, and yet, there was no denying it, little White felt that he was frightened. "It is not a ghost," he said to himself. "I *know* it cannot be a ghost"; but the perspiration burst out at every pore, and the air seemed to thicken with heat. "It is a living man," he said in his thoughts. "I hear his footstep, and I hear old Poquelin's footsteps, too, separately, over on the veranda. I am not discovered; the thing has passed; there is that odor again; what a smell of death! Is it coming back? Yes. It stops at the door of the cabin. Is it peering in at the sleeping mute? It moves away. It is in the path again. Now it is gone." He shuddered. "Now, if I dare venture, the mystery is solved." He rose cautiously, close against the cabin, and peered along the path.

The figure of a man, a presence if not a body—but whether clad in some white stuff or naked the darkness would not allow him to determine—had turned, and now, with a seeming painful gait, moved slowly from him. "Great Heaven! can it be that the dead do walk?" He withdrew again the hands which had gone to his eyes. The dreadful object passed between two pillars and under the house. He listened. There was a faint sound of feet upon a staircase; then all was still except the measured tread of Jean Poquelin walking on the veranda, and the heavy respirations of the mute slumbering in the cabin.

The little Secretary was about to retreat, but as he looked once more toward the haunted house a dim light appeared in the crack of a closed window, and presently old Jean Poquelin came, dragging his chair, and sat down close against the shining cranny. He spoke in a low, tender tone in the French tongue, making some inquiry. An answer came from within. Was it the voice of a human? So unnatural was it—so hollow, so discordant, so unearthly—that the stealthy listener shuddered again from head to foot, and when something stirred in some bushes near by—though it may have been nothing more than a rat—and came scuttling through the grass, the little Secretary actually turned and fled. As he left the enclosure he moved with bolder leisure through the bushes; yet now and then he spoke aloud: "Oh, oh! I see, I understand!" and shut his eyes in his hands.

How strange that henceforth little White was the champion of Jean Poquelin! In season and out of season—wherever a word was uttered against him—the Secretary, with a quiet, aggressive force that instantly arrested gossip, demanded upon what authority the statement or conjecture was made; but as he did not condescend to explain his own remarkable attitude, it was not long before the disrelish and suspicion which had followed Jean Poquelin so many years fell also upon him.

It was only the next evening but one after his adventure that he made himself a source of sullen amazement to one hundred and fifty boys, by ordering them to desist from their wanton hallooing. Old Jean Poquelin, standing and shaking his cane, rolling out his long-drawn maledictions, paused and stared, then gave the Secretary a courteous bow and started on. The boys, save one, from pure astonishment, ceased; but a ruffianly little Irish lad, more daring than any had yet been, threw a big hurtling clod, that struck old Poquelin between the shoulders and burst like a shell. The enraged old man wheeled with uplifted staff to give chase to the scampering vagabond; and—he may have tripped, or he may not, but he fell full length. Little White hastened to help him up, but he waved him off with a fierce imprecation and staggering to his feet resumed his way homeward. His lips were reddened with blood.

Little White was on his way to the meeting of the Board. He would have given all he dared spend to have stayed away, for he felt too fierce and too tremulous to brook the criticisms that were likely to be made.

"I can't help it, gentlemen; I can't help you to make a case against the old man, and I'm not going to."

"We did not expect this disappointment, Mr. White."

"I can't help that, sir. No, sir; you had better not appoint any more investigations. Somebody'll investigate himself into trouble. No, sir; it isn't a threat, it is only my advice, but I warn you that whoever takes the task in hand will rue it to his dying day—which may be hastened, too."

The President expressed himself "surprised."

"I don't care a rush," answered little White, wildly and foolishly. "I don't care a rush if you are, sir. No, my nerves are not disordered; my head's as clear as a bell. No, I'm *not* excited."

A Director remarked that the Secretary looked as though he had waked from a nightmare.

"Well, sir, if you want to know the fact, I have; and if you choose to cultivate old Poquelin's society you can have one, too."

"White," called a facetious member, but White did not notice. "White," he called again.

"What?" demanded White, with a scowl.

"Did you see the ghost?"

"Yes, sir; I did," cried White, hitting the table, and handing the President a paper which brought the Board to other business.

The story got among the gossips that somebody (they were afraid to say little White) had been to the Poquelin mansion by night and beheld something appalling. The rumor was but a shadow of the truth, magnified and distorted as is the manner of shadows. He had seen skeletons walking, and barely had escaped the clutches of one by making the sign of the cross.

Some madcap boys with an appetite for the horrible plucked up courage to venture through the dried marsh by the cattle-path, and come before the house at a spectral hour when the air was full of bats. Something which they but half saw— half a sight was enough—sent them tearing back through the willow-brakes and acacia bushes to their homes, where they fairly dropped down, and cried:

"Was it white?" "No—yes—nearly so—we can't tell— but we saw it." And one could hardly doubt, to look at their ashen faces, that they had, whatever it was.

"If that old rascal lived in the country we come from," said certain Américains, "he'd have been tarred and feathered before now, wouldn't he, Sanders?"

"Well, now he just would."

"And we'd have rid him on a rail, wouldn't we?"

"That's what I allow."

"Tell you what you *could* do." They were talking to some rollicking Creoles who had assumed an absolute necessity for doing *something*. "What is it you call this thing where an old man marries a young girl, and you come out with horns and"—

"*Charivari?*" asked the Creoles.

"Yes, that's it. Why don't you shivaree him?" Felicitous suggestion.

Little White, with his wife beside him, was sitting on their doorsteps on the sidewalk, as Creole custom had taught them, looking toward the sunset. They had moved into the lately-opened street. The view was not attractive on the score of beauty. The houses were small and scattered, and across the flat commons, spite of the lofty tangle of weeds and bushes, and spite of the thickets of acacia, they needs must see the dismal old Poquelin mansion, tilted awry and shutting out the declining sun. The moon, white and slender, was hanging the tip of its horn over one of the chimneys.

"And you say," said the Secretary, "the old black man has been going by here alone? Patty, suppose old Poquelin should be concocting some mischief; he don't lack provocation; the way that clod hit him the other day was enough to have killed him. Why, Patty, he dropped as quick as *that!* No wonder you haven't seen him. I wonder if they haven't heard something about him up at the drug-store. Suppose I go and see."

"Do," said his wife.

She sat alone for half an hour, watching that sudden going out of the day peculiar to the latitude.

"That moon is ghost enough for one house," she said, as her husband returned. "It has gone right down the chimney."

"Patty," said little White, "the drug-clerk says the boys are going to shivaree old Poquelin to-night. I'm going to try to stop it."

"Why, White," said his wife, "you'd better not. You'll get hurt."

"No, I'll not."

"Yes, you will."

"I'm going to sit out here until they come along. They're compelled to pass right by here."

"Why, White, it may be midnight before they start; you're not going to sit out here till then."

"Yes, I am."

"Well, you're very foolish," said Mrs. White in an undertone, looking anxious, and tapping one of the steps with her foot.

They sat a very long time talking over little family matters.

"What's that?" at last said Mrs. White.

"That's the nine-o'clock gun," said White, and they relapsed into a long-sustained, drowsy silence.

"Patty, you'd better go in and go to bed," said he at last.

"I'm not sleepy."

"Well, you're very foolish," quietly remarked little White, and again silence fell upon them.

"Patty, suppose I walk out to the old house and see if I can find out anything."

"Suppose," said she, "you don't do any such—listen!"

Down the street arose a great hubbub. Dogs and boys were howling and barking; men were laughing, shouting, groaning, and blowing horns, whooping, and clanking cow-bells, whinnying, and howling, and rattling pots and pans.

"They are coming this way," said little White. "You had better go into the house, Patty."

"So had you."

"No. I'm going to see if I can't stop them."

"Why, White!"

"I'll be back in a minute," said White, and went toward the noise.

In a few moments the little Secretary met the mob. The pen hesitates on the word, for there is a respectable difference, measurable only on the scale of the half century, between a mob and a *charivari*. Little White lifted his ineffectual voice. He faced the head of the disorderly column, and cast himself about as if he were made of wood and moved by the jerk of a string. He rushed to one who seemed, from the size and clatter of his tin pan, to be a leader. "*Stop these fellows, Bienvenu, stop them just a minute, till I tell them something.*" Bienvenu turned and brandished his instruments of discord in an imploring way to the crowd. They slackened their pace, two or three hushed their horns and joined the prayer of little White and Bienvenu for silence. The throng halted. The hush was delicious.

"Bienvenu," said little White, "don't shivaree old Poquelin to-night; he's"——

"My fwang," said the swaying Bienvenu, "who tail you I goin' to chahivahi somebody, eh? You sink bickause I make a little playfool wiz zis tin pan zat I am *dhonk?*"

"Oh, no, Bienvenu, old fellow, you're all right. I was afraid you might not know that old Poquelin was sick, you know, but you're not going there, are you?"

"My fwang, I vay soy to tail you zat you ah dhonk as de dev'. I am *shem* of you. I ham ze servan' of ze *publique*. Zese *citoyens* goin' to wickwest Jean Poquelin to give to the Ursuline' two hondred fifty dolla' "——

"*Hé quoi!*" cried a listener, "*Cinq cent piastres, oui!*"

"*Oui!*" said Bienvenu, "and if he wiffuse we make him some lit' *musique* ta-ra-ta!" He hoisted a merry hand and foot, then frowning, added: "Old Poquelin got no bizniz dhink s'much w'isky."

"But, gentlemen," said little White, around whom a circle had gathered, "the old man is very sick."

"My faith!" cried a tiny Creole, "we did not make him to be sick. W'en we say we going make *le charivari*, do you want that we hall tell a lie? My faith! 'sfools!"

"But you can shivaree somebody else," said desperate little White.

"*Oui!*" cried Bienvenu, "*et chahivahi* Jean-ah Poquelin tomo'w'!"

"Let us go to Madame Schneider!" cried two or three, and amid huzzas and confused cries, among which was heard a stentorian Celtic call for drinks, the crowd again began to move.

"*Cent piastres pour l'hôpital de charité!*"

"Hurrah!"

"One hongred dolla' for Charity Hospital!"

"Hurrah!"

"Whang!" went a tin pan, the crowd yelled, and Pandemonium gaped again. They were off at a right angle.

Nodding, Mrs. White looked at the mantel-clock.

"Well, if it isn't away after midnight."

The hideous noise down street was passing beyond earshot.

She raised a sash and listened. For a moment there was silence. Some one came to the door.

"Is that you, White?"

"Yes." He entered. "I succeeded, Patty."

"Did you?" said Patty, joyfully.

"Yes. They've gone down to shivaree the old Dutchwoman who married her step-daughter's sweetheart. They say she has got to pay a hundred dollars to the hospital before they stop."

The couple retired, and Mrs. White slumbered. She was awakened by her husband snapping the lid of his watch.

"What time?" she asked.

"Half-past three, Patty, I haven't slept a wink. Those fellows are out yet. Don't you hear them?"

"Why, White, they're coming this way!"

"I know they are," said White, sliding out of bed and drawing on his clothes, "and they are coming fast. You'd better go away from that window, Patty. My! what a clatter!"

"Here they are," said Mrs. White, but her husband was gone. Two or three hundred men and boys pass the place at a rapid walk straight down the broad, new street, toward the hated house of ghosts. The din was terrific. She saw little White at the head of the rabble brandishing his arms and trying in vain to make himself heard; but they only shook their heads, laughing and hooting the louder, and so passed, bearing him on before them.

Swiftly they pass out from among the houses, away from the dim oil lamps of the street, out into the broad starlit commons, and enter the willowy jungles of the haunted ground. Some hearts fail and their owners lag behind and turn back, suddenly remembering how near morning it is. But the most part push on, tearing the air with their clamor.

Down ahead of them in the long, thicket-darkened way there is—singularly enough—a faint, dancing light. It must be very near the old house; it is. It has stopped now. It is a lantern, and is under a well-known sapling which has grown up on the wayside since the canal was filled. Now it swings mysteriously to and fro. A goodly number of the more ghost-fearing give up the sport; but a full hundred move forward at a run, doubling their devilish howling and banging.

Yes; it is a lantern, and there are two persons under the tree. The crowd draws near—drops into a walk; one of the two is the old African mute; he lifts the lantern up so that it shines on the other; the crowd recoils; there is a hush of all clangor, and all at once, with a cry of mingled fright and horror from every throat, the whole throng rushes back, dropping every-thing, sweeping past little White and hurrying on, never stopping until the jungle is left behind, and then to find that not one in ten has seen the cause of the stampede, and not one of the tenth is certain what it was.

There is one huge fellow among them who looks capable of any villany. He finds something to mount on, and, in the Creole *patois*, calls a general halt. Bienvenu sinks down, and, vainly trying to recline gracefully, resigns the leadership. The herd gather round the speaker; he assures them that they have been outraged. Their right peaceably to traverse the public streets has been trampled upon. Shall such encroachments be endured? It is now daybreak. Let them go now by the open light of day and force a free passage of the public highway!

A scattering consent was the response, and the crowd, thinned now and drowsy, straggled quietly down toward the old house. Some drifted ahead, others sauntered behind, but every one, as he again neared the tree, came to a stand-still. Little White sat upon a bank of turf on the opposite side of the way looking very stern and sad. To each newcomer he put the same question:

"Did you come here to go to old Poquelin's?"

"Yes."

"He's dead." And if the shocked hearer started away he would say: "Don't go away."

"Why not?"

"I want you to go to the funeral presently."

If some Louisianian, too loyal to dear France or Spain to understand English, looked bewildered, some one would interpret for him; and presently they went. Little White led the van, the crowd trooping after him down the middle of the way. The gate, that had never been seen before unchained, was open. Stern little White stopped a short distance from it; the rabble stopped behind him. Something was moving out from under the veranda. The many whisperers stretched upward to see. The African mute came very slowly toward the gate, leading by a cord in the nose a small brown bull, which was harnessed to a rude cart. On the flat body of the cart, under a black cloth, were seen the outlines of a long box.

"Hats off, gentlemen," said little White, as the box came in view, and the crowd silently uncovered.

"Gentlemen," said little White, "here come the last remains of Jean Marie Poquelin, a better man, I'm afraid, with all his sins,—yes, a better—a kinder man to his blood—a man of more self-forgetful goodness—than all of you put together will ever dare to be."

There was a profound hush as the vehicle came creaking through the gate; but when it turned away from them toward the forest, those in front started suddenly. There was a backward rush, then all stood still again staring one way; for there, behind the bier, with eyes cast down and labored step, walked the living remains—all that was left—of little Jacques Poquelin, the long-hidden brother—a leper, as white as snow.

Dumb with horror, the cringing crowd gazed upon the walking death. They watched in silent awe, the slow *cortège* creep down the long, straight road and lessen on the view, until by and by it stopped where a wild, unfrequented path branched off into the undergrowth toward the rear of the ancient city.

"They are going to the *Terre aux Lépreux*," said one in the crowd. The rest watched them in silence.

The little bull was set free; the mute, with the strength of an ape, lifted the long box to his shoulder. For a moment more the mute and the leper stood in sight, while the former adjusted his heavy burden; then, without one backward glance upon the unkind human world, turning their faces toward the ridge in the depths of the swamp known as the Leper's Land, they stepped into the jungle, disappeared, and were never seen again.

GRACE ELIZABETH KING

Grace Elizabeth King was born in New Orleans, on November 29, 1851, and died in the same city, on January 14, 1932. Her father was a prominent lawyer and successful sugar planter before the war. A dominant member of her childhood family was her maternal grandmother, of Huguenot ancestry. Part Creole in blood, Miss King was wholly Creole in sympathy, and she wrote many stories and histories in analysis and praise of the Louisiana Creoles. In her *Memories of a Southern Woman of Letters* she relates dramatically her flight, as a child, with mother and grandmother, from New Orleans to a plantation which was held by the "beast" Butler and his soldiers. Her story "Bayou L'Ombre: An Incident of the War," although not autobiographical, gives a vivid picture of Louisiana plantation life during the war. After the war years she attended the Institut St. Louis, described in "Monsieur Motte"; she was instructed in the fashionable school conducted by the Mesdames Cenas, which appears in several of her stories as the Institute St. Denis; later she had excellent tutors in the languages. According to Miss Katherine Pope, "She speaks French like the French, has from girlhood been closely connected with the Creole element of New Orleans society, knows intimately the descendants of the Spanish and French who for generations held high place in the councils and social life in Louisiana." Memorable in her childhood was the friendship of Charles Gayarré, the Louisiana historian, and the days spent at his country home, Roncal. In her father's hospitable home she met literary celebrities, even at one time such an ill-assorted pair as Joaquin Miller and Julia Ward Howe. The visit of Richard Watson Gilder, editor of the *Century Magazine*, in 1884, aroused her to write "Monsieur Motte" in answer to his challenge, "If Cable is so false to you, why do not some of you write better?" The story was sent anonymously to Mr. Gilder, who returned it without a word of comment. But another visitor came to the city, Charles Dudley Warner, who praised the story and secured its publication in the *New Princeton Review* in January, 1886. This story and three others of Louisiana

and Creole life were published in the volume *Monsieur Motte*
(1888). Stories published in *Harper's Magazine* were collected
in *Tales of a Time and Place* (1892). Besides "Bayou L'Ombre,"
which has been mentioned, two of these stories are significant:
"Bonne Maman," a vivid picture of a poverty-stricken home
after the Civil War, in which proud, aristocratic Creoles are
served by loyal former slaves, and "Madrilene: Or the Festival
of the Dead," an account of interesting New Orleans customs
involving relations between quadroons and white people. Another group of stories, published in the *Century Magazine* in
1892–1893, were collected in *Balcony Stories* (1893). These
fifteen stories give interesting glimpses of New Orleans homes
in the period following the Civil War. Especially to be com-
mended are "A Drama of Three," and "A Crippled Hope."
She has written a few novelettes and novels, among which are
The Pleasant Ways of St. Médard (1916), a novel of reconstruction days in New Orleans, which Garnett called "a story
rare in historical significance," and *La Dame de Sainte Hermaine*
(1924) which Professor Quinn praised as "a charming novel
of Louisiana in the eighteenth century."

Of her historical works, Henry P. Dart, the editor of *The
Louisiana Historical Quarterly*, recommends in the order of importance *De Soto and His Men in the Land of Florida* (1898),
Jean Baptiste le Moyne, Sieur de Bienville (1892), the biography
of "the father of Louisiana," *Creole Families of New Orleans*
(1921), which "represents the pageantry of life in New Orleans"
during the eighteenth and early nineteenth centuries, and *New
Orleans: The Place and the People* (1895), with its fine revelation of the life and spirit of the city.

In her *Memories* we read about her personal acquaintance
with editors and authors, especially Gilder, Warner, Howells,
and Mark Twain. Her prized honors were from New Orleans,
as secretary of the Louisiana Historical Society and as the re-
cipient of an honorary degree from Tulane University.

From BAYOU L'OMBRE: AN INCIDENT
OF THE WAR

Of course they knew all about war—soldiers, flags, music,
generals on horseback brandishing swords, knights in armor

escalading walls, cannons booming through clouds of smoke. They were familiarized with it pictorially and by narrative long before the alphabet made its appearance in the nursery with rudimentary accounts of the world they were born into, the simple juvenile world of primary sensations and colors. Their great men, and great women too, were all fighters; the great events of their histories, battles; the great places of their geography, there they were fought (and generally the more bloody the battle, the more glorious the place); while their little chronology—the pink-covered one—stepped briskly over the centuries solely on the names of kings and sanguinary saliencies. Sunday added the sabbatical supplement to week-day lessons, symbolizing religion, concreting sin, incorporating evil, for their better comprehension, putting Jehovah himself in armor, to please their childish faculties—the omnipotent Intervener of the Old Testament, for whom they waved banners, sang hymns, and by the brevet title "little *soldiers* of the cross" felt committed as by baptism to an attitude of expectant hostility. Madamoiselle Couper, their governess, eased the cross-stitching in their samplers during the evenings, after supper, with traditions of "le grand Napoleon," in whose army her grandfather was a terrible and distinguished officer, le Capitaine Césaire Paul Picquet de Montignac; and although Mademoiselle Couper was most unlovable and exacting at times, and very homely, such were their powers of sympathetic enthusiasm even then that they often went to bed envious of the possessor of so glorious an ancestor, and dreamed fairy tales of him whose gray hair, enshrined in a brooch, reposed comfortably under the folds of mademoiselle's fat chin—the hair that Napoleon had looked upon!

When a war broke out in their own country they could hardly credit their good fortune; that is, Christine and Régina, for Lolotte was still a baby. . . .

Titine was about thirteen, Gina twelve, and Lolotte barely eight years old, when this, to them, happy break in their lives occurred. It was easily comprehensible to them that their city should be captured, and that to escape that grim ultimatum of

Mademoiselle Couper, *"passées au fil de l'epée,"* they should be bundled up very hurriedly one night, carried out of their home, and journey in troublesome roundabout ways to the plantation on Bayou l'Ombre.

That was all four years ago. School and play and city life, dolls and fêtes and Santa Claus, had become the property of memory. Peace hovered in the obscurity which once enveloped war, while "'61," "'62," "'63," "'64," filled immeasurable spaces in their short past. . . .

But—there were no soldiers, flags, music, parades, battles, or sieges. This war was altogether distinct from the wars contained in books or in Mademoiselle Couper's memory. There was an absence of the simplest requirements of war. They kept awaiting the familiar events for which they had been prepared; but after four years the only shots fired on Bayou l'Ombre were at game in the forest, the only blood shed was from the tottering herds of Texas beeves driven across the swamps to them, barely escaping by timely butchery the starvation they came to relieve, and the only heroism they had been called upon to display was still going to bed in the dark. . . . Sometimes a rumor of a battle "out in the Confederacy" would find its way across the swamps to them, and months afterward a newspaper would be thrown from a passing skiff to them; some old, useless, tattered, disreputable, journalistic tramp, garrulous with mendacities. . . . They would with mingled pride and envy read all the names, barely decipherable in the travel-stained record, from the President and Generals in big print to the diminishing insignificance of smallest-type privates; and they would shed tears, when the reaction would come a few days later, at the thought that in the whole area of typography, from the officers gaining immortality to the privates losing lives, there was not one name belonging to them; and they would ask why, of all the families in the South, precisely their father and mother should have no relations, why, of all the women in the South, they should be brotherless.

There was Beau, a too notorious guerilla captain;—but what glory was to be won by raiding towns, wrecking trains, plundering transports, capturing couriers, disobeying orders, defying regulations? He was almost as obnoxious to his own as to the enemy's flag.

Besides, Beau at most was only a kind of a cousin, the son of a deceased step-sister of their father's; the most they could expect from him was to keep his undisciplined crew of "'Cadians," Indians, and swampers away from Bayou l'Ombre. . . .

It was now early summer; the foliage of spring was lusty and strong, fast outgrowing tenderness and delicacy of shade, with hints of maturity already swelling the shape. The day was cloudless and warm, the dinner hour was long past, and supper still far off. . . . The plantation was quiet and still; not the dewy hush of early dawn trembling before the rising sun, nor the mysterious muteness of midnight, nor yet the lethargic dulness of summer when the vertical sun-rays pin sense and motion to the earth. It was the motionless, voiceless state of unnatural quietude, the oppressive consciousness of abstracted activity, which characterized those days when the whole force of Bayou l'Ombre went off into the swamps to cut timber. Days that began shortly after one midnight and lasted to the other; rare days, when neither horn nor bell was heard for summons; when not a skiff, flat-boat, nor pirogue was left at the "gunnels"; when old Uncle John alone remained to represent both master and men in the cares and responsibilities devolving upon his sex. The bayou lived and moved as usual, and carried its deceptive depths of brackish water unceasingly onward through the shadow and sunshine, rippling over the opposite low, soft banks, which seemed slowly sinking out of sight under the weight of the huge cypress-trees growing upon it. The long stretch of untilled fields back of the house, feebly kept in symmetrical proportion by crumbling fences, bared their rigid, seedless furrows in despairing barrenness to the sun, except in corner spots where a rank growth of weeds had inaugurated a reclamation in favor of barbarism. The sugar-house, superannuated and decrepit from unwholesome idleness, tottered against its own massive, smokeless chimney;

the surrounding sheds, stables, and smithy looked forsaken and neglected; the old blind mule peacefully slept in the shade of his once flagellated course under the corn-mill. Afar off against the woods the huge wheel of the draining-machine rose from the underbrush in the big ditch. The patient buzzards, roosting on the branches of the gaunt, blasted gum-tree by the bayou, raised their heads from time to time to question the loitering sun, or, slowly flapping their heavy wings, circled up into the blue sky, to fall again in lazy spirals to their watch-tower, or they took short flights by twos and threes over the moribund plantation to see if dissolution had not yet set in, and then all settled themselves again to brood and sleep and dream, and wait in tranquil certainty the striking of their banqueting hour.

The three girls were in the open hallway of the plantation house, Christine reading, Régina knitting, both listlessly occupied. Like everything else, they were passively quiet, and, like everything else, their appearance advertised an unwholesome lack of vitality, an insidious anamorphosis from an unexplained dearth or constraint. . . .

"Listen!" Like wood-ducks from under the water, the three heads rose simultaneously above their abstractions. "Rowlock! Rowlock!" The eyes might become dull, the tongue inert, and the heart languid on Bayou l'Ombre, but the ears were ever assiduous, ever on duty. Quivering and nervous, they listened even through sleep for that one blessed echo, the signal from another and distant world. Faint, shadowy, delusive, the whispering forerunner of on-coming news, it overrode the rippling of the current, the hooting of the owls, the barking of dogs, the splash of the gar-fish, the grunting of the alligator, the croaking of frogs, penetrating all turmoil, silencing all other sounds. "Rowlock! Rowlock!" Slow, deliberate, hard, and strenuous, coming up-stream; easy, soft, and musical, gliding down. "Rowlock! Rowlock!" Every stroke a very universe of hope, every oar frothing a sea of expectation! Was it the bayou or the secret stream of their longing that suggested the sound to-day? "Rowlock! Rowlock!" The smouldering

glances brightened in their eyes, they hollowed their hands behind their ears and held their breath for greater surety. "Rowlock! Rowlock!" In clear, distinct reiteration. It resolved
the moment of doubt.

"Can it be papa coming back?"

"No; it's against stream."

"It must be swampers."

"Or hunters, perhaps."

"Or Indians from the mound."

"Indians in a skiff?"

"Well, they sometimes come in a skiff."

The contingencies were soon exhausted, a cut-off leading
travellers far around Bayou l'Ombre, whose snaggy, rafted,
convoluted course was by universal avoidance relegated to an
isolation almost insulting. The girls quit their places and advanced to the edge of the gallery, then out under the trees,
then to the levee, then to the "gunnels," where they stretched
their long, thin, white necks out of their blue and brown check
gowns, and shaded their eyes and gazed down-stream for the
first glimpse of the skiff, their patience which had lasted months
fretting now over the delay of a few moments.

"At last we shall get some news again."

"If they only leave a newspaper!"

"Or a letter," said Lolotte.

"A letter! From whom?"

"Ah, that's it!"

"What a pity papa isn't here!"

"Lolotte, don't shake the gunnels so; you are wetting our
feet."

"How long is it since the last one passed?"

"I can tell you," said Lolotte—"I can tell you exactly; it
was the day Lou Ann fell in the bayou and nearly got drowned."

"You mean when you both fell in."

"I didn't fall in at all; I held on to the pirogue."

The weeping-willow on the point below veiled the view;
stretching straight out from the bank, it dropped its shock of
long green pliant branches into the water titillating and dimpling

the surface. The rising bayou bore a freight of logs and drift from the swamps above; rudely pushing their way through the willow boughs, they tore and bruised the fragile tendrils that clung to the rough bark, scattering the tiny leaves to follow hopelessly in their wake or dance up and down in the hollow eddies. Each time the willow screen moved, the gunnels swayed under the forward motion of the eager bodies.

"At last!"

They turned their eyes to the shaft of sunlight that fell through the plantation clearing, bridging the stream. The skiff touched, entered, and passed through it with a marvellous revelation of form and color, the oars silvering and dripping diamonds, arrows and lances of light scintillating from polished steel, golden stars rising like dust from tassels, cordons, buttons, and epaulets, while the blue clouds themselves seemed to have fallen from their empyrean heights to uniform the rowers with their own celestial hue—blue, not gray!

"Rowlock! Rowlock!" What loud, frightful, threatening reverberations! And the bayou flowed on the same, and the cypress-trees gazed stolidly and steadfastly up to the heavens, and the heavens were serenely blue and white! But the earth was sympathetic, the ground shook and swayed under their feet; or was it the rush of thoughts that made their heads so giddy? They tried to arrest one and hold it for guidance, but on they sped, leaving only wild confusion of conjecture behind.

"Rowlock! Rowlock!" The rudder headed the bow for the gunnels.

"Titine! Gina! Will they kill us all?" whispered Lolotte, with anxious horror. . . .

Under the wide-spreading, moss-hung branches, on the broad flat slope, a grand general washing of the clothes of the small community was in busy progress, a proper feminine consecration of this purely feminine day. The daily irksome routine was broken, the men were all away, the sun was bright and warm, the air soft and sweet, the vague recesses of the opposite forest were dim and silent, the bayou played under the gunnels in caressing modulations; all permitted the hearkening and the yielding to a debonair mood, and harmonized the disregard of concealment, the license of pose, the freedom of limb, the hilarity, the conviviality, the confidences, indiscretions, and audacities of tongue, the joyous indulgence in freak and impulse, the relaxation of unfriendliness, the banishment of thought, the return for one brief moment to the wild, sweet ways of nature, to the festal days of the golden age (a short return for them), as if the body still had claims, and the mind concessions, and the heart owed no allegiance, as if god and satyr eyes still peeped and glistened from leafy covert on their midsummer gambols. Their skirts were girt high around their broad full hips, their dark arms and necks came naked out of their low, sleeveless, white chemise bodies, and glistened with perspiration in the sun as if frosted with silver. Little clouds of steam rose from the kettles standing over heaps of burning chips. The splay-legged battling-boards fastened themselves firmer and firmer into the earth under the blows of the bats, pounding and thumping, squirting the warm suds in all directions, up into the laughing faces, down into the panting bosoms, against the shortened, clinging skirts, over the bare legs, trickling in frothy runnels over the soft red clay corrugated with innumerable toe-prints, and standing in pools everywhere. Out upon the gunnels the water swished and foamed under the vigorous movements of the rinsers, endlessly bending and raising their flexible muscular bodies, burying their arms to the shoulders in the cool green depths, piling higher and higher their heaps of tightly wrung clothes. The evenly filled pails sat with the ease of coronets on the heads of the water-carriers passing up and down the narrow slippery plankway. The children, under compulsion of continuous threats and occasional chastisement, fed the fire with chips from distant wood-piles, squabbling for the possession of the one cane-knife to split kindlers, imitating the noise and echoing with absurd fidelity the full-throated laughter that interrupted from time to time the work around the wash-kettles. High above the slop and tumult sat old Aunt Mary, the official sick-nurse of the plantation, commonly credited with conjuring powers. She held a corncob pipe between her yellow protruding teeth, and her little restless eyes travelled inquisitively from person to person as if in quest of professional information, twinkling with amusement at notable efforts of wit, and with malice at the general discomfiture expressed under their gaze. Heelen sat near, nursing her baby. She had taken off her kerchief, and leaned her uncovered head back against the trunk of the tree; the long wisps of wool, tightly wrapped in white knitting cotton, rose from irregular sections all over her elongated narrow skull, and encircled her wrinkled, nervous, toothless face like some ghastly serpentine chevelure.

"De Yankees! de Yankees! I seed 'em—at de big house! Little mistus she come for Uncle John. He fotch his gun—for to shoot 'em."

Lou Ann struggled to make her exhausted breath carry all her tidings. After each item she closed her mouth and swallowed violently, working her muscles until her little horns of hair rose and moved with the contortions of her face.

"An' dey locked a passel o' men up in de smoke-house—Cornfedrits."

The bats paused in the air, the women on the gunnels lifted their arms out of the water, those on the gang-plank, stopped where they were; only the kettles simmered on audibly.

Lou Ann recommenced, this time finishing in one breath, with the added emphasis of raising her arm and pointing in the direction from whence she came, her voice getting shriller and shriller to the end:

"I seed 'em. Dey was Yankees. Little mistus she come for Uncle John; he fotched his gun for to shoot 'em; and dey locked a passel o' men up in de smoke-house—Cornfedrits."

The Yankees! What did it mean to them? How much from the world outside had penetrated the unlettered fastnesses of their ignorance? What did the war mean to them? Had Bayou l'Ombre indeed isolated both mind and body? Had the subtle time-spirit itself been diverted from them by the cut-off? Could their rude minds draw no inferences from the gradual loosening of authority and relaxing of discipline? Did they neither guess nor divine their share in the shock of battle out there? Could their ghost-seeing eyes not discern the martyr-spirits rising from two opposing armies, pointing at, beckoning to them? If, indeed, the watershed of their destiny was forming without their knowledge as without their assistance, could not maternal instinct spell it out of the heart-throbs pulsing into life under their bosoms, or read from the dumb faces of the children at their breast the triumphant secret of superiority over others born and nourished before them? . . .

"My Gord A'mighty!"

The exclamation was uncompromising; it relieved the tension and encouraged rejoinder.

"My Lord!—humph!"

One bat slowly and deliberately began to beat again—Black Maria's. Her tall, straight back was to them, but, as if they saw it, they knew that her face was settling into that cold, stern rigidity, the keen eyes beginning to glisten, the long, thin nostrils nervously to twitch, the lips to open over her fine white teeth—the expression they hated and feared.

"O-h! o-h! o-h!"

A long, thin, tremulous vibration, a weird, haunting note: what inspiration suggested it?

"Glo-o-ry!"

Old Aunt Mary nodded her knowing head affirmatively, as if at the fulfilment of a silent prophecy. She quietly shook the ashes out of her pipe, hunted her pocket, put it in, and rising stiffly from the root, hobbled away on her stick in the direction of her cabin.

"Glo-o-ry!"

Dead-arm Harriet stood before them, with her back to the bayou, her right arm hanging heavy at her side, her left extended, the finger pointing to the sky. A shapely arm and tapering finger; a comely, sleek, half-nude body; the moist lips, with burning red linings, barely parting to emit the sound they must have culled in uncanny practices. The heavy lids drooped over the large sleepy eyes, looking with languid passion from behind the thick black lashes.

"Glo-o-ry!" Stripping their very nerves and baring secret places of sensation! The "happy" cry of revival meetings, as if midnight were coming on, salvation and the mourners' bench before them, Judgment-day and fiery flames behind them, and "Sister Harriet" raising her voice to call them on, on, through hand-clapping, foot-stamping, shouting, groaning, screaming, out of their sins, out of their senses, to rave in religious inebriation, and fall in religious catalepsy across the floor at the preacher's feet. With a wild rush, their hesitating emotions sought the opportune outlet, their hungry blood bounding and leaping for the mid-day orgy. Obediently their bodies began the imperceptible motion right and left and the veins in their throat swelled and stood out under their skins, while the short, fierce, intense responsive exclamations fell to relieve their own and increase the exaltation of the others.

"Sweet Christ! sweet Christ!"

"Take me, Saviour!"

"Oh, de Lamb! de Lamb!"

"I'm a-coming! I'm a-coming!"

"Hold back, Satan! we's a-catching on!"

"De blood's a-dripping! de blood's a-dripping!"

"Let me kiss dat cross! let me kiss it!"

"Sweet Master!"

"Glo-o-ry! Fre-e-dom!" It was a whisper, but it came like a crash, and transfixed them; their mouths stood open with the last words, their bodies remained bent to one side or the other, the febrile light in their eyes burning as if from their blood on fire. . . .

"Glory! Freedom! Freedom! Glory!"

"I'm bound to see 'em! Come along!"

Heelen's wild scream rang shrill and hysterical. She jerked her breast from the sucking lips, and dropped her baby with a thud on the ground. They all followed her up the levee, pressing one after the other, slipping in the wet clay, struggling each one not to be left behind. Emmeline, the wife of little Ben, the only yellow woman on the place, was the last. Her skirt was held in a grip of iron; blinded, obtuse, she pulled forward, reaching her arms out after the others.

"You stay here!"

She turned and met the determined black face of her mother-in-law.

"You let me go!" she cried, half sobbing, half angry.

"You stay here, I tell you!" The words were muttered through clinched teeth.

"You let me go, I tell you!"

"Glory! Freedom!"

The others had already left the quarters, and were on the road. They two were alone on the bank now, except Heelen's baby, whimpering under the tree; their blazing eyes glared at each other. The singing voices grew fainter and fainter. Suddenly the yellow face grew dark with the surge of blood underneath, the brows wrinkled, and the lips protruded in a grimace of animal rage. Grasping her wet bat tightly with both hands, she turned with a furious bound, and raised it with all the force of her short muscular arms. The black woman darted to the ground; the cane-knife flashed in the air and came down pitilessly toward the soft fleshy shoulder. A wild, terrified scream burst from Emmeline's lips; the bat dropped; seizing her skirt with both hands, she pulled forward, straining her back out of reach of the knife; the homespun tore, and she fled up the bank, her yellow limbs gleaming through the rent left by the fragment in the hand of the black woman.

They were so young, so handsome, so heroic, the very incarnation of the holy spirit of patriotism in their pathetic uniform of brimless caps, ragged jackets, toeless shoes, and shrunken trousers—a veteran equipment of wretchedness out of keeping with their fresh young faces. How proud and unsubdued they walked through the hall between the file of bayonets! With what haughty, defiant eyes they returned the gaze of their insultingly resplendent conquerors! Oh, if souls had been merchantable at that moment! Their hands tied behind their backs like runaway slaves! Locked up in the smoke-house! that dark, rancid, gloomy, mouldy depot of empty hogsheads, barrels, boxes, and fetid exhalations.

They were the first soldiers in gray the girls had ever seen; their own chivalrous knights, the champions of their radiant country. . . .

Maidens had mounted donjon towers at midnight, had eluded Argus-eyed sentinels, had drugged savage blood-hounds, had crossed lightning-scarred seas, had traversed robber-infested forests; whatever maidens had done they could do, for could ever men more piteously implore release from castle keep than these gray-clad youths from the smoke-house? Did ever maiden hearts beat more valiantly than theirs? (and did ever maiden limbs tremble more cowardly?) Many a tedious day had been lightened by the rehearsal of just such a drama as this; there had been rôles prepared for every imaginable san-guinary cell, but prevision had overlooked the unexpected. The erstwhile feasible conduct, the erstwhile feasible weapons, of a Jeanne d'Arc or Charlotte Corday, the defiant speeches, the ringing retorts—they were all inappropriate, inadequate, here and now. If God would only help them! but, like the bayou, the cypresses, and the blue sky, He seemed today eternally above their insignificant human necessities. . . .

"Glory! Freedom!"

In they came, Bacchantes drunk with the fumes of their own hot blood, Dead-arm Harriet leading them like a triumphant sorceress, waving and gesticulating with her one "live" arm, repeating over and over again the potent magical words, ob-livious of everything but their own ecstasy—the curious looks of the men, their own exposure, the presence of their mistresses.

"Freedom! Master! Freedom!"

What was the matter with them? What did they mean? What was it all about?

Christine and Régina raised their heads and looked per-plexed at the furious women in the yard, and the men gazing down to them.

"Freedom! Freedom!"

The light broke upon them; their fingers tightened in each other's clasp, and their cheeks flushed crimson.

"How dared they? What insolence! What—"

The opposite door stood open; they rushed across the hall and closed it between them and the humiliating scene. . . .

The door opened again; it was Black Maria, still holding the cane-knife in her hand. She crossed the room with her noise-less barefooted tread, and placed herself behind them. They did not expect her to say anything; Black Maria never talked much; but they understood as they always did.

Her skirts were still tied up, and they saw for the first time that the wool protruding from her disordered head-kerchief was snow-white.

Who was Black Maria? Where did she come from, with her white features and white nature under her ebon skin? What was the mystery that enveloped her? Why did the brain torture itself in surmises about her? Why did she not talk as the others did, and just for a moment uncover that coffin heart of hers? Why was she, alone of all the negroes, still an alien, a foreigner, an exile among them? Was she brooding on disgrace, outrage, revenge? Was she looking at some mirage behind her—a distant equatorial country, a princely rank, barbaric state, some inherited memory transmitted by that other Black Maria, her mother? Who was the secret black father whom no one had discovered? Was it, as the negroes said, the Prince of Darkness? And her own secret consort, the father of Ben? What religion had she to warrant the scornful repudiation of Christianity? What code that enabled her to walk as free through slavery, to assume slavery now when others hailed freedom?

"Look!" Lolotte held up a rusty irregular piece of iron. "I found this in the old Indian basket where I was looking for sinkers. Don't you see what it is? It is the old key of the smoke-house, and I am going to let those Confederates out." She spoke quietly and decidedly. There was something else in the other hand, concealed in the folds of her dress. She produced it reluctantly. It was the gun-wrench that filled so prominent a part in her active life—always coveting it, getting possession of it, being deprived of it, and accused unfailingly for its every absence and misplacement. "You see, it is so convenient; it screws so nicely on to everything," she continued, apologetically, as she demonstrated the useful qualification. "There! it is as good as a handle. All they've got to do is to slip away in the skiff while the others are eating. And I would like to know how they can ever be caught, without another boat on the place! But oh, girls"—her black eyes twinkled maliciously—"what fools the Yankees are!"

If the Federals, as they announced, were only going to remain long enough for the lady in the kitchen to prepare them something to eat, the length of their stay clearly rested in Peggy the cook's hands. . . . With minute particularity she set the table and placed the dishes. The sun was sinking, and sending almost horizontal rays over the roof of the smoke-house, whose ugly square frame completely blocked the view of the little window. Peggy carefully drew the red calico curtain across it, and after a moment's rehearsal to bring her features to the conventional womanly expression of cheerful obuseness to existing displeasure, she opened the dining-room door.

Gina and Lolotte stood close against the house under the window, looking at the locked door before them, listening to the sounds falling from the dining-room above. Once in the skiff, they were safe; but the little red curtain fluttering flimsily in the breeze coquetted with their hopes and the lives of three men. If the corners would but stay down a second! Titine and Black Maria were in front, about the skiff. Peggy's success appeared to be complimentary to her judgment. Food alone, however, does not suffice in the critical moments of life; men are half managed when only fed. There was another *menu*, the ingredients of which were not limited or stinted by blockade of war. She had prepared that also; and in addition to the sounds of plates, knives, forks, and glasses came the tones of her rich voice dropping from a quick tongue the *entremets* of her piquant imagination.

"Now! now!" whispered Gina. "We must risk something."

Woman-like, they paused midway and looked back; a hand stretched from the table was carelessly drawing the curtain aside, and the window stared unhindered at the jail.

Why had they waited? Why had they not rushed forward immediately? By this time their soldiers might have been free! They could hear Peggy moving around the table; they could see her bulky form push again and again across the window.

"Mammy! Mammy!"

Could she hear them? They clasped their hands and held their faces up in imploring appeal. The sun was setting fast, almost running down the west to the woods. The dinner, if good, was not long. The transport might even then be churning up the bayou. It all depended upon Peggy now.

"Mammy! Mammy!" They raised their little voices, then lowered them in agony of apprehension. "Mammy, do something! Help us!"

But still she passed on and about, around the table, across the window, blind to the smoke-house, deaf to them, while her easy, familiar voice recited the comical gyrations of "old Frizzly," the half-witted hen, who had first set her heart against being killed and stewed, and ran and hid, and screamed and cackled, and ducked and flew, and then, after her silly head was twisted off, "just danced, as if she were at a ' 'Cadian' ball, all over the yard."

It would soon be too late. It was too late now.

Black Maria had got the skiff away from the gunnels, but they might just as well give it up.

"Mammy!" A supreme effort of voice and look. The unctuous black face, the red bead ear-rings, the bandanna headkerchief, came out of the window with "old Frizzly's" last dying cackle. There was one flashing wink of the left eye.

They recognized then her "pièce de résistance oratoire"— a side-splitting prank once played upon her by her nursling, her pet, her idol, the plague of her life—Beau.

Who could have heard grating lock or squeaking hinges through the boisterous mirth that followed? Who could have seen the desperate bound of the three imprisoned soldiers for liberty through that screen of sumptuous flesh—the magnificent back that filled to overlapping the insignificant little window?

They did not wait to hear the captain's rapturous toast to Peggy in sassafras tea, nor his voluble protestations of love to her, nor could they see him forget his wounded arm to bring both clinched fists to the table, and then faint dead away.

"I knew it!"

"Just like him!"

"Take him in the air, quick!"

"No, sir! You take him in there, and put him on the best bed in the house." Peggy did not move from the window, but her prompt command turned them from the door in the hall, and her finger directed them to the closed bedchamber.

Without noticing Christine standing by the open window, they dropped their doughty burden, boots, spurs, sword, epaulets, and all, on the fresh white little bed, the feather mattress fluffing up all around as if to submerge him.

"Oh, don't bother about that; cut the sleeve off!"

"Who has a knife?"

"There."

"That's all right now."

"He's coming round."

"There's one nice coat spoiled."

"Uncle Sam has plenty more."

"Don't let it drip on the bed."

"Save it to send to Washington—trophy—wet with rebel blood."

The captain was evidently recovering.

"You stay here while I keep 'em eating," whispered Peggy, authoritatively, to Christine.

"How could they help seeing the tall form of Black Maria standing in the prow of the boat out in the very middle of the bayou? Suppose she had not been there to close the window quick as thought? Suppose instead of passing through her room she had run through the basement, as she intended, after pushing off the skiff?" Titine trembled as if she had an ague.

Rollicking, careless, noisy, the soldiers went back to their interrupted meal.

"How far was Black Maria now?" She opened the window a tiny crack. "Heavens! how slowly she paddled! lifting the oar deliberately from side to side, looking straight ahead. How clear and distinct she was in the soft evening light! Why did she not hurry? why did she not row? She could have muffled the oars. But no, she never thought of that; that was always the way—always something overlooked and forgotten. They could finish a dozen dinners before she got out of sight at this rate. Without the skiff they might just as well be locked still in the smoke-house. Did he suspect something, seeing her look out this way?" She closed the window tight.

"How dark the room was! She could hardly see him. How quiet he was! Was he sleeping, or had he fainted again? In her bed! her enemy lying in her bed! his head on her pillow, her own little pillow, the feverish confidant of so many sleepless nights! How far were they now? She must peep out again. Why, Maria had not moved! not moved an inch! Oh, if she could only scream to her! if she were only in the skiff!

"How ghastly pale he was! his face as white as the coverlet, his hair and beard so black; how changed without his bravado and impertinence! And he was not old; not older than the boys in gray. She had fancied that age and ugliness alone could go with violence and wrong. How much gold! how much glitter! Why, the sun did not rise with more splendor of equipment. Costumed as if for the conquest of worlds. If they dressed their captains this way, what was the livery of their generals? How curious the sleeveless arm looked! What a horrible mark the gash made right across the soft white skin! What a scar it would leave! What a disfigurement! And this, this is what men call love of country!" . . .

The blood was oozing up through the strips of plaster. She stanched and bathed and soothed the wound as she well knew how with her tender, agile fingers. Maria had disappeared now; she could open the window with impunity. The trackless water was flowing innocently along, the cooling air was rising in mist, the cypress-trees checked the brilliant sky with the filigree and net-work of their bristly foliage. The birds twittered, the chickens loitered and dallied on their way to roost. The expectant dogs were lying on the levee waiting for the swampers, who, they ought to know, could not possibly return before midnight. And Molly was actually on time this evening, lowing for mammy to come and milk her; what was the war to her? How happy and peaceful it all was! What a jarring contrast to swords and bayonets! Thank God that Nature was impartial, and could not be drilled into partisanship! If humanity were like Nature! If—if there had been no war! She paused, shocked at her first doubt; it was like saying, "If there had been no God!" . . .

He could observe her through his half-closed lids, which fell as she approached the bed, and closed tight as she bent above him. When she stood at the window he could look full at her. "How innocent and unsuspecting she looked!" The strained rigidity had passed away from her face. Her transparent, childlike eyes were looking with all their life of expression in the direction of the bed, and then at something passing in her own mind. "Thank heaven, the fright had all gone out of them! How horrible for a gentleman to read fear in the eyes of a woman! Her mind must be as pure and white, yes, and as impressionable too, as her bed. Did his presence lie like a blot upon it also? How she must hate him! how she must loathe him! Would it have been different if he had come in the other uniform—if he had worn the gray? would she then have cared for him, have administered to him? How slight and frail she was! What a wan, wistful little face between him and the gloomy old bayou! He could see her more plainly now since she had opened the window and let in the cool, fragrant air. There was no joyous development of the body in her to proclaim womanhood, none of the seductive, confident beauty that follows coronation of youth; to her had only come the care and anxiety of maturity. "This—this," he exclaimed to himself, "is the way women fight a war." Was she coming this way? Yes. To the bed? Hardly. Now she was pressing against it, now bending over him, now dropping a cooling dew from heaven on his burning arm, and now—oh, why so soon?—she was going away to stand and look out of the window again. . . .

Impulsive, thoughtless, hot-headed, he forgot again the wounded arm. With both hands he stayed her frightened start; he saw the expression of her eyes bending over him.

"Can you forgive me? It is a heartless, cowardly trick! I am not a Yankee; I am Beau, your cousin, the guerrilla."

The escaped soldiers ran like deer between the furrows of Uncle John's vegetable garden, where the waving corn leaves could screen them; then out to the bank of the bayou—not on the levee, but close against the fence—snagging their clothes and scratching their faces and hands on the cuckle-burrs; Lolotte in front, with a stick in her hand, beating the bushes for snakes, calling, directing, animating, in whisper; Régina in the rear, urging, pressing, sustaining the soldier lagging behind, but painfully striving with stiffened limbs to keep up with the pace of his older, more vigorous companions. Ahead of them Black Maria was steadily keeping the skiff out in the current. The bayou narrowed and grew dark as it entered between the banks of serried cypress-trees, where night had already fallen.

Régina looked hurriedly over her shoulder. "Had they found out yet? How slowly they ran! How long it took to get to the woods! Oh, they would have time over and over again to finish their dinner and catch them. Perhaps at this very moment, as she was thinking of it, a forgotten article in the skiff was betraying them! Perhaps a gun might even now be pointing down their path! Well, then, now! the bullet could start and the report come too late to warn them." From the little cottage under the trees the curtains fluttered, but no smooth-bore nor sharpened bayonet was visible.

She met his face, looking back also, but not for guns—for her. "If it had been different! If he had been a visitor, come to stay; days and evenings to be passed together!" The thought lifting the sulphurous war-clouds from her heart, primitive idyls burst into instantaneous fragrant bloom in it like spring violets. He was not only the first soldier in gray she had ever seen, but the first young man; or it seemed so to her.

"How near they were still to the house! how plainly they could yet be seen! He would be shot straight through the back, the gray jacket getting one stain, one bullet-hole, more, the country one soldier less. Would they shoot through a woman at him? Would they be able to separate them if she ran close behind him, moving this way and that way, exactly as he did? If she saw them in time she could warn him; he could lie flat down in the grass; then it would be impossible to hit him."

Increasing and narrowing the space between them at the hest of each succeeding contradictory thought, turning her head again and again to the house behind her, she lost speed. Lolotte and the two men had already entered the forest before she reached it. Coming from the fields, the swamps seemed midnight dark. They groped their way along, hand in hand, tripped by the slimy cypress knees that rose like evil gnomes to beset and entangle their feet, slipping over rolling logs, sinking in stagnant mire, noosed by the coils of heavy vines that dropped from unseen branches overhead. Invisible wings of startled birds flapped above them, the croaking of frogs ebbed and flowed around them, owls shrieked and screamed from side to side of the bayou. Lolotte had ceased her beating; swamp serpents are too sluggish to be frightened away. Their eyes, accustomed to the obscurity, could discern Black Maria turning the skiff to a half-submerged log, from which they could hear a turtle drop as if ballasted with lead. A giant cypress-tree arrested them; the smooth, fluted trunk, ringed higher and higher with whitish water-marks, recorded floods far over their heads; where they were scrambling once swam fish and serpents. He turned and faced her, the deliverer, whose manœuvres had not escaped him.

She had saved him from imprisonment, insult, perhaps death—the only heir of a heroic father, the only son of a

widowed mother; she had restored him to a precious heritage
of love and honor, replaced him in the interrupted ambitious
career of patriotic duty; she had exposed her life for him—she
was beautiful. She stood before him, panting, tremulous, ardent, with dumb, open red lips, and voluble, passionate eyes,
and with a long scratch in her white cheek from which the blood
trickled. She had much to say to him; but how in one moment
express four years—four long years—and the last long minutes.
The words were all there, had been rushing to her lips all day;
her lips were parted; but the eager, overcrowded throng were
jammed on the threshold; and her heart beat so in her ears!
He could not talk either; he could not explain. His companions were already in the boat, his enemies still in gun-shot.
He bent his face to hers in the dim light to learn by heart the
features he must never forget—closer, closer, learning, knowing more and more, with the eager precocity of youth.

Bellona might have flown disgusted away with the wings of
an owl, Columbia might have nodded as knowingly as old Aunt
Mary, when the hearts, learning and knowing, brought the faces
closer and closer together, until the lips touched.

"I shall come again; I shall come again. Wait for me. Surely
I shall come again."

"Yes! Yes!"

Black Maria pushed the skiff off. "Rowlock! Rowlock!"
They were safe and away.

Uncle John, with the daring of desperation, advanced, un-
armed as he was, to the vociferous group standing around the
empty gunnels.

"I-I-I-I don't keer ef you is de-de-de President o' de United
States hisself, I ain't gwine to allow no such cussin' and swearin'
in de hearin' o' de-de-de young ladies. Marse John he-he-he
don't allow it, and when Marse John ain't here I-I-I don't
allow it."

His remonstrance and heroic attitude had very little effect,
for the loud talk went on, and chiefly by ejaculation, imprecation, and self-accusation published the whole statement of
case; understanding which, Uncle John added his voice also:

"Good Gord A'mighty! Wy-wh-what's dat you say? Dey-dey-dey Yankees, an' you Cornfedrits? Well, sir, an' are you Marse Beau—you wid your arm hurted? Go 'long! You can't fool me; Marse Beau done had more sense en dat. My Gord! an' dey wuz Yankees? You better cuss—cussin's about all you kin do now. Course de boat's gone. You'll never ketch up wid 'em in Gord's world now. Don't come along arter me about it! 'Tain't my fault. How wuz I to know? You wuz Yankees enough for me. I declar', Marse Beau, you ought to be ashamed o' yourself! You wanted to l'arn dem a lesson! I reckon dey l'arnt you one! You didn't mean 'em no harm! Humph! dey've cut dey eye-teeth, dey have! Lord! Marse Beau, I thought you done knowed us better. Did you really think we wuz a-gwine to let a passel o' Yankees take us away off our own plantation? You must done forgot us. We jes cleaned out de house for 'em, we did—clo'es, food, tobacco, rum. De young ladies 'ain't lef' a mossel for Marse John. An'—an'—an' 'fore de good Gord, my gun! Done tuck my gun away wid 'em! Wh-wh-wh-what you mean by such doin's? L-l-look here, Marse Beau, I don't like dat, nohow! Wh-wh-what! you tuck my gun and gin it to de Yankees? Dat's my gun! I done had dat gun twenty-five year an' more! Dog-gone! Yes, sir, I'll cuss—I'll cuss ef I wants to! I 'ain't got no use for gorillas, nohow! Lem me 'lone, I tell you! lem me 'lone! Marse John he'll get de law o' dat! Who's 'sponsible? Dat's all I want to know—who's 'sponsible? Ef-ef-ef-ef—No, sir; dar ain't nary boat on de place, nor hereabouts. Yes, sir; you kin cross de swamp ef you kin find de way. No, sir—no, sir; dar ain't no one to show you. I ain't gwine to leave de young ladies twell Marse John he comes back. Yes, I reckon you kin git to de cut-off by to-morrow mornin', ef you ain't shot on de way for Yankees, an' ef your company is fool enough to wait for you. No, sir, I don't know nothin' 'bout nothin'; you better wait an' arsk Marse John. . . . My Gord! I'm obleeged to laugh; I can't help it. Dem fool nigger wimen a-sittin' on de brink o' de byer, dey clo'es tied up in de bedquilts, an' de shotes an' de pullits all kilt, a-waitin' for freedom! I lay dey'll git freedom enough to-night when de boys come home. Dey git white gentlemen to marry 'em! Dey'll git five hundred apiece. Marse Beau, Gord'll punish you for dis—He surely will. I done tole Marse John long time ago he oughter sell dat brazen nigger Dead-arm Harriet, an' git shet o' her. Lord! Lord! Lord! Now you done gone to cussin' an' swearin' agin. Dón't go tearin' off your jackets an' flingin' 'em at me. We don't want 'em; we buys our clo'es—what we don't make. Yes, Marse John'll be comin' along pretty soon now. What's your hurry, Marse Beau? Well, so long, ef you won't stay. He ain't got much use for gorillas neither, Marse John hain't."

The young officer wrote a few hasty words on a leaf torn from the pretty Russia-leather note-book, and handed it to the old darky. "For your Marse John."

"For Marse John—yes, sir; I'll gin hit to him soon's he comes in."

They had dejectedly commenced their weary tramp up the bayou; he called him back, and lowered his voice confidentially: "Marse Beau, when you captured dat transport and stole all dem fixin's an' finery, you didn't see no good chawin' tobacco layin' round loose, did you? Thanky! thanky, child! Now I looks good at you, you ain't so much changed sence de times Marse John used to wallop you for your tricks. Well, good-by, Marse Beau."

On the leaf were scrawled the words:

"All's up! Lee has surrendered.—BEAU."

MARY NOAILLES MURFREE
(Charles Egbert Craddock)

Mary Noailles Murfree was born near Murfreesboro, Tennessee, on January 24, 1850, and died in Murfreesboro, July 31, 1932. The Murfrees in successive generations had borne prominent parts in the settlement and development of North Carolina and Tennessee. Her father, William Law Murfree, was a Tennessean of considerable importance. Graduating from the University of Nashville he learned there or in later life to read Greek, Latin, French, and Spanish, and he read widely in English literature. Before the Civil War he prospered as a lawyer and as a plantation owner, with three plantations in Mississippi. Marrying his cousin, Priscilla Dickinson, daughter of a wealthy landowner, he lived on the twelve-hundred acre plantation of "Grantland," two miles from Murfreesboro. Mary had an older sister, Fanny, her inseparable lifelong companion, and a younger brother, William, who acquired a reputation as a law editor. When a child of four she suffered from a "fever," probably infantile paralysis, which resulted in a slight permanent lameness. The two sisters were taught by governesses, attended the Nashville Female Academy, the family having moved to Nashville in 1856, and later went to a finishing school in Philadelphia. For fifteen years the family spent long summers at Beersheba Springs, one hundred miles southeast of Murfreesboro, in the Cumberland Mountains, where Miss Mary became familiar with the mountain scenery and people, the material for a succession of stories and romances. In 1880 the family moved to St. Louis, where William had found legal success, but in 1889 the sisters returned to Murfreesboro, where they built a "New Grantland." There they lived happily, with both sisters writing, and Miss Mary receiving such honors as the state regency of the Daughters of the American Revolution and a doctorate of literature from the University of the South.

Her literary career began with the publication of a trivial essay, and a story, "My Daughter's Admirers" in *Lippincott's Magazine* (May, 1874; July, 1875), under the pseudonym of

"R. Emmet Dembry." In the May, 1878, number of the *Atlantic Monthly*, William Dean Howells published "The Dancin' Party at Harrison's Cove," as written by "Charles Egbert Craddock." In the next few years Howells and his successor Thomas Bailey Aldrich accepted for the *Atlantic* seven more stories by "Mr. Craddock," and in 1884 Houghton, Mifflin and Company published the stories under the title of *In the Tennessee Mountains*. These stories, in the order of periodical publication, are "The Dancin' Party at Harrison's Cove," "The Star in the Valley," "Electioneerin' on Big Injun Mounting," "The Romance of Sunrise Rock," "Over on the T'Other Mounting," "The 'Harnt' that Walks Chilhowee," "A-Playin' of Old Sledge at the Settlemint," and "Drifting Down Lost Creek." During the next year the *Atlantic* serialized *The Prophet of the Great Smoky Mountains*, which contains the character of Hi Kelsey, the mystic preacher. As vivid and romantic as one of her own local color tales is the story of the literary unveiling of the sturdy masculine Charles Egbert Craddock as the small, slightly crippled Mary Murfree in the *Atlantic Monthly* office.

Most readers know Miss Murfree only as the author of the two volumes mentioned, but she wrote many other stories and novels of the mountaineers, several historical novels, social tales, and even juveniles. Edd W. Parks states in his recent biography of Charles Egbert Craddock:

> In the fifteen years between 1884 and 1900, she published fifteen books. The first and last novels have nothing to do with mountain life; the thirteen intermediate books, eight novels and five volumes of short stories, deal exclusively with the mountains and mountaineers. Five novels and a novelette appeared serially in the *Atlantic Monthly;* another novel appeared in *Harper's*, before publication in book form. Almost every story in the five volumes of short stories had previously appeared in a well-established, reputable magazine. After 1900, she was to write two novels and several stories of the Tennessee mountains, but they were, in effect, repetitions of earlier stories. (Page 174.)

Some of the most distinctive novels and story collections are the following: *Where the Battle Was Fought* (1884), a novel of Civil War devastation; *In the Clouds* (1887), a tragic novel, with ecstatic descriptions of nature; *The Story of Broomsedge Cove* (1889), a longer mountain novel based on a mysterious murder; *In the "Stranger People's" Country* (1891), a dramatic tale grounded in realism; *His Vanished Star* (1894), the story of a young native, with various incidents about moonshiners and "furriners"; *The Phantoms of the Foot-Bridge, and Other Stories* (1895), five very good stories, the best one being "Way Down in Lonesome Cove," which is perhaps her most accurate portrayal of the life and dialect of mountaineers; *The Mystery of Witch-Face Mountain, and Other Stories* (1895), a group of three stories; *The Young Mountaineers* (1897), a collection of ten stories; *The Bushwhackers, and Other Stories* (1899), a group of three historical stories; *The Story of Old Fort Loudon* (1899), a legendary history of eighteenth-century pioneers and Indians; *A Spectre of Power* (1903), a historical tale of the struggles of the French and Indians in the eighteenth century; *The Storm Centre* (1905), a tale of growing understanding between Confederate and Federal sympathizers; *The Amulet* (1906), a novel dealing with fighting with the Cherokee Indians in frontier Tennessee; *The Windfall* (1907), a tale of various elements of Tennessee village and mountain life; *The Fair Mississippian* (1908), a romantic story of a lonely cotton plantation; and several others. Besides these published books, there are over a dozen uncollected stories and articles, issued in various magazines. For the descriptions of natural scenery, the creation of type characters, and the revelation of customs, loyalties, and prejudices of the people, her local color stories and novels of the Appalachian mountaineers were fresh and distinctive, and are still interesting and important.

THE DANCIN' PARTY AT HARRISON'S COVE

"Fur ye see, Mis' Darley, them Harrison folks over yander ter the Cove hev determined on a dancin' party."

The drawling tones fell unheeded on old Mr. Kenyon's ear, as he sat on the broad hotel piazza of the New Helvetia Springs, and gazed with meditative eyes at the fair August sky. An early moon was riding, clear and full, over this wild spur of the

Alleghanies; the stars were few and very faint; even the great Scorpio lurked, vaguely outlined, above the wooded ranges; and the white mist, that filled the long, deep, narrow valley between the parallel lines of mountains, shimmered with opalescent gleams.

All the world of the watering-place had converged to that focus, the ball-room, and the cool, moonlit piazzas were nearly deserted. The fell determination of the "Harrison folks" to give a dancing party made no impression on the preoccupied old gentleman. Another voice broke his reverie,—a soft, clear, well-modulated voice,—and he started and turned his head as his own name was called, and his niece, Mrs. Darley, came to the window.

"Uncle Ambrose,—are you there? So glad! I was afraid you were down at the summer-house, where I hear the children singing. Do come here a moment, please. This is Mrs. Johns, who brings the Indian peaches to sell,—you know the Indian peaches?"

Mr. Kenyon knew the Indian peaches, the dark crimson fruit streaked with still darker lines, and full of blood-red juice, which he had meditatively munched that very afternoon. Mr. Kenyon knew the Indian peaches right well. He wondered, however, what had brought Mrs. Johns back in so short a time, for although the principal industry of the mountain people about the New Helvetia Springs is selling fruit to the summer sojourners, it is not customary to come twice on the same day, nor to appear at all after nightfall.

Mrs. Darley proceeded to explain.

"Mrs. Johns's husband is ill and wants us to send him some medicine."

Mr. Kenyon rose, threw away the stump of his cigar, and entered the room. "How long has he been ill, Mrs. Johns?" he asked, dismally.

Mr. Kenyon always spoke lugubriously, and he was a dismal-looking old man. Not more cheerful was Mrs. Johns; she was tall and lank, and with such a face as one never sees except in these mountains,—elongated, sallow, thin, with pathetic, deeply sunken eyes, and high cheek-bones, and so settled an expression of hopeless melancholy that it must be that naught but care and suffering had been her lot; holding out wasted hands to the years as they pass,—holding them out always, and always empty. She wore a shabby, faded calico, and spoke with the peculiar expressionless drawl of the mountaineer. She was a wonderful contrast to Mrs. Darley, all furbelows and flounces, with her fresh, smooth face and soft hair, and plump, round arms half-revealed by the flowing sleeves of her thin, black dress. Mrs. Darley was in mourning, and therefore did not affect the ball-room. At this moment, on benevolent thoughts intent, she was engaged in uncorking sundry small phials, gazing inquiringly at their labels, and shaking their contents.

In reply to Mr. Kenyon's question, Mrs. Johns, stiting on the extreme edge of a chair and fanning herself with a pink calico sun-bonnet, talked about her husband, and a misery in his side and in his back, and how he felt it "a-comin' on nigh on ter a week ago." Mr. Kenyon expressed sympathy, and was surprised by the announcement that Mrs. Johns considered her husband's illness "a blessin', 'kase ef he war able ter git out'n his bed, he 'lowed ter go down ter Harrison's Cove ter the dancin' party, 'kase Rick Pearson war a-goin' ter be thar, an' hed said ez how none o' the Johnses should come."

"What, Rick Pearson, that terrible outlaw!" exclaimed Mrs. Darley, with wide-open blue eyes. She had read in the newspapers sundry thrilling accounts of a noted horse thief and outlaw, who with a gang of kindred spirits defied justice and roamed certain sparsely-populated mountainous counties at his own wild will, and she was not altogether without a feeling of fear as she heard of his proximity to the New Helvetia Springs, —not fear for life or limb, because she was practical-minded enough to reflect that the sojourners and employés of the watering-place would far outnumber the outlaw's troop, but fear that a pair of shiny bay ponies, Castor and Pollux, would fall victims to the crafty wiles of the expert horse thief.

"I think I have heard something of a difficulty between

your people and Rick Pearson," said old Mr. Kenyon. "Has a peace never been patched up between them?"

"No-o," drawled Mrs. Johns; "same as it always war. My old man'll never believe but what Rick Pearson stole that thar bay filly we lost 'bout five year ago. But I don't believe he done it; plenty other folks around is ez mean ez Rick, leastways mos' ez mean; plenty mean enough ter steal a horse, ennyhow. Rick *say* he never tuk the filly; say he war a-goin' ter shoot off the nex' man's head ez say so. Rick say he'd ruther give two bay fillies than hev a man say he tuk a horse ez he never tuk. Rick say ez how he kin stand up ter what he does do, but it's these hyar lies on him what kills him out. But ye know, Mis' Darley, ye know yerself, he never give nobody two bay fillies in this world, an' what's more he's never goin' ter. My old man an' my boy Kossute talks on 'bout that thar bay filly like she war stole yestiddy, an' 't war five year ago an' better; an' when they hearn ez how Rick Pearson hed showed that red head o' his'n on this hyar mounting las' week, they war fightin' mad, an' would hev lit out fur the gang sure, 'ceptin' they hed been gone down the mounting fur two days. An' my son Kossute, he sent Rick word that he had better keep out'n gunshot o' these hyar woods; that he didn't want no better mark than that red head o' his'n, an' he could hit it two mile off. An' Rick Pearson, he sent Kossute word that he would kill him fur his sass the very nex' time he see him, an' ef he don't want a bullet in that pumpkin head o' his 'n he hed better keep away from that dancin' party what the Harrisons hev laid off ter give, 'kase Rick say he's a-goin' ter it hisself, an' is a-goin' ter dance too; he ain't been invited, Mis' Darley, but Rick don't keer fur that. He is a-goin' ennyhow, an' he say ez how he ain't a-goin' ter let Kossute come, 'count o' Kossute's sass an' the fuss they've all made 'bout that bay filly that war stole five year ago,—'t war five year an' better. But Rick say ez how he is goin', fur all he ain't got no invite, an' is a-goin' ter dance too, 'kase you know, Mis' Darley, it's a-goin' ter be a dancin' party; the Harrisons hev determinated on that. Them gals of theirn air mos' crazed 'bout a dancin' party. They ain't been a bit of account sence they went ter Cheatham's Cross-Roads ter see thar gran'mother, an' picked up all them queer new notions. So the Harrisons hev determinated on a dancin' party; an' Rick say ez how he is goin' ter dance too; but Jule, *she* say ez how she know thar ain't a gal on the mounting ez would dance with him; but I ain't so sure 'bout that, Mis' Darley; gals air cur'ous critters, ye know yerself; thar's no sort o' countin' on 'em; they'll do one thing one time, an' another thing nex' time; ye can't put no dependence in em'. But Jule say ef he kin get Mandy Tyler ter dance with him, it's the mos' he kin do, an' the gang'll be no whar. Mebbe he kin git Mandy ter dance with him, 'kase the other boys say ez how non o' them is a-goin' ter ax her ter dance, 'count of the trick she played on 'em down ter the Wilkins settlemint—las' month, war it? no, 't war two months ago, an' better; but the boys ain't forgot how scandalous she done 'em, an' none of 'em is a-goin' ter ax her ter dance."

"Why, what did she do?" exclaimed Mrs. Darley, surprised. "She came here to sell peaches one day, and I thought her such a nice, pretty, well-behaved girl."

"Waal, she hev got mighty quiet say-nuthin' sort'n ways, Mis' Darley, but that thar gal do behave *re*diculous. Down thar ter the Wilkins settlemint,—ye know it's 'bout two mile or two mile 'n a half from hyar,—waal, all the gals walked down thar ter the party an hour by sun, but when the boys went down they tuk thar horses, ter give the gals a ride home behind 'em. Waal, every boy axed his gal ter ride while the party war goin' on, an' when 't war all over they all set out fur ter come home. Waal, this hyar Mandy Tyler is a mighty favo*rite* 'mongst the boys,—they ain't got no sense, ye know, Mis' Darley,—an' stiddier one of 'em axin' her ter ride home, thar war five of 'em axed her ter ride, ef ye'll believe me, an' what do ye think she done, Mis' Darley? She tole all five of 'em yes; an' when the party war over, she war the last ter go, an' when she started out'n the door, thar war all five of them boys a-standin' thar waitin' fur her, an' every one a-holdin' his horse by the bridle, an' none of 'em knowed who the others war a-waitin' fur.

An' this hyar Mandy Tyler, when she got ter the door an' seen
'em all a-standin' thar, never said one word, jest walked right
through 'mongst 'em, an' set out fur the mounting on foot with
all them five boys a-followin' an' a-leadin' thar horses an'
a-quarrelin' enough ter take off each others' heads 'bout which
one war a-goin' ter ride with her; which none of 'em did, Mis'
Darley, fur I hearn ez how the whole lay-out footed it all the
way ter New Helveshy. An' thar would hev been a fight 'mongst
'em, 'ceptin' her brother, Jacob Tyler, went along with 'em,
an' tried ter keep the peace atwixt 'em. An' Mis' Darley, all
them married folks down thar at the party—them folks in the
Wilkins settlemint is the biggest fools, sure—when all them
married folks come out ter the door, an' see the way Mandy
Tyler hed treated them boys, they jest hollered and laffed an'
thought it war mighty smart an' funny in Mandy; but she never
say a word till she kem up the mounting, an' I never hearn ez
how she say ennything then. An' now the boys all say none
of 'em is a-goin' ter ax her ter dance, ter pay her back fur them
fool airs of hern. But Kossute say he'll dance with her ef none
the rest will. Kossute he thought 't war all mighty funny too,—
he's sech a fool 'bout gals, Kossute is,—but Jule, she thought
ez how 't war scandalous."

Mrs. Darley listened in amused surprise; that these mountain
wilds could sustain a first-class coquette was an idea that had
not hitherto entered her mind; however, "that thar Mandy"
seemed, in Mrs. Johns's opinion at least, to merit the unenviable
distinction, and the party at Wilkins settlement and the pros-
pective gayety of Harrison's Cove awakened the same sentiments in her heart and mind as do the more ambitious germans
and kettledrums of the lowland cities in the heart and mind of
Mrs. Grundy. Human nature is the same everywhere, and the
Wilkins settlement is a microcosm. The metropolitan centres,
stripped of the civilization of wealth, fashion, and culture, would
present only the bare skeleton of humanity outlined in Mrs.
Johns's talk of Harrison's Cove, the Wilkins settlement, the
enmities and scandals and sorrows and misfortunes of the
mountain ridge. As the absurd resemblance developed, Mrs.

Darley could not forbear a smile. Mrs. Johns looked up with a momentary expression of surprise; the story presented no humorous phase to her perceptions, but she too smiled a little as she repeated, "Scandalous, ain't it?" and proceeded in the same lack-lustre tone as before.

"Yes,—Kossute say ez how he'll dance with her ef none the rest will, fur Kossute say ez how he hev laid off ter dance, Mis' Darley; an' when I ax him what he thinks will become of his soul ef he dances, he say the devil may crack away at it, an' ef he kin hit it he's welcome. Fur soul or no soul he's a-goin' ter dance. Kossute is a-fixin' of hisself this very minit ter go; but I am verily afeard the boy'll be slaughtered, Mis' Darley, 'kase thar is goin' ter be a fight, an' ye never in all yer life hearn sech sass ez Kossute and Rick Pearson done sent word ter each other."

Mr. Kenyon expressed some surprise that she should fear for so young a fellow as Kossuth. "Surely," he said, "the man is not brute enough to injure a mere boy; your son is a mere boy."

"That's so," Mrs. Johns drawled. "Kossute ain't more'n twenty year old, an' Rick Pearson is double that ef he is a day; but ye see it's the fire-arms ez makes Kossute more 'n a match fur him, 'kase Kossute is the best shot on the mounting, an' Rick knows that in a shootin' fight Kossute's better able ter take keer of hisself an' hurt somebody else nor ennybody. Kossute's more likely ter hurt Rick nor Rick is ter hurt him in a shootin' fight; but ef Rick didn't hurt him, an' he war ter shoot Rick, the gang would tear him ter pieces in a minit; and 'mongst 'em I'm actially afeard they'll slaughter the boy."

Mr. Kenyon looked even graver than was his wont upon receiving this information, but said no more; and after giving Mrs. Johns the febrifuge she wished for her husband, he returned to his seat on the piazza.

Mrs. Darley watched him with some little indignation as he proceeded to light a fresh cigar. "How cold and unsympathetic uncle Ambrose is," she said to herself. And after condoling effusively with Mrs. Johns on her apprehensions for her son's safety, she returned to the gossips in the hotel parlor, and Mrs. Johns, with her pink calico sun-bonnet on her head, went her way in the brilliant summer moonlight.

The clear lustre shone white upon all the dark woods and chasms and flashing waters that lay between the New Helvetia Springs and the wide, deep ravine called Harrison's Cove, where from a rude log hut the vibrations of a violin, and the quick throb of dancing feet, already mingled with the impetuous rush of a mountain stream close by and the weird night-sounds of the hills,—the cry of birds among the tall trees, the stir of the wind, the monotonous chanting of frogs at the water-side, the long, drowsy drone of the nocturnal insects, the sudden faint blast of a distant hunter's horn, and the far baying of hounds.

Mr. Harrison had four marriageable daughters, and had arrived at the conclusion that something must be done for the girls; for, strange as it may seem, the prudent father exists even among the "mounting folks." Men there realize the importance of providing suitable homes for their daughters as men do elsewhere, and the eligible youth is as highly esteemed in those wilds as is the much scarcer animal at a fashionable watering-place. Thus it was that Mr. Harrison had "determined on a dancin' party." True, he stood in bodily fear of the judgment day and the circuit-rider; but the dancing party was a rarity eminently calculated to please the young hunters of the settlements round about, so he swallowed his qualms, to be indulged at a more convenient season, and threw himself into the vortex of preparations with an ardor very gratifying to the four young ladies, who had become imbued with sophistication at Cheatham's Cross-Roads.

Not so Mrs. Harrison; she almost expected the house to fall and crush them, as a judgment on the wickedness of a dancing party; for so heinous a sin, in the estimation of the greater part of the mountain people, had not been committed among them for many a day. Such trifles as killing a man in a quarrel or on suspicion of stealing a horse, or wash-tub, or anything that came handy, of course, does not count; but a dancing party!

Mrs. Harrison could only hold her idle hands, and dread the heavy penalty that must surely follow so terrible a crime.

It certainly had not the gay and lightsome aspect supposed to be characteristic of such a scene of sin: the awkward young mountaineers clogged heavily about in their uncouth clothes and rough shoes, with the stolid-looking, lack-lustre maids of the hill, to the violin's monotonous iteration of The Chicken in the Bread-Trough, or The Rabbit in the Pea-Patch,—all their grave faces as grave as ever. The music now and then changed suddenly to one of those wild, melancholy strains sometimes heard in old-fashioned dancing tunes, and the strange pathetic cadences seemed more attuned to the rhythmical dash of the waters rushing over their stone barricades out in the moonlight yonder, or to the plaintive sighs of the winds among the great dark arches of the primeval forests, than to the movement of the heavy, coarse feet dancing a solemn measure in the little log cabin in Harrison's Cove. The elders, sitting in rush-bottomed chairs close to the walls, and looking on at the merriment, well-pleased despite their religious doubts, were somewhat more lively; every now and then a guffaw mingled with the violin's resonant strains and the dancers' well-marked pace; the women talked to each other with somewhat more animation than was their wont, under the stress of the unusual excitement of a dancing party, and from out the shed-room adjoining came an anticipative odor of more substantial sin than the fiddle or the grave jiggling up and down the rough floor. A little more cider too, and a very bad article of illegally-distilled whiskey, were ever and anon circulated among the pious abstainers from the dance; but the sinful votaries of Terpsichore could brook no pause nor delay, and jogged up and down quite intoxicated with the mirthfulness of the plaintive old airs and the pleasure of other motion than following the plow or hoeing the corn.

And the moon smiled right royally on her dominion: on the long, dark ranges of mountains and mist-filled valleys between; on the woods and streams, and on all the half-dormant creatures either amongst the shadow-flecked foliage or under the crystal waters; on the long, white, sandy road winding in and out through the forest; on the frowning crags of the wild ravine; on the little bridge at the entrance of the gorge, across which a party of eight men, heavily armed and gallantly mounted, rode swiftly and disappeared amid the gloom of the shadows.

The sound of the galloping of horses broke suddenly on the music and the noise of the dancing; a moment's interval, and the door gently opened and the gigantic form of Rick Pearson appeared in the aperture. He was dressed, like the other mountaineers, in a coarse suit of brown jeans somewhat the worse for wear, the trowsers stuffed in the legs of his heavy boots; he wore an old soft felt hat, which he did not remove immediately on entering, and a pair of formidable pistols at his belt conspicuously challenged attention. He had auburn hair, and a long full beard of a lighter tint reaching almost to his waist; his complexion was much tanned by the sun, and roughened by exposure to the inclement mountain weather; his eyes were brown, deep-set, and from under his heavy brows they looked out with quick, sharp glances, and occasionally with a roguish twinkle; the expression of his countenance was rather good-humored,—a sort of imperious good-humor, however,—the expression of a man accustomed to have his own way and not to be trifled with, but able to afford some amiability since his power is undisputed.

He stepped slowly into the apartment, placed his gun against the wall, turned, and solemnly gazed at the dancing, while his followers trooped in and obeyed his example. As the eight guns, one by one, rattled against the wall, there was a startled silence among the pious elders of the assemblage, and a sudden disappearance of the animation that had characterized their intercourse during the evening. Mrs. Harrison, who by reason of flurry and a housewifely pride in the still unrevealed treasures of the shed-room had well-nigh forgotten her fears, felt that the anticipated judgment had even now descended, and in what terrible and unexpected guise! The men turned the quids of tobacco in their cheeks and looked at each other in uncertainty; but the dancers bestowed not a glance upon the newcomers, and the musician in the corner, with his eyes half-closed, his head bent low upon the instrument, his hard, horny hand moving the bow back and forth over the strings of the crazy old fiddle, was utterly rapt by his own melody. At the supreme moment when the great red beard had appeared portentously in the doorway and fear had frozen the heart of Mrs. Harrison within her at the ill-omened apparition, the host was in the shed-room filling a broken-nosed pitcher from the cider-barrel. When he re-entered, and caught sight of the grave sun-burned face with its long red beard and sharp brown eyes, he too was dismayed for an instant, and stood silent at the opposite door with the pitcher in his hand. The pleasure and the possible profit of the dancing party, for which he had expended so much of his scanty store of this world's goods and risked the eternal treasures laid up in heaven, were a mere phantasm; for, with Rick Pearson among them, in an ill frame of mind and at odds with half the men in the room, there would certainly be a fight, and in all probability one would be killed, and the dancing party at Harrison's Cove would be a text for the bloody-minded sermons of the circuit-rider for all time to come. However, the father of four marriageable daughters is apt to become crafty and worldly-wise; only for a moment did he stand in indecision; then, catching suddenly the small brown eyes, he held up the pitcher with a grin of invitation. "Rick!" he called out above the scraping of the violin and the clatter of the dancing feet, "slip round hyar ef ye kin, I've got somethin' for ye"; and he shook the pitcher significantly.

Not that Mr. Harrison would for a moment have thought of Rick Pearson in a matrimonial point of view, for even the sophistication of the Cross-Roads had not yet brought him to the state of mind to consider such a half loaf as this better than no bread, but he felt it imperative from every point of view to keep that set of young mountaineers dancing in peace and quiet, and their guns idle and out of mischief against the wall. The great red beard disappeared and reappeared at intervals, as Rick Pearson slipped along the gun-lined wall to join his host and the cider-pitcher, and after he had disposed of the refreshment, in which the gang shared, he relapsed into silently watching the dancing and meditating a participation in that festivity.

Now, it so happened that the only young girl unprovided with a partner was "that thar Mandy Tyler," of Wilkins settlement renown; the young men had rigidly adhered to their resolution to ignore her in their invitations to dance, and she had been sitting since the beginning of the festivities, quite neglected, among the married people, looking on at the amusement which she had been debarred sharing by that unpopular bit of coquetry at Wilkins settlement. Nothing of disappointment or mortification was expressed in her countenance; she felt the slight of course,—even a "mounting" woman is susceptible of the sting of wounded pride; all her long-anticipated enjoyment had come to naught by this infliction of penance for her ill-timed jest at the expense of those five young fellows dancing with their triumphant partners and bestowing upon her not even a glance; but she looked the express image of immobility as she sat in her clean pink calico, so carefully gotten up for the occasion, her short black hair curling about her ears, and watched the unending reel with slow, dark eyes. Rick's glance fell upon her, and without further hesitation he strode over to where she was sitting and proffered his hand for the dance. She did not reply immediately, but looked timidly about her at the shocked pious ones on either side, who were ready but for mortal fear to aver that "dancin' ennyhow air bad enough, the Lord knows, but dancin' with a horse thief air jest scandalous!" Then, for there is something of defiance to established law and prejudice in the born flirt everywhere, with a sudden daring spirit shining in her brightening eyes, she responded, "Don't keer ef I do," with a dimpling half-laugh; and the next minute the two outlaws were flying down the middle together.

While Rick was according grave attention to the intricacies of the mazy dance and keeping punctilious time to the scraping of the old fiddle, finding it all a much more difficult feat than galloping from the Cross-Roads to the "Snake's Mouth" on some other man's horse with the sheriff hard at his heels, the solitary figure of a tall gaunt man had followed the long winding path leading deep into the woods, and now began the steep descent to Harrison's Cove. Of what was old Mr. Kenyon thinking, as he walked on in the mingled shadow and sheen? Of St. Augustin and his Forty Monks, probably, and what they found in Britain. The young men of his acquaintance would gladly have laid you any odds that he could think of nothing but his antique hobby, the ancient church. Mr. Kenyon was the most prominent man in St. Martin's church in the city of B—, not excepting the rector. He was a lay-reader, and officiated upon occasions of "clerical sore-throat," as the profane denominate the ministerial summer exodus from heated cities. This summer, however, Mr. Kenyon's own health had succumbed, and he was having a little "sore-throat" in the mountains on his own account. Very devout was Mr. Kenyon. Many people wondered that he had never taken orders. Many people warmly congratulated themselves that he never had; for drier sermons than those he selected were surely never heard, and a shuddering imagination shrinks appalled from the problematic mental drought of his ideal original discourse. But he was an integrant part of St. Martin's; much of his piety, materialized into contributions, was built up in its walls and shone before men in the costliness of its decorations. Indeed, the ancient name had been conferred upon the building as a sort of tribute to Mr. Kenyon's well-known enthusiasm concerning apostolic succession and kindred doctrines.

Dull and dismal was Mr. Kenyon, and therefore it may be considered a little strange that he should be a notable favorite with men. They were of many different types, but with one invariable bond of union: they had all at one time served as soldiers; for the war, now ten years passed by, its bitterness almost forgotten, had left some traces that time can never obliterate. What a friend was the droning old churchman in those days of battle and bloodshed and suffering and death! Not a man sat within the walls of St. Martin's who had not received some signal benefit from the hand stretched forth to impress the claims of certain ante-Augustin British clergy to consideration and credibility; not a man who did not remember stricken fields where a good Samaritan went about under shot and shell, succoring the wounded and comforting the dying; not a man who did not applaud the indomitable spirit and courage that cut his way from surrender and safety, through solid barriers of enemies, to deliver the orders on which the fate of an army depended; not a man whose memory did not harbor fatiguing recollections of long, dull sermons read for the souls' health of the soldiery. And through it all,—by the camp-fires at night, on the long white country-roads in the sunshiny mornings; in the mountains and the morasses; in hilarious advance and in cheerless retreat; in the heats of summer and by the side of frozen rivers, the ancient British clergy went through it all. And, whether the old churchman's premises and reasoning were false, whether his tracings of the succession were faulty, whether he dropped a link here or took in one there, he had caught the spirit of those staunch old martyrs, if not their falling churchly mantle.

The mountaineers about the New Helvetia Springs supposed that Mr. Kenyon was a regularly ordained preacher, and that the sermons which they had heard him read were, to use the vernacular, out of his own head. For many of them were accustomed on Sunday mornings to occupy humble back benches in the ball-room, where on week-day evenings the butterflies sojourning at New Helvetia danced, and on the Sabbath metaphorically beat their breasts, and literally avowed that they were "miserable sinners," following Mr. Kenyon's lugubrious lead.

The conclusion of the mountaineers was not unnatural, therefore, and when the door of Mr. Harrison's house opened and another uninvited guest entered, the music suddenly ceased. The half-closed eyes of the fiddler had fallen upon Mr. Kenyon at the threshold, and, supposing him a clergyman, he immediately imagined that the man of God had come all the way from New Helvetia Springs to stop the dancing and snatch the revelers from the jaws of hell. The rapturous bow paused shuddering on the string, the dancing feet were palsied, the pious about the walls were racking their slow brains to excuse their apparent conniving at sin and bargaining with Satan, and Mr. Harrison felt that this was indeed an unlucky party and it would undoubtedly be dispersed by the direct interposition of Providence before the shed-room was opened and the supper eaten. As to his soul—poor man! these constantly recurring social anxieties were making him callous to immortality; this life was about to prove too much for him, for the fortitude and tact even of a father of four marriageable young ladies has a limit. Mr. Kenyon, too, seemed dumb as he hesitated in the door-way, but when the host, partially recovering himself, came forward and offered a chair, he said with one of his dismal smiles that he hoped Mr. Harrison had no objection to his coming in and looking at the dancing for a while. "Don't let me interrupt the young people, I beg," he added, as he seated himself. The astounded silence was unbroken for a few moments. To be sure he was not a circuit-rider, but even the sophistication of Cheatham's Cross-Roads had never heard of a preacher who did not object to dancing. Mr. Harrison could not believe his ears, and asked for a more explicit expression of opinion.

"Ye say ye don't keer ef the boys an' gals dance?" he inquired. "Ye don't think it's sinful?"

And after Mr. Kenyon's reply, in which the astonished "mounting folks" caught only the surprising statement that dancing if properly conducted was an innocent, cheerful, and healthful amusement, supplemented by something about dancing in the fear of the Lord, and that in all charity he was disposed to consider objections to such harmless recreations a tithing of mint and anise and cummin, whereby might ensue a neglect of weightier matters of the law; that clean hands and clean hearts—hands clean of blood and ill-gotten goods, and hearts free from falsehood and cruel intention—these were the things well-pleasing to God,—after his somewhat prolix reply, the gayety recommenced. The fiddle quavered tremulously at first, but soon resounded with its former vigorous tones, and the joy of the dance was again exemplified in the grave joggling back and forth.

Meanwhile Mr. Harrison sat beside this strange new guest and asked him questions concerning his church, being instantly, it is needless to say, informed of its great antiquity, of the journeying of St. Augustin and his Forty Monks to Britain, of the church they found already planted there, of its retreat to the hills of Wales under its oppressors' tyranny, of many cognate themes, side issues of the main branch of the subject, into which the talk naturally drifted, the like of which Mr. Harrison had never heard in all his days. And as he watched the figures dancing to the violin's strains, and beheld as in a mental vision the solemn gyrations of those renowned Forty Monks to the monotone of old Mr. Kenyon's voice, he abstractedly hoped that the double dance would continue without interference till a peaceable dawn.

His hopes were vain. It so chanced that Kossuth Johns, who had by no means relinquished all idea of dancing at Harrison's Cove and defying Rick Pearson, had hitherto been detained by his mother's persistent entreaties, some necessary attentions to his father, and the many trials which beset a man dressing for a party who has very few clothes, and those very old and worn. Jule, his sister-in-law, had been most kind and complaisant, putting on a button here, sewing up a slit there, darning a refractory elbow, and lending him the one bright ribbon she possessed as a neck-tie. But all these things take time, and the moon did not light Kossuth down the gorge until she was shining almost vertically from the sky, and the Harrison Cove people and the Forty Monks were dancing together in high feather. The ecclesiastic dance halted suddenly, and a watchful light gleamed in old Mr. Kenyon's eyes as he became silent and the boy stepped into the room. The moonlight and the lamplight fell mingled on the calm, inexpressive features and tall, slender form of the young mountaineer. "Hy're, Kossute!" A cheerful greeting from many voices met him. The next moment the music ceased once again, and the dancing came to a standstill, for as the name fell on Pearson's ear he turned, glanced sharply toward the door, and drawing one of his pistols from his belt advanced to the middle of the room. The men fell back; so did the frightened women, without screaming, however, for that indication of feminine sensibility had not yet penetrated to Cheatham's Cross-Roads, to say nothing of the mountains.

"I told ye that ye warn't ter come hyar," said Rick Pearson imperiously, "and ye've got ter go home ter yer mammy, right off, or ye'll never git thar no more, youngster."

"I've come hyar ter put *you* out, ye cussed red-headed horse thief!" retorted Kossuth, angrily; "ye hed better tell me whar that thar bay filly is, or light out, one."

It is not the habit in the mountains to parley long on these occasions. Kossuth had raised his gun to his shoulder as Rick, with his pistol cocked, advanced a step nearer. The outlaw's weapon was struck upward by a quick, strong hand, the little log cabin was filled with flash, roar, and smoke, and the stars looked in through a hole in the roof from which Rick's bullet had sent the shingles flying. He turned in mortal terror and caught the hand that had struck his pistol,—in mortal terror, for Kossuth was the crack shot of the mountains and he felt he was a dead man. The room was somewhat obscured by smoke, but as he turned upon the man who had disarmed him, for the force of the blow had thrown the pistol to the floor, he saw that the other hand was over the muzzle of young Johns's gun, and Kossuth was swearing loudly that by the Lord Almighty if he didn't take it off he would shoot it off.

"My young friend," Mr. Kenyon began, with the calmness appropriate to a devout member of the one catholic and apostolic church; but then, the old Adam suddenly getting the upper hand, he shouted out in irate tones, "If you don't stop that noise, I'll break your head! Well, Mr. Pearson," he continued, as he stood between the combatants, one hand still over the muzzle of young Johns's gun, the other, lean and sinewy, holding Pearson's powerful right arm with a vise-like grip, "well, Mr. Pearson, you are not so good a soldier as you used to be; you didn't fight boys in the old times."

Rick Pearson's enraged expression suddenly gave way to a surprised recognition. "Ye may drag me through hell an' beat me with a soot-bag ef hyar ain't the old fightin' preacher agin!" he cried.

"I have only one thing to say to you," said Mr. Kenyon. "You must go. I will not have you here shooting boys and breaking up a party."

Rick demurred. "See hyar, now," he said, "ye've got no business meddlin'."

"You must go," Mr. Kenyon reiterated.

"Preachin's yer business," Rick continued; " 'pears like ye don't 'tend to it, though."

"You must go."

"S'pose I say I won't," said Rick, good-humoredly; "I s'pose ye'd say ye'd make me."

"You must go," repeated Mr. Kenyon. "I am going to take the boy home with me, but I intend to see you off first."

Mr. Kenyon had prevented the hot-headed Kossuth from firing by keeping his hand persistently over the muzzle of the gun; and young Johns had feared to try to wrench it away lest it should discharge in the effort. Had it done so, Mr. Kenyon would have been in sweet converse with the Forty Monks in about a minute and a quarter. Kossuth had finally let go the gun, and made frantic attempts to borrow a weapon from some of his friends, but the stern authoritative mandate of the belligerent peace-maker had prevented them from gratifying him, and he now stood empty-handed beside Mr. Kenyon, who had shouldered the old rifle in an absent-minded manner, although still retaining his powerful grasp on the arm of the outlaw.

"Waal, parson," said Rick at length, "I'll go, jest ter pleasure you-uns. Ye see, I ain't forgot Shiloh."

"I am not talking about Shiloh now," said the old man. "You must get off at once,—all of you," indicating the gang, who had been so whelmed in astonishment that they had not lifted a finger to aid their chief.

"Ye say ye'll take that—that"—Rick looked hard at Kossuth while he racked his brains for an injurious epithet—"that sassy child home ter his mammy?"

"Come, I am tired of this talk," said Mr. Kenyon; "you must go."

Rick walked heavily to the door and out into the moonlight. "Them was good old times," he said to Mr. Kenyon, with a regretful cadence in his peculiar drawl; "good old times, them War days. I wish they was back agin,—I wish they was back agin. I ain't forgot Shiloh yit, though, and I ain't a-goin' ter. But I'll tell ye one thing, parson," he added, his mind reverting from ten years ago to the scene just past, as he unhitched his horse and carefully examined the saddle-girth and stirrups, "ye're a mighty queer preacher, ye air, a-sittin' up an' lookin' at sinners dance an' then gittin' in a fight that don't consarn ye,—ye're a mighty queer preacher! Ye ought ter be in my gang, that's whar *ye* ought ter be," he exclaimed, with a guffaw, as he put his foot in the stirrup; "ye've got a damned deal too much grit fur a preacher. But I ain't forgot Shiloh yit, an' I don't mean ter, nuther."

A shout of laughter from the gang, an oath or two, the quick tread of horses' hoofs pressing into a gallop, and the outlaw's troop were speeding along the narrow paths that led deep into the vistas of the moonlit summer woods.

As the old churchman, with the boy at his side and the gun still on his shoulder, ascended the rocky, precipitous slope on the opposite side of the ravine above the foaming waters of the wild mountain stream, he said but little of admonition to his companion; with the disappearance of the flame and smoke and the dangerous ruffian his martial spirit had cooled; the last words of the outlaw, the highest praise Rick Pearson could accord to the highest qualities Rick Pearson could imagine— he had grit enough to belong to the gang—had smitten a tender conscience. He, at his age, using none of the means rightfully at his command, the gentle suasion of religion, must needs rush between armed men, wrench their weapons from their hands, threatening with such violence that an outlaw and desperado, recognizing a parallel of his own belligerent and lawless spirit, should say that he ought to belong to the gang! And the heaviest scourge of the sin-laden conscience was the perception that, so far as the unsubdued old Adam went, he ought indeed.

He was not so tortured, though, that he did not think of others. He paused on reaching the summit of the ascent, and looked back at the little house nestling in the ravine, the lamp-light streaming through its open doors and windows across the path among the laurel bushes, where Rick's gang had hitched their horses.

"I wonder," said the old man, "if they are quiet and peaceable again; can you hear the music and dancing?"

"Not now," said Kossuth. Then, after a moment, "Now, I kin," he added, as the wind brought to their ears the oft-told tale of the rabbit's gallopade in the pea-patch. "They're a-dancin' now, and all right agin."

As they walked along, Mr. Kenyon's racked conscience might have been in a slight degree comforted had he known that he was in some sort a revelation to the impressible lad at his side, that Kossuth had begun dimly to comprehend that a Christian may be a man of spirit also, and that bravado does not constitute bravery. Now that the heat of anger was over, the young fellow was glad that the fearless interposition of the warlike peacemaker had prevented any killing, "'kase ef the old man hed n't hung on ter my gun like he done, I'd have been a murderer like he said, an' Rick would hev been dead. An' the bay filly ain't sech a killin' matter nohow; ef it war the roan three-year-old now, 't would be different."

JOEL CHANDLER HARRIS

Joel Chandler Harris was born near Eatonton, Putnam County, Georgia, on December 9, 1848, and died in Atlanta, July 3, 1908. His mother, Mary Harris, was of a prominent family, but the identity of the father is disputed. "Miss Mary" reared the red-headed boy with difficulty, aided by relatives and neighbors, and cultivated in him a taste for reading and writing. The boy of thirteen went to Joseph Addison Turner's plantation, a few miles distant, where he set type for *The Countryman*, "probably the only newspaper ever printed on a Southern plantation." These were happy days, which later he wrote about in *On the Plantation*. He listened to Negro stories in the cabins, and inserted short essays and poems in the newspaper. This happy boyhood was ended abruptly in 1864, when Sherman's army swept through Putnam County. There followed years of wandering from one newspaper office to another, even as far as New Orleans. From 1870 to 1876 he was on the staff of the *Savannah Morning News*, of which the editor was William Tappan Thompson, the author of *Major Jones's Courtship*. As assistant editor he "reviewed books, composed a number of creditable poems, reported the legislative sessions in Atlanta and wrote some vivid and picturesque sketches of Georgia notables." In Savannah he met Esther La Rose whom he married in 1873. An epidemic of yellow fever in 1876 caused Harris to take his wife and two boys to Atlanta, where he joined as an editorial paragrapher the staff of the *Constitution*, of which Evan P. Howell was controlling owner and Harry W. Grady held an important position in the news department. Mrs. Julia Collier Harris writes that from 1886 "until his retirement from the paper, early in 1906, Joel Harris held the place of chief editorial writer. The combined work of Harris and Grady, under their liberal and able editor-in-chief, Evan P. Howell, brought national prestige to the *Constitution* at a crucial period of the South's history. Fortunately these men had the vision to realize what a powerful and honorable part might be played in the upbuilding of the South by a newspaper of intelligence, courage, and genuine patriotism." As editorial writer Harris wrote under three disguises, "The Cornfield Humorist," "Billy Sanders, the Philosopher of Shady Dale," and "The Sage of Snap-Bean Farm." Charcoal sketches and animal stories of Uncle Remus were published in the *Constitution* in 1878–1879, and in 1880 D. Appleton and Company published *Uncle Remus: His Songs and His Sayings.* This book has been issued in many reprints and editions, of which the one of 1895 is distinctive, with a new preface by Harris and illustrations by A. B. Frost. Throughout Harris's life, and even posthumously, Uncle Remus books appeared, ten in all, to the delight of children and adults. Students have listed and compared the stories, linguists have analyzed the Uncle Remus dialect, and folk-lorists have tried to thrust his sources back to century-old myths and legends.

In other volumes Harris wrote stories of diverse characters and scenes, which cover many phases of southern life: *Mingo and Other Sketches in Black and White* (1884), four stories of aristocratic plantation owners, poor farmers, old slaves, and mountaineers; *Free Joe, and Other Georgian Sketches* (1887), five stories of the harsher aspects of slavery, of the intense feelings against abolitionists, of revenue officers in the mountains, and of reconciliation after the war by marriage; *Daddy Jake the Runaway, and Other Stories Told After Dark* (1889), six stories of loyal Negro servants, the marriage of a Northerner to a Southerner, and the independence of mountaineers; *The Chronicles of Aunt Minervy Ann* (1899), eight stories involving characters which are types of southern gentlemen, farmers, editors, business men, and Negroes.

The student whose acquaintance with Harris is limited to the Uncle Remus stories read as a child, learns that Harris was a versatile writer of both romantic and realistic aspects of southern life, that he was a capable editorialist for the New South, and that he was a shrewd critic of politics and literature.

From FREE JOE AND OTHER GEORGIAN SKETCHES

Free Joe and the Rest of the World

The name of Free Joe strikes humorously upon the ear of memory. It is impossible to say why, for he was the humblest, the simplest, and the most serious of all God's living creatures, sadly lacking in all those elements that suggest the humorous. It is certain, moreover, that in 1850 the sober-minded citizens of the little Georgian village of Hillsborough were not inclined to take a humorous view of Free Joe, and neither his name nor his presence provoked a smile. He was a black atom, drifting hither and thither without an owner, blown about by all the winds of circumstances and given over to shiftlessness.

The problems of one generation are the paradoxes of a succeeding one, particularly if war, or some such incident, intervenes to clarify the atmosphere and strengthen the understanding. Thus, in 1850, Free Joe represented not only a problem of large concern, but, in the watchful eyes of Hillsborough, he was the embodiment of that vague and mysterious danger that seemed to be forever lurking on the outskirts of slavery, ready to sound a shrill and ghostly signal in the impenetrable swamps, and steal forth under the midnight stars to murder, rapine, and pillage,—a danger always threatening, and yet never assuming shape; intangible, and yet real; impossible, and yet not improbable. Across the serene and smiling front of safety, the pale outlines of the awful shadow of insurrection sometimes fell. With this invisible panorama as background, it was natural that the figure of Free Joe, simple and humble as it was, should assume undue proportions. Go where he would, do what he might, he could not escape the finger of observation and the kindling eye of suspicion. His lightest words were noted, his slightest actions marked.

Under all the circumstances it was natural that his peculiar condition should reflect itself in his habits and manners. The slaves laughed loudly day by day, but Free Joe rarely laughed. The slaves sang at their work and danced at their frolics, but no one ever heard Free Joe sing or saw him dance. There was something painfully plaintive and appealing in his attitude, something touching in his anxiety to please. He was of the friendliest nature, and seemed to be delighted when he could amuse the little children who had made a play-ground of the public square. At times he would please them by making his little dog Dan perform all sorts of curious tricks, or he would tell them quaint stories of the beasts of the field and birds of the air; and frequently he was coaxed into relating the story of his own freedom. The story was brief, but tragical.

In the year of our Lord 1840, when a negro-speculator of a sportive turn of mind reached the little village of Hillsborough on his way to the Mississippi region, with a caravan of likely negroes of both sexes, he found much to interest him. In that day and at that time there were a number of young men in the village who had not bound themselves over to repentance for the various misdeeds of the flesh. To these young men the negro-speculator (Major Frampton was his name) proceeded to address himself. He was a Virginian, he declared; and, to prove the statement, he referred all the festively inclined young men of Hillsborough to a barrel of peach-brandy in one of his covered wagons. In the minds of these young men there was less doubt in regard to the age and quality of the brandy than there was in regard to the negro-trader's birthplace. Major Frampton might or might not have been born in the Old Dominion—that was a matter for consideration and inquiry—but there could be no question as to the mellow pungency of the peach-brandy.

In his own estimation, Major Frampton was one of the most accomplished of men. He had summered at the Virginia Springs; he had been to Philadelphia, to Washington, to Richmond, to Lynchburg, and to Charleston, and had accumulated a great deal of experience which he found useful. Hillsborough was hid in the woods of middle Georgia, and its general aspect of innocence impressed him. He looked on the young men who had shown their readiness to test his peach-brandy, as overgrown country boys who needed to be introduced to some of the arts and sciences he had at his command. Thereupon the Major pitched his tents, figuratively speaking, and became, for the time being, a part and parcel of the innocence that characterized Hillsborough. A wiser man would doubtless have made the same mistake.

The little village possessed advantages and seemed to be providentially arranged to fit the various enterprises that Major Frampton had in view. There was the auction-block in front of the stuccoed court-house, if he desired to dispose of a few of his negroes; there was a quarter-track, laid out to his hand and in excellent order, if he chose to enjoy the pleasures of horse-racing; there were secluded pine thickets within easy reach, if he desired to indulge in the exciting pastime of cock-fighting; and various lonely and unoccupied rooms in the second story of the tavern, if he cared to challenge the chances of dice or cards.

Major Frampton tried them all with varying luck, until he began his famous game of poker with Judge Alfred Wellington, a stately gentleman with a flowing white beard and mild blue eyes that gave him the appearance of a benevolent patriarch. The history of the game in which Major Frampton and Judge Alfred Wellington took part is something more than a tradition in Hillsborough, for there are still living three or four who sat around the table and watched its progress. It is said that at various stages of the game Major Frampton would destroy the cards with which they were playing, and send for a new pack, but the result was always the same. The mild blue eyes of Judge Wellington, with few exceptions, continued to overlook "hands" that were invincible—a habit they had acquired during a long and arduous course of training from Saratoga to New Orleans. Major Frampton lost his money, his horses, his wagons, and all his negroes but one, his body-servant. When his misfortune had reached this limit, the major adjourned the game. The sun was shining brightly, and all nature was cheerful. It is said that the major also seemed to be cheerful. However this may be, he visited the court-house and executed the papers that gave his body-servant his freedom. This being done, Major Frampton sauntered into a convenient pine thicket, and blew out his brains.

The negro thus freed came to be known as Free Joe. Compelled, under the law, to choose a guardian, he chose Judge Wellington, chiefly because his wife Lucinda was among the

negroes won from Major Frampton. For several years Free
Joe had what may be called a jovial time. His wife Lucinda
was well provided for, and he found it a comparatively easy
matter to provide for himself; so that, taking all the circumstances into consideration, it is not matter for astonishment
that he became somewhat shiftless.

When Judge Wellington died, Free Joe's troubles began.
The judge's negroes, including Lucinda, went to his half-
brother, a man named Calderwood, who was a hard master and
a rough customer generally—a man of many eccentricities of
mind and character. His neighbors had a habit of alluding to
him as "Old Spite"; and the name seemed to fit him so completely that he was known far and near as "Spite" Calderwood.
He probably enjoyed the distinction the name gave him, at
any rate he never resented it, and it was not often that he missed
an opportunity to show that he deserved it. Calderwood's
place was two or three miles from the village of Hillsborough,
and Free Joe visited his wife twice a week, Wednesday and
Saturday nights.

One Sunday morning he was sitting in front of Lucinda's
cabin, when Calderwood happened to pass that way.

"Howdy, marster?" said Free Joe, taking off his hat.

"Who are you?" exclaimed Calderwood abruptly, halting and
staring at the negro.

"I'm name' Joe, marster, I'm Lucindy's ole man."

"Who do you belong to?"

"Marse John Evans is my gyardeen, marster."

"Big name—gyardeen. Show your pass."

Free Joe produced the document, and Calderwood read it
aloud slowly, as if he found it difficult to get at the meaning:

*"To whom it may concern: This is to certify that the boy Joe
Frampton has my permission to visit his wife Lucinda."*

This was dated at Hillsborough, and signed *"John W. Evans."*

Calderwood read it twice, and then looked at Free Joe, ele-
vating his eyebrows, and showing his discolored teeth.

"Some mighty big words in that there. Evans owns this
place, I reckon. When's he comin' down to take hold?"

Free Joe fumbled with his hat. He was badly frightened.

"Lucindy say she speck you wouldn't min' my comin', long ez I behave, marster."

Calderwood tore the pass in pieces and flung it away.

"Don't want no free niggers 'round here," he exclaimed. "There's the big road. It'll carry you to town. Don't let me catch you here no more. Now, mind what I tell you."

Free Joe presented a shabby spectacle as he moved off with his little dog Dan slinking at his heels. It should be said in behalf of Dan, however, that his bristles were up, and that he looked back and growled. It may be that the dog had the advantage of insignificance, but it is difficult to conceive how a dog bold enough to raise his bristles under Calderwood's very eyes could be as insignificant as Free Joe. But both the negro and his little dog seemed to give a new and more dismal aspect to forlornness as they turned into the road and went towards Hillsborough.

After this incident Free Joe seemed to have clear ideas concerning his peculiar condition. He realized the fact that though he was free he was more helpless than any slave. Having no owner, every man was his master. He knew that he was the object of suspicion, and therefore all his slender resources (ah! how pitifully slender they were!) were devoted to winning, not kindness and appreciation, but toleration; all his efforts were in the direction of mitigating the circumstances that tended to make his condition so much worse than that of the negroes around him—negroes who had friends because they had masters.

So far as his own race was concerned, Free Joe was an exile. If the slaves secretly envied him his freedom (which is to be doubted, considering his miserable condition), they openly despised him, and lost no opportunity to treat him with contumely. Perhaps this was in some measure the result of the attitude which Free Joe chose to maintain toward them. No doubt his instinct taught him that to hold himself aloof from the slaves would be to invite from the whites the toleration which he coveted, and without which even his miserable condition would be rendered more miserable still.

His greatest trouble was the fact that he was not allowed to visit his wife; but he soon found a way out of this difficulty. After he had been ordered away from the Calderwood place, he was in the habit of wandering as far in that direction as prudence would permit. Near the Calderwood place, but not on Calderwood's land, lived an old man named Micajah Staley and his sister Becky Staley. These people were old and very poor. Old Micajah had a palsied arm and hand; but, in spite of this, he managed to earn a precarious living with his turning-lathe.

When he was a slave Free Joe would have scorned these representatives of a class known as poor white trash, but now he found them sympathetic and helpful in various ways. From the back door of the cabin he could hear the Calderwood negroes singing at night, and he fancied he could distinguish Lucinda's shrill treble rising above the other voices. A large poplar grew in the woods some distance from the Staley cabin, and at the foot of this tree Free Joe would sit for hours with his face turned toward Calderwood's. His little dog Dan would curl up in the leaves near by, and the two seemed to be as comfortable as possible.

One Saturday afternoon Free Joe, sitting at the foot of this friendly poplar, fell asleep. How long he slept he could not tell; but when he awoke little Dan was licking his face, the moon was shining brightly, and Lucinda his wife stood before him laughing. The dog seeing that Free Joe was asleep, had grown somewhat impatient, and he concluded to make an excursion to the Calderwood place on his own account. Lucinda was inclined to give the incident a twist in the direction of superstition.

"I'z settin' down front er de fireplace," she said, "cookin' me some meat, w'en all of a sudden I year sumpin at de do'—scratch, scratch. I tuck'n tu'n de meat over, en make out I aint year it. Bimeby it come dar 'gin—scratch, scratch. I up en open de do', I did, en, bless de Lord! dar wuz little Dan, en it look like ter me dat his ribs done grow tergeer. I gin 'im some bread, en den, w'en he start out, I tuck'n foller 'im,

kaze I say ter myse'f, maybe my nigger man mought be some'rs
'roun'. Dat ar little dog got sense, mon."

Free Joe laughed and dropped his hand lightly on Dan's
head. For a long time after that, he had no difficulty in seeing
his wife. He had only to sit by the poplar tree until little
Dan could run and fetch her. But after a while the other
negroes discovered that Lucinda was meeting Free Joe in the
woods, and information of the fact soon reached Calderwood's ears. He said nothing; but one day he put Lucinda
in his buggy, and carried her to Macon, sixty miles away.
He carried her to Macon, and came back without her; and
nobody in or around Hillsborough, or in that section, ever
saw her again.

For many a night after that Free Joe sat in the woods and
waited. Little Dan would run merrily off and be gone a long
time, but he always came back without Lucinda. This happened
over and over again. The "willis-whistlers" would call and
call, like phantom huntsmen wandering on a far-off shore; the
screech-owl would shake and shiver in the depths of the woods;
the night-hawks, sweeping by on noiseless wings, would snap
their beaks as though they enjoyed the huge joke of which Free
Joe and little Dan were the victims; and the whip-poor-wills
would cry to each other through the gloom. Each night seemed
to be lonelier than the preceding, but Free Joe's patience was
proof against loneliness. There came a time, however, when
little Dan refused to go after Lucinda. When Free Joe mo-
tioned him in the direction of the Calderwood place, he would
simply move about uneasily and whine; then he would curl up
in the leaves and make himself comfortable.

One night, instead of going to the poplar-tree to wait for
Lucinda, Free Joe went to the Staley cabin, and, in order to
make his welcome good, as he expressed it, he carried with him
an armful of fat-pine splinters. Miss Becky Staley had a great
reputation in those parts as a fortune-teller, and the school-
girls, as well as older people, often tested her powers in that
direction, some in jest and some in earnest. Free Joe placed
his humble offering of light-wood in the chimney-corner, and

then seated himself on the steps, dropping his hat on the ground outside.

"Miss Becky," he said presently, "whar in de name er gracious you reckon Lucindy is?"

"Well, the Lord he'p the nigger!" exclaimed Miss Becky, in a tone that seemed to reproduce, by some curious agreement of sight with sound, her general aspect of peakedness. "Well, the Lord he'p the nigger! haint you been a-seein' her all this blessed time? She's over at old Spite Calderwood's, if she's anywhere, I reckon."

"No'm, dat I aint, Miss Becky. I aint seen Lucindy in now gwine on mighty nigh a mont'."

"Well, it haint a-gwine to hurt you," said Miss Becky, somewhat sharply. "In my day an' time it wuz allers took to be a bad sign when niggers got to honeyin' 'roun' an' gwine on."

"Yessum," said Free Joe, cheerfully assenting to the proposition—"yessum, dat's so, but me an' my ole 'oman, we 'uz raise tergeer, en dey aint bin many days w'en we 'uz 'way fum one 'n'er like we is now."

"Maybe she's up an' took up wi' some un else," said Micajah Staley from the corner. "You know what the sayin' is, 'New master, new nigger.'"

"Dat's so, dat's de sayin', but taint wid my ole 'oman like 'tis wid yuther niggers. Me en her wuz des natally raise up tergeer. Dey's lots likelier niggers dan w'at I is," said Free Joe, viewing his shabbiness with a critical eye, "but I know Lucindy mos' good ez I does little Dan dar—dat I does."

There was no reply to this, and Free Joe continued—

"Miss Becky, I wish you please, ma'am, take en run yo' kyards en see sump'n n'er 'bout Lucindy; kaze ef she sick, I'm gwine dar. Dey ken take en take me up en gimme a stroppin', but I'm gwine dar."

Miss Becky got her cards, but first she picked up a cup, in the bottom of which were some coffee grounds. These she whirled slowly round and round, ending finally by turning the cup upside down on the hearth and allowing it to remain in that position.

"I'll turn the cup first," said Miss Becky, "and then I'll run the cards and see what they say."

As she shuffled the cards the fire on the hearth burned slow, and in its fitful light the gray-haired, thin-featured woman seemed to deserve the weird reputation which rumor and gossip had given her. She shuffled the cards for some moments, gazing intently in the dying fire; then, throwing a piece of pine on the coals, she made three divisions of the pack, disposing them about in her lap. Then she took the first pile, ran the cards slowly through her fingers, and studied them carefully. To the first she added the second pile. The study of these was evidently not satisfactory. She said nothing, but frowned heavily; and the frown deepened as she added the rest of the cards until the entire fifty-two had passed in review before her. Though she frowned, she seemed to be deeply interested. Without changing the relative position of the cards, she ran them over again. Then she threw a larger piece of pine on the fire, shuffled the cards afresh, divided them into three piles, and subjected them to the same careful and critical examination.

"I can't tell the day when I've seed the cards run this a-way," she said after a while. "What is an' what aint, I'll never tell you; but I know what the cards sez."

"W'at does dey say, Miss Becky?" the negro inquired, in a tone the solemnity of which was heightened by its eagerness.

"They er runnin' quare. These here that I'm a lookin' at," said Miss Becky, "they stan' for the past. Them there, they er the present; and the t'others, they er the future. Here's a bundle"—tapping the ace of clubs with her thumb—"an' here's a journey as plain as the nose on a man's face. Here's Lucinda"—

"Whar she, Miss Becky?"

"Here she is—the queen of spades."

Free Joe grinned. The idea seemed to please him immensely.

"Well, well, well!" he exclaimed. "Ef dat don't beat my time! De queen er spades! W'en Lucindy year dat hit'll tickle 'er, sho'!"

Miss Becky continued to run the cards back and forth through her fingers.

"Here's a bundle an' a journey, and here's Lucinda. An' here's ole Spite Calderwood."

She held the cards toward the negro and touched the king of clubs.

"De Lord he'p my soul!" exclaimed Free Joe with a chuckle. "De faver's dar. Yesser, dat's him! W'at de matter 'long wid all un um, Miss Becky?"

The old woman added the second pile of cards to the first, and then the third, still running them through her fingers slowly and critically. By this time the piece of pine in the fireplace had wrapped itself in a mantle of flame, illuminating the cabin and throwing into strange relief the figure of Miss Becky as she sat studying the cards. She frowned ominously at the cards and mumbled a few words to herself. Then she dropped her hands in her lap and gazed once more into the fire. Her shadow danced and capered on the wall and floor behind her, as if, looking over her shoulder into the future, it could behold a rare spectacle. After a while she picked up the cup that had been turned on the hearth. The coffee grounds, shaken around, presented what seemed to be a most intricate map.

"Here's the journey," said Miss Becky, presently; "here's the big road, here's rivers to cross, here's the bundle to tote." She paused and sighed. "They haint no names writ here, an' what it all means I'll never tell you. Cajy, I wish you'd be so good as to han' me my pipe."

"I haint no hand wi' the kyards," said Cajy, and he handed the pipe, "but I reckon I can patch out your misinformation, Becky, bekaze the other day, whiles I was a-fishin' up Mizzer Perdue's rolling-pin, I hearn a rattlin' in the road. I looked out, an' Spite Calderwood was a-drivin' by in his buggy, an' thar sot Lucinda by him. It'd in-about drapt out er my min'."

Free Joe sat on the door-sill and fumbled at his hat, flinging it from one hand to the other.

"You haint see um gwine back, is you, Marse Cajy?" he asked after a while.

"Ef they went back by this road," said Mr. Staley, with the air of one who is accustomed to weigh well his words, "it must 'a' bin endurin' of the time whiles I was asleep, bekase I haint bin no furder from my shop than to yon bed."

"Well, sir!" exclaimed Free Joe in an awed tone, which Mr. Staley seemed to regard as a tribute to his extraordinary power of statement.

"Ef it's my beliefs you want," continued the old man, "I'll pitch 'em at you fair and free. My beliefs is that Spite Calderwood is gone an' took Lucindy outen the county. Bless your heart and soul! when Spite Calderwood meets the Old Boy in the road they'll be a turrible scuffle. You mark what I tell you."

Free Joe, still fumbling with his hat, rose and leaned against the door-facing. He seemed to be embarrassed. Presently he said:

"I speck I better be gittin' 'long. Nex' time I see Lucindy, I'm gwine tell 'er w'at Miss Becky say 'bout de queen er spades —dat I is. If dat don't tickle 'er, dey aint no nigger 'oman never bin tickle'."

He paused a moment, as though waiting for some remark or comment, some confirmation of misfortune, or, at the very least, some endorsement of his suggestion that Lucinda would be greatly pleased to know that she had figured as the queen of spades; but neither Miss Becky nor her brother said anything.

"One minnit ridin' in the buggy, 'longside er Mars Spite, en de nex' highfalutin' 'roun' playin' de queen er spades. Mon, deze yer nigger gals gittin' up in de pictur's; dey sholy is."

With a brief "Good-night, Miss Becky, Mars Cajy," Free Joe went out into the darkness, followed by little Dan. He made his way to the poplar, where Lucinda had been in the habit of meeting him, and sat down. He sat there a long time; he sat there until little Dan, growing restless, trotted off in the direction of the Calderwood place. Dozing against the poplar in the gray dawn of the morning, Free Joe heard Spite Calderwood's fox-hounds in full cry a mile away.

"Shoo!" he exclaimed, scratching his head, and laughing to himself, "dem ar dogs is des a-warmin' dat old fox up."

But it was Dan the hounds were after, and the little dog came back no more. Free Joe waited and waited, until he grew tired of waiting. He went back the next night and waited, and for many nights thereafter. His waiting was in vain, and yet he never regarded it as in vain. Careless and shabby as he was, Free Joe was thoughtful enough to have his theory. He was convinced that little Dan had found Lucinda, and that some night when the moon was shining brightly through the trees, the dog would rouse him from his dreams as he sat sleeping at the foot of the poplar-tree, and he would open his eyes and behold Lucinda standing over him, laughing merrily as of old; and then he thought what fun they would have about the queen of spades.

How many long nights Free Joe waited at the foot of the poplar-tree for Lucinda and little Dan no one can ever know. He kept no account of them and they were not recorded by Micajah Staley or by Miss Becky. The season ran into summer and then into fall. One night he went to the Staley cabin, cut the two old people an armful of wood, and seated himself on the door-steps, where he rested. He was always thankful— and proud, as it seemed—when Miss Becky gave him a cup of coffee, which she was sometimes thoughtful enough to do. He was especially thankful on this particular night.

"You er still layin' off for to strike up wi' Lucindy out thar in the woods, I reckon," said Micajah Staley, smiling grimly. The situation was not without its humorous aspects.

"Oh, dey er comin', Mars Cajy, dey er comin', sho," Free Joe replied, "I boun' you dey'll come; en w'en dey does come, I'll des take en fetch um yer, whar you kin see um wid you own eyes, you en Miss Becky."

"No," said Mr. Staley, with a quick and emphatic gesture of disapproval. "Don't! don't fetch 'em anywheres. Stay right wi' 'em as long as may be."

Free Joe chuckled, and slipped away into the night, while the two old people sat gazing in the fire. Finally Micajah spoke:

"Look at that nigger; look at 'im. He's pine-blank as happy

now as a killdee by a mill-race. You can't 'feze 'em. I'd in-
about give up my t'other hand ef I could stan' flat-footed, an'
grin at trouble like that there nigger."

"Niggers is niggers," said Miss Becky, smiling grimly,
"an' you can't rub it out; yet I lay I've seed a heap of white
people lots meaner'n Free Joe. He grins,—an' that's nigger,—
but I've ketched his under jaw a-trimblin' when Lucindy's
name uz brung up. An' I tell you," she went on bridling up a
little, and speaking with almost fierce emphasis, "the Old Boy's
done sharpened his claws for Spite Calderwood. You'll see it."

"Me, Rebecca?" said Mr. Staley, hugging his palsied arm;
"me? I hope not."

"Well, you'll know it then," said Miss Becky, laughing
heartily at her brother's look of alarm.

The next morning Micajah Staley had occasion to go into the
woods after a piece of timber. He saw Free Joe sitting at the
foot of the poplar, and the sight vexed him somewhat.

"Git up from there," he cried, "an 'go an' arn your livin'.
A mighty purty pass it's come to, when great big buck niggers
can lie a-snorin' in the woods all day, when t'other folks is
got to be up an' a-gwine. Git up from there!"

Receiving no response, Mr. Staley went to Free Joe, and
shook him by the shoulder; but the negro made no response.
He was dead. His hat was off, his head was bent, and a smile
was on his face. It was as if he had bowed and smiled when
death stood before him, humble to the last. His clothes were
ragged; his hands were rough and callous; his shoes were literally tied together with strings; he was shabby in the extreme.
A passer-by, glancing at him, could have no idea that such a
humble creature had been summoned as a witness before the
Lord God of Hosts.

AS TO SOUTHERN LITERATURE

(From *The Atlanta Constitution Nov. 3, 1879.*)

An interesting phase of the continual call for what is technically known as "Southern Literature" is the accompanying

demand for controversial fiction. Whether this is owing to the lack of healthy criticism or to the fact that we have been put upon the defensive so long that anything in relation to the South, its conditions or its institutions, past or present, which is suspiciously critical or even severely impartial, is construed into an attack, we have not time here to consider. We suspect, however, that it is due, rather, to the social and political isolation in which the South sought to preserve its peculiar property investment. It is natural that such isolation should produce remarkable pride of opinion and a belief that our civilization was perfect. The truth of the matter, however, is that Southern people are human beings and inherited, along with the rest of the world, their full share of the virtues as well as the faults of human nature; and when the Southern novelist comes to depict life in the South as it really was and is, his work, if he be a genuine artist, will be too impartial to suit the ideas of those who have grown fat through feeding upon the romantic idea that no additional polish could be put upon our perfections. The Southern Thackeray of the future will doubtless be surprised to learn that if he had put in an appearance half a century sooner he would probably have been escorted beyond the limits and boundaries of our Southern clime astraddle of a rail. Thackeray satirized the society in which he moved and held up to ridicule the hollow hypocrisy of his neighbors. He took liberties with the people of his own blood and time that would have led him hurriedly in the direction of bodily discomfort if he had lived in the South.

LITERATURE IN THE SOUTH

(From *The Atlanta Constitution Nov. 30, 1879.*)

The very spice and essence of all literature, the very marrow and essence of all literary art is its localism. No literary artist can lack for materials in this section. They are here all around him, untouched, undeveloped, undisturbed, unique and original, as new as the world, as old as life, as fair as flowers, as beautiful as the dreams of genius. But they must be mined. They must be run through the stamp mill. Where is the magician who will catch them and store them up? You may be sure that the man who does it will not care one copper whether he is developing and building up Southern or Northern literature, and he will feel that his work is considerably belittled if it be claimed by either on the score of sectionalism. In literature, art and society, whatever is truly Southern is likewise truly American; and the same may be said of what is truly Northern. Literature that is Georgian or Southern is necessarily American, and in the broadest sense. The sectionalism that is the most marked feature of our modern politics can [should] never intrude into literature. Its intrusion is fatal, and it is this fatality that has pursued and overtaken and destroyed literary effort in the South. The truth might as well be told. We have no Southern literature worthy of the name, because an attempt has been made to give it the peculiarities of sectionalism rather than to impart to it the flavor of localism.

SHERWOOD BONNER

Katherine Sherwood Bonner MacDowell (Sherwood Bonner) was born in a northern Mississippi town, Holly Springs, February 26, 1849, and died there July 22, 1883. Her father, a native of Ireland, came to Pennsylvania in early life, studied medicine, and as a young physician settled near Holly Springs, where he established his medical practice and married Mary Wilson, the daughter of a wealthy Holly Springs family. After his marriage, as the owner of several large plantations, his activities as a planter took precedence over his medical practice.

Katherine's childhood was spent in a prosperous ante-bellum home, noted for its gracious hospitality. A brother and a sister, both younger, were her companions, and she was cared for by a devoted colored nurse, the "Gran'mammy" of her stories. Her father, a cultivated man with a love of books and a good library, directed her reading. The following description from her novel *Like Unto Like* (1879) is undoubtedly based upon her own experience: "They were brought up on Walter Scott. They read Richardson, and Fielding, and Smollett. . . . They liked Thackeray pretty well, Bulwer very well, and Dickens they read under protest—they thought him low. They felt an easy sense of superiority in being 'quite English in our tastes, you know,' and knew very little of the literature of their own country, as it came chiefly from the North. Of its lesser lights they had never heard, and, as for the greater, they would have pitted an ounce of Poe against a pound of any one of them."

Katherine was about twelve years old when the Civil War cut sharply across her life. In December, 1862, Grant established in Holly Springs a depot of supplies protected by a small garrison, and on December 20 the Confederate General Van Dorn captured the post, taking about fifteen hundred prisoners and destroying Grant's stores. Less than fifty miles from Memphis, where Grant for a time had his headquarters, Holly Springs, as an important strategic point, was drawn into the magnetic field of Vicksburg and felt to the full the electric currents of war.

The effect upon Katherine must have been profound, but there is little evidence of it in her writing except perhaps in *Like Unto Like*, which pictures the effects of war and recon-. struction upon Holly Springs.

Of the main events of her life, we find, in the meagre sources now available, little but the barest statement. Her mother died when she was sixteen; in 1871 she married Edward MacDowell, a young man of good family in Holly Springs, and had one daughter. In 1873 she separated from her husband and "with youth, high health, and the courage of ignorance" went to Boston to earn her own living. Here she sought out Nahum Capen, the editor of *The Massachusetts Ploughman*, in which her first story had been published in 1864. Through Capen she met the Boston literary group and for a time acted as amanuensis to the sixty-six-year-old Longfellow, who encouraged the literary efforts of the brilliant young Southerner and to whom her novel, *Like Unto Like*, was dedicated. Sophia Kirk in her Preface to *Suwanee River Tales* (1884), Sherwood Bonner's second collection of stories, speaks of having in her possession some of Longfellow's letters to Katherine, many of them written in French.

Sherwood Bonner's first writings were articles, letters, and verses appearing in the Boston *Times*, the Memphis *Avalanche*, and other papers. The first to attract attention was a poem, "The Radical Club," in the Boston Sunday *Times* (reprinted in the *Massachusetts Historical Society Proceedings*, June, 1912). This parody of Poe's "The Raven" is said to have satirized out of existence the local organization which it described.

In 1876 she went to Europe with Mrs. Louise Chandler Moulton, sending back from Rome and Florence descriptive letters to Boston newspapers. In 1878 the yellow-fever epidemic called her from New England to Holly Springs to nurse her father and brother, both of whom died during the dreadful scourge of that year.

From this time she devoted herself almost entirely to writing short stories, many in dialect, dealing with Tennessee mountain life and with the "Egypt" district of Illinois, where she visited for a time. Her stories during this period appeared in such magazines as *Harper's New Monthly Magazine*, *Harper's Weekly*, *Lippincott's*, *The Youth's Companion*, and *Harper's Young People*.

In 1882 she learned that she had cancer, and in the following year she died in Holly Springs at the age of thirty-four. During the last months of her life she worked arduously in preparing collections of her stories for printing in book form. *Dialect Tales*, the first collection, was published by Harper and Brothers in 1883; *Suwanee River Tales*, the second collection, with an Introduction by Sophia Kirk, the friend who was with her in her last illness, was published by Harper and Brothers in 1884. Another collection, which was to have been called "Romances," was never completed. It would probably have included some of the longer stories, like "The Valcours," a novelette published in *Lippincott's*, in 1881; "Two Storms," in *Harper's New Monthly Magazine*, April, 1881; "The Revolution in the Life of Mr. Bolingall," a story of the yellow-fever epidemic, published in *Harper's New Monthly Magazine* in October, 1879; and "A Volcanic Interlude," a story of New Orleans, said to have caused many readers to cancel their subscriptions to *Lippincott's* (April, 1880), because of its "intensity and frankness."

In the notice of her death in *Harper's Weekly*, August 11, 1883, the publishers of many of her stories give the best contemporary estimate of Sherwood Bonner and her work. They testify to the beauty and vitality of her physical presence and to the quality of her writing. Her literary sympathies, they say, "were not pessimistic. . . . She was no censor of her times. . . . She was a simple naturalist in art, with a strong hand and a delicate touch. Life as she had seen it and lived it in the Southern States of the Union was the object of her attention and she sketched it in the spirit and the method of a master." There can be little doubt that Sherwood Bonner at the time of her death was on the way to being a major writer in the field of the American short story. Her gift for clear, swift-moving, untrammeled narrative, her developing technical skill in the handling of plot, her increasing realism, her admirable sense of humor, her freedom from the sentimentality that ruins, for today's readers, so much of the fiction of her period, and the widening field of her interests, all point toward distinctive achievement, had her literary life been extended beyond its brief ten years. What she did produce deserves increased attention.

From DIALECT TALES

The Bran Dance at the Apple Settlement

"They's mostly Apples in that settle*ment*," said Mr. Jack Officer. "When they has a blow-out they kind o' jines together, and makes the feathers fly. Lucky thing for preachers 'f they take a camp-meetin' in han'. They'll have the mo'ners lively 'f they have to press every waggin an' old mule in the Cumberland to git 'em thar. They pretty much rule things round here. 'F one of 'em takes a fancy to a good-lookin' girl, the other boys keep away—they are shooters, them Apples. Thar's a powerful lot of 'em. Old Grandpa Apple— him that started the settle*ment*—is a-livin' yet. He come over from Carliny some sixty years back, in a canopied waggin, with all he had, includin' his gret-uncle, ready to light out fur Jordan, an' a yaller dog—female, that's mothered the best breed o' pups on the mountain. He had two blooded cows, an' a stavin' young woman for a wife; an' calves an' children came's fast's he could house 'em—faster too, I reckin, for they had to tent it one hot summer. The boys they growed up, an' they married aroun' the country, an' somehow they've had luck—big, smart, han'some families. An' their childern is a-marryin' an' child-bearin'. So, you see, old Grandpa Apple he sees the fourth generation. An' I guess the Lord ain't any pleaseder in surveyin' the earth he has made than that old man in a-countin' Apple noses.

"They're goin' to have a bran dance to-morrer over in the settle*ment*. Ever seen a bran dance? 'T's a powerful nice entertainment. Better stop over an' go 'long with me."

We "stopped over." Starting the next morning by earliest cock-crow, we reached the Apple Settlement, so exhilarated— ah! delicious air of the Cumberland!—that we were ready to cut pigeon wings in a bran dance until the bran flew about our ears as dry as the dust of a powdered mummy.

The scene was as animated as one of Hogarth's pictures. Horses, mules, ox-wagons, spring-carts, were huddled at the gate. People were moving about under the trees with the fantastic gravity that hides inward joy. Half a dozen slim young fellows, in blue calico shirts, opening to show their sunburnt throats, were masters of ceremonies. They shook our hands with serious cordiality, and nodded silently to Mr. Officer. They do not say much, these mountain people. How should they? They might be early-language makers, for the few words they know. Jack Officer was garrulous. But, as he said of himself, he was "born with the gab." Besides, he read the Bible and a weekly paper.

Grandpa Apple was sitting under a tree in the yard.

"Looks like a peeled Apple, *he* does," said Mr. Officer, facetiously.

This startling simile was not inappropriate, the old man was so white and clean. His head was bare, and shone like the snow. A long white beard dropped from his chin, and white overhanging eyebrows almost hid his eyes. His face was white and wrinkled as a yeasty tub of beer. His trousers and shirt were of white linsey, and he was fanning himself with a white turkeytail fan. He would have served gloriously, backed up in a Christmas window, as Santa Claus, or the Old Year.

In the heart of a lovely grove Grandpa Apple had built his log-cabin. It was so comfortable-looking, so entirely the right sort of house to be set among those trees! The logs were sawed in two, and were worn to a rich polish; the spaces between were new chinked with white mortar. There were many rooms connected by little porches wide as foot-paths. Doors and windows were opened wide. The floors were bare, and freshly scrubbed. There were beds in every room, four red posters guarding feather-beds of forty-goose power. Woodcuts from newspapers and fashion magazines were gummed on the walls. Althea boughs were thrust into the cavernous depths of the wide fireplaces, and in one room there was a wonderful screen made of hundreds of little pictures.

The kitchen was the place to melt your soul. A mass of coals that would have frightened Daniel glowed in the fireplace. A black pot hung from a crane. Half a dozen ovens were ranged on the hearth, coals under and above them. From time to time the oven lids were lifted with the burnt end of a broomhandle, revealing six little pigs in various stages of brownness. The deities of this place were somewhat wizened Apples, so to speak. They danced once; now they cooked. So passes the glory of mountain pinks. They looked warm, and a little anxious. But now and then they would plunge their heads into a basin of cool water, and come up, like Duffy after the third round, confident and smiling.

The women were nearly all assembled in the room with the screen. They sat against the walls solemnly. They were dressed in clean, bright calicoes, cut as low as the collar-bone. Some—vain, dressy creatures—wore broad, flat, crocheted collars, and bows shaped like flying birds. The girls were supple and straight, with ankles not offensive to the eye of man; but among the matrons were some queer figures, whose lacks or redundancies were concealed by hoops and set off with trails.

"Looks 's if them sort ought to perch in the trees," said Mr. Officer, watching a green calico dragged across the floor.

The young men glowered in through the windows, and poked each other in the sides, making a noise between tongue and cheek not unlike a prolonged cluck to a horse.

Mr. Officer held a violin under his chin. "Take your partners!" he called, with a piercing scrape of the bow across the strings.

"My fust fiddled," remarked Mrs. Officer, "but not with the skill'dness of Mr. Officer."

The young men came in and led out the girls; one mountain maid—and a pretty one—lingered.

"You needn't ask me," she said, coquettishly. "I've promised to dance the first dance with Mr. Tom Jared."

"Should like to know why he don't come," said young Jack Apple; "'pears 's if he ain't in a hurry."

At this instant a little black bullet head was thrust inside the door, and an African voice called, with a subdued chuckle,

"Mars' Tom say he done gin out de notion."

Sensation. Up jumped the offended fair, and rushed after the messenger, who ran from the slap to come.

"She's as mad as forty thousand wet hens," said Mrs. Officer, mildly.

And we thought she had a right to be.

From the grove sounded the inspiring strain of "Billy in the Low Grounds." We found the dancers in a rustic arbor, roofed with green boughs intertwined with hickory withes. Floor there was none save the smooth earth covered three inches deep with wheat-bran. Slightly dampened, it was pleasant to dance on; but Heaven preserve them when they danced it dry!

Men on one side, women on the other, stiff as a line of bayonets. It was a reel they were to dance. Jack Officer sat on an inverted barrel at one end of the arbor.

Down the middle danced the leading pair, and, separating with an air of being braced for duty, began their advances at opposite ends of the line. It was rather heavy. Here was their stamping ground, and they came down flat-footed. Suddenly a screech created a pleasant confusion.

"He trod on my foot a-purpose, he did!" cried a woman with elfish black hair, shaking her fist at a young fellow.

Another woman, wife or sweetheart, responded, with a provoking drawl,

"What made yer come t' a party bar'-footed?"

"P'r'aps I'd have as good shoes as you, Jane Oscar, 'f my man wuz in th' ground-hog whiskey business."

"Come, come!" interposed a peaceful Apple. "Speaking o' ground-hog, who'll have a drink?"

A blue water-bucket, in which a tin dipper floated, was brought forward.

All took Titanic gulps. There was a smacking of lips such as would have done credit to a tournament of lovers.

"Ah-h! That's the true Cumberland punch!" cried the refreshed fiddler.

We tasted the Cumberland punch. It was not made on the one, two, three principle, but was even more simple. It was sugarless, lemonless, waterless. It was smoky, strong, and brought tears to the eyes. In short, it was white whiskey mixed with white whiskey.

"An' very strengthenin' to the legs it is," said Jack Apple, pressing its offer.

The dancing began again with vigor, with fire and fury. The music sped in tripping notes, and Mr. Officer added his cracked but cheerful voice:

> "Oh! whar did you come from?—
> Knock a nigger down—
> Oh! whar did you come from,
> Jerry Miah Brown?"

The bran dried under their warm feet and blew up in little swirls. The mountain boys jumped until their heads knocked against the boughs above, and green leaves whirled through the flying dust. Rills of laughter bubbled forth, checked by sudden coughs. Girls' loosened hair caught around the wet necks of their partners.

> "Don't you weep no more, Sister Mary;
> Don't you weep no more, Brother John,"

sang Mr. Officer, kicking his feet against the barrel;

> "For Satan is dead, an' the word is said
> For to save you a heavenly crown.
> Yes, it is"—thump, thump—
> "Yes, it is"—thump, thump—
> "For to save you a *heavy*-anly crown."

"The devil!" suddenly exclaimed one of the Bleylock boys. The dancing stopped; Jack Officer leaped from the barrel.

"Look yonder!" said young Bleylock, pointing up to the forest roof of the arbor.

There darted a sunbeam, here fluttered a dogwood blossom, and between flower and ray the evil head of a snake wriggled socially.

"Clear out!" cried Mr. Officer, gesticulating wildly. In two minutes the place was cleared. The bran settled slowly. His snakeship was monarch, but there was naught to survey.

Jack Apple stepped in, however, an open clasp-knife in one hand. He poured some whiskey on the ground, and stooping, rubbed his other hand in the wet earth until it was gummy and black. Whether there was some mysterious significance in this rite, or he did it to secure a firmer grip, we did not know. But he seized the snake just back of the head, and before it could hiss for wonder one snake of the world had been cut in two, and could not come again.

Grandpa Apple had surveyed the scene with interest and pride.

"Purty well done, Jack—purty well," he said. "'T comes natural to the Apples to hate snakes. D' I ever tell you o' my scrimmage with the snakes on Council Rock?"

"Reckon 't 'll b'ar tellin' over agin," said Jack Officer's wife.

"'Twuz when I fust settled in Tennessee," said Grandpa Apple; "an' I built my house on a rock, like the man in Scripter, you know. We moved in befo' it wuz finished, an' the roof wuz but partly shingled. 'Twuz coolish, snappish weather, an' I made rousin' big fires, an' warmed the old rock up. An' one mornin' me an' my wife an' the baby (Jack's grandpa) wuz in bed, an' I heerd a soft, ugly sound—hiss-s-s-s-s! The mornin' wuz dark, but I peered with young eyes at the floor, an' it seemed to be a-risin' in curls an' waves—put me in mind o' Cany Fork when the wind is of a moderate gustiness. I raised on my elbow, an' I squinted up my eyes for a closer look, an' I said, 'Lord o' creation!'—not that I'm a swarin' man; but them wuz snakes! an' that sight wuz enough to make a man throw rocks at his grandmother. What a lot of 'em, little an' big!—'s many's there are Apples here to-day. Maybe 'twuz kind o' prophetic. Well, I woke Nancy, an' told her to roll up head, ears, an' baby (Jack's grandpa) in the blankets; an' I crawled up the bed-post an' out through that blessed hole in the roof. Fortunate I had a neighbor with a family o' boys, an' we got on boots, an' with rifles an' whips we went in for the biggest snake-

fight ever seen this side o' Jordan. You see, thar nests wuz
under the rock, an' my fires had made it warm for 'em, an'
they had come a-corkscrewin' out o' thar winter quarters.
Tell you we slayed an' we slew! The old woman she stayed
kivered up, ekally afeard, she said, o' men an' snakes, we got
so bloody an' fierce to kill. I do s'pose we killed a million o'
them rattlers—they wuz all rattlers."

"Oh! oho! Mr. Apple," said Jack Officer; "them figgers is
too high. 'F you killed one thousand a day, 'twould take you
a matter o' twenty years to git shet of a million."

"Now, look at that!" said the old man, admiringly; and,
"Mr. Officer's a powerful smart man—powerful," said Jack's
wife.

It was now noon, and dinner was served in the grove. The
table was made of pine boards stretched across chair backs.
It was crowded with savory dishes, and as for the dear little
pigs, never were pigs so good since the first that it took the
burning of a hut to roast.

After dinner the dance began again, but we were tired and
spent with laughter. We sought a far-off tree, and, gazed upon
admiringly by three small Apples, slept until the bran dance
was over.

Jack and the Mountain Pink

Young Selden was bored. Who was not bored among the
men? It was the tense summer of '78. A forlorn band of
refugees from the plague crowded a Nashville hotel. There
was nothing for the men to do but to read the fever bulletins,
play billiards in an insensate sort of way, and keep out of the
way of the women crying over the papers.

Young Selden felt that another month of this sort of thing
would leave him melancholy mad. So he jammed some things
into a light bag and started off for a tramp over Cumberland
Mountain.

"I envy you," said a decrepit old gentleman, with whom he
was shaking hands in good-bye. "I was brought up in the
mountain country fifty years ago. Gay young buck I was!

Go in, my boy, and make love to a mountain pink! Ah, those jolly, barefooted, melting girls! No corsets, no back hair, no bangs, by Heaven!"

It was the afternoon of a hot September day. Young Selden had started that morning from Bloomington Springs in the direction of the Window Cliff—a ridge of rocks from which he had been told a very fine view could be obtained. The road grew rougher and wilder, seeming to lose itself in hills, stumps, and fields, and was as hard to trace out as a *Bazar* pattern. He finally struck a foot-path leading to a log-cabin, where a very brown woman sat peacefully smoking in the doorway.

"Good-day," he said, taking off his hat.

The brown woman nodded in a friendly manner—the little, short, meaning nod of the mountains, that serves, so to speak, as the pro-word of these silent folk. Young Selden inquired the way to Window Cliff.

"You carn't git thar's the crow flies," she drawled, slowly; "but I reckin my daughter k'n g'long with yer."

"Aha!" thought Selden—"a mountain pink!"

"Take a cheer," said the mother, rising and going within. He seated himself on the steps, and made friends with a dog or two.

A young girl soon appeared, tying on a sun-bonnet. She greeted him with a nod, the reproduction of her mother's, and drawled, in the same tone, "Reckin you couldn't git tu Winder Clift 'thout somebody to show you the way."

"And you will be my guide?"

"'F co'se."

They started off, young Selden talking airily. He soon felt, however, that he shouldn't make love to *this* mountain pink. To begin with, there was no pink about her. She was brown, like her mother.

"Coffee!" thought Selden, with a grim remembrance of a black, muddy liquid he had drunk a few nights before at a log-cabin, over which the very babies smacked their lips.

Her eyes had the melancholy of a cow's, without the ruminative expression that gives sufficient intellectuality to a cow's sad gaze. To put it tersely, they looked stupid. Her mouth curled down a little at each corner. Her hair was not visible under her pea-green sun-bonnet. Her dress of whitish linsey was skimpy in its cut, and she wriggled in it as if it were loose skin she was trying to get out of.

She was not a talker. She looked at Selden with big eyes, and listened impassively. He elicited from her that her name was Sincerity Hicks; that her mother was the widder Hicks, and there were no others in the family; that she had never been to school, but could read, only she had no books.

"Should you like some?"

"Dunno. 'Pears 's if thar's too much to do t' fool over books."

Perhaps because he had talked so much young Selden began to get out of breath. They had crossed a field, climbed a fence, and were descending a great hill, breaking a path as they walked. He panted, and could hardly keep up with Sincerity, though she seemed not to walk fast. But she got over the ground with a light-footed agility that aroused his envy. It looked easy, but, since he could not emulate her, he concluded that long practice had trained her walk to its perfection. He noticed, too, that she walked "parrot-footed," placing each new track in the impression of the other. Imitating this, awkwardly enough, he got on better.

Reaching the clear level at the bottom of the hill, he saw at a glance that he had penetrated to a wild and virginal heart of beauty. Like a rough water-fall melting into a silver-flowing river, the vexatious and shaggy hill sloped to a dreaming valley. Streams ran about, quietly as thoughts, over pale rocks. Calacanthus bushes, speckled with their ugly little red blooms, filled the air with fragrance like that of crushed strawberries. Upspringing from this low level of prettiness rose the glory of the valley—the lordly, the magnificent birch-trees. Their topmost boughs brushed against the cliffs that shut in the opposite side. How fine these cliffs were! They rose up almost perpendicularly, and, freed halfway of their height from the thick growth of underbrush, stood out in bare, bold picturesqueness. Window Cliffs! Aha! these were the windows. Two wide spaces, square and clean-blown, framing always a picture—now a bit of hard blue sky; other times pink flushes of sunrise, or the voluptuous moon and peeping eyes of stars.

"Want ter go t' the top?" inquired Sincerity.

"I—dunno," rejoined Selden, lazily. Truth was, he did not wish to move. He liked the vast shadows, the cool deeps, the singing tones of the valley. Then he was sure he had a blister on his heel. Still, to come so far—"How long a walk is it?"

"Oh, jest a little piece—'bout a quarter."

"Up and away, then!" cried young Selden.

A long "quarter" he found that walk. They crossed the valley, climbed a fence, and dropped into a corn-field to be hobbled over. Up and down those hideous little furrows— it was as sickening as tossing on a chopping sea. Selden stopped to rest. Sincerity, not a feather the worse, looked him over with mild patience.

"Lemme tote yo' haversack," she said.

"No, no," said the young man with an honest blush. But he was reminded of a flask of brandy in his knapsack, of which he took a grateful swig.

"Now," said his guide, as, the corn-field crossed, they emerged into forest—"now we begins to climb the mountain."

Selden groaned. He had thought himself nearly on a level with the Window Cliff. To this day that climb is an excruciating memory to young Selden. He thought of

> "Johnny Schnapps,
> Who bust his shtraps,"

and wondered if the disaster was not suffered in going up a mountain. He felt himself melting away with heat. He knew that his face was blazing like a Christmas pudding, and dripping like a roast on a spit. He resigned the attempt to keep up with Sincerity. When they started on this excruciating tramp the droop of her pea-green sun-bonnet had seemed to him abject; now he knew that it expressed only contempt—contempt for the weakling and the stranger.

But one gets to the top of most things by trying hard enough, and they gained at last the rough crags that commanded the valley.

Ah! the fair, grand State! There was a spot for a blind man to receive sight! The young man drew a long breath as he gazed over the bewitching expanse. All so fresh, so un-breathed-on, the only hints of human life the little log-cabins perched about, harmonious as birds' nests amid their surroundings.

Sincerity Hicks stood fanning herself with the green sun-bonnet. There was something pretty about her, now that this disfigurement was removed. But a mountain pink—what a pretty implication in the name!—no.

"So this is Window Cliff?" he said. "And is there any particular name for the ledge yonder?"

"'Tis called Devil's Chimney, 'nd the cut between is Long Hungry Gap."

"Long Hungry Gap?—where have I heard that famished name? Oh yes, some of Peters's scouts. You know Peters?"

"Yaas, I've heerd tell o' Jim Peters."

Sincerity's drawl was not quickened, but Selden was surprised to see a light leap into her eyes as suddenly as a witch through a key-hole.

"These fellows had a room next to mine at the Bloomington Hotel," Selden went on, "and the walls are like paper; so I heard all they said."

"And what d' they say?"

"Well, that the captain was up the country on a moonshine raid; but that they were on the track of something better—had heard of a 'powerful big still' up in Long Hungry Gap—and would mash it up as soon as the captain got back."

"D' they say when Peters wuz expected?"

"The next day."

Sincerity tied on her bonnet.

"Guess you kin find the way back," she remarked.

"Hello! what does this mean?"

"I've got sometin' t' attend to across the mounting."

"I'll go with you."

Sincerity stopped and turned a serious face. "Likely's not you'll git hurt."

"Oho! I'm *in*, if there's any chance of a scrimmage. Go ahead."

She did go ahead. If the path had been vexatious before, now it was revengeful and aggressive. In fact, there was no path. But Sincerity, like love, found out a way. Suddenly, like a comic mask popped on a friend's face, something sinister and strange burst upon them through the familiar woods. Or, rather, they burst upon it—a wild-cat still, securely sheltered under an innocent combination of rocks, ferns, and magnolia-trees.

Four or five wild-looking fellows sprang up, their hands on their rifles.

"None o' yo' shootin'," said Sincerity Hicks; "he's a friend."

"Sho' he ain't a spy? 'Cause if that's the case, mister, you'll stay in these woods face down."

"My impetuous moonshiner, I don't call myself the friend of you law-breakers, but I'm no spy. I brought the news to the faithful Sincerity of Captain Peters being on your track."

Hurried questions were asked and answered. Several resolute voices suggested to fight it out, but all seemed to await the decision of an old man they called Jack, who leaned against a tub, with a touching expression of meekness under unmerited ill-luck.

"No, boys," he said; "we ain't strong enough. But we'll run off what we can. Save the copper—we'll never git another so big an' satisfactory—an' the mash tun, an' as many of the tubs 's you can git off."

It was a transformation scene. Things seemed to fly to pieces all at once, like a bomb-shell. The great copper still was hoisted on the shoulders of two or three men; the worm, the mash tun, the coolers, were taken down with celerity, and the unlucky moonshiners made off through the woods.

"Reckin th' rest 'll have ter go," said Jack, pensively; "but tell you what, Sincerity Hicks, seems 's if I couldn't b'ar to have 'em git th' old sow an' her pigs."

"Run 'em off."

"They're too young, honey.   Come 'ere."

He led to a mimosa-tree behind a rock; and under its sensitive shade reposed, like Father Nile, a portly porcine mother, overrun with little, pink, blind pigs.

"Ain't you got a spar' tub?" asked the girl.

His face lighted.   "I catches," he said, gently.

He brought an empty whiskey puncheon, and covered the bottom with straw.   Then he lifted the pink pigs into it, assisted by Sincerity and the elegant Selden.

The mother squealed.   "Stuff her mouth," ordered the old man.

Sincerity thrust an ear of corn into the open jaws.

"Now," said Jack, "I'll run briefly through the woods, a-toting this, an' the old sow she'll follow—"

"No, you don't, Jack Boddy!" said a quiet voice.   "Smell o' that."

The ugly end of a rifle protruded itself.   A Tennessee giant leaned against the rock.   Peters?   Of course it was Peters. What other man had that easy swagger, three feet of black beard, and as wide a grin in saying checkmate?

Jack Boddy smiled innocently.

"Why, captain, you see me jest attendin' to a litter o' pigs o' mine."

"Yes, I see.   An' my men is attendin' to some pigs o' yourn. Walk out, old 'coon."

Peters' scouts were destroying all that was left of the mountain still.

"Whar's the others?" asked one of the men.

"I run this here still all by myself," said Jack, with an air of ingenuous pride.

"What a lie!" said the captain.   "Have you cut his copper boiler, boys?"

"'Tain't here."

"Whar's your copper, Jack?"

"Gone to heaven," said Jack, rolling his eyes.

"You can't make anything out o' Jack Boddy," said a scout, grinning.

"Well, I've got you, anyhow," cried the captain.

"An' the oldest one in the business, Jim."

"An' I'll ketch the rest in time. Come on, boys. We'll stop at the widder Hicks's to-night. Can your mother put us up, Sissy?"

"Dunno," said Sincerity.

"Mighty know-nothin' all of a sudden." And turning to Selden. "You're a stranger, I see, mister. On the cirkit?"

"Not at all; only a traveller. Climbed the Window Cliff, and stumbled over here."

"'F you'd been in these parts a year or so ago," said an old man, relieving his mouth of the white whiskers he was chewing, "you'd 'a seen a sight o' stills. They were thick as weevils in flour. But a man of might arose in the land and he cleared 'em out."

"Peters, I suppose?"

"Yessir—James Cook Peters, whose name ought to be Gideon, the Sword of the Lord; formerly an ignorant blacksmith of Tipper County, but advanced, by the grace of God an' the app'intment of gov'ment, to bust wild-cat stills, an' flood the earth with hot whiskey a-steamin' from the vats."

"Any—er—murderin' involved in the blacksmithin' trade?" inquired Jack Boddy, with a casual air of interest.

Captain Peters turned an angry red, but said nothing.

"Becaze," continued the artless old man, "it's a pretty bloody business you've took up now. How many men have you killed? Five, I b'lieve, with your own hand, an' twenty-one with yer men."

"It wuz a fair fight," said the captain. "I killed 'em honorable, an' wuz acquitted by the laws o' my country."

"And though their numbers should be seventy times seven," said the white-haired satellite of the captain, "and the land run with blood, this thing has got to be put a stop to."

"Look a-here, James Riggs," said Jack, "this here moon-shinin' is jest like a wriggle-worm. Don't you know, how-soever many pieces you chop 'em into, a fresh head'll grow, an' a new worm swim away? Tell you, you can't stop moon-shinin' 's long's there's an honest man in Old Hickory's State."

"The Lord commanded, and the sun stood still," said James Riggs, "'twon't be no harder job 'n that."

As they talked they were descending the mountain. The noble Jack alas! was handcuffed and guarded between two men. From time to time he scratched his head against the end of a rifle that was nearer his ear than some men would have liked. Evidently, though open to reproach, Mr. Boddy was a knight without fear.

The widow Hicks manifested no surprise at the coming of her guests. They found her with her hands plunged into a great tray of meal and water—enough to make hoe-cake for a regiment.

"Hurry up with supper, old woman," caid Captain Peters. "I'm dead tired. I rid all last night, an' ain't slept for three nights runnin'."

At supper he could hardly keep his eyes open.

"I'll turn in right off," he said.

There were some preliminaries to be gone through with— not of prayers or undressing, however. The captain eyed his prisoner thoughtfully, and remarked, "B'lieve they call you Slippery Jack?"

"I am kind of hard to hold," said Mr. Boddy, with a modest twinkle.

"So!"

Another moment, and Jack was tightly bound by a stout rope around the captain's own body. "I reckon you don't git away to-night."

"Dunno!" said Jack.

The cabin had two rooms. In one the widow, Sincerity, and Mr. James Riggs went to bed. Mr. Boddy and the captain occupied the one bed in the other. A third of it was offered young Selden, but he preferred a blanket and the floor. The scouts were divided, and guarded doors and windows.

Young Selden could not sleep. The wild novelty of the situation excited him, and his aching limbs made him toss uneasily. A little fire smouldered on the hearth, and big, shapeless shadows clutched at each other in the corners. Plenty of sounds broke the silence. The captain, happy in having made a Siamese twin of Slippery Jack, snored as if he were choking to death. The guards talked and jested roughly. A whippoor-will's three wild notes sounded just above the roof. He wondered if Jack was asleep. No; there was a slight alert movement of his body, and young Selden caught the gleam of a wild blue eye under a shaggy eyebrow. With perceptions sharpened, intensified, Selden waited for he knew not what. Mr. Boddy's eye rolled upward—and what! a wilder, brighter eye, a star, shone with answering ray through a crevice in the roof. The crevice widened; other stars stole in sight. Selden felt as if his senses were leaving him. Now the crevice was obscured; and now something shining, glimmering, and cold as the light of eye or star, protruded itself cautiously as peeping mouse through the hole in the roof. It was the point of an open knife.

Selden almost sprang to his feet. Was he to witness murder? But somehow he trusted Jack Boddy—and he waited.

The knife was affixed to a knotted rope. It soon dangled within reach of Mr. Boddy's hand. And the sly moonshiner, with a silent grin at the sleeping captain, cut the ropes that bound them together. Then hand over hand, lightly as a sailor, he climbed the ropes, slipped through the opening, and was gone,

"Over the hills, and far away."

Young Selden wanted to shout. But he contented himself with a quiet chuckle, and went to sleep.

He was awakened in the morning by blue-blaze swearing. The captain was foaming at the mouth, James Riggs was wiping his eyes with a spotted handkerchief, and the scouts were swearing by all that was blessed or damned that they had not closed their eyes.

"How is it with you, stranger?" said Captain Peters. "Did you see or hear anything?"

"Oh no. I slept straight through," said young Selden, with that cheerful readiness to lie that comes to great souls.

"Well, the devil must 'a helped him."

"Lor, boys," said the widow Hicks, with a slight twitch at the corners of her mouth, "you know Jack Boddy is a powerful cunnin' man—slippery as an eel."

"Jest let me get these hands on him once more—jes' *once* more!"

"S'pose you'd kill him, wouldn't you?" said the widow, sweetly. "Lor, now, I s'pose you don't make no more of killin' a man 'n I do of wringin' a chicken's neck?"

"Don't excite him," implored James Riggs; "he's powerful plagued over this misfortune."

"Come to breakfast," said the widow. "I won't make no laughin'-stawk of him 'f I can help it."

"Damnation!" said the captain.

As for Sincerity Hicks, she looked as stolid as a wooden Indian. Selden pressed some money in her hand at parting, and whispered, "My dear girl, I was delighted; you climb like a cat."

"Guess this'll be good for some blue beads," she said, without moving a muscle; "I've been a-wantin' some a right smart while."

Young Selden shook with silent laughter as he strode away.

"A mountain pink!" he murmured. "Oh no, a bean stalk—a Cumberland bean stalk."

SIDNEY LANIER

Sidney Lanier was born in Macon, Georgia, February 3, 1842, and died at Lynn, in the mountains of North Carolina, September 7, 1881, with burial in Baltimore. His grandfather came from Virginia to Georgia, where he prospered; his father was an educated, cultured lawyer; and his religious, music-loving mother was the daughter of a Virginia planter. His younger brother Clifford he loved almost extravagantly. As a child he cared passionately for music and learned to play the guitar, violin, organ, and flute. At fourteen he entered Oglethorpe College, then at Midway, two miles from Milledgeville. He was so good a student that his father took him out of college for a year, holding that seventeen was too young to graduate. After his graduation in 1860 he spent a year at his grandfather's hotel at Montvale Springs in eastern Tennessee, and then returned to Oglethorpe as a tutor. Among his colleagues there were James Woodrow, uncle of Woodrow Wilson, and Milton H. Northrup, later a newspaper man in Washington and Syracuse. These friends liberalized the youth's puritanical ideas about religion and science, and spurred his ambition for scholarly study. While he was considering further study, the approaching war settled his immediate future for him. After the citizens of Macon had passed a declaration of independence from the United States and Georgia had followed South Carolina in seceding from the Union, Lanier volunteered in June, 1861, for military service. With the Macon Volunteers he was stationed near Norfolk, helped build Ft. Fisher at Wilmington, North Carolina, and engaged in major battles in Virginia. Assigned to a blockade-running vessel, he was taken prisoner and suffered "death in life" in several Federal prisons. In February, 1865, he was released from prison, ill with lung trouble and fever. Friends and sympathetic strangers helped him on his way home, first by sea to Virginia and then down through the Carolinas on foot or by farm wagons.

After convalescence, he completed the writing of the novel *Tiger-Lilies*, begun during the war, and went to New York in 1867 to secure its publication. This is an autobiographical

novel of five years of Lanier's life, including observations of
mountain life as seen from Montvale Springs, realistic war and
prison scenes, and ideas about nature and art, which were to be
elaborated in later writings.

In 1867 he married Mary Day in Macon, who reared his
children, edited his writings, and for fifty years after his
death kept alive his literary reputation. After his marriage
the years passed in a painful struggle to regain health, to earn
a living, and to become known as a writer. After an attempt
at teaching, he submitted reluctantly to the study of law and
worked in his father's law office. He gained a local reputation
as a flute-player, a poet, and an orator.

In 1873 Lanier determined to give his remaining years to
music and poetry. He settled in Baltimore as flautist in the
Peabody Symphony Orchestra, holding the position for seven
years. In 1873 he published "Corn" and "The Symphony"
in *Lippincott's Magazine*, which brought him the friendship of
Bayard Taylor, a literary man of influence. Taylor invited
Lanier to write the words for a cantata to be sung at the Centennial Exposition of 1876 in Philadelphia, and he responded
with "The Centennial Meditation of Columbia," which aroused
critical controversy. In 1877 Lanier published a volume of
ten poems which had appeared in *Lippincott's Magazine*,
with a dedication to the actress Charlotte Cushman, who had
been his friend and adviser. Feeling the need of increasing his
income, Lanier had tried to obtain a professorship in the recently founded Johns Hopkins University. President Daniel
Coit Gilman was interested in him, but could not convince
the trustees. In 1878 a Georgia lady, Mrs. Edgeworth Bird,
organized in her Baltimore home a class to hear Lanier lecture
on Elizabethan poetry. Lanier prepared for his lectures by
reading widely in the writings of Old and Middle English,
even acquiring a knowledge of Anglo-Saxon. He lectured so
intelligently that in 1879 President Gilman appointed him lecturer in English literature. Lanier was immensely pleased at
becoming a university professor with a permanent income.
Years later, in 1902, his formal lectures were printed as *Shakespeare and His Forerunners*. During 1879 Lanier wrote a manual
of prosody, published in 1880 as *The Science of English Verse*,
which received both praise and disapproval. The last twelve
Johns Hopkins lectures were later published in 1883, with a

revised form in 1897, as *The English Novel,* in which Lanier emphasized George Eliot as the greatest of all English artists in fiction. In his last years, he turned out several juvenile books, such as *The Boys' Froissart* (1879). His collected poems were issued posthumously in 1884. Other posthumous books include *Music and Poetry* (1898) and *Retrospects and Prospects* (1899), which were essays collected from magazines and manuscripts.

From TIGER–LILIES

The Call to Arms

The early spring of 1861 brought to bloom, besides innumerable violets and jessamines, a strange, enormous, and terrible flower.

This was the blood-red flower of war, which grows amid thunders; a flower whose freshening dews are blood and hot tears, whose shadow chills a land, whose odors strangle a people, whose giant petals droop downward, and whose roots are in hell.

It is a species of the great genus, sin-flower, which is so conspicuous in the flora of all ages and all countries, and whose multifarious leafage and fruitage so far overgrow a land that the violet, or love-genus, has often small chance to show its quiet blue.

The cultivation of this plant is an expensive business, and it is a wonder, from this fact alone, that there should be so many fanciers of it. A most profuse and perpetual manuring with human bones is absolutely necessary to keep it alive, and it is well to have these powdered, which can be easily done by hoofs of cavalry-horses and artillery-wheels, not to speak of the usual method of mashing with cannon-balls. It will not grow, either, except in some wet place near a stream of human blood; and you must be active in collecting your widows' tears and orphans' tears and mothers' tears to freshen the petals with in the mornings.

It requires assiduous working; and your labor-hire will be a large item in the expense, not to speak of the amount disbursed in preserving the human bones alive until such time as they may be needed, for, I forgot to mention, they must be fresh, and young, and newly-killed.

It is, however, a hardy plant, and may be grown in any climate, from snowy Moscow to hot India.

It blooms usually in the spring, continuing to flower all summer until the winter rains set in: yet in some instance it has been known to remain in full bloom during a whole inclement winter, as was shown in a fine specimen which I saw the other day, grown in North America by two wealthy landed propri-etors, who combined all their resources of money, of blood, of bones, of tears, of sulphur and what not, to make this the grandest specimen of modern horticulture, and whose success was evidenced by the pertinacious blossoms which the plant sent forth even amid the hostile rigors of snow and ice and furious storms. It is supposed by some that seed of this Ameri-can specimen (now dead) yet remain in the land; but as for this author (who, with many friends, suffered from the unhealthy odors of the plant), he could find it in his heart to wish fervently that these seed, if there be verily any, might perish in the germ, utterly out of sight and life and memory and out of the remote hope of resurrection, forever and ever, no matter in whose granary they are cherished!

But, to return.

It is a spreading plant, like the banyan, and continues to in-sert new branch-roots into the ground, so as sometimes to overspread a whole continent. Its black-shadowed jungles afford fine cover for such wild beasts as frauds and corruptions and thefts to make their lair in; from which, often, these issue with ravening teeth and prey upon the very folk that have planted and tended and raised their flowery homes!

Now, from time to time, there have appeared certain indi-viduals (wishing, it may be, to disseminate and make profit upon other descriptions of plants) who have protested against the use of this war-flower.

Its users, many of whom are surely excellent men, contend

that they grow it to protect themselves from oppressive hail-storms, which destroy their houses and crops.

But some say the plant itself is worse than any hailstorm; that its shades are damp and its odors unhealthy, and that it spreads so rapidly as to kill out and uproot all corn and wheat and cotton crops. Which the plant-users admit; but rejoin that it is cowardly to allow hailstorms to fall with impunity, and that manhood demands a struggle against them of some sort.

But the others reply, fortitude is more manly than bravery, for noble and long endurance wins the shining love of God; whereas brilliant bravery is momentary, is easy to the enthusi-astic, and only dazzles the admiration of the weak-eyed since it is as often shown on one side as the other.

But then, lastly, the good war-flower cultivators say, our preachers recommend the use of this plant, and help us mightily to raise it in resistance to the hailstorms.

And reply, lastly, the interested other-flower men, that the preachers should preach Christ; that Christ was worse hailed upon than anybody, before or since; that he always refused to protect himself, though fully able to do it, by any war-banyan; and that he did, upon all occasions, not only discourage the resort to this measure, but did inveigh against it more earnestly than any thing else, as the highest and heaviest crime against Love—the Father of Adam, Christ, and all of us.

Friends and horticulturists, cry these men, stickling for the last word, if war was ever right, then Christ was always wrong; and war-flowers and the vine of Christ grow different ways, insomuch that no man may grow with both!

But these sentiments, even if anybody could have been found patient enough to listen to them, would have been called sen-timentalities, or worse, in the spring of 1861, by the inhabitants of any of those States lying between Maryland and Mexico. An afflatus of war was breathed upon us. Like a great wind, it drew on and blew upon men, women, and children. Its sound mingled with the solemnity of the church-organs and arose with the earnest words of preachers praying for guidance in the matter. It sighed in the half-breathed words of sweethearts conditioning impatient lovers with war-services. It thundered splendidly in the impassioned appeals of orators to the people. It whistled through the streets, it stole in to the firesides, it clinked glasses in bar-rooms, it lifted the gray hairs of our wise men in conventions, it thrilled through the lectures in college halls, it rustled the thumbed book-leaves of the school-rooms.

This wind blew upon all the vanes of all the churches of the country, and turned them one way—toward war. It blew, and shook out, as if by magic, a flag whose device was unknown to soldier or sailor before, but whose every flap and flutter made the blood bound in our veins.

Who could have resisted the fair anticipations which the new war-idea brought? It arrayed the sanctity of a righteous cause in the brilliant trappings of military display; pleasing, so, the devout and the flippant which in various proportions are mixed elements in all men. It challenged the patriotism of the sober citizen, while it inflamed the dream of the statesman, ambitious for his country or for himself. It offered test to all allegiances and loyalties; of church, of state; of private loves, of public devotion; of personal consanguinity; of social ties. To obscurity it held out eminence; to poverty, wealth; to greed, a gorged maw; to speculation, legalized gambling; to patriotism, a country; to statesmanship, a government; to virtue, purity; and to love, what all love most desires—a field wherein to assert itself by action.

From RETROSPECTS AND PROSPECTS
Music

Music defies calculation, it baffles prophecy, it vanishes during analysis. It has more avatars than Vishnu, more metamorphoses than Jupiter, more transmigrations than Pythagoras's soul. It is, at one and the same time, an angel and a devil; a muse and a fury; a tarantula and an anodyne; a free Proteus and a Prometheus bound. It is a spiritual analogue to carbon; which appears one moment as charcoal, the next moment as rose-leaf, and the next as diamond. Yonder, as drum and horn, music marches at the head of armies like a general; here, as voice or lute, it sings by the cradles of children like a mother. In the cathedral it is chanting *Laudamus* for the birth of a king; in the graveyard it is chief mourner at the burial of a beggar. Last night in slippers and spangles it led a dance; to-day in sober black it leads a church-service. It conducts virtue along the aisle to the marriage-altar; it inflames vice to unholy embrace in the brothel. In the music-room it is a piano, in the forest it is a whistling bird, in the heavens it is a groaning wind, in the firmament it is a whirling star, and in the soul it is like a serene fire.

Why does not our age, which claims to be a Prospero of eras, subject and tame this singular spirit, Music, which is at once an Ariel and a Caliban, and will indifferently girdle the earth or chop firewood for us?

To the soul, music combines in itself the power of steam, the agility of electricity, and the fidelity of printing-type. It is a civilization in a conch-shell.

Love is a fast lily whose petals gleam faintly just under the wave of life, and sometimes sway and float out above it. Up from this lily, then, arises an odor: it is Music.

"The orator," said Quintilian, "should know everything." How much more should the musician understand all things! For the true musician is as much higher than the orator as love is higher than law. The Greeks did well therefore when they made their word *Mousiké* signify a symmetrical and harmonious education of all the powers of a man.

From MUSIC AND POETRY

The Legend of St. Leonor

Once upon a time St. Leonor, with sixty disciples, came to an inhospitable region at the mouth of the Rance in Armorica, and settled. Their food was of the rudest description, being only what they could obtain from the woods and waters. One day the good Bishop Leonor, while praying, happened to see a small bird carving a grain of wheat in its beak. He immediately set a monk to watching the bird, with instructions to follow it when it flew away. The monk followed the bird, and was led to a place in the forest where he found several stalks of wheat growing. This was probably the last relic of some ancient Gallo-Roman farm. St. Leonor, on learning the news, was overjoyed. "We must clear the forest and cultivate the ground," he exclaimed, and immediately put the sixty at work. Now the work was hard, and the sixty disciples groaned with tribulation as they toiled and sweated over the stubborn oaks and the briary underbrush. But when they came to plough, the labor seemed beyond all human endurance. I do not know how they ploughed; but it is fair to suspect that they had nothing better than forked branches of the gnarly oaks with sharpened points for ploughs, and as there is no mention of cattle in the legend, the presumption is fair that these good brothers hitched themselves to the plough and pulled. This presumption is strengthened by the circumstance that, in a short time, the sixty rebelled outright. They begged the Bishop to abandon agriculture and go away from that place. "Pater" (naively says the Bollandist recounter of the legend),—"Pater," cried the monks, "oramus te ut de loco isto recedas."

But the stout old father would not recede. No; we must get into beneficial relations with this soil. Then the monks assembled together by night, and, having compared opinions, found it the sense of the meeting that they should leave the very next day, even at pain of the abandonment of the Bishop. So, next morning, when they were about to go, behold! a miracle stopped them: twelve magnificent stags marched proudly out of the forest and stood by the ploughs, as if inviting the yoke. The monks seized the opportunity. They harnessed the stags, and these diligently drew the ploughs all that day. When the day's work was done, and the stags were loosed from harness, they retired into the forest. But next morning the faithful wild creatures again made their appearance and submitted their royal necks to the yoke. Five weeks and three days did these animals labor for the brethren.

When the ground was thoroughly prepared, the Bishop pronounced his blessing upon the stags, and they passed quietly back into the recesses of the forest. Then the Bishop sowed his wheat, and that field was the father of a thousand other wheat-fields, and of a thousand other homes, with all the amenities and sweetnesses which are implied in that ravishing word.

Now, here is the point of this legend in this place. Of course, the twelve stags did not appear from the forest and plough; and yet the story is true. The thing which actually happened was that the Bishop Leonor, by his intelligence, foresight, practical wisdom, and faithful perseverance, reclaimed a piece of stubborn and impracticable ground, and made it good, arable soil. (It is also probable that the story was immediately suggested by the re-taming of cattle which the ancient Gallo-Roman people had allowed to run wild. The bishops did this sometimes.) This was a practical enough thing; it is being done every day; it was just as prosaic as any commercial transaction. But, mark you, the people—for this legend is a pure product of the popular imagination of Brittany—the people who came after saw how the prosaic wheat-field of the Bishop had flowered into the poetical happiness of the rude and wild inhabitants who began to gather about his wheat patch, and to plant fields and build homes of their own; and, seeing that the prose had actually become thus poetic, the people (who love to tell things as they really are, and in their deeper relations) the people have related it in terms of poetry. The bird and the stags are terms of poetry. But, notice again, that these are not silly, poetic licenses; they are not merely a child's embellishments of a story; the bird and the stags are *not* real; but they *are* true. For what do they mean? They mean the powers of Nature. They mean, as here inserted, that if a man go forth, sure of his mission, fervently loving his fellow-men, working for their benefit; if he adhere to his mission through

good and evil report; if he resist all endeavor to turn him from
it, and faithfully stand to his purpose,—presently he will succeed; for the powers of Nature will come forth out of the recesses of the universe and offer themselves as draught-animals
to his plough. The popular legend is merely an affirmation in
concrete forms of this principle; the people, who are all poets,
know this truth. We moderns, indeed,—we whose practical
experiences beggar the wildest dreams of antiquity,—have
seen a wilder (beast) creature than a stag come out of the woods
for a faithful man. We have seen steam come and plough the
seas for Fulton; we have seen lightning come and plough the
wastes of space for Franklin and Morse.

From THE NEW SOUTH
The New South

It is impossible to end without adverting to a New South
which exists in a far more literal sense than that of small farming. How much of this gracious land is yet new to all real
cultivation, how much of it lies groaning for the muscles of
man, and how doubly mournful is this newness, in view of the
fair and fruitful conditions which here hold perpetual session,
and press perpetual invitation upon all men to come and have
plenty! Surely, along that ample stretch of generous soil,
where the Appalachian ruggednesses calm themselves into
pleasant hills before dying quite away into the sea-board levels,
a man can find such temperances of heaven and earth—enough
of struggle with nature to draw out manhood, with enough of
bounty to sanction the struggle—that a more exquisite co-
adaptation of all blessed circumstances for man's life need not
be sought. It is with a part of that region that this writer is
most familiar; and one cannot but remember that, as one stands
at a certain spot thereof and looks off up and across the Ocmul-
gee River, the whole prospect seems distinctly to yearn for men.
Everywhere the huge and gentle slopes kneel and pray for
vineyards, for cornfields, for cottages, for spires to rise up from

beyond the oak-groves. It is a land where there is never a day of summer nor of winter when a man cannot do a full day's work in the open field; all the products meet there, as at nature's own agricultural fair; rice grows alongside of wheat, corn alongside of sugar-cane, cotton alongside of clover, apples alongside of peaches, so that a small farm may often miniature the whole United States in growth; the little valleys everywhere run with living waters, asking grasses and cattle and quiet grist-mills; all manner of timbers for economic uses and trees for finer arts cover the earth; in short, here is such a neighborly congregation of climates, soils, minerals, and vegetables, that within the compass of many a hundred-acre farm a man may find wherewithal to build his house of stone, of brick, of oak, or of pine, to furnish it in woods that would delight the most curious eye, and to supply his family with all the necessaries, most of the comforts, and many of the luxuries, of the whole world. It is the country of homes.

And, as said, it is because these blissful ranges are still clamorous for human friendship; it is because many of them are actually virgin to plough, pillar, axe, or mill-wheel, while others have known only the insulting and mean cultivation of the earlier immigrants who scratched the surface for cotton a year or two, then carelessly abandoned all to sedge and sassafras, and sauntered on toward Texas: it is thus that these lands are, with sadder significance than that of small farming, also a New South.

THOMAS NELSON PAGE

Thomas Nelson Page was born at "Oakland," Hanover County, Virginia, on April 23, 1853, and died at "Oakland" November 1, 1922. He was the descendant of two remarkable Virginia families, the Pages and the Nelsons. Two great-grandfathers had served Virginia as governors, and his father was a major throughout the War Between the States. The family suffered "the burdens of war and the distressing effects of reconstruction." In 1869 he entered Washington College, now Washington and Lee University, of which General Robert E. Lee was president. Of Lee Page wrote: "Their idolized general . . . returned to the little college town of Lexington, Va., to devote the rest of his life to educating the young men of the South." Page's biographies of Lee contain interesting incidents of Lee as president of the college. Page withdrew in 1872 to read law for a year under his father; next he tutored in a family near Louisville, Kentucky; and then he took a law degree under John B. Minor in the law school of the University of Virginia. From 1874 to 1893 he practised law in Richmond, where he took an active part in the civic and social life of the city. In 1886 he married Anna Seddon Bruce, who died two years later.

In 1889 he went abroad with Rosewell Page, his younger brother and later biographer. With Francis Hopkinson Smith he went on lecture and reading tours in 1889–1893. In 1893 he married Mrs. Florence Lathrop Field and removed to Washington. His books and lectures brought him financial rewards and broad reputation. This successful southern writer could spend his winters in Washington, New York, or Europe, and his summers in Virginia or Maine. In 1913 President Wilson appointed Page as ambassador to Italy. Until 1919 he served the United States conscientiously and successfully, bringing mutual good feeling between Italy and the United States. During the same period Walter Hines Page of North Carolina was ambassador to England.

Although he had contributed a Negro dialect poem, "Uncle Gabe's White Folks," and an essay, "Old Yorktown," to

Scribner's Monthly, literary recognition first came with the publication of the story "Marse Chan" in the *Century Magazine* in 1884. Other Negro stories were contributed to magazines, and in 1887 he collected six of them in the volume, *In Ole Virginia, or Marse Chan and Other Stories*. "Marse Chan," "Unc' Edinburg's Drowndin'," a romantic story of plantation life before the war, "Meh Lady," a vivid account of the griefs and hardships of the war, "Ole Stracted," an excellent picture of Negro cabin life, and "Polly," a vivid picture of the relations between plantation owners, slaves, and the white farming class, are based upon life in Hanover County, Virginia. The last story, "No Haid Pawn," (no head pond), is a vivid story of the supernatural. Critics regard *Red Rock* (1898), as his best novel. Its setting is on the plantations north of Richmond from 1858 to 1872, and it is a vivid tale of Reconstruction days. Other novels have been popular, especially *The Old Gentleman of the Black Stock* (1897), *Gordon Keith* (1903), which pictures a Southerner in New York City and has some good scenes in a mining town of the South, and *John Marvel, Assistant* (1909), the story of a young lawyer who leaves the South and lives in a large city of the West, probably Chicago.

Among his collection of essays are *The Old South* (1892), *Social Life in Old Virginia* (1897), *The Negro, the Southerner's Problem* (1904) and *The Old Dominion* (1908). His earlier study of *Robert E. Lee, the Southerner* (1908) was expanded into *Robert E. Lee, Man and Soldier* (1911). This is an incomplete list, as indicated by the eighteen volumes in the Scribner's Plantation Edition of his *Novels, Stories, Sketches, and Poems*.

Page's stories and novels are valued for their vivid characterization, well-organized plots, and skillful use of Negro dialect. His Negro stories may be compared with those of Harris, and his treatment of Virginia life may be sharply contrasted with that by Ellen Glasgow. Students will continue to dispute the completeness of his pictures of ante-bellum plantation life. These pictures are not inaccurate, but they are incomplete and fragmentary. Dr. F. P. Gaines, now the president of Washington and Lee University, Page's alma mater, says about Page in his *Southern Plantation* that he was "far more passionate than Harris in the maintenance of a hypothesis of departed glory, paints in more glowing colors, is uniformly more idealistic, descends less frequently—if ever—from the heights of

romantic vision; in short, he expresses the supreme glorifica-
ion of the old regime; he 'wrote the epitaph of a civilization.'"

From PASTIME STORIES
How Jinny Eased Her Mind

Uncle Ben Williamson was as well known in town as the
mayor or the governor. He was an "old-time darky," and to
this character owed his position, which was a good one. He
had been "Boy" about law offices in the Law Building ever since
the first evening some years before when he had knocked gently
at Judge Allen's door, and then, after a tardy invitation, had
slipped slowly in sideways, with his old beaver hat in his hand,
and, having taken in in his comprehensive glance the whole
room, including the Judge himself, had said, apparently satisfied, that he had heard they wanted a boy, and he wanted a
place. It was an auspicious moment for the old fellow; the last
"boy," a drunkard and a thief, had just been discharged, and the
judge had been much worried that day trying to wait on himself. His thoughts had turned in the waning evening light to
his home, from which the light had faded for all time, and his
heart was softened. The old lawyer had looked Ben over too,
and had been satisfied. Something about him had called up
tender recollections of his little office at the old Court-house
before he became a successful lawyer and a celebrated judge,
and when his best friend was the old drunken negro who waited
on him, "cleaned up" (?) his room, and was his principal client
and most sympathetic friend and counsellor in his long love-
affair with his sweetheart, the old colonel's brown-eyed daughter. He had just been dreaming of her, first as she wore his
first violets, and then as she lay for the last time, with her head
pillowed in his roses, and her white, slender hands, whiter than
ever, clasped over his last violets on her quiet breast.

He had recalled all the sweet difficulties in winning her; his
falling back into dissipation, his picking himself up again, and
again his failure; and then the lonely evening when he had sat

in front of the dying fire, sad, despairing, and had wondered if life were worth holding longer; then old William slipping in, hat in hand. He recalled the old man's keen look at him as he sat before the fire with the pistol half hidden under the papers on his desk, and his sudden breaking of the silence with: "Don't you give her up, Marse Johnny; don't you nuver give her up. Ef she's wuth havin', she's wuth fightin' for; an' ef she say No, she jes beginnin' to mean Yes. Don't you give her up." And he had not given her up, and she had called him from the dead and had made him. He would not have given the right to put those violets in her calm hands for a long life of unbroken happiness with any one else. So, when the door opened quietly, and Uncle Ben, in his clean shirt, time-browned coat, and patched breeches, slipped in, it was an auspicious moment for him.

"Where did you come from?" he asked him.

"From old Charlotte, suh; used to 'longst to de Bruces."

"Can you clean up?"

He laughed a spontaneous, jolly laugh. "Kin I clean up? Dat's what I come to do. Jinny ken, too."

"Can you read?"

"Well, nor, suh, not edzactly. I ain't no free-issue nigger ner preacher." The shade of disappointment on his face counterbalanced this, however.

"Do you get drunk?"

"Yes, sir, sometimes."—Cheerfully. "Not so often. I 'ain't got nuttin to get de whiskey. But ef I's drunk, Jinny cleans up."

"Who is Jinny?"

"She's my wife."

"What sort of a woman is she?"

"She's a black woman. Oh!—she's a good sort o' ooman— a toler'ble good sort o' ooman, ef you know how to git 'long wid her. Sort o' raspy sometimes, like urr wimmens, but I kin manage her. You kin try us. Ef you don't like us we ken go. We 'ain't got no root to we foots."

"You'll do. I'll try you," said the judge; and from that time

Uncle Ben became the custodian of the offices. He was a treasure. As he had truly said, he got drunk sometimes, but when he did, Jinny took his place and cleaned up. Her temper was, as he had said, certainly "raspy." Even flattery must have admitted this, and Uncle Ben wore a bandage or plaster on some part of his head a considerable part of his time; but no one ever heard him complain. "Jinny jes been kind o' easin' her mine," he said, in answer to questions.

At length it culminated: one night Jinny went to work on him with a flat-iron to such good purpose that first a policeman came in, and then a doctor had to be called to bring him to, and Jinny was arrested.

Next morning, when Jinny was sent on to the grand jury for striking with intent to maim, disfigure, disable, and kill, Ben was a trifle triumphant. When the justice announced his decision, he rose, and shaking his long finger at her, exclaimed, "Aye, aye, what I tell you?"

"Silence!" roared the big tipstaff, and Ben sat down with a puzzled look on his face.

When the police court closed he went up to his wife, and said, in a commanding tone: "Now come 'long home wid me an' 'have yourself. I'll teach you to sling flat-iron at folks' head!"

The officer announced, however, that Jinny would have to go to jail—the case had passed beyond his jurisdiction. She had been "sent on to the grand jury."

Ben's countenance fell. "Got to go to jail!" he repeated, mechanically, in a dazed kind of way. "Got to go to jail!" Then the prisoners were taken down to the jail. He followed behind the line of stragglers that generally attended that interesting procession, and he sat on a stone outside the iron door nearly all day.

That afternoon he spent in the judge's office. The grand jury was in session, and next day "a true bill" was found against Jinny Williamson for an attempt to maim, disfigure, disable, and kill—a felony. The same day her case was called, the first on the docket.

She had good counsel. She could have had every lawyer in

the building had she wanted them, so efficiently had old Ben
polled the bar. But the case was a dead open-and-shut one.
Unhappily, the judge was ill with gout. The Commonwealth
called Ben, first man, and he told simply the same story he had
told at the police court and to the grand jury. Jinny had always
had a vicious temper, and had often exercised it towards him.
That evening she had gone rather far, and finally he had attempted to remonstrate with her, had "tapped her with his
open hand," and she had pounded his head with the flat-iron.
The officer was called, and corroborated the story. He had
heard the noise; had gone in and found Ben unconscious, and
the woman in a fury, swearing to kill him. The surgeon pronounced the wound one which came near being very serious;
but for Ben's exceptionally hard head, the skull would have
been fractured; as it was, only the outer plate of the frontal bone
was broken. He had known several men killed by blows much
less vigorous. No cross-examination affected the witnesses.
Ben had evidently told his story unwillingly. The jury was
solemn. Earnest if short speeches were made. The judge
gave a strong instruction upon the evil of women being lawless
and murderous, and the jury retired. The counsel leaned over
and told Ben he thought they had lost the case, and the jury
would probably send his wife up for at least a year. Ben said
nothing. He only looked once at Jinny sitting sullen and lower-
ing in the prisoners' box beside a thief. Then, after a while, he
got up and went out, and a minute later slipped in again at the
door sideways, and making his way over to her, put an orange—
not a very large or fresh one—into her lap. She did not look
at him.

The appearance of the jury filing in glum and important sent
him to his seat. The clerk called the names and asked, "Gentlemen of the jury, have you agreed on a verdict?" The con-
sumptive-looking foreman bowed, and handed in the indictment, amid a sudden silence, and the clerk read, slowly, "We,
the jury, find the prisoner guilty," etc., "and sentence her to
confinement in the penitentiary for two years." Neither Jinny
nor Ben stirred, nor did the counsel. He was evidently con-

sidering. The judge, in a voice slightly troubled, said he would pronounce sentence at once, and asked the prisoner if she had anything she wished to say. She rocked a little and glanced shyly over towards Ben with a sort of appealing look—her first—, said nothing, looked down again, and turned her orange over in her lap.

"Stand up," said the judge; and she stood up.

Just then Ben stood up too, and making his way over to her, said, "Jedge, ken I say a wud?"

"Why—ah—yes," said the judge, doubtfully. "It is very unusual, but go on." He sat back in his arm-chair.

"Well, gent'mens," began Ben, "I jes wants to say" (he paused, and took in the entire court-room in the sweep of his glance)—"I jes wants to say dat I don't think you ought to do Jinny dat a-way. Y'all 'ain' got nuttin 't all 'ginst Jinny. She 'ain' do nuttin to you all—nuttin 't all. She's my wife, an' what she done she done to me. Ef I kin stan' it, y'all ought to be able to, dat's sho'. Now hit's dis a-way. Y'all is married gent'mens, an' yo' knows jes how 'tis. Yo' knows sometimes a ooman gits de debil in her. 'Tain't her fault; 'tis de debil's. Hit jes like wolf in cows. Sometimes dee gits in de skin an' mecks 'em kick up an' run an' mean. Dat's de way 'tis wid wimmens. I done know Jinny ever sence she wuz a little gal at home in de country. I done know how mean she is. I done know all dat, an' I done marry her, 'cuz she suit me. I had plenty o'urr gals I could 'a' marry, but I ain' want dem. I want Jinny, an' I pester her tell she had me. Well, she meaner eben 'n I think she is; but dat ain' nuttin: I satisfied wid her, an' dat's 'nough. Y'all don' know how mean she is. She mean as a narrer-faced mule. She kick an' she fight an' she quoil tell sometimes I hardly ken stay in muh house; but dat ain' nuttin. I stay dyah, an' when she git thoo I right dyah jes same as befo', an' I know den I gwine have a good supper, an' I ain' got to pester my mine 'bout nuttin. Y'all done been all 'long dyah, 'cuz y'all is married gent'mens. Well, dat's de way 'twuz turr night. Jinny been good so long, I feared she got some'n de matter wid her, an' I kind o' git oneasy, an' sort o' poke her

up. But she ain't; she all right. I so glad to find her dat way,
I sort o' uppish, an' when she hit me I slapped her. I didn'
mean to hu't her; I jes hit her a little tap side her head, so, an'
she went all to pieces in a minute. I done hurt her feelin's.
Y'all knows how 'tis yo'self. Wimmen's got mighty cu'ious
feelin's, ain' like chillern's nor men's. Ef you slap 'em, dey
goes dat a-way. Dey gits aggervated, an' den dey got to ease
dee mine. Well, Jinny she got mighty big mine, an' when she
dat a-way it tecks right smart to ease it—to smoove it. Fust
she done try broom, den cheer, den shovel, den skillet; but ain'
none o' dem able to ease her, an' den she got to try de flat-
iron. She got to do it. Y'all knows how 'tis. Ef wimmen's
got to do anything dey got to do it, an' dat's all. Flat-iron
don' hu't none. I ain' eben feel it. Hit jes knock me out muh
head little while, an' I jes good as I wuz befo'. When I come to
I fine dee done 'rest Jinny. Dat's what hu't me. Jinny done
been easin' her mine all dese years, an' we 'ain' nuver had no
trouble befo'. An' now y'all say she got to go to de pen'ten-
tia'y. How'd y'all like somebody to sen' you' wife to pen'ten-
tia'y when she jes easin' her mine? I ax you dat. How she
gwine ease her mine dyah? I ax yo dat. I know y'all gwine
sen' her dyah, gent'mens, 'cuz you done say you is. I know you
is, an' I 'ain' got nuttin to say 'bout it, not a wud; but all I ax
you is to le' me go dyah too. I don' want stay here b'dout
Jinny, an' y'all ain' gwine to know how to manage her b'dout
me. I is de on'iest one kin do dat. Jinny got six chillern—
little chillern—dis las' crap; she didn' hab none some sevrul
years, an' den she had six. I gwine bring 'em all right upheah
to y'all to teck keer on, 'cuz I gwine wid her—ef you le' me.
I kyarn stan' it dyah by myself. I lettle mo' went 'stracted last
night. Y'all kin have 'em, 'cuz y'all ken teck keer on 'em, an'
I kyan't. I would jes like you to let her go home for a leetle
while 'fo yo' sen' her up, I jes would like dat. She got a right
new baby dyah squealin' for her dis minute, an' I mighty feared
hit gwine to die widout her, an' dat'll be right hard 'pon Jinny.
She 'ain' never los' but byah one, an' I had right smart trouble
wid her 'bout dat. She sort o' out her head arter dat some

sevrul months, till she got straight agin. I git 'long toler'ble well wid de urr chillerns, but I ain' able to nuss dat new one, an' she squeal all night. I got a ooman to come dyah an' look arter it, but she say she want Jinny, an' I think Jinny want her—I think she do. Jes let her go dyah a little while. Dat's all I want to ax you."

He sat down.

A glance at Jinny proved his assertion. Her eyes were shut fast, and with her arms tightly folded across her ample bosom, she was rocking gently from side to side. Two tears had pushed out from under her eyes, and stood gleaming on her black cheeks.

The counsel glanced up at the judge, whose face wore a look of deep perplexity, and then at the jury. "I would like to poll the jury," he said.

The clerk read the verdict over, and called the first name. "Is that your verdict?"

The juror arose. "Well, judge, I thought it was; but" (he looked down at his fellows) "I think if I could I would like to talk to one or two of the other jurors a minute, if it is not too late. My wife's got a right new baby at home herself that squealed a little last night, and I'd like to go back to the room and think about it."

"Sheriff, take the jury back to their room," said the judge, firmly.

In a few minutes they returned, and the verdict was read:

"We, the jury, all married men, find the prisoner guilty of only easing her mind."

WALTER HINES PAGE

Walter Hines Page was born in Cary (near Raleigh), North Carolina, on August 15, 1855 and died in Pinehurst, North Carolina, December 21, 1918. His father, Allison F. Page, was a man of some importance in the state, for he built the railroad from Aberdeen to Asheboro, which helped develop the central region. Although a slave-holder in his early years, he was a Union man; and although opposed to secession, he served the Confederate States when conflict became unavoidable. Page had a remarkably liberal and thorough education in different institutions. As a boy he attended the locally famous Bingham Academy at Mebane, North Carolina, under the military and classical direction of Colonel William Bingham. After a year at Trinity College (now Duke University), in 1871–1872 he transferred to Randolph-Macon College, then located at Ashland above Richmond. There Professor Thomas Randolph Price taught him Greek and aroused in him a love for England and English literature. When Johns Hopkins University opened its doors in 1876, Page entered as one of the twenty Fellows and sat under Professor Basil L. Gildersleeve. Not caring to continue the study of classics and philology, he left in 1878. After a few years of work of various kinds, he went out to Missouri, where he rose in five months from "cub" reporter to editor of the St. Joseph *Gazette*, and the next year (1880) he married Willia Alice Wilson, a childhood friend from Cary. After an interval (1881 to 1883) as reporter and editorial writer for the *New York World*, North Carolina pulled him home, and he purchased and edited the *Raleigh Chronicle*. His pen had a "javelin-like quality" in pointing out the "Ghosts" that were strangling the state, "the Ghost of the Confederate dead, the Ghost of religious orthodoxy, the Ghost of Negro domination." But he aroused many enemies, for as R. D. W. Connor writes, ". . . he was fighting the ghosts of a dead past and didn't know it. He should have let the dead alone and devoted his energies and abilities to stimulating the activities of the living." Under the discouragement of hostile attack and financial failure, he turned his newspaper over to Josephus

Daniels, and returned to New York. From 1885 to 1895 he was active, and finally successful, in New York journalism, writing editorials for the *Brooklyn Union*, contributing literary and political notes to the *Nation* and *Harper's Weekly*, and working under E. L. Godkin on the *New York Evening Post*. For three years he struggled with the *Forum* as its business manager, but made the magazine a distinctive success when he became its editor, for he wrote himself, or secured from able men, stirring literary and political articles. Next he spent the years from 1895 to 1899 in Boston as literary adviser for Houghton, Mifflin and Company, which owned the *Atlantic Monthly*, and as associate editor and editor of that magazine. Although the *Atlantic Monthly* had lived a glorious life for forty years, with the best of American writers as editors and contributors, it had become too parochial and was being ignored by readers and subscribers. Page put life into it. As his successor, Bliss Perry, wrote to him: "No one who has not seen something of its inside history can appreciate how great a debt the *Atlantic* owes to you for breathing into it the breath of life. If it had not been for your impatient energy in getting the magazine out of its ruts, the grass would be growing over its grave today."

But the editorship of this leading magazine did not satisfy Page long. Back he went to New York, to aid in founding the new publishing house of Doubleday, Page, and Company, and to found the *World's Work*, which he edited until 1918. In this year President Wilson appointed him Ambassador to England. Historians will long argue about his influence in bringing the United States into the World War, for he was strenuously anti-German. Only ill-health in 1918 could bring his resignation from this mission.

Although Page was often very critical of the South, an attitude which has brought him opponents, he was active in forwarding its welfare, as he saw it. He made three extended tours of the South, and wrote much about each, and he served on such important boards as the Southern Education Board, the General Education Board, the International Health Commission, and Theodore Roosevelt's Country Life Commission.

Page's writings were numerous, for he was a prolific journalist in the rapid production of editorials, addresses, articles, and letters. Many of these have never been collected from the newspapers and magazines. Two books are of especial importance to the student of southern life and literature, especially of the New South movement. In 1902 was published *The Rebuilding of Old Commonwealths: Being Essays toward the Training of the Forgotten Man in the Southern States*. This consists of a reprinted article and two addresses. "The Rebuilding of Old Commonwealths," first printed in the *Atlantic Monthly*, is a plea for the rebuilding of the rural South through industry and public education. The two addresses, "The Forgotten Man" and "The School That Built a Town" are also pleas for education—not the classical education which Page himself had obtained—but special, vocational training of the children of "forgotten men." In his high praise of this book Professor Mims says that "It ought to be read and reread by every Southern man who would understand the significant forces that are now making a new order of society." According to Page, this new order can be brought about by industry and education.

In 1909 he published anonymously *The Southerner, a Novel; Being the Autobiography of Nicholas Worth*. This is a reworking and expansion of a serial published in the *Atlantic Monthly*, from July to October, 1906, under the title of "The Autobiography of a Southerner Since the Civil War" by "Nicholas Worth." Although both contain facts from Page's own life, both are generally fictitious. It is doubtful if any incident is accurate, and the most striking incidents are imaginary. It is best to read *The Southerner* as a novel, interesting and valuable for its pictures of southern life after the Civil War, and not try to verify the persons and places.

In these books, and in all his writings, Page viewed his native South from a national point of view. As R. D. W. Connor says: "Page refused to look at Southern conditions and problems through the eye of a Southerner, but insisted upon seeing them from the point of view of a broad and ever-widening Nationalism. A South, illiterate, unhealthy, poverty-stricken, was a national peril, therefore, the South must be encouraged and helped to build schools, establish boards of health, develop her natural resources, and make adequate provisions for the social and spiritual welfare of the average man."

THE SOUTHERNER: A NOVEL
Being the Autobiography of Nicholas Worth

Chapter I. The Fringe of War

One day when the cotton fields were white and the elm leaves were falling, in the soft autumn of the Southern climate wherein the sky is fathomlessly clear, the locomotive's whistle blew a much longer time than usual as the train approached Millworth. It did not stop at so small a station except when there was somebody to get off or to get on; and so long a blast meant that someone was coming. Sam and I ran down the avenue of elms to see who it was. Sam was my slave, philosopher, and friend. I was ten years old and Sam said that he was fourteen.

There was constant talk about the war. Many men of the neighbourhood had gone away somewhere—that was certain; but Sam and I had a theory that the war was only a story. We had been fooled about old granny Thomas's bringing the baby, and long ago we had been fooled also about Santa Claus. The war might be another such invention, and we sometimes suspected that it was. But we found out the truth that day, and for this reason it is among my clearest early recollections.

For, when the train stopped, they put off a big box and gently laid it in the shade of the fence. The only man at the station was the man who had come to change the mail-bags; and he said that this was Billy Morris's coffin and that he had been killed in a battle. He asked us to stay with it till he could send word to Mr. Morris, who lived two miles away. The man came back presently and leaned against the fence till old Mr. Morris arrived, an hour or more later.

The lint of cotton was on his wagon, for he was hauling his crop to the gin when the sad news reached him; and he came in his shirt sleeves, his wife on the wagon seat with him.

All the neighbourhood gathered at the church, a funeral was preached and there was a long prayer for our success against "the invaders," and Billy Morris was buried. I remember that I wept the more because it now seemed to me that my doubt about the war had somehow done Billy Morris an injustice.

Old Mrs. Gregory wept more loudly than anybody else; and she kept saying, while the service was going on, "It'll be my John next." In a little while, sure enough, John Gregory's coffin was put off the train, as Billy Morris's had been, and I regarded her as a woman gifted with prophecy. Other coffins, too, were put off from time to time. About the war there could no longer be a doubt. And, a little later, its realities and horrors came nearer home to us, with swift, deep experiences.

One day my father took me to the camp and parade ground ten miles away, near the capital. The General and the Governor sat on horses and the soldiers marched by them and the band played. They were going to "the front." There surely must be a war at the front, I told Sam that night.

Still more coffins were brought home, too, as the months and the years passed; and the women of the neighbourhood used to come and spend whole days with my mother, sewing for the soldiers. So precious became woollen cloth that every rag was saved and the threads were unravelled to be spun and woven into new fabrics. And they baked bread and roasted chickens and sheep and pigs and made cakes, all to go to the soldiers at the front.

My father had not gone into the army. He was a "Union man" and he did not believe in secession. I remember having heard him once call it a "foolish enterprise." But he could not escape the service of the Confederate Government, if he had wished; and, although he opposed the war, he did not wish to be regarded by his neighbours as a "traitor." The Government needed the whole product of his little cotton mill, and of a thousand more which did not exist. He was, therefore, "detailed" to run the mill at its utmost capacity and to give its product to the Government. He received pay for it, of course, in Confederate money; and, when the war ended, there were thousands of dollars of these bills in the house. My mother made screens of one-hundred-dollar bills for the fireplaces in summer.

I once asked her, years afterwards, why my father did not buy something that was imperishable with all this money, while it had a certain value—land, for instance.

"Your father would have regarded it as dishonourable to use money in this way which he knew would lose its value; for this would have been taking advantage of the delusion of his neighbours."

Thus the thread that the little mill spun went to the making of clothes for soldiers and bandages for the wounded—mitigated human suffering somewhat, it is now pleasant to think; and thus it happened that my father was at home when the noise of cannon came. It was in the first soft days of spring. There was a battle at Marlborough, they said. Would they fight here, too? The slaves were terror-stricken. What was going to happen to them? Would they be carried off and shot? Old Aunt Maria, the cook, shouted throughout the day:

"Dey say dat de niggers'll be free. I ain't gwine ter have none o' deir freedom, I ain't. May de good Lord carry me erway in er chariut o' fire."

Officers in gray came to the house all day and all night and all the next day. Their horses pawed the lawn and ate the bark from the mimosa trees. Coming and going, asking for food and drink, all talked loudly, their swords clanking, and big pistols hung from their saddles.

Colonel Caldwell, my father's old friend, was one of these officers; and he and my father sat by the fire a long time that night talking in sad excitement. My mother in after years recalled their conversation to me.

My father said that the war ought immediately to be ended, that our army ought to give up, that there was no chance of success, and that no more men ought to be killed.

"True, true," said Colonel Caldwell, "but they are invading our homes. They are despoiling and starving the innocent. Shall we tamely submit? Shall we be cowards? Your own home, Worth, may be plundered before another night."

"As for me," he went on, "even if I were relieved of my command on this line of retreat, I should not dare be found at home when they come. That would mean death or capture. God knows what will become of my family. My wife expects me to call at home to-morrow to tell her what to do. I can but ride by and go on."

"Sacrificing more men," said my father, "every cruel day."

"Men!" exclaimed the Colonel. "What of it? So long as the conflict goes on, we cannot regard the life of a soldier. Its very cheapness is the basis of all war. We have become used to death. It is better than to go to starve in prison. If I must die, let me die fighting."

"But, after that, what?" my father asked. "Even if we could win, the country is dead. That is the thought that troubles me—the coming anarchy."

Then the roll of musketry was heard down the road.

"God save you, Caldwell"; and the Colonel and his companions rushed to their waiting horses and rode away in the moonlight.

We now all lived in my mother's room. I remember that my father sat by the fire with his face buried in his hands. The bed had been taken from the bedstead and put on the floor, because the floor, being below the windows, was a safer place from bullets. I was lying on it, my brother Charles beside me, and my mother held the baby in her arms.

I had feverishly heard all that had been said; and it seemed to me that the end of the world was about to come. The earth rolled toward me. In a moment it would crush us all. Then, as I held my breath, the great globe became light as air and floated away. The feverish dream came again and I cried out. My mother caressed me. Then she took the baby again and sat at the fire by my father, with one hand on his knee.

And soon after daylight the blue-coated cavalry of the "Yankees" came down the road. They had a little cannon on a horse and they put it on the high ground behind our garden and shot a ball clean through John Root's shanty, far down the road. John's old mother believed the rest of her days that when it struck the house she was killed and went to heaven. She met her husband there, and he told her that they had plenty of rations in the army of the Lord and that they slept in houses with gold window sashes. He had been a carpenter.

And that night the Union officers occupied my father's house. A colonel made his headquarters in the parlor, and he appropriated two bedrooms upstairs. But a good deal of work had to be done during the afternoon to make them comfortable for him; for, before he came, looting cavalrymen of his regiment had run their swords through the beds, looking for hidden silver; and the hearth had been torn up on the same quest. I saw one soldier who had three silver pitchers hanging from his saddle.

Old George, a lame slave, a simple old man, hovered during the day about the back porch, to be near the white people, and a Union soldier thrust a pistol in his face.

"Say, old man, tell it quick or I'll blow your head off—where is everything hidden here?"

Old George fell on his knees.

"'Fore God, Marster, don' shoot a poo' old nigger—your 'umble sarvant"; and, in an ashamed, frightened way, he led the "bummer" up the back stairs to the place in the ceiled wall through which many things had been put into the garret of the "ell." The soldiers broke into this hiding place and found food, and little else. In their chagrin they brought out sacks of flour, cut the bags and emptied it on the floor through the bedrooms and down the stairs. Thus the Colonel walked to his bayonetted bed up a stairway strewn and packed with flour, and slept in a room where the bricks that had been torn from the hearth were piled to right and left.

I slept that night on a trundle bed by my mother's, for her room was the only room left for the family, and we had all lived there since the day before. The dining room and the kitchen were now superfluous, because there was nothing more to cook or to eat.

An army corps built its camp-fires under the great oaks and cut their emblems on their trunks, where you may see them to this day; and, while they were there, the news came one day that Lincoln had been killed. I heard my father and the Union General talking about it; and, so solemn was their manner, I remember it clearly. The news that somebody had been killed had become so common that more than the usual solemnity was required to impress any particular death on the mind.

A week or more after the army corps had gone, I drove with my father to the capital one day, and almost every mile of the journey we saw a blue coat or a gray coat lying by the road, with bones or hair protruding—the unburied and forgotten of either army.

Thus I had come to know what war was, and death by violence was among the first deep impressions made on my mind. My emotions must have been violently dealt with and my sensibilities blunted—or sharpened? Who shall say? The wounded and the starved straggled home from hospitals and from prisons. There was old Mr. Sanford, the shoemaker, come back again, with a body so thin and a step so uncertain that I expected to see him fall to pieces. Mr. Larkin and Joe Tatum went on crutches; and I saw a man at the post-office one day whose cheek and ear had been torn away by a shell. Even when Sam and I sat on the river-bank fishing, and ought to have been silent lest the fish swim away, we told over in low tones the stories that we had heard of wounds and of deaths and of battles.

But there was the cheerful gentleness of my mother to draw my thoughts to different things. I can even now recall many special little plans that she made to keep my mind from battles. She hid the military cap that I had worn. She bought from me my military buttons and put them away. She would call me in and tell me pleasant stories of her own childhood. She would put down her work to make puzzles with me, and she read gentle books to me and kept away from me all the stories of the war and of death that she could. Whatever hardships befell her (and they must have been many) she kept a tender manner of resignation and of cheerful patience. There was a time—how long I do not know—while Aunt Maria was wan-

dering about looking for the "freedom" for which she had
said she did not care, when my mother did the cooking for the
family; and I remember to have seen her many times in the
wash-house scrubbing our clothes.

I have often wondered, and no doubt you have, too, at the
deficiencies of the narratives that we call history; for, although
they tell of what men did with governments and with armies,
they forget the pathetic lack of tender experiences that has
ever fallen to war-shortened childhood, and the childlessness
of women who never had mates because the men who would
have wed them fell in battle in their youth. In histories of this
very war I have read boasts about the number of men who
perished from a single State!

After a while the neighbourhood came to life again. There
were more widows, more sonless mothers, more empty sleeves
and wooden legs than anybody there had ever seen before. But
the mimosa bloomed, the cotton was planted again, and the
peach trees blossomed; and the barnyard and the stable again
became full of life. For, when the army marched away, they,
too, were as silent as an old battlefield. The last hen had been
caught under the corn-crib by a "Yankee" soldier, who had
torn his coat in this brave raid. Aunt Maria told Sam that all
Yankees were chicken thieves whether they "brung freedom
or no."

The little cotton mill was again started, for I must tell you,
in the very beginning, that the river ever ran and the mill kept
turning; and I should be ungrateful if I allowed you to forget
that on every year, whose events will be told in this book, the
cotton bloomed and ripened and opened white to the sun; for
the ripening of the cotton and the running of the river and the
turning of the mills make the thread not of my story only but
of the story of our Southern land—of its institutions, of its
misfortunes and of its place in the economy of the world; and
they will make the main threads of its story, I am sure, so long
as the sun shines on our white fields and the rivers run—a
story that is now rushing swiftly into a happier narrative of a
broader day.

The same women who had guided the spindles of war-time were again at their tasks—they at least were left; but the machinery was now old and worked ill. Negro men, who had wandered a while looking for an invisible "freedom," came back and went to work on the farm from force of habit. They now received wages and bought their own food. That was the only apparent difference that freedom had brought them.

My Aunt Katherine came from the city for a visit, my Cousin Margaret with her. Through the orchard, out into the newly ploughed ground beyond, back over the lawn which was itself bravely repairing the hurt done by horses' hoofs and tent-poles, and under the oaks, which bore the scars of camp-fires, we two romped and played gentler games than camp and battle. One afternoon, as our mothers sat on the piazza and saw us come loaded with apple-blossoms, they said something (so I afterward learned) about the eternal blooming of childhood and of nature—how sweet the early summer was in spite of the harrying of the land by war; for our gorgeous pageant of the seasons came on as if the earth had been the home of unbroken peace.

Chapter III. *Two Backgrounds of My Life*

Now, if you would clearly understand the story that I am to tell, and the confused vision and the groping through the mist (for this was a dark time of our country for youth to find its way) you must know the background of my life. What a medley of experiences go to the making of a man! Therefore, I say that, if you wish to get the key to my story, you must remember that an autobiography is like a gentleman in this—that it begins with a grandfather. And, as for me, it is surely true that my grandfather was the beginning of me.

He was Nicholas Worth, for whom first my father was named, and then I. He was yet hale at a very old age. He lived at the Old Place a few miles from the state capital (the capital city, we called it), and he had lived there all his long life, in the very house where he was born. It had received additions first on one side, then on another, and a "new house," itself now

fifty years old, had been built and the two houses were connected by a porch. The Old Place and the old man antedated
the State and, of course, the capital itself.

The story was untrue that he had been a drummer-boy in the
Revolutionary war, for he was not born in time. But his father
served under General Washington; and, after the war, he came
from an older colonial settlement into this wilderness, as it was
then, where good land could be had for the taking; and thus
the Old Place came to be built by Revolutionary hands.

And it was a real piece of the past. Later wars, even this
most desperate latest war between the states, had seemed to
touch it only lightly. True, two sons of the house had been
killed; but even this ghastly experience had not changed the
historic relations of the place nor of the man. They seemed to
belong to the century before. The Old Place was the oldest
house in the region, the old man was the ruling patriarch, and
the traditions and the flavour and the manner of the old times
clung so firmly to both that intervening events, even tragedies,
were easily forgotten. Besides, every family had lost sons in
this war, and the loss of sons conferred no special distinction.

And the old man had done his thinking before the period of
secession. He used both idioms and premises that had long gone
out of fashion. He regarded the war as an error. He had lived
through it as a good sailor goes through a storm. However
strong the wind may blow, he knows that, when it passes, the
sea will be calm again. The old man was too old, as I was too
young, to take part in the thought or in the fighting of the
time. We, at least, had been saved from danger to body and
from the worst distortions of mind. If his thought had for a
time been interrupted, he had taken it up where he had left it
off, as a man becomes himself again after a bad dream.

As every lucky child has a Great Place to go to, the Old
Place served this gracious use for me. It was ten miles away
from my father's home, and the drives between them had been
my chief journeyings. The Old Place was the background of
my life, therefore, a sort of home back of my own home. The
visits that I had made there were the happiest times of my

childhood, for I felt that all things were stable there. The mellowness of the place, the ripened wisdom of the old man, the cool quiet of the library were parts of the foundation of things; the garden with box-hedges and beds of sage and thyme and a row of fig trees by the fence—the odours of these have made my memory of the place savoury and pleasing through whatever barren stretches I have traveled in any period of my life. Plenty and Welcome, too, had their abode there, even during the days of severest privation.

The slave quarters were still kept, most of them, by the same families of Negroes that had lived there in bondage. My grandfather's especial servant, Uncle Ephraim, had not been away in search of freedom at all, for no one could think of the old master without Ephraim, nor of Ephraim without his old master. They had for a long generation been the embodied wisdom for big house and quarters. Each had the habit of talking to the other even when the other was out of hearing. When my grandfather would rouse himself from a nap on the piazza, he would ask, "What d'you think of that, Ephraim?" even if Ephraim were a mile away; and Ephraim used to mutter to himself, as he walked alone to the stable or to his cabin, "Yes, old marster, I 'grees wid yer."

It was our habit to visit the old man before any important enterprise was undertaken; and now the time was come when I was to go to the famous Graham boarding-school, and I went to bid him good-bye.

This was the school where the sons of generals and of colonels and of other gentlemen were trained under military discipline, made severer now by the grim memory of Stonewall Jackson, under whom Colonel Graham had served and whose spirit he revered as his knights their lord, King Arthur.

I found my grandfather eager to discover my expectations and ambitions, and he asked me many questions, making smiling test of my readiness to answer difficult ones.

For the saddest and vividest of reasons, even the little incidents of that particular day, stay in my memory yet. I recall my grandfather's manner when he asked:

"My son, do you write a fair script?"

I sat down at his secretary and wrote a line for him that I recalled from a copy-book and I wrote my name under it— "Nich's Worth III."

"Not that way," said he, and he took his quill and wrote "Nicholas Worth."

"Spell it out." His "script" was like George Washington's, now become a little tremulous, but still strong and clear.

Write fair script, sit your horse erect, do not pull the trigger till your aim is clear—these were maxims that fixed themselves in my mind that day. For he had me mount my horse and ride for him; and, when one of my cousins and I shot at a target behind the garden, he walked there to see how well we did it.

After an early supper I bade my grandfather "far'well" (he always said far'well); and he reminded me that some day I should be the head of the family.

"Dat's so," said Uncle Ephraim, "for Mars' Nick, he is de ol'est, and Mars' Littlenick is de ol'est in de line."

"Far'well, my son; I shall hear good reports of you—be sure. Far'well."

"Mars' Littlenick gwine t' sen' good 'ports, you be boun', ol' Marster. He's de smartest of 'em all. He ain't done name' fur you and Mars' Nick bof, fur nothin'."

My aunt Eliza, who had been the mistress of the Old Place since my grandmother's death, wished me a safe ride home, and Uncle Ephraim assured me that the moon would not go down till midnight. "Mighty good night for 'possums," he remarked; and I rode home in the cool of the evening. Most of the road lay through woodland. The cabins that stood here and there were lighted chiefly by pine knots, which gave a cheerful glow, and a fice now and then ran out and barked till I was beyond its hearing. Now and then, too, a hog would run from a fence corner with a sudden grunt which startled me to tighten my grip on the reins.

It was a beautiful night with moonlight shadows of the pines across the road and with dense, dark places here and there through which I galloped. It is just as well to pass deep shadows as fast as you can—not from fear, of course, but because we are children of light.

The night and the earth and the pine forest—when you come in direct contact with all these at once, you feel yourself akin to fundamental things, especially if you are a boy and your alert imagination is quickened by every sound and perfume. And you will carry the odour of the earth and of the trees in your memory at whatever distance you may live from them and however many years thereafter. Go into the woods at night now, if you are old, and you will be likely to recall a road and a wood that gave forth the same odours half a century ago; and you may even conjure up some particular night and recall with distinctness all that happened then. You may call back old friends that you had half forgotten; for the memory of those whose childhood was spent on the soil likes to make its return circuit on the ground.

And so I rode on, over the bridge beside which the mill-dam roared, then up the steep hill, and at last I came into the main road. I quickened my pace for fear my mother might be uneasy about me, and in a little while I was near the public well by old Jonas Good'in's. As I galloped around the short turn in the road there, my horse snorted and stopped and began to rear. In front of me was a company of horsemen in white, with white cloths over their horses—a little army of them, it seemed to me. I coaxed my horse nearer.

"Ku-Klux," said I to myself. Although my pulse beat somewhat more quickly, I knew that they would do no harm to me if I rode on. Besides, why should I run?

A deep-voiced member of the clan dismounted and said:

"Your horse don't like us, young fellow. Has he been doin' any deviltry?" And he led him along by the bridle.

There was a Negro man drawing water at the well with all his might, and a group of white, masked figures stood about him.

"I want a hundred more gallons to fill me up," said one of them. "It was hot in hell to-day and I got thirsty. Hurry up, old man."

"Say, young fellow, do you know of any niggers that need attention?" another gruff voice asked. My horse by this time had passed the group and ran as if the whole clan were chasing us.

I fear to omit this unexciting single experience of my life with the Ku-Klux Klan; for my whole story might be discredited if I had no encounter with them at all. And many a time these many years I have had occasion to think of the romances and the political tracts and the political speeches that abler men than I would have made out of even this encounter. But a truthful record like this can make nothing more of the incident than the report, which was spread the next day, that they flogged an old Negro in the neighbourhood whom they frightened into a confession of having stolen a pig. I can only express regret that it was not at least a mule that he had stolen, so that my own adventure with them might thereby have a greater dignity. . . .

Chapter IV. *The Flower of the South*

The son of a general, if he were at all a decent fellow, had, of course, a higher social rank among the boys at the Graham School than the son of a colonel. There was some difficulty in deciding the exact rank of a judge or of a governor, as a father; but the son of a preacher had a fair chance of a good social rating, especially of an Episcopalian clergyman. A Presbyterian preacher came next in rank.

I was at first at a social disadvantage. My father had been a Methodist—that was bad enough; but he had had no military title at all. If it had become known among the boys that he had been a "Union man"—I used to shudder at the suspicion in which I should be held. And the fact that my father had had no military title did at last become known; and one day Tom Warren, a boy from the "capital city," twitted me with this unpleasing fact. In a moment or two, we were clinched in a hand-to-hand fight. Of course a crowd gathered, and presently Colonel Graham himself appeared.

"Stand back and see it done fairly," said he, and the boys made the circle wider.

"What is it about?"

"He called me a liar, sir," said Tom.

"Well, no gentleman will take that," said the Colonel.

"I didn't call him a liar, but I do now, and I'll choke him, too," and I made a grasp at Tom's throat, and we were again a whirling mass of swinging arms and dodging heads.

"Halt!" Instantly we stood and saluted. My collar was torn and my face was bleeding from Tom's scratches. But we stood erect in silence.

"Sir," said I.

"Speak."

"He cast reflections on my family, sir."

"What have you to say, Tom?"

"I said, sir, that his father was not in the war."

"He said my father was a coward, sir."

Some boy in the crowd cried out, "I'd fight at that."

"Halt!" cried the Colonel, and we kept from clinching again and again we stood erect, each quivering with anger.

"I see you'll have to fight it out," said the Colonel in a moment, "before you feel better. Square off. Give them room."

Then the fight began again. After we had scratched and pounded one another and torn one another's clothes, I at last threw Tom, and the Colonel called out, "Halt!"

We were on our feet in a second. Each saluted. We were commanded to shake hands. The Colonel explained to the crowd in a sort of oratorical fashion that he had known Mr. Worth, that he had given his time and fortune to his country, and that there was no better man in any part of the Government's service. The incident was over. The crowd of boys went away. The Colonel went back to his office smiling. I was unspeakably grateful to him.

At his office, which was a wooden shanty at one end of the barracks, the Colonel renewed his conversation with a gentleman who had come to plead for his son's reinstatement in the school.

"I cannot tell you, sir," he said, "how deeply I am grieved.

But I cannot argue the subject. In fact, I have no power to reinstate your son. I could not keep the honour of the school— I could not even keep the boys, if he were to return. They would appeal to their parents and most of them would be called home. They are the flower of the South, sir."

This boy had cheated on an examination and had been sent home by the first train after his conviction.

That night, a half hour before taps, when my three room-mates were absent, one of my best friends came into my room.

"Worth," he asked, "wasn't your father a colonel?"

"No, but he was in the service of the Confederate Government and he wasn't a coward."

"I didn't mean that he was a coward. But I want to tell you something," and he went on in the sad tone in which we speak of great misfortunes. "You won't tell anybody, Worth, will you? My father—my father isn't a colonel nor nothin'. But I swear he isn't a coward. I saw him whip a man once. Worth, don't you ever tell anybody—he's a good father to me"; and the boy had a sob in his voice. When another fellow came into the room, he warmly shook my hand—since, as he saw it, we had a common misfortune—and he went away.

The rough beds were turned down from their edges whereon they rested all day against the wall of the log room, the poles were drawn that held the blankets and the mattresses in place; and we four room-mates went to bed. Taps were sounded; all lights were out; and the day of my first fight with Tom Warren was done.

The boys said that I had shown my mettle; among my friends I had a day or two of some little glory; and at the beginning of my second year I was made an officer of the battalion, and only "brave" boys were chosen as officers.

Lest you should imagine (and thereby, too, fall into a grave error) that fighting was the only manly art cultivated at the Graham school, you must be informed that, between military exercises, successful onslaughts were made on Latin and mathematics. The master's educational code contained three laws:

A boy must have a sound body, and the more roughly you

use him the sounder his body will become and the greater his physical bravery.

A boy must know Latin or he cannot be a gentleman.

A boy must know mathematics or his mind will not be trained.

And the years swiftly passed at these barracked labours, as the years pass swiftly elsewhere at that time of life. Our forced growth—for we had reached the emotional level of manhood while we were yet boys—gave us rapid development. . . .

JAMES LANE ALLEN

James Lane Allen was born on a farm near Lexington, Kentucky, on December 21, 1849, and died in New York on February 18, 1925. He was the seventh and youngest child of Richard and Helen Foster Allen. The Allens were of Virginian ancestry and had lived for three generations in Kentucky as gentleman farmers, but without slaves. The mother, however, was the dominating influence in his career, arousing his interests in books and nature. The youth toiled on the farm and secured an education under financial difficulties. His own childhood memories and the stories of neighbors recalled the happier ante-bellum days of aristocracy and chivalry. Like that by Thomas Nelson Page his early fiction glorified an idealized plantation life. After attending a preparatory school in Lexington, he entered in 1868 Transylvania College, now Kentucky University. Upon his graduation in 1872 he delivered the salutary address in Latin. For twelve years he was a teacher in preparatory schools and colleges. In 1873–1874 he was instructor of Greek and mathematics in Richmond College, Missouri, and in 1880–1883 he was professor of Latin at Bethany College, Bethany, West Virginia. From 1883 until his death he lived in New York, with frequent sojourns in Lexington and with several trips to Europe. Even as an aging man he continued his lifelong regime of study and careful writing. He was never married.

Always a great reader, he sought out the current French and British literature, which seemed to reach the trans-Appalachian region rather promptly. George Eliot's and Hardy's novels influenced his literary style and theory of fiction. Darwin and Huxley brought him the new science.

His early writings were reviews, stories, and poems, published in *Harper's Magazine*, *Century Magazine*, and other periodicals, which rapidly brought him some reputation. Literary success came in 1891 with the publication of *Flute and Violin and Other Kentucky Tales*, a collection of tales previously published in periodicals. Besides "Flute and Violin," a sentimental story of the Reverend James Moore and the lame boy David, the "other" tales are "King Solomon of Kentucky," the story of a vagabond; "Two Gentlemen of Kentucky," of the tender attachment of a master and slave; "The White Cowl," in which a monk is torn between his vows and his passion for a woman; "Sister Dolorosa," the tragic love of a nun for a young man; and "Posthumous Fame; or a Legend of the Beautiful," an allegory. This was followed by *The Blue Grass Region of Kentucky, and Other Kentucky Articles* (1892), a collection of essays from magazines. In the same year *Lippincott's Magazine* published *John Gray*, which was issued the next year in book form. This is a romantic tale of the love of a Kentucky schoolmaster for a pretty but shallow girl who marries another man. A better and more successful romance is *A Kentucky Cardinal* (1894), an idyl of provincial life, with colorful nature passages. Influenced by Hardy, he turned from the "Genteel Tradition" and the Cult of the Gentleman in writing "Butterflies: A Tale of Nature," first appearing in *The Cosmopolitan Magazine*, 1895–1896, and published as the book, *Summer in Arcady: A Tale of Nature* (1896), a surprisingly bold story of boy and girl passion. *The Choir Invisible* (1897), an enlargement of *John Gray*, has won both the approbation and scorn of critics, but it was one of the best sellers of the last decade of the century and brought Allen popular and financial success. *The Reign of Law: A Tale of the Kentucky Hemp Fields* (1900) is technically well-written, but its liberal thesis of the conflict between science and religion brought protests, of which the most vigorous was by President McGarvey of the University of Kentucky. *The Mettle of the Pasture* (1903) is a realistic novel dealing with the question of the "double standard." Still studying science, and later anthropology, he wrote two symbolic tales of an incompleted Christmas trilogy: *The Bride of the Mistletoe* (1909) and *The Doctor's Christmas Eve* (1910). Deeply offended by the severities of critics and the neglect by readers, he went back to writing romances, but his volumes from 1912 to the posthumous *The Landmark* (1925) are comparatively unimportant. Thus he swung full circle, from idealistic romance, to Hardy-like realism, to Maeterlinck symbolism, and to the idealism of the old days of Kentucky.

From THE REIGN OF LAW

I

The century just past had not begun the race of its many-footed years when a neighborhood of Kentucky pioneers, settled throughout the green valleys of the silvery Elkhorn, built a church in the wilderness, and constituted themselves a worshipping association. For some time peace of one sort prevailed among them, if no peace of any other sort was procurable around. But by and by there arose sectarian quarrels with other backwoods folk who also wished to worship God in Kentucky, and hot personal disputes among the members—as is the eternal law. So that the church grew as grow infusorians and certain worms,—by fissure, by periodical splittings and breakings to pieces, each spontaneous division becoming a new organism. The first church, however, for all that it split off and cast off, seemed to lose nothing of its vitality or fighting qualities spiritual and physical (the strenuous life in those days!); and there came a time when it took offence at one particular man in its membership on account of the liberality of his religious opinions. This settler, an old Indian fighter whose vast estate lay about halfway between the church and the nearest village, had built himself a good brick house in the Virginian style; and it was his pleasure and his custom to ask travelling preachers to rest under his roof as they rode hither and thither throughout the wilderness—Zion's weather-beaten, solitary scouts.

While giving entertainment to man and beast, if a Sunday came round, he would further invite his guest, no matter what kind of faith the vessel held, if it only held any faith, to ride with him through the woods and preach to his brethren. This was the front of his offending. For since he seemed brother to men of every creed, they charged that he was no longer of *their* faith (the only true one). They considered his case, and notified him that it was their duty under God to expel him.

After the sermon one Sunday morning of summer the scene

took place. They had asked what he had to say, and silence had followed. Not far from the church doors the bright Elkhorn (now nearly dry) swept past in its stately shimmering flood. The rush of the water over the stopped mill-wheel, that earliest woodland music of civilization, sounded loud amid the suspense and the stillness.

He rose slowly from his seat on the bench in front of the pulpit—for he was a deacon—and turned squarely at them; speechless just then, for he was choking with rage.

"My brethren," he said at length slowly, for he would not speak until he had himself under control, "I think we all remember what it is to be persecuted for religion's sake. Long before we came together in Spottsylvania County, Virginia, and organized ourselves into a church and travelled as a church over the mountains into this wilderness, worshipping by the way, we knew what it was to be persecuted. Some of us were sent to jail for preaching the Gospel and kept there; we preached to the people through the bars of our dungeons. Mobs were collected outside to drown our voices; we preached the louder and some jeered, but some felt sorry and began to serve God. They burned matches and pods of red pepper to choke us; they hired strolls to beat drums that we might not be heard for the din. Some of us knew what it was to have live snakes thrown into our assemblages while at worship; or nests of live hornets. Or to have a crowd rush into the church with farming tools and whips and clubs. Or to see a gun levelled at one of us in the pulpit, and to be dispersed with firearms. Harder than any of these things to stand, we have known what it is to be slandered. But no single man of us, thank God, ever stopped for these things or for anything. Thirty years and more this lasted, until we and all such as we found a friend in Patrick Henry. Now, we hear that by statute all religious believers in Virginia have been made equal as respects the rights and favors of the law.

"But you know it was partly to escape intolerable tyranny that we left our mother country and travelled a path paved with suffering and lined with death into this wilderness. For in this virgin land we thought we should be free to worship God according to our consciences.

"Since we arrived you know what our life has been,—how we have fought and toiled and suffered all things together. You recall how lately it was that when we met in the woods for worship,—having no church and no seats,—we men listened and sang and prayed with our rifles on our shoulders."

He paused, for the memories hurt him cruelly.

"And now you notify me that you intend to expel me from this church as a man no longer fit to worship my Maker in your company. Do you bring any charge against my life, my conduct? None. Nothing but that, as a believer in the living God—whom honestly I try to serve according to my erring light—I can no longer have a seat among you—not believing as you believe. But this is the same tyranny that you found unendurable in Spottsylvania. You have begun it in Kentucky. You have been at it already how long? Well, my brethren, I'll soon end your tyranny over me. You need not *turn* me out. And I need not change my religious opinions. I will *go* out. But—"

He wheeled round to the rough pulpit on which lay the copy of the Bible that they had brought with them from Virginia, their Ark of the Covenant on the way, seized it, and faced them again. He strode toward the congregation as far as the benches would allow—not seeing clearly, for he was sightless with his tears.

"But," he roared, and as he spoke he struck the Bible repeatedly with his clenched fist, "by the Almighty, I will build a church of my own to Him! To Him! do you hear? not to your opinions of Him nor mine nor any man's! I will cut off a parcel of my farm and make a perpetual deed of it in the courts, to be held in trust forever. And while the earth stands, it shall stand, free to all Christian believers. I will build a school-house and a meeting-house, where any child may be free to learn and any man or woman free to worship."

He put the Bible back with shaking arms and turned on them again.

"As for you, my brethren," he said, his face purple and distorted with passion, "you may be saved in your crooked,
narrow way, if the mercy of God is able to do it. But you are
close to the jaws of Hell this day!"

He went over into a corner for his hat, took his wife by the
hand and held it tightly, gathered the flock of his children
before him, and drove them out of the church. He mounted
his horse, lifted his wife to her seat behind him, saw his children
loaded on two other horses, and, leading the way across the
creek, disappeared in the wilderness.

II

Some sixty-five years later, one hot day of midsummer in
1865—one Saturday afternoon—a lad was cutting weeds in a
woodland pasture; a big, raw-boned, demure boy of near
eighteen.

He had on heavy shoes, the toes green with grass stain; the
leather so seasoned by morning dews as to be like wood for
hardness. These were to keep his feet protected from briers or
from the bees scattered upon the wild white clover or from the
terrible hidden thorns of the honey-locust. No socks. A pair
of scant homespun trousers, long outgrown. A coarse clean
shirt. His big shock-head thatched with yellow straw, a
dilapidated sun-and-rain shed.

The lanky young giant cut and cut and cut; great purple-
bodied poke, strung with crimson-juiced seed; great burdock,
its green burrs a plague; great milkweed, its creamy sap gushing
at every gash; great thistles, thousand-nettled; great ironweed,
plumed with royal purple; now and then a straggling bramble
prone with velvety berries—the outpost of a patch behind him;
now and then—more carefully, lest he notch his blade—low
sprouts of wild cane, survivals of the impenetrable brakes of
pioneer days. All these and more, the rank, mighty measure of
the soil's fertility—low down.

Measure of its fertility aloft, the tops of the trees, from
which the call of the redheaded woodpecker sounded as faint as
the memory of a sound and the bark of the squirrels was elfin-

thin. A hot crowded land, crammed with undergrowth and overgrowth wherever a woodland stood; and around every woodland dense cornfields; or, denser still, the leagues of swaying hemp. The smell of this now lay heavy on the air, seeming to be dragged hither and thither like a slow scum on the breeze, like a moss on a sluggish pond. A deep robust land; and among its growths he—this lad, in his way a self-unconscious human weed, the seed of his kind borne in from far some generations back, but springing out of the soil naturally now, sap of its sap, strength of its strength.

He paused by and by and passed his forefinger across his forehead, brushing the sweat away from above his quiet eyes. He moistened the tip of his thumb and slid it along the blade of his hemp hook—he was using that for lack of a scythe. Turning, he walked back to the edge of the brier thicket, sat down in the shade of a black walnut, threw off his tattered headgear, and, reaching for his bucket of water covered with poke leaves, lifted it to his lips and drank deeply, gratefully. Then he drew a whetstone from his pocket, spat on it, and fell to sharpening his blade.

The heat of his work, the stifling air, the many-toned woods, the sense of the vast summering land—these things were not in his thoughts. Some days before, despatched from homestead to homestead, rumors had reached him away off here at work on his father's farm, of a great university to be opened the following autumn at Lexington. The like of it with its many colleges Kentucky, the South, the Mississippi valley had never seen. It had been the talk among the farming people in their harvest fields, at the cross-roads, on their porches—the one deep sensation among them since the war.

For solemn, heart-stirring as such tidings would have been at any other time, more so at this. Here, on the tableland of this unique border state, Kentucky—between the halves of the nation lately at strife—scene of their advancing and retreating armies—pit of a frenzied commonwealth—here was to arise this calm university, pledge of the new times, plea for the peace and amity of learning, fresh chance for study of the revelation of the Lord of Hosts and God of battles. The animosities were over, the humanities re-begun.

Can you remember your youth well enough to be able to recall the time when the great things happened for which you seemed to be waiting? The boy who is to be a soldier—one day he hears a distant bugle: at once *he* knows. A second glimpses a bellying sail: straightway the ocean path beckons to him. A third discovers a college, and toward its kingly lamps of learning turns young eyes that have been kindled and will stay kindled to the end.

For some years this particular lad, this obscure item in Nature's plan which always passes understanding, had been growing more unhappy in his place in creation. By temperament he was of a type the most joyous and self-reliant—those sure signs of health; and discontent now was due to the fact that he had outgrown his place. Parentage—a farm and its tasks— a country neighborhood and its narrowness—what more are these sometimes than a starting-point for a young life; as a flower-pot might serve to sprout an oak, and as the oak would inevitably reach the hour when it would either die or burst out, root and branch, into the whole heavens and the earth; as the shell and yolk of an egg are the starting-point for the wing and eye of the eagle. One thing only he had not outgrown, in one thing only he was not unhappy: his religious nature. This had always been in him as breath was in him, as blood was in him: it was his life. Dissatisfied now with his position in the world, it was this alone that kept him contented in himself. Often the religious are the weary; and perhaps nowhere else does a perpetual vision of Heaven so disclose itself to the weary as above lonely toiling fields. The lad had long been lifting his inner eye to this vision.

When, therefore, the tidings of the university with its Bible College reached him, whose outward mould was hardship, whose inner bliss was piety, at once they fitted his ear as the right sound, as the gladness of long awaited intelligence. It was bugle to the soldier, sail to the sailor, lamp of learning to the innate student. At once he knew that he was going to the university—sometime, somehow—and from that moment felt no more discontent, void, restlessness, nor longing.

It was of this university, then, that he was happily day-dreaming as he whetted his hemp hook in the depths of the woods that Saturday afternoon. Sitting low amid heat and weeds and thorns, he was already as one who had climbed above the earth's eternal snow-line and sees only white peaks and pinnacles—the last sublimities.

He felt impatient for to-morrow. One of the professors of the university, of the faculty of the Bible College, had been travelling over the state during the summer, pleading its cause before the people. He had come into that neighborhood to preach and to plead. The lad would be there to hear.

The church in which the professor was to plead for learning and religion was the one first set up in the Kentucky wilderness as a house of religious liberty; and the lad was a great-grand-child of the founder of that church, here emerging mysteriously from the deeps of life four generations down the line.

III

The church which David's grim old Indian-fighting great-grandfather had dedicated to freedom of belief in the wilderness, cutting off a parcel of his lands as he had hotly sworn and building on it a schoolhouse also, stood some miles distant across the country. The vast estate of the pioneer had been cut to pieces for his many sons. With the next generation the law of partible inheritance had further subdivided each of these; so that in David's time a single small farm was all that had fallen to his father; and his father had never increased it. The church was situated on what had been the opposite bound-ary of the original grant. But he with most of the other boys in the neighborhood had received his simple education in that school; and he had always gone to worship under that broad-minded roof, whatsoever the doctrines and dogmas haply preached.

These doctrines and dogmas of a truth were varied and con-flicting enough; for the different flocks and herds of Protestant believers with their parti-colored guides had for over fifty years found the place a very convenient strip of spiritual pasture: one congregation now grazing there jealously and exclusively; afterwards another.

On this quiet bright Sunday morning in the summer of 1865, the building (a better than the original one, which had long before been destroyed by accidental burning) was overcrowded with farming folk, husbands and wives, of all denominations in the neighborhood, eager to hear the new plea, the new pleader. David's father and mother, intense sectarians and dully pious souls, sat among them. He himself, on a rearmost bench, was wedged fast between two other lads of about his own age— they dumb with dread lest they should be sent away to this university.

The minister soon turned the course of his sermon to the one topic that was uppermost and bottommost in the minds of all.

He bade them understand now, if they had never realized it before, that from the entrance of educated men and women into the western wilderness, those real founders and builders of the great commonwealth, the dream of the Kentuckians had been the establishment of a broad, free institution of learning for their sons. He gave the history of the efforts and the failures to found such an institution, from the year 1780 to the beginning of the Civil War; next he showed how, during those few awful years, the slow precious accumulations of that preceding time had been scattered; books lost, apparatus ruined, the furniture of lecture rooms destroyed, one college building burned, another seized and held as a hospital by the federal government; and he concluded with painting for them a vision of the real university which was now to arise at last, oldest, best passion of the people, measure of the height and breadth of the better times: knowing no North, no South, no latitude, creed, bias, or political end. In speaking of its magnificent new endowments, he dwelt upon the share contributed by the liberal-minded farmers of the state, to some of whom he was speaking: showing how, forgetful of the disappointments and failures of their fathers, they had poured out money by the thousands and tens of thousands, as soon as the idea was presented to them again—the rearing of a great institution by the people and for the people in their own land for the training of their sons, that they might not be sent away to New England or to Europe.

His closing words were solemn indeed; they related to the college of the Bible, where his own labors were to be performed. For this, he declared, he pleaded not in the name of the new state, the new nation, but in the name of the Father. The work of this college was to be the preparation of young men for the Christian ministry, that they might go into all the world and preach the Gospel. One truth he bade them bear in mind: that this training was to be given without sectarian theology; that his brethren themselves represented a revolution among believers, having cast aside the dogmas of modern teachers, and taken, as the one infallible guide of their faith and practice, the Bible simply; so making it their sole work to bring all modern believers together into one church, and that one church the church of the apostles.

For this university, for this college of the Bible especially, he asked, then, the gift and consecration of their sons.

Toward dusk that day David's father and mother were sitting side by side on the steps of their front porch. Some neighbors who had spent the afternoon with them were just gone. The two were talking over in low, confidential tones certain subjects discussed less frankly with their guests. These related to the sermon of the morning, to the university, to what boys in the neighborhood would probably be entered as students. Their neighbors had asked whether David would go. The father and mother had exchanged quick glances and made no reply. Something in the father's mind now lay like wormwood on the lips.

He sat leaning his head on his hand, his eyes on the ground, brooding, embittered.

"If I had only had a son to have been proud of!" he muttered. "It's of no use; he wouldn't go. It isn't in him to take an education."

"No," said the mother, comforting him resignedly, after a pause in which she seemed to be surveying the boy's whole life; "it's of no use; there never was much in David."

"Then he shall work!" cried the father, striking his knee with clenched fist. "I'll see that he is kept at work."

Just then the lad came round from behind the house, walking rapidly. Since dinner he had been off somewhere, alone, having it out with himself, perhaps shrinking, most of all, from this first exposure to his parents. Such an ordeal is it for us to reveal what we really are to those who have known us longest and have never discovered us.

He walked quickly around and stood before them, pallid and shaking from head to foot.

"Father!"—

There was filial dutifulness in the voice, but what they had never heard from those lips—authority.

"I am going to the university, to the Bible College. It will be hard for you to spare me, I know, and I don't expect to go at once. But I shall begin my preparations, and as soon as it is possible I am going. I have felt that you and mother ought to know my decision at once."

As he stood before them in the dusk and saw on their countenances an incredible change of expression, he naturally mistook it, and spoke again with more authority.

"Don't say anything to me now, father! And don't oppose me when the time comes; it would be useless. Try to learn while I am getting ready to give your consent and to obtain mother's. That is all I have to say."

He turned quickly away and passed out of the yard gate toward the barn, for the evening feeding.

The father and mother followed his figure with their eyes, forgetting each other, as long as it remained in sight. If the flesh of their son had parted and dissolved away into nothingness, disclosing a hidden light within him like the evening star, shining close to their faces, they could scarce have been struck more speechless. But after a few moments they had adjusted themselves to this lofty annunciation. The mother, unmindful

of what she had just said, began to recall little incidents of the
lad's life to show that this was what he was always meant to be.
She loosened from her throat the breastpin containing the hair
of the three heads braided together, and drew her husband's
attention to it with a smile. He, too, disregarding his disparagement of the few minutes previous, now began to admit
with warmth how good a mind David had always had. He
prophesied that at college he would outstrip the other boys
from that neighborhood. This, in its way, was also fresh
happiness to him; for, smarting under his poverty among rich
neighbors, and fallen from the social rank to which he was
actually entitled, he now welcomed the secondary joy which
originates in the revenge men take upon each other through the
superiority of their children.

One thing both agreed in: that this explained their son. He
had certainly always needed an explanation. But no wonder;
he was to be a minister. And who had a right to understand a
minister? He was entitled to be peculiar. . . .

WILLIAM SYDNEY PORTER
(O. Henry)

William Sydney Porter, better known as "O. Henry," was born on September 11, 1862, in Greensboro, North Carolina, and died on June 5, 1910, in New York. He was christened William Sidney, which he changed to William Sydney in 1898. His father, Dr. Algernon Sidney Porter, was a highly esteemed physician, whose patients decreased in number with his absorption in a succession of impractical inventions. After the death of his mother, when he was three yers old, the boy was cared for by his aunt, Miss Evalina Porter, and later attended her private school. He read widely in fiction by British and American authors, and throughout life seemed capable of informing and educating himself by reading. His late afternoons and evenings were spent in the drugstore of his uncle, Clarke Porter, where he acquired enough knowledge of drugs to become a registered pharmacist. Having pictorial skill, the young clerk amused himself and his friends by drawing cartoons of the customers and loafers. These sketches were much enjoyed, and the reputation of the shy, reticent boy spread. Colonel William Bingham of the well-reputed Bingham School at Mebane, a few miles distant, offered him free tuition and board "in order to get use of his talent as a cartoonist for the amusement of our boys," but the youth could not accept this offer, for he had no money for uniform and books. The older citizens of Greensboro relate legends of Will Porter's life and lament that the newspapers too often print his name as O'Henry.

In 1881 he went out to Texas with Dr. and Mrs. J. K. Hall, on a visit to their sons of Texas-Ranger fame, who had performed daring exploits along the Mexican border. Dick, or Richard M. Hall, later rose to political importance in the state, serving as State Land Commissioner, and even running for governor. Lee, or "Red" Hall, was a Ranger of successful exploits against Comanches and desperadoes. Will Porter, a pale-faced boy, weighing about a hundred pounds, lived with Dick Hall in his log-cabin home in La Salle County, learned to ride and rope range-ponies, and to become an expert pistol

shot. There was spare time for some studying of French and
German and for learning to speak Spanish.

After this experience he went to Austin, where, after learning
bookkeeping, he worked as clerk and bookkeeper (1885–1887),
as draftsman in the Texas Land Office (1887–1891), and as
teller in the First National Bank (1891–1894). In 1887 he
married Athol Estes, a girl of seventeen, with whom, as Carl
Van Doren says, "he dashingly eloped." In 1894 he resigned
his bank position to give all his time to editing a humorous weekly, *The Rolling Stone*. Although he printed across
the full-page head, "OUT FOR THE MOSS," the periodical failed
within a year. While serving as reporter and columnist on the
Houston *Daily Post*, a shortage was belatedly discovered in
his account as teller of the Austin bank. C. Alphonso Smith
states that "he was summoned back to Austin to stand trial for
the alleged misappropriation of $1158.68. Had he gone [back]
he would certainly have been acquitted." Acting like a guilty
man, he fled to New Orleans and Honduras. A few months
later, learning that his wife was dying from tuberculosis, he returned to Austin and stood trial. In February, 1898, he was
convicted, and sent to the federal prison at Columbus, Ohio.
His five-year sentence was shortened to three years and three
months by good behavior and by his services as prison drug
clerk. Throughout the rest of his life Porter was trying to
conceal this incident from relatives, friends, and readers. His
daughter was over thirty years old before she knew about it.
He stated his birth as of 1867, instead as of 1862, thus wiping
out five years.

Porter wrote at least twelve stories in prison, publishing them
under various pseudonyms. The first story under the pen-
name of "O. Henry" was "Whistling Dick's Christmas Stocking," published in *McClure's Magazine* for December, 1899.
According to C. Alphonso Smith, Porter's pen-name of "O.
Henry" is a popular abbreviation of Etienne-Ossian Henry
(1798–1873), a distinguished French chemist, to whom there
are frequent references in *The United States Dispensatory*,
(14th edition, 1877), a common reference book in drugstores.
After his release from the Columbus prison, he stayed for a
short time in Pittsburgh, where he rejoined his daughter; then
he went to New York in 1902 upon the invitation of the editors
of *Ainslee's Magazine*. The eight-year residence in New York,

until his death in 1910, was marked by prolific story writing and rapidly acquired reputation. About one hundred and fifty stories appeared in New York newspapers and magazines, to be swiftly collected in books. The first of these volumes, *Cabbages and Kings* [1914], a collection of stories laid in Latin America, was followed by one or more volumes each year, also several posthumous volumes. In 1907 he married a friend of his North Carolina youth, Sarah Lindsay Coleman. He died at the Polyclinic Hospital, New York, and was buried at Asheville.

The real O. Henry, the elusive New York resident, with a few intimate friends, is difficult to understand, although these friends have written reminiscent sketches and even a biography. But there is a fictitious, legendary O. Henry who is very different from the real William Sydney Porter. In his bit of autobiographica, which he published in the *New York Times*, April 4, 1909, Porter himself contributed to this legend. George MacAdam expanded the autobiography and enlarged the legend, and one finds that some hasty literary historians have accepted many of the mythical incidents as true biography. Nor are the critics agreed regarding O. Henry's literary rank— even such students of the short story as C. Alfonso Smith, Carl Van Doren, and Fred Lewis Pattee. But he is worthy of a place in a volume of southern prose, for some of his best stories deal with the South. Even Professor Pattee admits that "A few times the glow of insight and sympathy hovers over the fifteen studies he made of his native South—by all means the best of his fiction." Nearly sixty tales deal with the Southwest, of which forty are placed in Texas. "Nevertheless," as Arthur B. Maurice writes, "the heart of O. Henry Land is here in the middle South. Often it is the spirit of the South that carries a story where the scene is elsewhere."

From OPTIONS

Thimble, Thimble

These are the directions for finding the office of Carteret & Carteret, Mill Supplies and Leather Belting:

You follow the Broadway trail down until you pass the Cross-town Line, the Bread Line, and the Dead Line, and come to the Big Cañons of the Moneygrubber Tribe. Then you turn to the left, to the right, dodge a push-cart and the tongue of a two-ton four-horse dray, and hop, skip, and jump to a granite ledge on the side of a twenty-one-story synthetic mountain of stone and iron. In the twelfth story is the office of Carteret & Carteret. The factory where they make the mill supplies and leather belting is in Brooklyn. Those commodities—to say nothing of Brooklyn—not being of interest to you, let us hold the incidents within the confines of a one-act, one-scene play, thereby lessening the toil of the reader and the expenditure of the publisher. So, if you have the courage to face four pages of type and Carteret & Carteret's office boy, Percival, you shall sit on a varnished chair in the inner office and peep at the little comedy of the Old Nigger Man, the Hunting-Case Watch, and the Open-Faced Question—mostly borrowed from the late Mr. Frank Stockton, as you will conclude.

First, biography (but pared to the quick) must intervene. I am for the inverted sugar-coated quinine pill—the bitter on the outside.

The Carterets were, or was (Columbia College professors please rule), an old Virginia family. Long time ago the gentlemen of the family had worn lace ruffles and carried tinless foils and owned plantations and had slaves to burn. But the war had greatly reduced their holdings. (Of course you can perceive at once that this flavor has been shoplifted from Mr. F. Hopkinson Smith, in spite of the "et" after "Carter.") Well, anyhow:

In digging up the Carteret history I shall not take you farther back than the year 1620. The two original American Carterets came over in that year, but by different means of transportation. One brother, named John, came in the *Mayflower* and became a Pilgrim Father. You've seen his picture on the covers of the Thanksgiving magazines, hunting turkeys in the deep snow with a blunderbuss. Blandford Carteret, the other brother, crossed the pond in his own brigantine, landed on the Virginia coast, and became an F. F. V. John became distinguished for piety and shrewdness in business; Blandford for his pride, juleps, marksmanship, and vast slave-cultivated plantations.

Then came the Civil War. (I must condense this historical interpolation.) Stonewall Jackson was shot; Lee surrendered; Grant toured the world; cotton went to nine cents; Old Crow whiskey and Jim Crow cars were invented; the Seventy-ninth Massachusetts Volunteers returned to the Ninety-seventh Alabama Zouaves the battle flag of Lundy's Lane which they bought at a second-hand store in Chelsea, kept by a man named Skzchnzski; Georgia sent the President a sixty-pound watermelon—and that brings us up to the time when the story begins. My! but that was sparring for an opening! I really must brush up on my Aristotle.

The Yankee Carterets went into business in New York long before the war. Their house, as far as Leather Belting and Mill Supplies was concerned, was as musty and arrogant and solid as one of those old East India tea-importing concerns that you read about in Dickens. There were some rumors of a war behind its counters, but not enough to affect the business.

During and after the war, Blandford Carteret, F. F. V., lost his plantations, juleps, markskmanship, and life. He bequeathed little more than his pride to his surviving family. So it came to pass that Blandford Carteret, the Fifth, aged fifteen, was invited by the leather-and-mill supplies branch of that name to come North and learn business instead of hunting foxes and boasting of the glory of his fathers on the reduced acres of his impoverished family. The boy jumped at the chance; and, at the age of twenty-five, sat in the office of the firm equal partner with John, the Fifth, of the blunderbuss-and-turkey branch. Here the story begins again.

The young men were about the same age, smooth of face, alert, easy of manner, and with an air that promised mental and physical quickness. They were razored, blue-serged, straw-hatted, and pearl stick-pinned like other young New Yorkers who might be millionaires or bill clerks.

One afternoon at four o'clock, in the private office of the firm, Blandford Carteret opened a letter that a clerk had just

brought to his desk.   After reading it, he chuckled audibly for
nearly a minute.   John looked around from his desk inquiringly.

"It's from mother," said Blandford.   "I'll read you the funny
part of it.   She tells me all the neighborhood news first, of
course, and then cautions me against getting my feet wet and
musical comedies.   After that come vital statistics about calves
and pigs and an estimate of the wheat crop.   And now I'll
quote some:

" 'And what do you think!   Old Uncle Jake, who was
seventy-six last Wednesday, must go travelling.   Nothing
would do but he must go to New York and see his "young
Marster Blandford."   Old as he is, he has a deal of common
sense, so I've let him go.   I couldn't refuse him—he seemed
to have concentrated all his hopes and desires into this one
adventure into the wide world.   You know he was born on
the plantation, and has never been ten miles away from it in
his life.   And he was your father's body servant during the war,
and has been always a faithful vassal and servant of the family.
He has often seen the gold watch—the watch that was your
father's and your father's father's.   I told him it was to be
yours, and he begged me to allow him to take it to you and to
put it into your hands himself.

" 'So he has it, carefully enclosed in a buckskin case, and is
bringing it to you with all the pride and importance of a king's
messenger.   I gave him money for the round trip and for a two
weeks' stay in the city.   I wish you would see to it that he
gets comfortable quarters—Jake won't need much looking after
—he's able to take care of himself.   But I have read in the
papers that African bishops and colored potentates generally
have much trouble in obtaining food and lodging in the Yankee
metropolis.   That may be all right; but I don't see why the
best hotel there shouldn't take Jake in.   Still, I suppose it's
a rule.

" 'I gave him full directions about finding you, and packed
his valise myself.   You won't have to bother with him; but I do
hope you'll see that he is made comfortable.   Take the watch
that he brings you—it's almost a decoration.   It has been worn

by true Carterets, and there isn't a stain upon it nor a false movement of the wheels. Bringing it to you is the crowning joy of old Jake's life. I wanted him to have that little outing and that happiness before it is too late. You have often heard us talk about how Jake, pretty badly wounded himself, crawled through the reddened grass at Chancellorsville to where your father lay with the bullet in his dear heart, and took the watch from his pocket to keep it from the "Yanks."

" 'So, my son, when the old man comes consider him as a frail but worthy messenger from the old-time life and home.

" 'You have been so long away from home and so long among the people that we have always regarded as aliens that I'm not sure that Jake will know you when he sees you. But Jake has a keen perception, and I rather believe that he will know a Virginia Carteret at sight. I can't conceive that even ten years in Yankeeland could change a boy of mine. Anyhow, I'm sure you will know Jake. I put eighteen collars in his valise. If he should have to buy others, he wears a number $15\frac{1}{2}$. Please see that he gets the right ones. He will be no trouble to you at all.

" 'If you are not too busy, I'd like for you to find him a place to board where they have white-meal corn-bread, and try to keep him from taking his shoes off in your office or on the street. His right foot swells a little, and he likes to be comfortable.

" 'If you can spare the time, count his handkerchiefs when they come back from the wash. I bought him a dozen new ones before he left. He should be there about the time this letter reaches you. I told him to go straight to your office when he arrives.' "

As soon as Blandford had finished the reading of this, something happened (as there should happen in stories and must happen on the stage).

Percival, the office boy, with his air of despising the world's output of mill supplies and leather belting, came in to announce that a colored gentleman was outside to see Mr. Blandford Carteret.

"Bring him in," said Blandford, rising.

John Carteret swung around in his chair and said to Percival: "Ask him to wait a few minutes outside. We'll let you know when to bring him in."

Then he turned to his cousin with one of those broad, slow smiles that was an inheritance of all the Carterets, and said:

"Bland, I've always had a consuming curiosity to understand the differences that you haughty Southerners believe to exist between 'you all' and the people of the North. Of course, I know that you consider yourselves made out of finer clay and look upon Adam as only a collateral branch of your ancestry; but I don't know why. I never could understand the differences between us."

"Well, John," said Blandford, laughing, "what you don't understand about it is just the difference, of course. I suppose it was the feudal way in which we lived that gave us our lordly baronial airs and feeling of superiority."

"But you are not feudal, now," went on John. "Since we licked you and stole your cotton and mules you've had to go to work just as we 'damyankees,' as you call us, have always been doing. And you're just as proud and exclusive and upper-classy as you were before the war. So it wasn't your money that caused it."

"Maybe it was the climate," said Blandford, lightly, "or maybe our negroes spoiled us. I'll call old Jake in, now. I'll be glad to see the old villain again."

"Wait just a moment," said John. "I've got a little theory I want to test. You and I are pretty much alike in our general appearance. Old Jake hasn't seen you since you were fifteen. Let's have him in and play fair and see which of us gets the watch. The old darky surely ought to be able to pick out his 'young marster' without any trouble. The alleged aristocratic superiority of a 'reb' ought to be visible to him at once. He couldn't make the mistake of handing over the timepiece to a Yankee, of course. The loser buys the dinner this evening and two dozen 15½ collars for Jake. Is it a go?"

Blandford agreed heartily. Percival was summoned, and told to usher the "colored gentleman" in.

Uncle Jake stepped inside the private office cautiously. He was a little old man, as black as soot, wrinkled and bald except for a fringe of white wool, cut decorously short, that ran over his ears and around his head. There was nothing of the stage "uncle" about him: his black suit nearly fitted him; his shoes shone, and his straw hat was banded with a gaudy ribbon. In his right hand he carried something carefully concealed by his closed fingers.

Uncle Jake stopped a few steps from the door. Two young men sat in their revolving desk-chairs ten feet apart and looked at him in friendly silence. His gaze slowly shifted many times from one to the other. He felt sure that he was in the presence of one, at least, of the revered family among whose fortunes his life had begun and was to end.

One had the pleasing but haughty Carteret air; the other had the unmistakable straight, long family nose. Both had the keen black eyes, horizontal brows, and thin, smiling lips that had distinguished both the Carteret of the *Mayflower* and him of the brigantine. Old Jake had thought that he could have picked out his young master instantly from a thousand Northerners; but he found himself in difficulties. The best he could do was to use strategy.

"Howdy, Marse Blandford—howdy, suh?" he said, looking midway between the two young men.

"Howdy, Uncle Jake?" they both answered pleasantly and in unison. "Sit down. Have you brought the watch?"

Uncle Jake chose a hard-bottom chair at a respectful distance, sat on the edge of it, and laid his hat carefully on the floor. The watch in its buckskin case he gripped tightly. He had not risked his life on the battlefield to rescue that watch from his "old marster's" foes to hand it over again to the enemy without a struggle.

"Yes, suh; I got it in my hand, suh. I'm gwine give it to you right away in jus' a minute. Old Missus told me to put it in young Marse Blandford's hand and tell him to wear it for the family pride and honor. It was a mighty longsome trip for an old nigger man to make—ten thousand miles, it must be, back to old Vi'ginia, suh. You've growed mightily, young marster. I wouldn't have reconnized you but for yo' powerful resemblance to the old marster."

With admirable diplomacy the old man kept his eyes roaming in the space between the two men. His words might have been addressed to either. Though neither wicked nor perverse, he was seeking for a sign.

Blandford and John exchanged winks.

"I reckon you done got you ma's letter," went on Uncle Jake. "She said she was gwine to write to you 'bout my comin' along up this er-way."

"Yes, yes, Uncle Jake," said John briskly. "My cousin and I have just been notified to expect you. We are both Carterets, you know."

"Although one of us," said Blandford, "was born and raised in the North."

"So if you will hand over the watch—" said John.

"My cousin and I—" said Blandford.

"Will then see to it—" said John.

"That comfortable quarters are found for you," said Blandford.

With creditable ingenuity, old Jake set up a cackling, high-pitched, protracted laugh. He beat his knee, picked up his hat and bent the brim in an apparent paroxysm of humorous appreciation. The seizure afforded him a mask behind which he could roll his eye impartially between, above, and beyond his two tormentors.

"I sees what!" he chuckled, after a while. "You gen'lemen is tryin' to have fun with the po' old nigger. But you can't fool old Jake. I knowed you, Marse Blandford, the minute I sot eyes on you. You was a po' skimpy little boy no mo' than about fo'teen when you lef' home to come No'th; but I knowed you the minute I sot eyes on you. You is the mawtal image of old marster. The other gen'leman resembles you mightily, suh; but you can't fool old Jake on a member of the old Vi'ginia family. No suh."

At exactly the same time both Carterets smiled and extended a hand for the watch.

Uncle Jake's wrinkled, black face lost the expression of amusement into which he had vainly twisted it. He knew that he was being teased, and that it made little real difference, as far as its safety went, into which of those outstretched hands he placed the family treasure. But it seemed to him that not only his own pride and loyalty but much of the Virginia Carterets' was at stake. He had heard down South during the war about that other branch of the family that lived in the North and fought on "the yuther side," and it had always grieved him. He had followed his "old marster's" fortunes from stately luxury through war to almost poverty. And now, with the last relic and reminder of him, blessed by "old missus," and entrusted implicitly to his care, he had come ten thousand miles (as it seemed) to deliver it into the hands of the one who was to wear it and wind it and cherish it and listen to it tick off the unsullied hours that marked the lives of the Carterets—of Virginia.

His experience and conception of the Yankees had been an impression of tyrants—"low-down, common trash"—in blue, laying waste with fire and sword. He had seen the smoke of many burning homesteads almost as grand as Carteret Hall ascending to the drowsy Southern skies. And now he was face to face with one of them—and he could not distinguish him from his "young marster" whom he had come to find and bestow upon him the emblem of his kingship—even as the arm "clothed in white samite, mystic, wonderful" laid Excalibur in the right hand of Arthur. He saw before him two young men, easy, kind, courteous, welcoming, either of whom might have been the one he sought. Troubled, bewildered, sorely grieved at his weakness of judgment, old Jake abandoned his loyal subterfuges. His right hand sweated against the buckskin cover of the watch. He was deeply humiliated and chastened. Seriously, now, his prominent, yellow-white eyes closely scanned the two young men. At the end of his scrutiny he was conscious of but one difference between them. One wore a narrow black tie with a white pearl stickpin. The other's "four-hand" was a narrow blue one pinned with a black pearl.

And then, to old Jake's relief, there came a sudden distraction. Drama knocked at the door with imperious knuckles, and forced Comedy to the wings, and Drama peeped with a smiling but set face over the footlights.

Percival, the hater of mill supplies, brought in a card, which he handed, with the manner of one bearing a cartel, to Blue-Tie.

" 'Olivia De Ormond,' " read Blue-Tie from the card. He looked inquiringly at his cousin.

"Why not have her in," said Black-Tie, "and bring matters to a conclusion?"

"Uncle Jake," said one of the young men, "would you mind taking that chair over there in the corner for a while? A lady is coming in—on some business. We'll take up your case afterward."

The lady whom Percival ushered in was young and petulantly, decidedly, freshly, consciously, and intentionally pretty. She was dressed with such expensive plainness that she made you consider lace and ruffles as mere tatters and rags. But one great ostrich plume that she wore would have marked her anywhere in the army of beauty as the wearer of the merry helmet of Navarre.

Miss De Ormond accepted the swivel chair at Blue-Tie's desk. Then the gentlemen drew leather-upholstered seats conveniently near, and spoke of the weather.

"Yes," said she, "I noticed it was warmer. But I mustn't take up too much of your time during business hours. That is," she continued, "unless we talk business."

She addressed her words to Blue-Tie, with a charming smile.

"Very well," said he. "You don't mind my cousin being present, do you? We are generally rather confidential with each other—especially in business matters."

"Oh, no," carolled Miss De Ormond. "I'd rather he did hear. He knows all about it, anyhow. In fact, he's quite a material witness because he was present when you—when it happened. I thought you might want to talk things over before—well, before any action is taken, as I believe the lawyers say."

"Have you anything in the way of a proposition to make?" asked Black-Tie.

Miss De Ormond looked reflectively at the neat toe of one of her dull kid pumps.

"I had a proposal made to me," she said. "If the proposal sticks it cuts out the proposition. Let's have that settled first."

"Well, as far as—" began Blue-Tie.

"Excuse me, cousin," interrupted Black-Tie, "if you don't mind my cutting in." And then he turned, with a good-natured air, toward the lady.

"Now, let's recapitulate a bit," he said cheerfully. "All three of us, besides other mutual acquaintances, have been out on a good many larks together."

"I'm afraid I'll have to call the birds by another name," said Miss De Ormond.

"All right," responded Black-Tie, with unimpaired cheerfulness; "suppose we say 'squabs' when we talk about the 'proposal' and 'larks' when we discuss the 'proposition.' You have a quick mind, Miss De Ormond. Two months ago some half-dozen of us went in a motor-car for a day's run into the country. We stopped at a road-house for dinner. My cousin proposed marriage to you then and there. He was influenced to do so, of course, by the beauty and charm which no one can deny that you possess."

"I wish I had you for a press agent, Mr. Carteret," said the beauty, with a dazzling smile.

"You are on the stage, Miss De Ormond," went on Black-Tie. "You have had, doubtless, many admirers, and perhaps other proposals. You must remember, too, that we were a party of merry-makers on that occasion. There were a good many corks pulled. That the proposal of marriage was made to you by my cousin we cannot deny. But hasn't it been your experience that, by common consent, such things lose their seriousness when viewed in the next day's sunlight? Isn't there something of a 'code' among good 'sports'—I use the

word in its best sense—that wipes out each day the follies of
the evening previous?"

"Oh, yes," said Miss De Ormond. "I know that very well.
And I've always played up to it. But as you seem to be con-
ducting the case—with the silent consent of the defendant—
I'll tell you something more. I've got letters from him repeating the proposal. And they're signed, too."

"I understand," said Black-Tie gravely. "What's your price
for the letters?"

"I'm not a cheap one," said Miss De Ormond. "But I had
decided to make you a rate. You both belong to a swell family.
Well, if I *am* on the stage nobody can say a word against me
truthfully. And the money is only a secondary consideration.
It isn't the money I was after. I—I believed him—and—and
I liked him."

She cast a soft, entrancing glance at Blue-Tie from under her
long eyelashes.

"And the price?" went on Black-Tie, inexorably.

"Ten thousand dollars," said the lady, sweetly.

"Or—"

"Or the fulfilment of the engagement to marry."

"I think it is time," interrupted Blue-Tie, "for me to be
allowed to say a word or two. You and I, cousin, belong to a
family that has held its head pretty high. You have been
brought up in a section of the country very different from the
one where our branch of the family lived. Yet both of us are
Carterets, even if some of our ways and theories differ. You
remember, it is a tradition of the family, that no Carteret ever
failed in chivalry to a lady or failed to keep his word when it
was given."

Then Blue-Tie, with frank decision showing on his countenance, turned to Miss De Ormond.

"Olivia," said he, "on what date will you marry me?"

Before she could answer, Black-Tie again interposed.

"It is a long journey," said he, "from Plymouth Rock to
Norfolk Bay. Between the two points we find the changes
that nearly three centuries have brought. In that time the old

order has changed. We no longer burn witches or torture slaves. And today we neither spread our cloaks on the mud for ladies to walk over nor treat them to the ducking-stool. It is the age of common sense, adjustment, and proportion. All of us—ladies, gentlemen, women, men, Northerners, Southerners, lords, caitiffs, actors, hardware-drummers, senators, hod-carriers and politicians—are coming to a better understanding. Chivalry is one of our words that changes its meaning every day. Family pride is a thing of many constructions—it may show itself by maintaining a moth-eaten arrogance in a cob-webbed Colonial mansion or by the prompt paying of one's debts.

"Now, I suppose you've had enough of my monologue. I've learned something of business and a little of life; and I somehow believe, cousin, that our great-great-grandfathers, the original Carterets, would endorse my view of this matter."

Black-Tie wheeled around to his desk, wrote in a checkbook and tore out the check, the sharp rasp of the perforated leaf making the only sound in the room. He laid the check within easy reach of Miss De Ormond's hand.

"Business is business," said he. "We live in a business age. There is my personal check for $10,000. What do you say, Miss De Ormond—will it be orange blossoms or cash?"

Miss De Ormond picked up the check carelessly, folded it indifferently, and stuffed it into her glove.

"Oh, this'll do," she said, calmly. "I just thought I'd call and put it up to you. I guess you people are all right. But a girl has feelings, you know. I've heard one of you was a Southerner—I wonder which one of you it is?"

She arose, smiled sweetly, and walked to the door. There, with a flash of white teeth and a dip of the heavy plume, she disappeared.

Both of the cousins had forgotten Uncle Jake for the time. But now they heard the shuffling of his shoes as he came across the rug toward them from his seat in the corner.

"Young marster," he said, "take yo' watch."

And without hesitation he laid the ancient timepiece in the hand of its rightful owner.

WOODROW WILSON

Woodrow Wilson was born at Staunton, Virginia, December 28, 1858, and died in Washington, D.C., February 3, 1924. His father, Joseph Ruggles Wilson, served as minister in various Presbyterian churches. The family lived in Augusta, Georgia (1858–1870), Columbia, South Carolina (1870–1874), and in Wilmington, North Carolina. Prepared by tutors, the youth spent part of a year at Davidson College, North Carolina, and four years (1875–1879) at Princeton University, where he distinguished himself as a debater and as a writer of historical essays. He then attended the law school of the University of Virginia (1879–1880). In 1882 he was admitted to the bar and began practising law in Atlanta. Abandoning a profitless law practice, he renewed his studies in Johns Hopkins University (1882–1885), and after a brilliant career was awarded the Ph.D. degree in 1886. His dissertation, *Congressional Government*, which has widely circulated in a succession of editions, is highly praised by critics.

As a professor of history he served Bryn Mawr College (1885–1888), Wesleyan University (1888–1890), and Princeton University (1890–1892). As president of Princeton University (1902–1911), he raised the scholarly standards by insisting that "the object of a University is simply and entirely intellectual." Convinced that the scholarly aspects of a university cannot be divorced from the social aspects, he attempted to reform the clubs at Princeton. That his "Quad Plan" was not visionary is now realized in the college and house plans at Yale and Harvard. From 1911 to 1913 he served as Democratic governor of New Jersey and led a reform administration. He was President of the United States from 1913 to 1921, striving to keep the country out of war, yielding to the apparent necessity of the participation of the United States in the World War, and working for the attainment of democratic objectives in the Peace Conference, which he attended.

In September, 1919, he made a series of addresses on a tour of the country, explaining the Treaty of Peace and the League of Nations, and urging the country to support them. This final effort to accomplish the great ends toward which he had bent all his energies since 1918 was interrupted suddenly when he suffered a collapse and a paralytic stroke. Until his death in 1924 he was a very ill man, although at times he recovered sufficiently to issue letters and messages.

Although Woodrow Wilson's political activities have in our day overshadowed his scholarly and literary accomplishments, and although he will doubtless continue to be studied as a statesman rather than as a man of letters, he is nevertheless important to the student of southern literature both as a writer of strong, trenchant prose and as an effective advocate of southern political and social ideals.

ROBERT E. LEE: AN INTERPRETATION

In one sense, it is a superfluous thing to speak of General Lee, —he does not need the eulogy of any man. His fame is not enhanced, his memory is not lifted to any new place of distinction by any man's word of praise, for he is secure of his place. It is not necessary to recount his achievements; they are in the memory not only of every soldier, but of every lover of high and gifted men who likes to see achievements which proceed from character, to see those things done which are not done with the selfish purpose of self-aggrandizement, but in order to serve a country, and prove worthy of a cause. These are the things which make the name of this great man prominent not only, but in some regards unapproachable in the history of our country.

I happened the other day to open a book not printed in this part of the country, the *Century Cyclopedia of Names*, and to turn to the name of Lee, and I was very much interested, and I must say a little touched, by the simple characterization it gave of the man: "A celebrated American general in the Confederate service." How perfectly that sums the thing up,— a celebrated American general, a national character who won his chief celebrity in the service of a section of the country, but who was not sectionalized by the service, is recognized now as a national hero; who was not rendered the less great because he bent his energies towards a purpose which many men conceived not to be national in its end.

I think this speaks something for the healing process of time. I think it says something for the age, that it should have taken so short a time for the whole nation to see the true measure of this man, and it takes me back to my own feelings about one's necessary connection with the region in which he was born. . . .

It is a notable thing that we see when we look back to men of this sort. The Civil War is something which we cannot even yet uncover in memory without stirring embers which may spring into a blaze. There was deep colour and the ardour of blood in that contest. The field is lurid with the light of passion, and yet in the midst of that crimson field stands this gentle figure,—a man whom you remember, not as a man who loved war, but as a man moved by all the high impulses of gentle kindness, a man whom men did not fear, but loved; a man in whom everybody who approached him marked singular gentleness, singular sweetness, singular modesty,—none of the pomp of the soldier, but all the simplicity of the gentleman. This man is in the centre of that crimson field, is the central figure of a great tragedy. A singular tragedy it seems which centres in a gentleman who loved his fellow-men and sought to serve them by the power of love, and who yet, in serving them with the power of love, won the imperishable fame of a great soldier! A singular contradiction! . . .

I want to say that the lesson of General Lee's life to me is that it is not the immediate future that should be the basis of the statesman's calculation. If you had been in Lee's position, what would have been your calculation of expediency? Here was a great national power, material and spiritual, in the North. In the Northwest there had grown up by a slow process, as irresistible as the glacial movement, a great national feeling, a feeling in which was quite obliterated and lost the old idea of the separate sovereignty of states. In the South there had been a steadfast maintenance of the older conception of the union. What in such a case would you have said to your countrymen? "It will be most proper, as it will certainly be most expedient, for you to give in to the majority, and vote for the Northern conception?" Not at all. If you had been of Lee's kind you would have known that men's consciences, men's habits of thought, lie deeper than that, and you would have said: "No; this is not a time to talk about majorities; this is a time to express convictions; and if her conviction is not expressed by the South in terms of blood she will lose her character. These are her convictions, and if she yields them out of expediency she will have proved herself of the soft fibre of those who do not care to suffer for what they profess to love." Even a man who saw the end from the beginning should, in my conception as a Southerner, have voted for spending his people's blood and his own, rather than pursue the weak course of expediency. There is here no mere device, no regard to the immediate future. What has been the result?—ask yourself that. It has been that the South has retained her best asset, her self-respect. . . .

Now, what does it mean that General Lee is accepted as a national hero? It means simply this delightful thing, that there are no sections in this country any more; that we are a nation and are proud of all the great heroes whom the great processes of our national life have elevated into conspicuous places of fame. I believe that the future lies with all those men who devote themselves to national thinking, who eschew those narrow calculations of self-interest which affect only particular communities and try to conceive of communities as a part of a great national life which must be purified in order that it may be successful. For we may pile up wealth until it exceed all fables of riches in ancient fiction and the nation which possesses it may yet use it to malevolent ends. A poor nation such as the United States was in 1812, for example, if it is in the right, is more formidable to the world than the richest nation in the wrong. For the rich nation in the wrong destroys the fair work that God has permitted and man has wrought; whereas, the poor nation, with purified purpose, is the stronger. It looks into men's hearts and sees the spirit there; finds some expression of that spirit in life; bears the fine aspect of hope and exhibits in all its purposes the irresistible quality of rectitude. These are the things which make a nation formidable. There is nothing so self-destructive as selfishness, and there is nothing so permanent as the work of hands that are unselfish. You may pile up fortunes and dissolve them, but pile up ideals and they will never be dissolved. A quiet company of gentlemen sitting through a dull summer in the city of Philadelphia worked out for a poor and rural nation an immortal constitution, which has made statesmen all over the world feel confidence in the political future of the race. They knew that human liberty was a feasible basis of government.

There is always danger that certain men thinking only of the material prospects of their section, wishing to get the benefit of the tariff, it may be, or of this thing, or of that, when it comes to the distribution of favors, will write only the history which has been written again and again, whose reiteration has been repeated since the world began; from which no man will draw fresh inspiration; from which no ideal can spring, from which no strength can be drawn. Whereas the nation which denies itself material advantage and seeks those things which are of the spirit works not only for each generation, but for all generations, and works in the permanent and durable stuffs of humanity.

I spoke just now in disparagement of the vocation of the orator. I wish there were some great orator who could go about and make men drunk with this spirit of self-sacrifice. I wish there were some man whose tongue might every day carry abroad the golden accents of that creative age in which we were born a nation; accents which would ring like tones of reassurance around the whole circle of the globe, so that America might again have the distinction of showing men the way, the certain way, of achievement and of confident hope.

MERE LITERATURE

A singular phrase this, "mere literature,"—the irreverent invention of a scientific age. Literature we know, but "mere" literature? We are not to read it as if it meant *sheer* literature, literature in the essence, stripped of all accidental or ephemeral elements, and left with nothing but its immortal charm and power. "Mere literature" is a serious sneer, conceived in all honesty by the scientific mind, which despises things that do not fall within the categories of demonstrable knowledge. It means *nothing but literature*, as who should say, "mere talk," "mere fabrication," "mere pastime." The scientist, with his head comfortably and excusably full of knowable things, takes nothing seriously and with his hat off, except human knowledge. The creations of the human spirit are, from his point of view, incalculable vagaries, irresponsible phenomena, to be regarded only as play, and, for the mind's good, only as recreation,— to be used to while away the tedium of a railway journey, or to amuse a period of rest or convalescence; mere byplay, mere make-believe. . . .

It is by the number and charm of the individualities which it contains that the literature of any country gains distinction. We turn anywhither to know men. The best way to foster literature, if it may be fostered, is to cultivate the author himself,—a plant of such delicate and precarious growth, that special soils are needed to produce it in its full perfection. The conditions which foster individuality are those which foster simplicity, thought and action which are direct, naturalness, spontaneity. What are these conditions?

In the first place, a certain helpful ignorance. It is best for the author to be born away from literary centres, or to be excluded from their ruling set if he be born in them. It is best that he start out with his thinking, not knowing how much has been thought and said about everything. A certain amount of ignorance will insure his sincerity, will increase his boldness and shelter his genuineness, which is his hope of power. Not ignorance of life, but life may be learned in any neighborhood; —not ignorance of the greater laws which govern human affairs, but they may be learned without a library of historians and commentators, by imaginative sense, by seeing better than by reading;—not ignorance of the infinitudes of human circumstance, but these may be perceived without the intervention of universities;—not ignorance of one's self and of one's neighbor; but innocence of the sophistications of learning, its research without love, its knowledge without inspiration, its method without grace; freedom from its shame at trying to know many things as well as from the pride of trying to know but one thing; ignorance of that faith in small confounding facts which is contempt for large reassuring principles. . . .

It is your direct, unhesitating, intent, headlong man, who has his sources in the mountains, who digs deep channels for himself in the soil of his times and expands into the mighty river, to become a landmark forever; and not your "broad" man, sprung from the schools, who spreads his shallow, extended waters over the wide surfaces of learning, to leave rich deposits, it may be, for other men's crops to grow in, but to be himself dried up by a few score summer noons. The man thrown early upon his own resources, and already become a conqueror of success before being thrown with the literary talkers; the man grown to giant's stature in some rural library, and become exercised there in a giant's prerogatives before ever he has been laughingly told, to his heart's confusion, of scores of other giants dead and forgotten long ago; the man grounded in hope and settled in conviction ere he has discovered how many hopes time has seen buried, how many convictions cruelly given the lie direct by fate; the man who has carried his youth into middle age before going into the chill atmosphere of *blasé* sentiment; the quiet, stern man who has cultivated literature on a little oatmeal before thrusting himself upon the great world as a prophet and seer; the man who pronounces new eloquence in the rich dialect in which he was bred; the man come up to the capital from the provinces,—these are the men who people the world's mind with new creations, and give to the sophisticated learned of the next generation new names to conjure with. . . .

It would be not a little profitable if we could make correct analysis of the proper relations of learning—learning of the critical, accurate sort—to origination, of learning's place in literature. Although learning is never the real parent of literature, but only sometimes its foster-father, and although the native promptings of soul and sense are its best and freshest sources, there is always the danger that learning will claim, in every court of taste which pretends to jurisdiction, exclusive and preëminent rights as the guardian and preceptor of authors. An effort is constantly being made to create and maintain standards of literary worldliness, if I may coin such a phrase. The thorough man of the world affects to despise natural feeling; does at any rate actually despise all displays of it. He has an eye always on his world's best manners, whether native or imported, and is at continual pains to be master of the conventions of society; he will mortify the natural man as much as need be in order to be in good form. What learned criticism essays to do is to create a similar literary worldliness, to establish fashions and conventions in letters.

I have an odd friend in one of the northern counties of Georgia,—a county set off by itself among the mountains, but early found out by refined people in search of summer refuge from the unhealthful air of the southern coast. He belongs to an excellent family of no little culture, but he was surprised in the midst of his early schooling by the coming on of the war; and education given pause in such wise seldom begins again in the schools. He was left, therefore, to "finish" his mind as best he might in the companionship of the books in his uncle's library. These books were of the old sober sort: histories, volumes of travels, treatises on laws and constitutions, theologies, philosophies more fanciful than the romances encased in neighbor volumes on another shelf. But they were books which were used to being taken down and read; they had been daily companions to the rest of the family, and they became familiar companions to my friend's boyhood. He went to them day after day, because theirs was the only society offered him in the lonely days when uncle and brothers were at the war, and the women were busy about the tasks of the home. How literally did he make those delightful old volumes his familiars, his cronies! He never dreamed the while, however, that he was becoming learned; it never seemed to occur to him that everybody else did not read just as he did, in just such a library. He found out afterwards, of course, that he had kept much more of such company than had the men with whom he loved to chat at the post-office or around the fire in the village shops, the habitual resorts of all who were socially inclined; but he attributed that to lack of time on their part, or to accident, and has gone on thinking until now that all the books that come within his reach are the natural intimates of man. And so you shall hear him, in his daily familiar talk with his neighbors, draw upon his singular stores of wise, quaint learning with the quiet colloquial assurance, "They tell me," as if books contained current rumor; and quote the poets with the easy unaffectedness with which others cite a common maxim of the street! He has been heard to refer to Dr. Arnold of Rugby as "that school teacher over there in England."

Surely one may treasure the image of this simple, genuine man of learning as the image of a sort of masterpiece of Nature in her own type of erudition, a perfect sample of the kind of learning that might beget the very highest sort of literature; the literature, namely, of authentic individuality. It is only under one of two conditions that learning will not dull the edge of individuality: first, if one never suspect that it is creditable and a matter of pride to be learned, and so never become learned for the sake of becoming so; or, second, if it never suggest to one that investigation is better than reflection. Learned investigation leads to many good things, but one of these is not great literature, because learned investigation commands, as the first condition of its success, the repression of individuality.

His mind is a great comfort to every man who has one; but a heart is not often to be so conveniently possessed. Hearts frequently give trouble; they are straightforward and impulsive, and can seldom be induced to be prudent. They must be schooled before they will become insensible; they must be coached before they can be made to care first and most for themselves: and in all cases the mind must be their schoolmaster and coach. They are irregular forces; but the mind may be trained to observe all points of circumstance and all motives of occasion.

No doubt it is considerations of this nature that must be taken to explain the fact that our universities are erected entirely for the service of the tractable mind, while the heart's only education must be gotten from association with its neighbor heart, and in the ordinary courses of the world. Life is its only university. Mind is monarch, whose laws claim supremacy in those lands which boast the movements of civilization, and it must command all the instrumentalities of education. At least such is the theory of the constitution of the modern world. It is to be suspected that, as a matter of fact, mind is one of those modern monarchs who reign, but do not govern. That old House of Commons, that popular chamber in which the passions, the prejudices, the inborn, unthinking affections long ago repudiated by mind, have their full representation, controls much the greater part of the actual conduct of affairs. To come out of the figure, reasoned thought is, though perhaps the presiding, not yet the regnant force in the world. In life and literature it is subordinate. The future may belong to it; but the present and past do not. Faith and virtue do not wear its livery; friendship, loyalty, patriotism, do not derive their motives from it. It does not furnish the material for those masses of habit, of unquestioned tradition, and of treasured belief which are the ballast of every steady ship of state, enabling it to spread its sails safely to the breezes of progress, and even to stand before the storms of revolution. And this is a fact which has its reflection in literature. There is a literature of reasoned thought; but by far the greater part of those writings which we reckon worthy of that great name is the product, not of reasoned thought, but of the imagination and of the spiritual vision of those who see,—writings winged, not with knowledge, but with sympathy, with sentiment, with heartiness. Even the literature of reasoned thought gets its life, not from its logic, but from the spirit, the insight, and the inspiration which are the vehicle of its logic. Thought presides, but sentiment has the executive powers; the motive functions belong to feeling. . . .

It is devoutly to be wished that we might learn to prepare the best soils for mind, the best associations and companionships, the least possible sophistication. We are busy enough nowadays finding out the best ways to fertilizing and stimulating mind; but that is not quite the same thing as discovering the best soils for it, and the best atmospheres. Our culture is, by erroneous preference, of the reasoning faculty, as if that were all of us. Is it not the instinctive discontent of readers seeking stimulating contact with authors that has given us the present almost passionately spoken dissent from the standards set themselves by the realists in fiction, dissatisfaction with mere recording or observation? And is not realism working out upon itself the revenge its enemies would fain compass? Must not all April Hopes exclude from their number the hope of immortality?

The rule for every man is, not to depend on the education which other men prepare for him,—not even to consent to it; but to strive to see things as they are, and to be himself as he is. Defeat lies in self-surrender.

NOTES

WILLIAM BYRD

The selections are from *William Byrd's Histories of the Dividing Line Betwixt Virginia and North Carolina.* With Introduction and Notes by William K. Boyd. Raleigh, N.C.: 1929. Pages 60–65; 162–169. The selections include entries from both the *Secret History* and *The History of the Dividing Line*, for the purposes of comparison. The *Secret History* manuscript, written earlier than the *Dividing Line* manuscript, came into the possession of the American Philosophical Society, Philadelphia, which has preserved it. It reveals Byrd's antipathy for Fitz-William and Irvine, narrates accounts of insult or violence to frontier women, which Byrd condemned, contains three letters and five speeches not in the *History of the Dividing Line*, and admits only one unfavorable reflection on North Carolina. The manuscript of the *History of the Dividing Line* passed on to the descendants of Byrd, and is now, in Boyd's words, "in the custody of a New York trust company." It is twice the length of the *Secret History*, contains much information about colonization in America, includes descriptions of the region traversed by the surveying expedition, and features descriptions of fauna, flora, Indians, and pioneers. It contains much unfavorable criticism of the "lubbers" of North Carolina.

Byrd assigns fictitious names, in his *Secret History*, to the chief men of the survey, as follows: Virginia Commissioners: William Byrd, "Steddy"; William Dandridge, "Meanwell"; Richard Fitz-William, "Firebrand," (Surveyor-General of Customs for the Southern Colonies). Virginia Surveyors: Alexander Irvine, "Orion," (Professor of Mathematics at the College of William and Mary); William Mayo, "Astrolabe." North Carolina Commissioners: Chief Justice Gale, "Judge Jumble"; Edward Moseley, "Plausible"; John Lovich, "Shoebrush"; William Little, "Puzzlecause." North Carolina Sur-

veyor: Samuel Swann, "Bootes." The Chaplain: Rev. Peter
Fountain (Fontine), "Dr. Humdrum." Some of the fifteen
"able Woodsmen" were James Petillo (Patillo), John Ellis,
Charles Kimball, George Hamilton (Hambleton), and John
Evans.

1 Periaugas: periaguas; a canoe made from the trunk of a
single tree hollowed out.

2 Peruvian bark: Cinchona bark, which yields quinine.

3 Beavers, formerly plentiful in this region and long extinct,
have been brought into the Appalachian region by game commissioners in recent years.

4 Buffaloes, or the American bison, were plentiful in sections
of the South in colonial days.

5 Hipocoacanah: Ipecacuanha, which yields ipecac.

6 The Saponi tribe was of the Sioux family, and lived in some
numbers in this Dan River region.

7 The Tuskarooda tribe was of the Iroquois family. In two
Indian wars between 1711 and 1713, most of the twelve hundred
warriors were killed, and the remnant removed to New York
to join the Five Nations.

WILLIAM WIRT

The first selection is from William Wirt. *A Discourse on the
Lives and Characters of Thomas Jefferson and John Adams who
both died on the Fourth of July, 1826.* Washington: 1826. In
Claiborne Pamphlets, Volume I, Number 13.

Wirt delivered this speech in Washington, in the House of
Representatives, on October 19, 1826, the anniversary of the
surrender of Yorktown and the birthday of John Adams. His
speech shows his close friendship with Jefferson, and his intimate knowledge of Monticello, where he had often visited.
His biographer, John Pendleton Kennedy, said about this
address: "It is one of the most masterly effusions that our literature can boast of. . . . There are passages in this oration that
will long be preserved amongst the most classical and graphic
sketches that belong to the rich stock of our language."

Sketches of the Life and Character of Patrick Henry was published in Philadelphia in 1817, and was so popular that fifteen editions were issued by 1859. The extract chosen is from pages 132–143 of the revised edition of 1836.

It may come as a surprise to students of American literature that the famous "Liberty or Death" speech in its extant version was written by Wirt. In obtaining material for the biography Wirt was especially indebted to Judge St. George Tucker of Williamsburg, and in a letter acknowledging his large debt for aid Wirt wrote, "I have taken almost entirely Mr. Henry's speech in the convention of '75 from you, as well as your description of its effect on you verbatim." (*Life of Patrick Henry*, p. 252.) That qualifying word *almost* has aroused controversy. A few historians, including Lyon G. Tyler, are convinced that the speech is not "apocryphal." The consensus of opinion among Henry's biographers, including Moses Coit Tyler and William Wirt Henry, is that Wirt was largely responsible for the form that we have today. It is a warm topic for professorial and student controversy.

JOHN C. CALHOUN

The selection from "A Discourse on Government" is from Volume I, pages 52–64, *The Works of John C. Calhoun*. Edited by Richard K. Crallé. New York: 1853–1855. 6 vols.

The selection from the "Speech on the Slavery Question, Delivered in the Senate, March 4, 1850," is from Volume IV, pages 571–573.

HUGH SWINTON LEGARÉ

The selection from the "Fourth of July, 1823, Oration" is from Volume I, pages 262–263; 268–269, of *Writings of Hugh Swinton Legaré*. Charleston, S.C.: 1846. 2 vols.

The selection from Legaré's review of Hall's *Travels in America* is from *The Southern Review*, IV, 321–369 (November, 1829).

8 A memorial was presented to the King at this period by his Majesty's American subjects then in London. Of the thirty who signed it, *seventeen* were citizens of Charleston—and sent thither for their education.—See *Garden's Anecdotes*, Second Series, p. 4. (Legaré's note.)

9 This gentleman was pre-eminent in his classes at Westminster, and was for a long time Captain of the Town-Boys. (Legaré's note.)

10 More accurately a *sixth*. (Legaré's note.)

Captain Basil Hall had been a traveler many years before he came to America in 1827, for he entered the Royal Navy in his fourteenth year. He made a leisurely journey with his family, first spending some time in Canada, then traveling extensively through the United States, from New England south through the coastal states to Georgia and north up the Mississippi valley. In his Preface he implies that his reception in America was hospitable and that he has kindly feelings. Since his *Travels in North America* was violently criticized by Legaré and other reviewers, one reads some of his statements with surprise.

I have studiously avoided mentioning circumstances, or even making allusions, calculated to give pain to any person; and . . . I shall deeply lament having written on the subject at all, if these pages shall be thought to contain a single expression inconsistent with the gratitude, which, in common with my family, I must ever feel for the attention and hospitality we received from the Americans, or with the hearty good-will we bear to every individual whom we met with in their widely extended country.

Edinburgh, 15th June, 1829.

Jane L. Mesick, in *The English Traveller in America, 1785–1835* (New York: 1922), relates the story of the reception by Americans. Captain Hall and Mrs. Frances M. Trollope were the most hated of all the British travelers.

Captain Basil Hall, a visitor in 1827–8, was the arch-traitor to American hospitality in the opinion of those who tried to endure his fault-finding. (Page 12)

Though the captain came to this country in such a professedly kindly mood, his book had the effect of arousing a storm of angry feelings in the Americans. Travellers who passed through the country after his visit complained that hospitality was withheld from them because of the feeling this work had aroused. (Page 288)

Miss Mesick quotes from the considerable number of reviews and books in which Captain Hall was attacked.

AUGUSTUS BALDWIN LONGSTREET

The sketches in *Georgia Scenes* were first published in Georgia newspapers. In 1833–1834 Longstreet published eight sketches in the Milledgeville *Southern Recorder:* "The Dance," "The Song," "The Horse Swap," "The Turf," "The Fight," "The Turn Out," "The Character of a Native Georgian," and "The Gander Pulling." He transferred the series to his own paper, the Augusta *State Rights Sentinel,* where he published eight sketches: "The 'Charming' Creature as a Wife," "Militia Drill," "The Mother and Her Child," "The Fox Hunt," "The Wax Works," "Dropping to Sleep," "The Debating Society," and "A Sage Conversation." It has not been determined where and when four remaining sketches were first published: "Georgia Theatrics," "The Ball," "An Interesting Interview," and "A Shooting Match." Of these twenty sketches he published nineteen (omitting "Dropping to Sleep") from his own *Sentinel* press in 1835, as *Georgia Scenes, Characters, Incidents, Etc., in the First Half Century of the Republic.* By a Native Georgian. Longstreet disavowed authorship of "The Militia Company Drill," stating that "This is from the pen of a friend, who has kindly permitted me to place it among the *Georgia Scenes.*" John D. Wade states in his biography of Longstreet that this friend was probably Oliver Hillhouse Prince. Although Longstreet states in the Preface that "*Hall* is the writer of those sketches in which *men* appear as the principal actors, and *Baldwin* of those in which *women* are the prominent figures," this is obviously a device, probably transparent to his readers, for attempted anonymity.

David Crockett

The bibliographical problems in the study of Crockett are many, and very interesting. Perhaps a listing of his writings, with comments, will be of value.

Sketches and Eccentricities of Col. David Crockett, of West Tennessee. New York: J. and J. Harper, 1833. (Not by Crockett, although he copied some of the stories in writing his *Narrative*. Miss Rourke states that the same book was published in 1833 in Cincinnati under the title, *The Life and Adventures of Colonel David Crockett of West Tennessee,* copyrighted by J. S. French. "The two volumes show a single variation. At the end of *Sketches and Eccentricities* a note is added on the results of the election in 1833, favoring Crockett. At the end of *Life and Adventures* appears a hunting sketch, entitled Billy Buck.")

Crockett, David. *A Narrative of the Life of David Crockett.* . . . Written by Himself. Philadelphia: E. L. Carey and A. Hart, Baltimore: Carey, Hart & Co., 1834. (Commonly referred to as the *Narrative* or the *Autobiography*. Crockett states in his Preface that he had the manuscript "run over by a friend or so, and that some little alterations have been made in the spelling and grammar." This is understatement, for Crockett doubtless had a "ghost writer." Miss Rourke tells about an extant letter, written by Crockett to his publishers, in which he states that Thomas Chilton was to receive one-half the profits of the book. Thomas Chilton (1778–1854) was a Member of Congress from Kentucky in 1827–1831 and 1833–1835.)

Crockett, David. *An Account of Col. Crockett's Tour to the North and Down East.* . . . Philadelphia: Carey and Hart, 1835. (In a letter to the publishers Crockett mentions a "Mr. Clark" and states that the book "was written from

notes furnished by myself." Miss Rourke asserts that the
"Mr. Clark" "was almost surely Matthew St. Clair Clarke
. . . Clerk of the House, compiler of many volumes of con-
gressional records, documents, and other archives, and
Crockett's friend.")

*The Life of Martin Van Buren, Heir-Apparent to the "Govern-
ment."* . . . By David Crockett. Philadelphia: David Wright,
1835. (This biography was not written by Crockett. As
several persons have asserted, and John D. Wade has undoubtedly proved, the author was Augustin Smith Clayton
(1783–1839) a Georgian who knew Crockett in Congress.)

Col. Crockett's Exploits and Adventures in Texas. Philadelphia:
T. K. and P. G. Collins, 1836. (This book, published after
Crockett's death, was not written by him. Crockett possibly
left letters and a diary narrating some of his adventures in
Texas, which the author may have read. Certainly the
author gleaned freely from recent publications on Texas.
The attribution of authorship to Richard Penn Smith, a
Philadelphia author, is untenable. John D. Wade suggests
that Augustin Smith Clayton was the author, and the inclusion of the episode of "Georgia Theatrics" from Longstreet's *Georgia Scenes* may support this opinion. The
identity of the writer—or compiler—is still a matter of
speculation.)

Crockett Almanacs. (From 1835 to 1856 about fifty of these
almanacs were published. Miss Rourke lists over forty
titles. The copyrights of the first two issues were in Crockett's
name, and later numbers were issued as by the "Heirs of
Col. Crockett.")

William Gilmore Simms

"The Lazy Crow" was first published in *The Gift for 1840*,
and collected in *The Wigwam and the Cabin.* New York: 1845.
Scipio and the other Negroes are Gullah Negroes, who
speak a different dialect from that of the characters in Joel
Chandler Harris's Uncle Remus stories and those in Thomas

Nelson Page's *In Ole Virginia*. According to Reed Smith
"the term Gullah is applied to a special group type of Negroes,
limited historically and geographically to the sea-islands and
the narrow tidewater strip bordering the coast counties of
Georgia and a small section of northwest Florida. . . . Both
the word Gullah and the Negroes so named came from the
west coast of Africa."

The Gullah dialect has been called "the worst English in the
world," a "quaint linguistic mongrel," and "the most peculiar
of all American forms of speech." As Reed Smith says:
"What the Gullahs seem to have done was to take a sizable
part of the English vocabulary as spoken on the coast by the
white inhabitants from about 1700 on, wrap their tongues
around it, and reproduce it changed in tonality, pronunciation,
cadence, and grammar to suit their native phonetic tendencies,
and their existing needs of expression and communication."
See Reed Smith, *Gullah*. Bulletin of the University of South
Carolina. No. 190. Columbia, S.C.: 1926.

A more recent book is *Gullah: Negro Life in the Carolina Sea
Islands* (Durham, N.C.: 1940), by Mason Crum, who has
written about the Gullah dialect, life, religion, and customs.
He gives the following list of Gullah words which are most
likely of African origin.

Ki, an exclamation, or used to express wonder.
Buckra, a white man; *po' buckra,* poor white trash.
Nyam, to eat, as " 'e nyam 'e bittle."
Yam, probably related to *unyamo,* sweet potato.
Cona or *yoonah,* you or your.
Goober, peanut.
Pinder, peanut.
Cooter, turtle.
Okra, the vegetable.
Plat-eye, a prowling ghost or evil spirit.

The Gullah dialect in "The Lazy Crow" is comparatively
simple, and the student will have no trouble in reading the story.
Notice the several meanings of *enty.*

Simms wrote four other Negro stories: "Caloya," "The Snake in the Cabin," "The Bride of the Battle," and "The Passage of Arms in '76." J. Allen Morris says that "The Lazy Crow" "is important because it shows that Simms recognized the literary value of Negro superstitions that he learned from a first-hand acquaintance with the superstitious Negroes of the ante-bellum South."

JOHN ESTEN COOKE

In the restoration of Williamsburg extensive research has been made by the Research and Record Department Colonial Williamsburg, Inc. There were *two* theatres in Williamsburg before the Revolution. The authorities agree that the first theatre in Virginia, and in America, was erected in 1716 on the Palace Green, Williamsburg, and was in use until about 1740. No records are available about early performances in this theatre, before the announcement in *The Virginia Gazette* for Sept. 10, 1736, of the production of *Cato*, *The Busybody*, *The Recruiting Officer*, and *The Beaux Stratagem*. These plays and others were probably produced by a professional company which had been acting in New York and Charleston. In 1750 the Kean-Murray Company was invited to come to Williamsburg, and a new theatre was built for them behind the Capitol. According to *The Virginia Gazette* of October 21, 1751, the company produced *King Richard III* and "a tragic dance composed by Monsieur Denoir called the Royal Captive." Theatrical and dramatic history really begins, however, with the coming in 1752 of Lewis Hallam's Company, which consisted of Hallam, his wife, their three children, Lewis, Jr., Adam, and Beatrice, and ten adult members. On September 15, 1752, Hallam's Company produced the *Merchant of Venice* with a farce, *The Anatomist, or Sham Doctor* "before a numerous and polite Audience with great applaus." Mrs. Hallam played the part of Portia, for Beatrice was a child. There is no record that Beatrice had a part. Lewis Hallam, Jr., a boy of twelve years, had only one line to speak, but he was so overcome with fright that he rushed off the stage in tears, leaving his line un-spoken. In later years both Lewis and Beatrice became popu-lar actors.

See A. H. Quinn, *A History of the American Drama: From the Beginning to the Civil War* (New York: 1923); V. A. Jones, "The Theatre in Colonial Virginia," *The Reviewer*, V, 81–88 (January, 1925); *The Reviewer*, V, 81–88 (January, 1925); J. O. Beaty, *John Esten Cooke* (New York: 1925.)

GEORGE WASHINGTON CABLE

Although the dictionaries give various definitions of *Creoles*, the student of the Creole stories by Cable, Grace King, and Kate Chopin should limit the definition to the descendants of the original Spanish and French colonists in the Louisiana region. The Creoles should not be confused with quadroons, who have Negro blood, or with Cajuns, who are the descend-ants of the French Acadians who came to Louisiana in the eighteenth century. The Creoles are an aristocratic group, proud of their lineage and traditions.

Edward L. Tinker gives Cable credit as a pioneer in using new material which is widely exploited to-day by many southern writers.

Cable will always be remembered for two books, *Old Creole Days* and *The Grandissimes*, and also because he is the legitimate father of the literary movement which is producing such splendid fruit in the South today. Cable first, among southern writers, treated objectively and realistically the life he saw around him, and was first to break the taboo against writing about the Negro. His courage freed the authors who followed him of the necessity of fulsome praise for all things sectional; taught them their right and duty to analyze and portray truth-fully, even, if necessary to criticize, the social conditions under which they and those around them live. All this Cable accom-plished at the cost of practical ostracism among his own people; so he may well be called the first martyr to the cause of literary freedom in the South.

See "Cable and the Creoles," *American Literature*, V, 326 (January, 1934).

GRACE ELIZABETH KING

In his unpublished dissertation on "Diversity in the Characters Portrayed in Southern Regional Short Stories in the Nineteenth Century" (University of North Carolina, 1944), Ben Gray Lumpkin writes as follows about Grace King.

Short histories of American literature frequently introduce Grace King by a statement to the effect that she wrote her short stories to give a more accurate treatment of the Creoles than that found in Cable's stories. Such may be the fact, but it nevertheless remains true that she portrayed fewer Creole characters in leading roles than Cable's stories present. Aside from the well-known character of Marie Modeste, Grace King's stories contain only six other characters which appear clearly as Creoles. Marie Modeste first appears as an orphan girl kept in the most aristocratic school in New Orleans by an octoroon hairdresser, Marcelite, who is hiding the fact that Marie is the daughter of Monsieur Motte, a Creole planter killed during the Civil War. In the story "On the Plantation" she is in the background, but in "The Drama of an Evening" her identity and family are revealed, and in the "Marriage of Marie Modeste" her engagement and marriage to Charles Montyon, a native Frenchman, is narrated. In the same group of stories, collected in the volume, *Monsieur Motte*, a group of secondary Creole characters appears: Madame Lareveillere is the teacher and part owner of St. Denis, the most fashionable school for girls in New Orleans: Monsieur Armand Goupilleau runs through all four stories as a notary public, but in "On the Plantation" his love for Madame Lareveillere and his engagement to her is developed; and the Creole mistress of a plantation, Madame Aurore, appears in "On the Plantation" as the busy wife of Monsieur Felix, owner of Bel Angely, a sugar plantation.
. . . Madame Nénaine is the Bonne Maman of the story entitled "Bonne Maman." . . . Another poverty-stricken Creole woman who had lost all her property during the Civil War is portrayed in "La Grande Demoiselle" as Mademoiselle Idalie

Sainte Foy Mortemart, who at the time of the story is teaching
a Negro school in Louisiana for $7.50 a month. In "Pupasse"
Grace King portrayed the character of a dull Creole girl named
Marie Pupasse, who had spent seven years in the first two
classes of Madame Joubert's private school in New Orleans,
without learning the irregular French verbs. The principal
finally sends her home to her impoverished grandmother who
had been maintaining the school:

Mary Noailles Murfree (Charles Egbert Craddock)

In his biography, *Charles Egbert Craddock*, Edd W. Parks
writes about the publishing of "The Dancin' Party" story:

Mary and Fanny had planned to write together a novel about
Beersheba Springs and the mountaineers who lived in that
neighborhood. Mary wrote the first chapter, but somehow it
seemed so complete in itself that a second chapter was never
written, and Mary started another mountain story. One day
Mr. Murfree read the chapter, and suggested that it was an
admirable tale in itself. Why not send it to the *Atlantic
Monthly?*

But no member of the family liked her old pen-name of
Dembry. . . . The name of Egbert Craddock had been given
to a character in an earlier story—that name was lifted, and
Charles attached, to give a convincing rounded sound.

Mr. Howells accepted the story immediately. "The Dancin'
Party at Harrison's Cove" appeared in the May, 1878, *Atlantic*.
The great days of that magazine were not yet over. To appear
in its pages was to receive a literary accolade. True, the great
siege-guns who once dominated American letters were almost
gone. Longfellow, Holmes, and Whittier still wrote occasional
poems, but Lowell had turned to the *North American Review*.
New names had come to replace the giants, and soon in their
turn appeared giant-like: Mark Twain, Henry James, Thomas
Bailey Aldrich, Sarah Orne Jewett, Charles Dudley Warner,
Bret Harte, and the editor, William Dean Howells. It was a
goodly company.

But "The Dancin' Party" easily deserved a place at the
board. Mary's experimental days were over. This story had
finish and vitality, from the first sentence . . . to the inevitable

moral at the end. It is a story of mountaineers, as seen through the eyes of persons from "outside"—exactly the mountain life that Miss Murfree knew best. (Pages 92–94.)

JOEL CHANDLER HARRIS

C. Alphonso Smith's excellent chapter on "Dialect Writers" in the *Cambridge History of American Literature*, II, 347–366, contains several pages on Joel Chandler Harris. About the Uncle Remus dialect he states, in part: "The characteristics of this dialect consist wholly in adaptation of existing English words and endings, not in the introduction of new words or new endings. The plurals of all nouns tend to become regular. Thus Uncle Remus says *foots* (*feet*), *toofies* (*teeth*), and *gooses* (*geese*), though the old plural *year* is retained. The relative pronoun *who* is not used, its place being taken by *which* (or *w'ich*), *what* (or *w'at*), *dat*, and the more interesting *which he* and *which dey*, corresponding to Chaucer's *that he* and *that they*. Thus: 'She holler so loud dat Brer Rabbit, *which he* wuz gwine by, got the idee dat she wuz callin' him.'"

In his unpublished dissertation on "Diversity in the Characters Portrayed in Southern Regional Short Stories in the Nineteenth Century" (University of North Carolina, 1944), Ben Gray Lumpkin writes about Joel Chandler Harris's poor-white characters.

The best examples of poor-whites in Harris's stories are Bud Stucky and his mother in "Azalia." . . . Another poor-white family was portrayed by Harris as Becky Staley and her brother Micajah in "Free Joe and the Rest of the World." Both are poor. Becky tells fortunes to eke out the income which her brother makes by operating a lathe in his home. Neither is unkind to Free Joe, yet they are not financially able to help the distressed negro substantially, and both are unaware of Free Joe's troubles after his slave wife is sold out of the community by her master so that Free Joe cannot visit her. Just before Free Joe dies of starvation, exposure, and grief, Micajah Staley sees him and decides that the free negro is as happy as a kildee. In addition to this failure to understand the negro, another reason for classifying the Staleys as poor-whites is found in a statement by Harris about them: "When he was a slave Free Joe would have scorned these representatives of a class known as poor white trash, but now he found them sympathetic and helpful in various ways." The chief significance of this statement, and of the Staleys' treatment of Free Joe, is that the oft-repeated generalization about traditional poor-whites' being enemies of all negroes is qualified by Harris's portrayal. It suggests that poor-whites, like other white people, can live peaceably with negroes whom they know and understand.

SIDNEY LANIER

Aubrey H. Starke, in his *Sidney Lanier: A Biographical and Critical Study* (Chapel Hill, N.C.: 1933), gives a complete account of the writing and publication of *Tiger-Lilies*, analyzes the contents, and quotes contemporary reviews. One paragraph is pertinent to the passages quoted.

. . . *Tiger-Lilies* is in no sense a war-novel, for Lanier would not have glorified war by writing an account of it, and he shrank even from recalling in minute detail the horrors necessary to an indictment of it. An allegorical account in one chapter and in another a confession of sins and a brief defense of Jefferson Davis (suffering, at the time *Tiger-Lilies* was written, in a prison where Lanier himself had been confined): that is all. Though the scenes of the second part of *Tiger-Lilies* are laid in war-stricken Virginia, the war serves only to add further adventures to the lives of the characters previously introduced, and curiously enough the tone here is much less serious than that of the first part. . . . But as fiction the two chapters that make up the episode of Gorm Smallin's desertion are the best in the book, and almost a short story in themselves—a very real and moving short story in which Lanier, long before Mary Noailles Murfree (Charles Egbert Craddock) used the Tennessee mountaineer, his dialect and his background, with dramatic effectiveness. (Page 100.)

The extract entitled "Music" is from the first essay in *Retrospects and Prospects: Descriptive and Historical Essays* (New

York: 1899). Charles Day Lanier, the son of the poet, states that this essay was composed by Lanier "at the age of twenty-four—the compelled overflow of a buoyant, strenuous soul."

"The Legend of St. Leonor" was first published in the *Independent*, XXXVII (December 17, 1885) and was reprinted in *Music and Poetry* (New York: 1885). Aubrey H. Starke states that it was "planned as part of an essay on 'The Relations of Poetry and Science.'"

The selection is from the essay, "The New South," which appeared in *Scribner's Monthly* for October, 1880, and was reprinted in *Retrospects and Prospects*.

WILLIAM SYDNEY PORTER (O. HENRY)

"Thimble, Thimble" is from *Options*, New York: c. 1909, Harper and Brothers.

For the study of O. Henry's stories which are based upon southern material the student will find help in the "O. Henry Index," compiled by E. F. Saxton, published in a pamphlet, *O. Henry Papers*, by Doubleday, Page & Company, and reprinted in an abridgement in *Waifs and Strays*. O. Henry wrote over sixty stories containing southern material, of which forty have Texas settings or characters. H. E. Collins says that "O. Henry did not attempt to give realistic pictures of cowboys, outlaws, and Rangers: his Texas stories are merely romances of the unexpected, the commonplace." F. L. Pattee states that "A few times the glow of insight and sympathy hovers over the fifteen studies he made of his native South—by all means the best part of his fiction." The following books contain nearly all of his stories with southern material.

Waifs and Strays (1906). Three southern stories out of twelve.
The Heart of the West (1907). Fourteen southern stories out of nineteen.
The Gentle Grafter (1908). Seven southern stories out of fourteen.

Roads of Destiny (1909).   Ten southern stories out of twenty-two.

Options (1909).   Seven southern stories out of sixteen.

Strictly Business (1910).   "A Municipal Report" has a Tennessee setting.

Whirligigs (1910).   Eight southern stories out of twenty-three.

Sixes and Sevens (1911).   Five southern stories out of twenty-five.

Rolling Stones (1913).   Among the stories, sketches, and poems are eight stories containing Texas material.